The Art of Self-Persuasion

The Art of Self-Persuasion

The Social Explanation of False Beliefs

Raymond Boudon

Translated by Malcolm Slater

Polity Press

This translation © Polity Press 1994.
First published in France as *L'art de se persuader* © Librairie Arthème Fayard
1990.
First published in 1994 by Polity Press in association with
Blackwell Publishers.
Published with the assistance of the French Ministry of Culture.

Editorial office:
Polity Press
65 Bridge Street
Cambridge CB2 1UR, UK

Marketing and production:
Blackwell Publishers
108 Cowley Road
Oxford OX4 1JF, UK

238 Main Street
Cambridge, MA 02142, USA

ISBN 0 7456 0898 1

A CIP catalogue record for this book is available from the British Library and the
Library of Congress.

Typeset in 10 on 11½ pt Bembo by Photoprint.
Printed in Great Britain by T.J. Press Ltd, Padstow, Cornwall

This book is printed on acid-free paper.

Contents

Preface

This book does not claim to be the final word on a traditional subject to which a significant contribution, following on from those of moralists and philosophers, has been made by the classical and contemporary human sciences. This is true for example of classical sociology; the writings of Max Weber and Durkheim on the phenomena of belief indicate the importance they attached to this subject. One of the crucial contributions of these two pioneers was to have seen that even the strangest beliefs can, like any other object, be subjected to scientific analysis and explained in objective terms. How is this possible? Weber's lucid and clear-cut answer to this difficult and controversial question of method, and one to which he held consistently, was that understanding a belief meant finding the reasons for it, whether these were explicit or merely implicit.

This was also the answer given by Durkheim, not so much in his theoretical and doctrinal writing as in those analyses which have best stood the test of time and which appear to the present-day reader as the most sound.

Although Pareto, regarded by Parsons[1] as one of the three great founders of sociology, deals in his Treatise of General Sociology mainly with the art of self-persuasion in such a way that it could be regarded as the main theme of the book, he nevertheless gives a completely different answer to the same question. For him, it is mainly *feelings*, and unconsious ones at that, that are the cause of beliefs. For him, the only exception are beliefs directly inspired by the controlled observation of reality, or by 'logico-experimental' reasoning. In other words, only objectively valid arguments can provoke adherence. All others he took to be quibbles having little influence in our beliefs, and his approach was to regard them as effects rather than causes – their function was as a cover-up, hiding feelings which were often unutterable, and which ought to be regarded as the true causes of the beliefs. By his treatment of this classic theme, Pareto was in any case making it clear that he regarded it as an essential concern of sociology.

The theme is a central one in present-day human sciences. Habermas made it the focus of his ambitious approach in *The Theory of the Communicative Action*.[2] Previously, it had been brilliantly analysed in *The New Rhetoric – a treatise on argumentation* by Perelman and Olbrechts-Tyteca.[3] These writers, by their explicit disagreement with Pareto,[4] raised once again the central methodological question, to which I referred, of how to explain beliefs. Contrary to what Pareto says, they argue that people are quite capable of persuasion and self-persuasion – best written as (self-)persuasion – by reasoning which has no true objective basis.

Similarly, Toulmin was rightly regarded as having written a pioneering work when he showed, in *The Uses of Argument*,[5] that many arguments are convincing, even though their structure bears no resemblance to that of a line of reasoning which logic would regard as valid. For example, a legal argument generally cannot be reformulated in a way that is compatible with the rules of logic; nevertheless, it can not only legitimate, but also be the basis of, conviction.

As a general rule, many of the modern human sciences, in different and often autonomous ways, made a significant contribution to the analysis of persuasion and self-persuasion. Writing on this theme is so considerable that a whole volume would be needed to cover it. This present book therefore does not claim to be a treatise on the art of (self-)persuasion, but a mere *contribution* to this central concern of the human sciences.

Most of what I have to say is a variation on a theme of George Simmel. Simmel recognized, as did Pareto and indeed the whole of classical philosophy, that the most effective way of (self-)persuasion is of course to develop a valid demonstrative argument. However, unlike Pareto, he suggests, in a way which seems quite paradoxical, that this approach can lead to one's being convinced not only of correct ideas, but also – no doubt the exception rather than the rule – of ideas which are dubious, weak or false. All that is needed for this to happen is that the explicit line of argument is contaminated by hidden *a priori* notions.

In this way, says Simmel, a line of argument which logic, and in a more general sense, scientific thinking would regard as irreproachable, can produce false ideas. Moreover, this is one of the main ways in which false ideas occur.

The allusive writing where Simmel sketches out this theme, rather than going into it in detail, at first intrigued me enormously. How can it be that the soundest arguments can be a source – even an essential source – of dubious ideas? Subsequently, I became convinced not only that this model could easily be illustrated by numerous examples, but also that

Simmel had, in passing, come up with a profoundly original view about the origin of dubious and false ideas.

This theme runs through the whole of this book. However, I want to make it clear immediately that, to my mind, the analyses which follow in no way exhaust the potentialities of what I call the Simmel model.

One could simply apply the model to what is nowadays usually called 'ordinary knowledge'. It is easy to spot in everyday thinking examples where unacceptable conclusions are drawn from sound premises.

However, since Simmel's view is that false ideas can arise from the most unexceptionable thought processes, it was more relevant, or in any case more tempting (in that the paradox became a challenge), to apply his model to the results of thinking that is *methodical* – I prefer, where possible, to use this word, rather than *scientific*, which is more ambiguous.

For this reason, apart from the second chapter – dealing with failures of 'intuition' in ordinary thinking – all my examples are drawn from scientific analyses or theories. Since one can speak accurately only about what one knows well, I have taken from the pool of human sciences a collection of theories all of which have two characteristics: firstly, they can be regarded as based on unexceptionable reasoning; and secondly, they lead to conclusions that are weak, dubious, questionable, or even downright false.

Within the human sciences, my examples could have been taken from a wide variety of disciplines and fields. In reality, they come from the philosophy and sociology of science, for reasons which will be examined in Chapter 1. However, the book will also include examples from other registers. The common ground of all the examples is that they confirm the importance of Simmel's model: the persuasive force of their strange conclusion stems from the fact that these are the product of sound reasoning.

Chapter 1 ('The powers that induce us to agree') establishes the framework for these analyses and tries to show that one of the essential contributions of the present-day human sciences in the area of the phenomena of knowledge is to have shown in very different ways that, contrary to the teachings of a long-standing and respectable philosophical tradition, people often have good reason to believe in dubious or false ideas. They may often subscribe to these ideas under the influence of irrational forces – the mind is often fooled by the heart. However, such beliefs also develop very often (more often than one thinks) from reasons provided by the subject – reasons which, as Simmel makes it clear, can be well founded.

Chapter 2 ('Good reasons for believing in false ideas') tries to show that distortions of the intuition often occur for good reason. In this, I have used some particularly instructive analyses from contemporary cognitive psychology, and I have tried to show that they could be explained and reinterpreted using Simmel's model.

Chapter 3 ('Simmel's model') shows how Simmel's model might be reconstituted on the basis of two extracts from the writing of this great German sociologist and philosopher.

Chapter 4 ('Hyperbole machines') shows how the model can be applied to two classical examples from the philosophy of science and from political science.

Simmel's model can be illustrated by a whole range of examples; but, over and above this diversity, various categories can be discerned, and it is to this question that Chapters 5 to 8 are devoted. Here it is shown how apparently innocuous everyday *a priori* notions can lead to dubious ideas on the strength of sound arguments. Each of these chapters deals with a particular type of *a priori*: Chapter 5 ('Questions and answers') with the logical kind of everyday *a priori*; Chapters 6 ('No effect without cause') and 7 ('Truth is unique') with the epistemological type of *a priori*; and Chapter 8 ('Words and things') with the linguistic type of *a priori*.

I repeat that I do not believe that these chapters exhaust the potential of the Simmel model, and it is easy to conceive of other categories more or less important and typical. But they are perhaps sufficient to show its considerable interest from the point of view of 'knowledge of knowledge'.

I said that one of the contributions of present-day sciences has been to show that belief in dubious ideas often stems from *good reasons*. I needed to be clear about this notion, which implies a fresh look at the theory of rationality; this I have done in Chapter 9 ('Reason with a small r').

Finally, Chapter 10 ('Simmel and the theory of knowledge') tries to show the relationship between the model that constitutes the central theme of this book and Simmel's theory of knowledge. Discussion of it is warranted by its importance, originality and correctness, and the fact that it is not widely known.

Should we speak of 'the art of persuasion', or 'the art of (self-) persuasion'? In fact, the expressions are virtually interchangeable in the context of the book, since the fundamental point in Simmel's model is that not only interlocutors, but also knowing subjects, can see their own arguments through all kinds of *a priori* which may distort their meaning. A valid argument can in this way produce dubious ideas in the mind of the speaker as well as in that of the interlocutor.[6]

Simmel's model identifies an essential mechanism of persuasion and self-persuasion, but it must be stressed that it is not the only one. Toulmin's model offers another possibility: a 'legal' kind of reasoning, even though it is not reducible to scientific reasoning, can in fact be convincing. People can also be convinced by modes of reasoning that are vague yet not without rules, which Perelman calls 'rhetorical'. Moreover, the reasons which people come up with can, as Pareto suggests, serve merely to 'rationalize' beliefs inspired by 'feelings'.

Doubtless every process whereby ideas are spread brings into play these different mechanisms which are complementary. But the mechanism briefly analysed by Simmel – which might be called *the Simmel effect* – certainly plays in most cases a pivotal or lead role, in that a dubious or false idea is more likely to catch on – at least in the kind of society in which we live – when it has a scientific label attached to it.

For this reason, this process seems to me to be an essential theme in the sociology of knowledge. It suggests in fact that collective belief in weak, dubious or false ideas can sometimes become established simply because the ideas are legitimated by reasoning which there is no reason not to regard as valid.

However, it has a further dimension which is of interest to cognitive sociology. Implication is an essential component of social interaction, and many writers have emphasized the role of implicit *frameworks* in social perception. Goffman, for example, recommended the phrase *frame analysis* to describe this area of sociology. What Simmel suggests in his writings which form the starting point of the analyses in this book is that, in the same way, all reasoning is set in an *implicit framework* – a system of propositions which knowing subjects have good reasons for regarding as *self-evident*. Of course, this framework can affect their conclusions and sometimes their beliefs, just as the perceptual frameworks which they deploy can affect their perceptions.

Since there is nothing to prevent these *a priori* from being exposed to criticism, it must again be emphasized that this omnipresence of the *a priori*, in ordinary knowledge as in scientific knowledge, does not in any way imply scepticism. It no more jeopardizes the ability of knowledge to arrive at truth and objectivity than frameworks of perception condemn subjects to perceptual illusion.

I have used the phrases *sociology of knowledge* and *cognitive sociology* interchangeably. Is one preferable to the other? The question is of no great importance. The former is no doubt more common, but it often suggests a very restricted programme, where the main aim is to identify the social causes of the phenomena of knowledge and belief. This definition, however, is of recent, neo-Marxist origin, and the programme of writers such as Durkheim or Weber, whose works are full of analyses attempting to explain knowledge and belief, is not limited to this approach. More ambitiously, they try to explain why particular social subjects believe what they do, to consider how best to explain belief, and also to identify the mechanisms which give rise to beliefs. Similarly, writers such as Pareto and Simmel have outlined grammars creating the mental processes that lead subjects to subscribe to propositions which may appear strange to an observer. Generally speaking, classical sociology has examined very intensely the question – a theoretical and methodological one – of adherence to ideas. This should not surprise us since, on this point as on others, great classical sociology is the direct heir of philosophy, a constant theme of which has always been 'the powers which lead us to consent'.

To differentiate between this classical programme and the more limited programme often associated with the phrase 'sociology of knowledge' (despite the intentions of Karl Mannheim, who invented it), one might suggest, without insisting, the semi-neologism *cognitive sociology*.

The analyses in this book make a deliberately circumscribed contribution to this programme by developing the hypothesis that weak and false ideas often owe their status of *received ideas* to the fact that they derive from sound arguments contaminated by implicit *frameworks* which impose themselves on the subject because the latter has good reasons for regarding them as 'self-evident'. What I call in this book the *Simmel effect* represents of course only one of the ways in which beliefs are crystallized.[7]

It has doubtless become clear that I am taking the word *belief* in a sense that is both particular and limited. I will come back briefly to this point about vocabulary at the end of Chapter 1, but I would like to say now that I regard the term as shorthand for 'adherence to dubious, weak or false ideas'.[8]

I would also like to make it clear that, although I am dealing here – in the perspective which I have just outlined – with the *cognitive* causes of beliefs, I am quite aware that they are generally mixed in with *affective* causes. However, I will not pursue this much further, but simply say something in Chapter 1 about the reasons why, in my opinion, there is a tendency to exaggerate the importance of the latter and underestimate that of the former.

I would like once more to stress the open character, in my view, of this book: when, in Chapter 2, I offer an interpretation of certain findings from cognitive psychology, I am perfectly aware of the hypothetical nature of the processes whose existence I am postulating. I am also aware that empirical research would be necessary to move the discussion on. Moreover, the implicit *frameworks* whose contamination effects I am now examining are in my view only examples, and need to be developed into a more complete typology. Chapters 5, 6, 7 and 8 are restricted to the examination of epistemological or linguistic *a priori* which, while important, are particular. Moreover, my examples deal mainly with controlled knowledge. Of course, the application of the processes of crystallization of beliefs I am analysing here could be extended to ordinary knowledge: the same effects, magnified, would be observed without difficulty, with the intervention of implication giving rise, here as before, to adherence to dubious statements, even beliefs, which an outside observer would very likely regard as 'magical'.

I leave it to the reader to draw from the studies in this book certain philosophical conclusions that arise, but on which I decided not to dwell: in this way, the halo surrounding reasoning limits the transparency sometimes accorded to consciousness. But this limitation has nothing to do with the phenomena of blindness well analysed in 'hot' theories of belief. The relative opacity of knowing subjects to themselves in a way puts speaker and interlocutor on the same footing and meanings that we can understand the essentially intersubjective (some would say 'dialogical') nature of knowledge, a point rightly stressed by Habermas.

Moreover, this book is a contribution, not only to the theory of rationality, but also to current interdisciplinary research on the 'multiple self'.[9]

Finally, my criticism of cognitive relativism by means of examples of the Simmel model (the conclusions of which are summarized at the end of Chapter 8) could, I think, be extended without any real problem to the other forms of relativism – ethical relativism and aesthetic relativism.

In an effort to provoke initial discussion of the ideas I am putting forward, I presented some of the analyses in this book as unpublished talks and lectures, and in articles published in various languages.[10]

I have made reference to the background of this book in order to explain why there are a small number of repetitions. I decided not to eliminate them, since their presence gives chapters a certain autonomy – an autonomy further underlined by my decision to condense each chapter into a summary at the end.

My warm thanks go to A. Boyer, G. Businon, M. Clavelin, J. Elster and A. Petroni, as well as to A. Devinant and F. Rousseau, for their valuable comments on a work for which the final responsibility is mine alone.

Part I

1

The powers that induce us to agree

The question how and why one subscribes to a particular idea, of what exactly are, to quote Pascal, 'the powers that induce us to agree',[1] is a subject so important for philosophy and the human sciences alike that it has given rise to an enormous body of literature. From the number and variety of works on this matter, the conclusion is that writers, as well as common-sense thought, make concurrent use of *three* principal models to account for adherence to ideas.

However, although common sense has no problem in recognizing that the three models are all necessary, and that, depending on the circumstances, one or the other applies, classical theorists of beliefs, from moralists to sociologists, tend to opt for one of the three.

THREE MODELS

Firstly, the fact that subject X subscribes to idea Y, that the subject believes in Y, can be explained (and indeed the explanation is quite frequent) by the *reasons* that the subject has for believing in it. Thus few people would refuse to recognize that belief in the truth of the statement 'two and two make four' is explained by the reason that two and two do in fact make four. Similarly, belief in the fact that 'fire burns' is explained by the fact that fire does burn.

This is why Karl Mannheim, who pioneered the sociology of knowledge, drew a clear demarcation line between beliefs which fall within the sociologist's area, and those which fall outside.[2] Religious beliefs come within it, he tells us – they can be understood and explained only by taking them in the social context in which they appear. Conversely, no social factor needs to be evoked to explain why one believes that 'two and two are four'. It is sufficient to note that there are *objective reasons* for endorsing this statement.

At this point, I will simply note that when I say that 'few people' would reject this distinction, this is not an example of litotes. After all, there is at least one group of thinkers who refuse to admit that the *reasons* for a belief can ever be the *cause* of that belief. I am referring to the proponents of the 'strong programme' in the sociology of science.[3] This programme is defined in particular by the postulate that adherence to a statement – even a statement in physics or mathematics, or a simple statement of fact – can in no way be explained exclusively by the objective reasons for believing in it.

I will have another look later at this surprising view, which is nowadays influential and perhaps less paradoxical than it seems. For the moment, I will merely indicate its existence.

I will call a '*type I* explanation' that which sees in the *reasons* which the subject might have for believing in the truth of statement Y the *cause* of belief in statement Y.

In many cases, it is impossible to have recourse to a type I model, and we must explain a particular belief of subject X in the statement Y by causes which it is clear cannot be reasons. It is of course a *passion* – jealousy – which leads Othello to believe that Desdemona is unfaithful. Doubtless he thinks he has reasons – those which Iago puts into his mind – for subscribing to the idea of his wife's guilt. But everybody except Othello himself can see plainly that the credence he gives to these reasons is itself an effect of his jealousy. In this case, it is a passion which is the cause of the particular belief. As for the reasoning by which the subject justifies the belief, this is itself the effect rather than the cause of the belief.

Let us call a *type II* model the explanation of beliefs by causes which are not reasons.

This classical model is defined succinctly by La Rochefoucauld ('the mind is always the dupe of the heart'), and more subtly and fully by Pascal:

> Everyone knows that the two ways by which opinions enter the soul are its two principal powers – the understanding and the will. The more natural one is the understanding, in that one ought never to agree to anything except demonstrable truths; but the more common one, though it goes against nature, is the will; for people are almost always induced into believing not by proof, but by attractiveness. This way is base, unworthy and alien: therefore everybody disclaims it. People profess to believe and even to love only if they know they deserve it.[4]

Thus many beliefs are explained by affective causes or, as Pascal says later on, by 'the rash whims of the will'. But nobody readily agrees that their beliefs are due to passions ('this way is base, unworthy and alien: therefore everybody disclaims it'); because of this, one always finds reasons for one's beliefs, and even for one's feelings ('people profess to

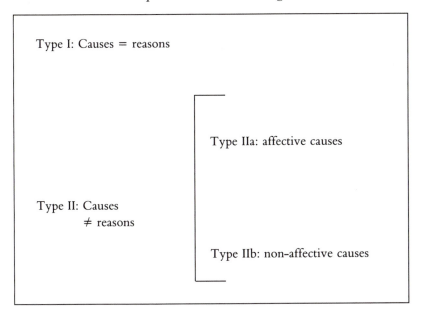

Figure 1.1

believe and even to love only if they know it is deserved'). However, these reasons are a mere smokescreen.

It is beyond doubt, of course, that this classical model applies to many beliefs. However, should we make it the only model? Can it explain, for example, the 'agreement' accorded to ideologies?

Since the time of the moralists, many theorists have tended to give a positive answer to this question. This position is at variance, as I have said, with common sense, which seems to be much more flexible in its spontaneous explanations of beliefs. As we shall see, it is also contradicted by findings from contemporary human sciences, which end up by substituting in many areas a *type I* model (explanation through *reasons*) for the type II models (explanation through *causes* of another sort) in operation.

But it must also be noted that there are two variants within what I call the type II model. I will speak of *type IIa* in relation to the Pascal–La Rochefoucauld model, which sees in passions or, using the vocabulary of the seventeenth century, in the 'will', the virtual monopoly of explanation of belief in dubious, weak or false ideas. It is distinct from the model I will call *type IIb*, which sets out to explain beliefs through causes which are *neither reasons nor passions*. These types are shown synoptically in figure 1.1.[5]

Various examples could be given to illustrate this type of explanation of beliefs, but a classic one is the theory of 'primitive mentality', which had its moment of glory. Although this theory is nowadays regarded by some as definitely outmoded, for others it is still of vital significance.[6] In any event, it offers the best illustration possible of what I am calling type IIb.

The causes referred to by Lévy-Bruhl to explain the magic beliefs of 'primitive people'[7] are not in fact reasons, but neither are they passions. They are located rather in that mental organization peculiar, according to Lévy-Bruhl, to 'primitive people', which leads them to follow rules of logic different from those which we ourselves obey. We must, says Lévy-Bruhl,

> abandon the idea of reducing mental operations in advance to a single type, whatever the society under consideration, and of explaining all collective representations in terms of a psychological and logical mechanism which is always the same.[8]

In other words, the logical and psychological mechanisms must be thought of as variable according to the culture and society, and therefore as being dependent on social causes.

It is understandable why Lévy-Bruhl's theory, in its day, attracted a great deal of attention, and why even today it is extolled by the proponents of cultural relativism: it destroyed the idea of the universality of logic as we practise it, and showed the rules of thinking to be variable between societies. This is not to imply that Lévy-Bruhl suggested putting our logic and that of 'primitive people' on the same plane. Like Comte and most positivists, he thought that the highest stage of evolution, which according to him Western civilization had reached, was characterized by a reconciliation between human thought and the real world. The logic which operated in primitive societies was therefore condemned as a residue.

Magical beliefs are, according to Lévy-Bruhl, explained by the fact that primitive people conform to a system of thought different from our own. This system, called by Lévy-Bruhl 'primitive mentality', consists of laws which, in the same way, for example, as our laws of contradiction or excluded middle, guide the 'primitive person' in inference about the real world, but the content of which is quite different from these logical laws. Thus, the system of the 'primitive mentality' admits of a 'law' to which Lévy-Bruhl gives the name 'law of participation':

> In the collective representations of the primitive mentality, objects, beings and phenomena can, in a way which to us is incomprehensible, be both

themselves and something other than themselves. In a way which is no less incomprehensible, they emit and take in forces, virtues, qualities, mystical[9] actions which make themselves felt outside themselves, while not ceasing to be where they are.[10]

Later, Lévy-Bruhl makes it clear that the 'prelogical' mentality, as he says once again, 'does not compel itself first and foremost, like our thinking, to renounce contradiction. It obeys the law of participation primarily.'[11]

Thus Lévy-Bruhl explains the magical beliefs of 'primitive people' in terms of psychic factors which, unlike the passions of classical tradition, are not affective in nature, and which, moreover, are characterized by the fact that, being inaccessible to direct observation, they must be inferred from observed beliefs. As for the *reasons* which 'primitive people' give for their beliefs, these are regarded by Lévy-Bruhl as having no causal influence on those beliefs. He considers them on the contrary to be justifications which can simply be ignored by the observer anxious to explain in a scientific and objective manner the beliefs of 'primitive people'.

This model of explanation of beliefs, of which Lévy-Bruhl offers a telling example, is also very widespread. Common sense has frequent recourse to it. Thus, when a belief seems strange to us and we explain it, for example, by reference to the hypothesis that the person holding the belief is 'deranged' or 'gullible', we are also invoking unseen psychic causes whose real nature is nevertheless guaranteed by the effects that they are supposed to produce. As for the reasons which subjects have for their beliefs, they are usually regarded, in a case of this kind, as effects rather than causes of the belief in question.

In its *form*, an 'analysis' such as this is therefore of the same kind as the one suggested by Lévy-Bruhl for magical beliefs, even though the latter is obviously much more elaborate.

Because this explanatory model is widely used, both in 'ordinary' and 'scientific' analyses of beliefs, it is not hard to find a large number of illustrations of it.

Durkheim has frequent recourse to a model of this type. Thus, according to *The Elementary Forms of the Religious Life*,[12] totemic beliefs impose themselves on social subjects. They are as far from being masters of them as they are of their passions. These beliefs must be analysed as a sort of projection of the respect which society normally inspires in its members and from which they cannot escape. Nevertheless, in other parts of the same book, Durkheim prefers the type I model (explanations in terms of *reasons*): thus his analysis of magic tries to show that 'primitive people' believe in magic because they have *good reasons* for believing in it.

The fact that Durkheim uses a type I model to account for magical beliefs and a type IIb model to explain religious beliefs raises significant exegetical questions which I cannot go into now.

Marx also has recourse – often but not invariably – to the IIb model, for example in *The German Ideology*, where he sets out to look at whether the fact of belonging to a particular social class imposes on social subjects – unbeknown to them – collective beliefs from which they can no more escape than Durkheim's Australian aborigine can escape from totemic beliefs.[13]

Marx's analyses of ideological beliefs, and Durkheim's and Lévy-Bruhl's analyses of religious beliefs, are of course very different in their detail and content. But on the formal level they have one point in common – they make beliefs the effect of factors which are not directly observable, but which are inferred by the observer from the subject's behaviour or utterances. It is these unconscious factors – operating unbeknown to the subject – which are regarded as the true causes of the beliefs.

To round off this casuistry, Pareto and Freud would represent a fourth case in point, corresponding to a type IIc, with type IIa being exemplified by Pascal and La Rochefoucauld and type IIb by Lévy-Bruhl.

On the argument of the more esoteric aspects of their writing, all in fact use a model which says that beliefs are the result mainly of causes of an affective nature, but inaccessible to direct observation. The first characteristic puts this model closer to type IIa, the second to type IIb. Pareto's 'feelings' are no more accessible to the subject and the observer than Freud's 'unconscious desires'.

However, in order to avoid having to differentiate too much, we will assimilate this model with type IIb: the important thing from the point of view of the explanation of beliefs is that, for Lévy-Bruhl as well as for Pareto, these beliefs are interpreted as the effect, not of reasons, but of causes inaccessible to observation. We must also stress again that writers who favour Type IIb explanations (Marx, Pareto, etc.), just like those who go for the IIa model (La Rochefoucauld, Pascal, etc.) usually accept that the *reasons* which subjects give for the validity of their beliefs are of a purely *illusory* nature: although subjects themselves have reasons, these should be regarded as having no real effect on the beliefs. This means that the Othello case is considerably broadened, since the subject himself is in fact in the worst position to know why he believes what he does believe.

This typology means, we can note in passing, that convergences are shown up which may well seem surprising.

According to moralists and classical philosophers such as Pascal, people tend to hide the affective causes of their beliefs by means of reasons which are ostensibly objective, but which in fact mislead them. The Freudian tradition says roughly the same thing when it suggests that the reasons subjects give for their beliefs should be regarded as a *rationalization*. In Marxist thought, the concept of *false consciousness* aims to convey a similar idea. Pareto thinks that beliefs – with the exception of those which are explained by objective reasons – are always the effect of feelings, and he crudely dubs 'logical varnish' what he calls *distortions*, in other words, the 'pseudo-logical' justifications that we give for our beliefs. Basically, there is no great difference between this 'logical varnish' and Freudian 'rationalization'. As for the idea which these notions convey, it is explicit in the Pascal quotation on page 4.

THE INFLUENCE OF THE TYPE II MODEL

When a belief seems strange, odd, false or discredited, the explanation which tends spontaneously to be given of why people subscribe to it often falls within type II: the causes rather than the reasons are sought, and the tendency is to regard the reasons which subjects give for them as mere illusions having no real effect on their beliefs.

To avoid any misunderstanding, it is useful to clarify a point of vocabulary and note that since the *reasons* which subjects come up with can be taken in certain cases as the causes of their beliefs, when I say that model II explains beliefs in terms of causes rather than reasons, I mean of course that these causes are not reasons, even though 'reasons' are a species of the genus 'causes'. In other words, the word 'cause' can be understood in two ways, depending on whether the species 'reasons' is included in the genus or not. In the majority of cases, this ambiguity should cause no problems.

Numerous examples show how easy it is, when faced with a strange belief or surprising behaviour, to evoke type II as an explanatory model. Why do Swedish peasants reject a particular innovation when it is in their interest to accept it? The cause of this is their ingrained traditionalism. Why is there a high birthrate among Indian peasants, contributing to their collective poverty? Because they slavishly follow centuries-old ways. Why do American automobile workers appear satisfied with their lot when they are condemned to a very ordinary life without a future? Because they have internalized and unconsciously accepted a norm – the need to *succeed* – which imposes itself on them with the same strictness as respect for society on Durkheim's aborigines.

I will not dwell on the fact – which I have tried to substantiate elsewhere – that these explanations using type II models can quite well be substituted in the three examples just given by type I explanations.[14] The so-called traditionalism of Swedish peasants is simply the manifestation of prudent behaviour: why place immediate trust in a source of information – in this case the government – which tries to convince me that what is in *its* interest is also in *mine*? The persistence of high birthrates in developing countries is explained to a large extent by the fact that infant mortality is higher there and that the idea of one generation helping another is much more crucial in traditional societies than in modern ones. As for the American automobile workers, the type II explanation given by the author of the study referred to is an example of what might be called a *projection* effect: I am not able to put myself in the shoes of people who are satisfied with *aurea mediocritas*, and, failing to conceive their reasons, I look for the causes of their attitude.[15] In the same way, Lévy-Bruhl, unable to conceive of the reasons why primitive people believe their rituals can produce rain, imagines that they are subject to logical principles different from ours.

Many more examples of this type could be given, each more telling than the last. When the social distance which separates the observer from the observed crosses a certain threshold, the former tends to explain the *strange* beliefs of the latter in terms of *causes* rather than *reasons*. However, in examples such as those I have given and in many others, further enquiry often reveals that the real causes of the beliefs are in fact reasons. By having many children, the Indian peasant certainly contributes to collective poverty, but this negative effect is infinitesimal for each family unit and becomes significant only for the population as a whole. The important point is that what directly concerns the peasant is not the collective effect, but rather that if he conformed to the small family model, he would expose the members of his family to gratuitous risks and would certainly reduce his standard of living as well as his future security.

Therefore, in many cases, it is seen that for a spontaneous type II explanation (causes ≠ reasons), one can usefully substitute a type I explanation (causes = reasons).

However, type IIa, and especially IIb (or IIc), explanations are readily thought, in a curious way, to be more *profound*, in that they are more likely to describe reality in all its complexity than type I explanations. In fact, they *often* seem – but *not always* – at the same time easy and false.

There are doubtless also examples where spontaneous explanation of strange beliefs turns naturally towards type I rather than type II. Thus, since scientists – even those from the distant past – cannot readily be treated in the same casual way as Indian peasants, General Motors workers or 'primitive people', outdated scientific beliefs (including those which we regard today as very odd and extravagant) are usually explained in terms of the *reasons* which there may have been for believing in them. We accept, for example, that eighteenth-century scientists had reasons for believing in the now totally discredited theory of phlogiston, just as those at the beginning of the twentieth century had reasons for adhering to the ether hypothesis. Nobody would dream of explaining the lasting preoccupation with these theories by the *fanaticism* of scientists or their submissiveness to some *primitive mentality*.

Examples such as these, however, are somewhat exceptional. Generally, somebody observing beliefs which seem strange shows a strong tendency to call on type II explanations. Why is this?

Firstly, because of sociocentrism: when a belief seems strange to us – as happens with magical beliefs, for example – it is almost by definition that we do not see the reasons for it. We therefore tend to regard it as the product of causes rather than reasons. Moreover, it is always easy to find purely verbal explanations for strange beliefs in the framework of the type II model. These explanations range from conceptual processes widely used in everyday sociology or psychology (for example, X believes that Y is true because X is 'stupid', 'crooked', etc.) to those of 'professional' sociology or psychology (for example, X believes in Y because X has 'internalized' a particular view of the world). Explanations such as these can of course be relevant. But they can also be meaningless, even false, leading to the conclusion that, contrary to the claims of such writers as Gaston Bachelard, scientific explanation, far from being distinct from common sense, is often in a direct line with it.

Other more subtle factors go to explain the attraction of the type II model. One of these has to do with the influence of the very ancient philosophical tradition which conceives of knowledge as a sort of reflection of reality in the mind. As soon as one takes this image seriously, one is easily led to explain asymmetrically adherence to a true idea and adherence to a dubious or false idea. In the second case, recourse will normally be had to the hypothesis of psychic factors able to upset the subject's contemplation of reality and operating unbeknown to the subject. In the first case, adherence to a true idea will be explained by its objective validity, which will be regarded as giving the subject sufficient reason to adhere to it.

The influence of this classical philosophy of knowledge is all the greater in that, far from being based only on the authority of a venerable tradition, there is a literal verification in thousands of everyday occurrences. I believe that a particular object is on my table because I have just put it there, and I can easily observe that it is in fact there: in a case such as this, the coincidence between reality and belief will generally be considered to be a sufficient reason for the latter. On the other hand, if I believe that an object which I have just put on the table is still there, whereas in fact it is not and nobody has entered the room, then this illusion has to be explained by certain psychic factors. The explanation will naturally be based in the first case on *reasons*, and in the second case on *causes* (not having the status of reasons).

This type of situation is so commonplace that it tends to impose as something which is self-evident the classic view that correct beliefs stem from correct reasoning, whereas false beliefs are generally the result of factors that distort the subject's reasoning without the subject's being aware of it.

In other words, type II models are influential both because they represent a kind of corollary of the classical theory of knowledge, which itself was always influential, and because they give a clear account of failures and successes alike in what today is usually called ordinary knowledge.

We must also add that this classical theory of knowledge – that of Bacon, Descartes and Pascal – and at the same time the predominance of the type II model in explaining adherence to dubious ideas, was revived by some of the modern writers referred to before, who have in common the fact that they have had a significant influence even over those who were unaware of it: Freud and Marx, as well as Durkheim, Lévy–Bruhl and Pareto.

Thus there is an *asymmetrical* theory of knowledge and error, with a central core identical in all suggested variants, which links Bacon and Pascal across the centuries with Marx, Freud and Pareto.

TYPE I OR TYPE II?

Once again, it is not difficult to think of a thousand examples of beliefs, some of which are explained by a type I model and others by a type IIa or IIb model, and there is no question of giving any of them the stamp of universality, even though it is frequently claimed that they should have it.

I have tried to indicate the reasons why type II models were often wrongly applied. I will not repeat them, except to stress a crucial point which up to now I have simply noted: that very often substituting a type I for a type II explanation gives rise to a positive feeling that progress has been made – so positive that eminent writers, from Weber to Popper, felt justified in seeing such a substitution as the main task of human sciences.

Why this partiality – so contrary to tradition, to principles of ordinary knowledge, and quite simply to accepted thinking – in favour of type I? I will try to answer the question by referring to a classical example – the explanation of magical beliefs.

On page 6 I recalled the famous type II explanation for magical beliefs put forward by Lévy-Bruhl at the beginning of the twentieth century. What I said there, even though brief, was enough to understand the crux of his theory. 'Primitive people' believe in causal relationships which have no objective justification, because they are subject to rules of logic which lead them to confuse causal relationships between things with similarities between phenomena or between words that denote the things. These 'mystical' principles lead them, in other words, to accept that A can influence B when there is a verbal relationship or a physical resemblance between A and B.

Although Durkheim often goes for the type II model, he suggests a type I explanation where magic is concerned.

Nowadays Lévy-Bruhl's explanation is generally regarded as false and irrevocable, and Durkheim's as so correct and acceptable that modern theorists of magic reproduce its principles verbatim, while merely refining the details.[16]

According to Durkheim, a theorist of magic ought to consider, firstly, that primitive people who believe in magic cannot, in the nature of things, know the many theories developed by Western civilization over the centuries. There is no reason why 'primitive people' should know the laws of energy transformation, or the theory of levels of explanation. Secondly, activities as complex as fishing or agriculture imply of course not just mastery of technique, but, beyond that, the use of more general theories such as the origin and growth of plants, interaction between plants and soil, or the influence of humankind on agricultural production. People in the West tend to borrow these general theories, at least in part, from the corpus of knowledge which for them has a monopoly of legitimacy – science. 'Primitive people' borrow them from theories which, equally, give them a general interpretation of the world and are for this reason invested with legitimacy, that is, the theories of religion obtaining in their society. Magical beliefs should therefore, according to Durkheim, be regarded as 'applied' theories drawn by traditional societies from religious doctrines recognized as true, just as in modern societies techniques used by engineers are drawn from the corpus of science.

Here Durkheim addresses to himself an obvious objection, namely that the magical processes to which 'primitive people' have recourse are not as effective as techniques drawn from science. However, showing that magic is not effective assumes, says Durkheim, the deployment of methods of causal analysis developed by science, the mastery of which it would be incongruous to assume was possessed by 'primitive people'. Moreover, it is clearly not always easy to conclude that 'A causes B', either in everyday life or in scientific research. For example, it is often difficult to answer the question of whether a particular pattern of behaviour can in fact be regarded as the cause of a particular illness.

A further point is that, as Durkheim says, we observe scientists themselves continuing to believe, sometimes for many years, in theories disproved by the facts. Often, they have good reasons for this. Who can say in advance that a particular fact, shown to be contradictory with a particular theory, is not an artifact, that is, an illusion arising from empirical methods? Who can say for sure that a small modification to the theory will not manage to save it?[17] In other words, suggests Durkheim, for equally good reason, one can either abandon or continue to believe in a theory disproved by the facts. In this way, the magician whose methods fail and who tries to save them by auxiliary hypotheses (the ritual was not followed properly, opposing forces impaired its effectiveness, and so on) is behaving in a way which is no different from that of the scientist, and is even of the same fundamental nature.[18]

Moreover, even assuming, as is warranted, that primitive people, with no mastery of methods of casual analysis, have a rudimentary and intuitive knowledge of the procedures by which a casual relationship can be accepted or rejected, this foreknowledge is often of little help. Moreover it is not difficult to conclude that in 'modern' societies themselves, ordinary people as well as scientists believe in all kinds of causal relationships which have no sound empirical basis. This is because, very often, testing a relationship such as 'A causes B' assumes complex procedures whose application is very often rendered more difficult by the endemic existence of phenomena of co-linearity. We need only quote the example of beliefs about the effectiveness of a particular treatment or practice on longevity, physical health or psychic 'equilibrium'. There is no doubt at all that *magical* beliefs, that is, beliefs in dubious causal relationships, are common currency in this sort of area. They are largely explained by the fact that it is very difficult – because of the phenomena of co-linearity which blur the relationships between these variables – to establish or disprove the corresponding causal relationships.

The same is true of many other areas – for example, political beliefs. Frequently, it is fundamentally impossible to determine whether policy A is likely to produce result B or not, quite simply because by adopting A, results A', A'' and so on are produced at the same time. This objective co-linearity explains why those scientists who are the most imbued with a scientific, even a scientistic, ethos are often prone to magical beliefs when they express opinions about politics.

Correcting Lévy-Bruhl's rigidly evolutionist view, Durkheim says that magical beliefs still predominate to a large extent in modern societies, and concludes that although the magician is closer to the scientist than is often thought, it is also true that the scientist can also be close to the magician.

Durkheim's demonstration is crowned by an argument of remarkable subtlety. By a kind of trick of nature, magical beliefs, however false, can be *reinforced*, as Durkheim explains, rather than contradicted by reality, such as when rituals to bring rain are practised at times when rain would help crops and when it is also more likely to fall, so that there is more rain when the rituals are practised than when they are not. In this way, causal belief is boosted by a statistical correlation between the two variables in question.

Therefore, suggests Durkheim, there is nothing strange in magical beliefs. Far from following a peculiar logic, primitive people follow strictly the same principles as us. They subscribe to all kinds of weak or false 'A causes B' statements for reasons that are exactly analogous to those which lead us to believe in similar statements that are just as false. The *content* of these statements may vary, depending on the state of science or stage of society. But very often there is no difference between the processes followed by the scientist who still believes in phlogiston, the magician who believes fertility rites are effective, or the modern person who believes a particular practice is good for health or individual happiness.

There are three reasons, I think, why Durkheim's theory of magic – also found in abridged form in Weber,[19] though any mutual influence is difficult to establish – is nowadays as widely accepted as Lévy-Bruhl's is discredited.[20]

Firstly, Durkheim's theory comprises a set of *'psychological'*[21] propositions – or more accurately statements on the subjective states of magicians and their public – which are all perfectly and readily acceptable; for example:

- an activity such as agriculture requires that subjects have a theory on the origin and growth of the planets;
- a theory contradicted by experience can be rescued by auxiliary hypotheses;
- one can have good reasons for not rejecting a theory contradicted by experience;
- social subjects tend to take their interpretations of the world from the corpus of knowledge regarded as legitimate;
- 'applied' knowledge is built up on the basis of basic knowledge;
- one tends to rely on a causal statement confirmed by the corresponding correlation;
- subjects who are unaware of the laws of the transformation of energy will distinguish less clearly between the case of the firemaker from that of the rainmaker than those who are aware of them;
- subjects without the statistical arsenal to validate a causal inference are in a worse position to judge whether a set of observations justifies the assertion 'A causes B'.

The list is of course not exhaustive.

Secondly, Durkheim's theory allows us, from a sociological viewpoint, to explain the *variations*, in space and time, of the phenomenon of magic. By further exploring the avenues opened up by Durkheim, it can be argued that, to give rise to magic, the religious theories obtaining in a particular society must develop a world view where nature seems to be governed by capricious spirits.[22] On the other hand, when it is conceived as being dominated by fixed rules, by a coherent and harmonious constitution, magic is hardly likely to flourish. This is why the phenomenon is only marginally important in traditional societies such as Ancient Greece or China, whereas it is practised in many others.

Moreover, as Mauss has observed, the dominant activities in the society in question must be both complex and uncertain enough for magic processes to develop and become institutionalized.[23]

In the same way, it has been convincingly suggested that the increase in magic and witchcraft in the sixteenth century until its relatively sudden disappearance in the eighteenth century needs to be seen, among other factors, in the light of changes in dominant *Weltanschauungen*. As long as the dominant world view in the Christian West was of Aristotelian inspiration, magic and withcraft remained relatively marginal. However, the Renaissance enthusiasm for neo-Platonism – which introduced the notion of analogy between natural, supernatural and psychic phenomena – promoted their development.[24] Then, at the end of the seventeenth century, Cartesianism triumphed among the elites and imposed the idea of the impersonality of nature: God created an ordered world, but no longer intervenes in its functioning. The spread of this new world view meant that magic and witchcraft lost ground.[25]

All these *variations* are easily explained within the framework of Durkheimian theory; but they are completely incomprehensible within that of Lévy-Bruhl's theory, where one would have to assume some very unlikely swings of *primitive mentality* to account for cycles of magic and withcraft.

Finally, from an *epistemological* viewpoint, Durkheim's theory is neither *ad hoc* nor tautological. It is not *ad hoc* in that the set of propositions which allow us to analyse the adherence of people from certain traditional societies to magical beliefs has a validity independent of the consequences to which they give rise. It is not tautological in that the explanatory propositions which it introduces are certainly not a mere translation into another language of the phenomenon to be explained.

The defects in Lévy-Bruhl's theory are the inverse of the good points in Durkheim's. Firstly, it includes *psychological* hypotheses which are very cumbersome. It is not, for example, an insignificant hypothesis to assume that subjects follow rules of logic which vary according to the society and that they have to accept these rules without being able in any way to distance themselves critically from them. Lévy-Bruhl's 'primitive people' place on their associations of ideas a causal interpretation without exercising over this process any more control than over the chemical processes in their body. These cumbersome psychological hypotheses and the notion of primitive mentality itself are an invitation to the critic to wield Occam's razor.

Sociologically, Lévy-Bruhl's theory does not explain how magic is distributed in time and space. As soon as magical beliefs are seen as the product of cognitive organization characteristic of people in traditional societies, it is impossible to see why magic practices should not be present in all such societies. But their presence or absence depends on the types of dominant activities, as well as on the types of world view peddled by religious systems.

Lévy-Bruhl's theory is completely unable to account for the relationship between the development of magic and these morphological and ideological variables. Of course, unlike Durkheim's theory, it is also unable to account for the appearance and spread of magic practices in *modern* societies.

Finally, his theory is, from an *epistemological* point of view, both *ad hoc* and tautological. It is *ad hoc* in that its key notions – the concept of primitive mentality or *mystical* explanation – were devised exclusively to account for the phenomena which Lévy-Bruhl was trying to explain, that is, magical phenomena. It is *tautological* in that these notions simply paraphrase magical beliefs. They explain why primitive people confuse verbal associations and causal relationships by saying they have a tendency to confuse the two, a tendency shown to be true by the fact that they do in reality confuse them.

It is therefore easy to understand why the theory outlined by Durkheim tends to meet with approval, whereas Lévy-Bruhl's has hardly survived, despite initial success. The former explains the phenomenon of magic by a set of basic propositions, each of which is readily acceptable and which are clearly independent of the phenomenon thereby explained. The logical quality of the theory produces, moreover, a significant sociological dividend, in that it means that the theory can account for the distribution of magic in time and space.

For these reasons, we regard Durkheim's theory as *objectively* preferable to Lévy-Bruhl's; and there is a definite feeling of having made progress by moving from the latter to the former.

But the important thing as far as my present contribution to the debate is concerned is that all these differences stem from a basic difference between the two theories: Durkheim's theory is type I and Lévy-Bruhl's[26] type II. The former explains magical beliefs in terms of the reasons which magicians and their public have for believing in it. Lévy-Bruhl attempts on the other hand to account for it by psychic forces of *causes* bearing on the subject. However, whereas Durkheim's *reasons* are convincing, the same hardly applies to Lévy-Bruhl's *causes*.

This difference of type is easily shown by an effective linguistic test. Durkheim's theory can of course be introduced by saying 'magicians have good reasons to believe that their rituals are effective, because . . .'. On the other hand, Lévy-Bruhl's theory cannot be introduced by using this kind of wording; instead we have to say 'magicians *have no reasons* for believing that their rituals are effective, *but* (they are subject to a logic which makes them confuse homonymy and resemblance . . .)'.

I have gone into some detail on this example because I think it has a certain degree of generality and it allows us to understand the apparently surprising advice given by Weber and Popper in various forms and in any case applied consistently by them: *to account for a belief, or an action, always try to find the reasons for it.*

This advice is based on a simple fact: since spontaneous sociology is prone to misuse 'irrational' explanations of behaviour and beliefs, scientific sociology is often led to set sound explanations in terms of *reasons* against weak explanations in terms of alleged *causes* which common sense supplies so copiously.

Many other examples could be cited where, as in the case of the explanation of magic, a move from a type II to a type I theory is associated with a feeling of having made progress.

There is often an implicit application of this methodology by Durkheim, as shown by my analysis of his theory of magic, but also in many other analyses in his two books *Suicide* and *The Elementary Forms of the Religious Life.*[27]

The methodology is much more consistent and explicit in, for example, Max Weber. For him, explaining the religious beliefs of a particular group always involves accounting for the reasons that group members have for those beliefs. This is why most of his analyses in the sociology of religion can be introduced by the following kind of wording: 'members of X group, society, class, etc, had good reasons to believe Y, because . . .'. This is seen in some very well-known quotations: 'Roman administrators had good reasons for believing in the cult of Mithra, because . . .', 'Prussian civil servants had good reasons for being attracted by freemasonry, because . . .', 'Roman peasants had good reasons for being polytheist, because . . .'[28].

A discussion of the theory of magic also allows me to refer – without going into detail, since I will come back to it later – to a major problem which is a difficult one: the *reasons* which Durkheim's magicians have for believing in the effectiveness of their rituals, or Weber's Prussian civil servants in the truth of masonic dogma, are clearly not *objective* reasons. They are not reasons of the kind that lead me to agree with the statement 'two and two are four'. Nevertheless, they are *good reasons*, which is why they can be interpreted as the causes of the beliefs in question.

If we accept that an analysis such as Durkheim's is relevant, we then have to admit the existence of a category of reasons which may seem strange since, while they are *good* enough to have an effect on beliefs, they are *without objective foundation*. The case of magic is in this respect paradigmatic, since magical beliefs are by definition false beliefs:

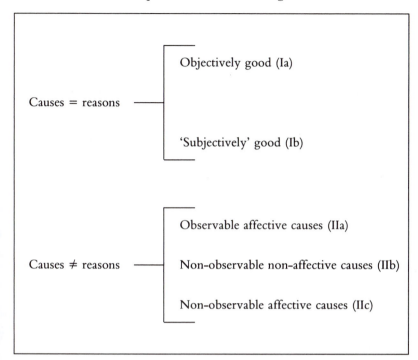

Figure 1.2 — labels:

Causes = reasons
- Objectively good (Ia)
- 'Subjectively' good (Ib)

Causes ≠ reasons
- Observable affective causes (IIa)
- Non-observable non-affective causes (IIb)
- Non-observable affective causes (IIc)

Figure 1.2

although their beliefs are without objective foundation, magicians have good reasons for believing what they believe.

For the sake of clarity, I will call these kinds of reasons 'subjective' reasons, with the inverted commas indicating that although they are subjective, they are neither arbitrary, nor connected with the singularity of the subject. The question, *self-evidently*, is how reasons can be at the same time *good* and without objective foundation.

I will come back to this difficult point on several occasions. For now, however, I would emphasize that the genius of writers such as Max Weber, as well as Pareto,[29] Durkheim and even Marx,[30] lies in the fact that, in their more incisive analyses, they saw clearly that it was vital, to explain all kinds of beliefs, to create an intermediate category in the no-man's-land between the case where beliefs are explicable in terms of objectively justified reasons and the case where they are explained in terms of causes that are not reasons[31].

To avoid all misunderstanding, I would like to say as emphatically as I can that, just because the idea that substituting a type I theory ('X has *good reasons* for believing Y, *because . . .*') for a type II theory ('X has *no* reasons for believing Y, *but* . . .') is often associated with a feeling of progress, I do not in any way draw the conclusion that all beliefs have to be explained by reasons. The Pascal – La Rochefoucauld and Freud – Pareto models are also frequently relevant, and it is true that many beliefs have *affective causes*, whether observable or not.

Generally speaking the three basic models to which I referred at the beginning – now increased to five because of more subtle distinctions (between, on the one hand, *objective* and *subjective* reasons, and on the other, observable and non-observable affective causes) – are all relevant (see figure 1.2).[32]

I do not therefore underestimate in any way the *irrational* causes (if one wishes to use the phrase) of beliefs. All I am saying is that the feeling of having made progress which often occurs when one is able to replace a type II theory by a type I theory can be set against the tendency to misuse type II models, in ordinary knowledge as well as in the human sciences, particularly as a result of the intellectual traditions referred to earlier.

THE RESURGENCE OF TYPE I THEORIES

It is perhaps because of the vague feeling that type I theories tend very often to be more satisfying than type II theories that nowadays, in all the human sciences, there is a proliferation of the former. It can even be argued that the human sciences today give the impression of taking really seriously for the first time the advice of Weber (and Karl Popper, who is simply following Weber on this point), namely, to assume that all beliefs and behaviour are inspired by *reasons*, and to abandon this premise only if one is convinced that one cannot do otherwise.

I would go even further: not only do the contemporary human sciences apply this advice (not always, but often), but they show the good use to which it can be put. The cases where they give the feeling of really having something new to teach us about the world are frequently those where, far from paraphrasing ordinary knowledge, they seem to have been able to explain in terms of a type I theory phenomena which common sense tends to explain by a type II theory.

While not wishing to attempt the impossible task of a comprehensive list in this area, I would like briefly to emphasize that the modern human sciences, often independently, have produced a valuable collection of thinking about the subject: writers in the fields of philosophy, sociology of knowledge, cognitive psychology and economics have, in studying the theory of rationality, come up with a whole range of type I models explaining belief in ideas which are false, dubious, weak or simply without objective foundation.

In short, there is easily accessible in the various human sciences a whole range of writing which breaks with the tradition of the moralists, of classical philosophy, and of a great deal of the classical human sciences – that part which argues that beliefs without objective foundation cannot be explained in terms of the reasons which the subject has for subscribing to them.

a) Philosophy

As for philosophers, type I theories are the particular concern of those studying the theory of rhetoric. In this context, reference must again be made to Toulmin and Perelman, two pioneering writers who, though very different from each other, have between them been responsible for a profound renewal of the theory not only of rhetoric, but of persuasion, communication, and communicational influence.[33]

The basic hypothesis for these writers is that many kinds of reasoning processes have a real capacity to convince, though they differ in form from canonical processes recognized by logic. It is not an accident that Perelman suggests that the 'new rhetoric' should be resolutely anti-Paretan. For writers such as Pareto (or Pascal) the only arguments with the power to convince are ones which would find a place in scientific debate. Others, such as those occurring with the beliefs of magicians, should be analysed, according to Pareto, as covering arguments having no causal influence on beliefs.

The central intuition of Toulmin and Perelman is totally against this view, which the latter ascribes to Pareto probably because among modern writers he is the most directly inspired by it and the one who articulates it in the most schematic way.

This intuition starts from a simple statement, further developed by Aristotle, that there are many kinds of subjects which cannot, by their very nature, be tackled in a demonstrative mode. They must therefore be approached using modes of reasoning which, while unable to furnish proof, are nevertheless not without persuasive force. These arguments will produce reasons which are perhaps without objective foundation, but which exert a real causal influence on the beliefs of the speaker or the speaker's audience. Perelman suggests that these modes of reasoning should be grouped under the heading of 'rhetoric', in its Aristotelian sense, not in the modern, superficial sense given to it under Jesuit influence.[34]

We may note in passing that this modern meaning of rhetoric as a catalogue of the embellishments of oratory became prevalent at the same time as the idea, which Pascal expressed well in the passage quoted earlier, that reason and passion – 'understanding' and 'will' – are the two 'powers which induce us to agree'. This coincidence is significant, since the classical model does not accept that non-demonstrative reasons can have any influence on conviction.

Although their paths diverge, Toulmin's starting point is the same as Perelman's. It seems to me that Toulmin has shown convincingly that reasoning of a legal *kind* – which of course does not occur only in legal debates in the strict meaning of the term – is neither superior nor inferior to scientific reasoning, but that it is different in nature, because it answers different questions. In this way, the way in which 'backing' operates, which Toulmin analyses in detail and which he sees as the central feature of 'legal' reasoning, is hardly used in scientific reasoning. However, ignoring the classical tradition, Toulmin suggests that one would not go to the trouble of constructing complex edifices of reasoning if they had a mere covering function. In fact, they give speakers and their audience the *reasons* for believing in the truth of a particular statement, and it is because of these reasons that they do in fact believe in it. These reasons may of course be at the same time *good* and non-demonstrative.[35]

A brief summary of the contribution of Toulmin and Perelman would say that they are responsible for the idea that reasons without objective foundation can nevertheless be *good*, and determine our beliefs.

The works of Toulmin and Perelman were very influential and undoubtedly helped to break down the idea that only demonstrative reasoning could be convincing. In this sense, both writers bear out the principle that explaining that X believes Y often means looking for the reasons – even though these may have no objective foundation – which X might have for subscribing to Y.

In other words, to explain beliefs, both Toulmin and Perelman are in favour of substituting type I theories for type II theories.

b) Sociology

Writers on the theory of reasoning have shown that reasoning processes of a non-demonstrative type could be sounder and have a greater bearing on beliefs than classical tradition allowed, and in the same way philosophers and sociologists of science have shown that scientific reasoning was exclusively demonstrative only in exoteric presentations. Operations of a 'backing' kind associated with Toulmin are, according to writers such as Kuhn, Ziman or Holton, just as much a feature of reasoning processes used by scientists to persuade themselves that a particular conclusion is correct as they are of legal reasoning.[36] However, though they play a decisive role in the generation of beliefs, they are merely temporary props and play no part in the public presentation of results, since this has to be in keeping with the demonstrative style.

In any event, what these developments in the sociology of science show is that scientific beliefs are often the result of reasons which are at the same time *good* and non-demonstrative, like those used by lawyers, and even lay people, to convince themselves.

In this regard, modern sociologists and philosophers of science find inspiration in the most productive area of classical sociology – that which says that beliefs should be explained (except when it seems implausible) by reference to the reasons which inspire them, and that these reasons can be with or without objective foundation.

I will not dwell on the fact that one of the strokes of genius of the two main founders of sociology, Weber and, in his best writing, Durkheim (when he analyses magic, but in many other places as well), is the suggestion that one should explain beliefs, including those which at first sight are the most bizarre ones, in terms of good reasons.

I hasten to add that it is impossible to say there is general acceptance in the social sciences of the Weberian premise – which Popper calls the 'zero hypothesis'[37] – that even the strangest beliefs should be regarded as inspired by good reasons, unless the contrary is proved. On the contrary, we must recognize that many sociologists are satisfied with the view that arguments presented by subjects to bolster their beliefs ought to be analysed as having a mere covering function, with the *real* causes of the beliefs being located elsewhere.

In any event, modern sociology has also made a significant contribution to type I theories.[38]

c) Psychology

Among the human sciences, cognitive psychology is today one of the most prolific and cumulative. The current vitality of the discipline stems largely from the way in which, in a conscious, even deliberate, manner, it develops type I theories at the expense of type II theories which have for too long shown an overweening hegemonism, according to cognitive psychologists. They set what they call 'hot theories' against 'cold theories' of belief, and their whole research is based on the idea of giving the latter the importance they deserve.

This distinction between *cold* theories and *hot* theories partly coincides with my distinction between type I theories and type II theories. More accurately, the hot theories of Nisbett and Ross[39] more or less correspond to what I earlier called type IIa and IIc theories (explanation of beliefs in terms of observable or non-observable *affective* causes), while their cold theories correlate with my type I theories (causes of beliefs = *reasons*). The distinction between hot and cold theories does not therefore take in type IIb theories, exemplified by Lévy-Bruhl's theory of magic. The divergence between the two typologies stems from the criterion on which they are based: the hot/cold pairing is produced by the *psychological* distinction between reasons and *affects*; the type I/type II pairing by the *epistemological* distinction between *reasons* and *causes*.

Hot theories, according to Nisbett and Ross, are those which fall under the heading of La Rochefoucauld's maxim 'the spirit is always the dupe of the heart'.

Behaviourism and psychoanalysis, the two major twentieth-century schools of psychology, have upheld an essentially 'motivational' conception of illusion and error. Nisbett recalls on this point that no less a pioneer of behaviourism than Tolman himself spoke of 'motivational imperialism', and it was only after lengthy argument by Nisbett that it became accepted that errors observed during learning processes were not always due to affective causes.

As for cold theories, cognitive psychologists place them under the heading of a quotation from J. S. Mill: 'Every erroneous inference, though originating in moral causes, involves the intellectual operation of admitting insufficient evidence as sufficient.'

In its simplicity, this sentence opens up a research programme completely different from the one which had become established under the influence of classical tradition; false ideas doubtless originate in 'moral causes', that is, what classical writers called feelings, urges, the imagination, and other causes, all of which in the seventeenth century were summed up in the concept of 'will'. But, at the same time, adherence to false ideas depends on one vital condition: there must be produced in the mind of subjects, under the effect of mechanisms whose nature J. S. Mill tried to analyse in his treatise on the distortion of inference,[40] distortions which lead them to accept reasons as sufficient when they are in fact insufficient.

In other words, in cognitive psychology, Mill was responsible for, or at least suggested, a research shift similar to the one which Weber later advocated in sociology. In any event, it can be argued without great fear of contradiction that, by opting for this avenue of research, modern cognitive psychology has contributed significantly to the explanation of belief.

d) Economics

As for economists, they have contributed to the development of *cold* theories of belief in a way which can be described as involuntary. In effect, their contribution is a by-product of the gradual enhancement and increasing complexity of the economic theory of rationality. Starting with a rigid conception of rationality (an action or decision is rational when it is based on reasons which are *objectively* the best), they gradually replaced it by a flexible theory, stressing the uncertain, limited and imperfectly reliable nature of 'rational' procedures. In doing this, they laid the foundations, without realizing it, of a theory that beliefs can be based on good reasons.

It is not therefore surprising that it was an economist, Anthony Downs, who proved that 'ideology' is a necessary ingredient of 'rationality'.[41] Faced with a complex decision, says Downs, economic or political actors have no access to the information they need to act in full knowledge of the facts. They have therefore to make decisions on the basis of beliefs with a more or less sound foundation. Translated back into Weberian idiom, Downs's theorem can be expressed thus: in a complex situation, axiological rationality substitutes for the deficiencies of instrumental rationality or, more simply, *good reasons* replace objectively valid, but inaccessible, reasons.

Downs's book was particularly influential, and led to the complete renewal of the theory of action and decision by taking explicit account of the fact that actors are usually in situations of imperfect information.[42]

However, the most influential contribution from economics is without doubt Herbert Simon's theory of subjective rationality, which goes furthest in exploiting Downs's theorem. In any event, it starts explicitly from the principle that economic and social actors can in normal circumstances have all kinds of acceptable and defensible reasons for believing in conjectural ideas which may be correct and relevant, but also very dubious or false.

e) Other contributions

The list of contributions could be extended by adding models developed by logicians (particularly by the proponents of 'flexible logic') or by theorists of artificial intelligence to analyse the processes of natural inference.[43] In one respect, works in these fields tend to show that methods of inference used intuitively in 'ordinary knowledge' are much more flexible than is often thought. By trying to formalize them, these theorists have also indirectly contributed, in their way, to the enhancement of *cold* theories (that is, type I theories) of belief, and have shown, following the example of cognitive psychologists, that processes of natural inference, even though often giving reliable results, are also responsible for false beliefs.

This short list is perhaps sufficient to show that, though the classical philosophical tradition (that which is expressed particularly brilliantly in Pascal's theory of error), common sense and much of human sciences tend to give an undisputed prominence to hot theories of belief, it is clear also that several of the human sciences – cognitive psychology, non-

Weberian sociology, economics, philosophical theories of argumentation, the theory of natural inference, non-classical logic, and so on, jointly (if involuntarily) contribute to the development of a *cold* theory of belief, that is, a theory which emphasizes the premise that, before exploring other avenues, we must look for the good reasons subjects might have for believing in ideas that seem strange to us.

WHY THIS RESURGENCE OF TYPE I THEORIES?

If we try to find the reasons for this resurgence of type I theories in the human sciences, we can say that, while this complicity between the human sciences is certainly not absolutely new, since, on this subject, J. S. Mill links up with Weber and with the Durkheim of the theory of magic, it has become significantly stronger in recent decades.

It is impossible to give a complete answer to the question of why this should be; the resurgence of *cold* theories of belief and behaviour is certainly the result of multiple causes, and I would like to emphasize this point.

I referred earlier to the hypothesis of a possible link between the *classic* conception of knowledge, which assimilates knowledge to a *perception* of reality, and the causal view of belief; the former in fact implies that, when subjects are the victim of an illusion, this is the result of disruptive causes.

Conversely, the development of cold theories is the result (at least partially) of the slow spread of the *modern* theory of knowledge. To use Rorty's phrase[44], we lived for a long time with the idea that knowledge is a 'mirror of nature', that it is a 'knowledge of' and not a 'knowledge that', until the appearance and acceptance of the constructivist conception introduced by the Kantian revolution. As soon as knowledge becomes a 'knowledge that' and is conditioned by the *a priori* of the knowing subject, there is a symmetry between adherence to the true idea and adherence to the false idea. This conclusion is of course not drawn by Kantianism itself, which is protected by its universalist conception of the *a priori* of knowledge; but it is clearly perceived by certain neo-Kantians, particularly Weber and Simmel.

These two philosophers/sociologists are Kantian in that they retain the Kantian idea that knowledge assumes *a priori*, and also that this intervention by the knowing subject does not deny access to what is true, but on the contrary makes access possible. However, by rejecting the fixed nature of Kantian *a priori*, they introduce into the Kantian construct a 'nuance' with a potential for disruption.

Simmel is perhaps more explicit in this respect, and he is the stoutest defender of the idea that truth and objectivity are accessible to the knowing subject not, as he says, *although* but *because* knowledge always expresses a point of view.[45]

At the same time, the intervention of these *a priori* can also (and this stems almost immediately from this softer version of Kantianism) be a source of illusions and bring about adherence to weak, dubious or strange ideas. As soon as the *a priori* used in knowledge lose their universal and immutable character and become more like what Popper calls *conjectures* (and which sociologists and psychologists prefer to call frames or *frameworks*), they can in fact easily give rise to illusion.

This is why neo-Kantianism can be seen as an invitation to explain adherence to dubious ideas in terms of type I theories, of cold theories.

Neo-Kantianism, which Simmel articulates particularly clearly, is today of course very widespread, though in most cases still in a latent, semiconscious or amorphous state. In any event, hardly anybody now believes that knowledge is a reflection of reality in the mind of the knowing subject. Therefore it is perhaps because the human sciences are guided by this modern philosophy of knowledge that they now reject knowledge as a 'mirror of nature', preferring to see it as the result of a move which is active, uncertain, floundering, often obliged to compromise, and thereby subject to failure as well as success.

In the end, this modern theory of knowledge replaces, in all kinds of areas, categorical statements by fine distinctions. In this perspective, therefore, scientific knowledge and ordinary knowledge are different in degree rather than in nature. The important thing is that the theory means that we can see more easily that belief in false ideas can be the result not only of breakdowns in the way thought functions, or distortions produced by the intervention of psychic forces outside the subject's control, but also when the subject applies common thought processes, even the normal processes of scientific thought.

Perhaps a shared Kantian heritage also explains the unexpected convergence of writers such as Weber and Durkheim on the question of the explanation of magical beliefs.

A THEORY OF ILLUSION

In any event, what Simmel does is to derive an explanatory theory of illusion from his neo-Kantian conception of knowledge. He suggests that dubious ideas can be produced by the most natural and commendable processes of reasoning and inference, and explains this by saying that, with realizing it and in a natural and normal manner, we combine with theories or acceptable ideas, implicit propositions (*a priori*) based on good reasons but which can lead us to dubious conclusions.

More precisely, when we construct a theory to explain a phenomenon, we always introduce, as well as explicit propositions on which we base our reasoning, implicit propositions which do not appear directly in the field of our consciousness. In the classical vocabulary of logicians, our lines of reasoning are often *enthymemes*, that is, shortened forms of reasoning (such as syllogisms with one premise unexpressed). Of course it may well be, as he says, that the structure of the theory is modified when these implicit propositions are made explicit; or that the conclusions we draw from the theory are overturned as soon as the implicit propositions are revealed.

Therefore many false ideas arguably spring from the most unimpeachable ideas and reasoning.

Simmel's argument can be even further extended: often, the most firmly established dubious ideas owe their strength quite simply to the fact that they stem from very sound arguments.

I will give a detailed analysis later of what I will from now on call the 'Simmel model', but for now I will merely note that it means we can probably extend – doubtless in a particular direction, but an important one – this cold theory of belief which appears in a diffuse way in all kinds of disciplines.

We will see in any case that Simmel's model is not a simple intellectual construct but has innumerable applications. Because of this, it is a fascinating model for explaining belief in dubious ideas.

Of course, the appearance of dubious, weak or false ideas never derives exclusively from this *Simmel effect*, and we must regard explanatory models of adherence to ideas suggested by traditional philosophy and human sciences as idealized models likely to combine in reality. When a received idea appears, some people will subscribe to it *above all* because it corresponds to their passions (Pascal), or their 'feelings' (Pareto); some will subscribe to it because of *reasons* of the kind analysed by, for example, Toulmin (reasons derived from 'legal'-type reasoning) and some because of *rhetorical*-type reasoning in Perelman's sense, while others will subscribe to it because of *demonstrative* or *scientific* reasoning. But, although Simmel's model describes only *one* of the ideal-typical ways in which people subscribe to dubious or weak ideas, it is particularly important because an idea is more likely to be generally accepted when it is seen to derive from demonstrative arguments. For this reason, the model is a vital element in cognitive sociology.[46] We can even hypothesize that many received ideas circulate first in small groups following the logic of Simmel's model, then spread to other groups because of a Perelman – or Toulmin-type process, and spread even more widely through a Pareto-type process.[47]

FIELDS OF APPLICATION

We know therefore from Simmel's model that *perfectly valid* reasoning can lead to false ideas in that we do not perceive the implicit statements which surround it, and we do not realize that our conclusions are *also* drawn from these implicit statements which we tacitly adopt because we have good reasons for adopting them.

This suggests that we should apply the model to the products of methodical reasoning rather than of ordinary knowledge, and because of this I have taken the trouble to spell out, elaborate, illustrate, or quite simply show the validity and the explanatory power of Simmel's model, using examples from the human sciences.

Of course, in keeping with the principles of the model, my examples are taken from theories which are totally respectable from a scientific point of view, so I am not concerned here with false beliefs arising from sophistical theories.[48]

I limit myself to the human sciences not just for reasons of familiarity, but also for less superficial reasons. It is rare for ideas to come down from above, and the dubious, weak or false ideas (as well as correct ones) which we have about the world often come, after detours and interventions of a more or less complex kind, from the human sciences. Received ideas about the natural sciences sometimes themselves come from the human sciences – particularly the philosophy and sociology of science.

I will try to show by my examples that, as Simmel suggests, many dubious ideas are based on sound arguments, or, more precisely, are the result of a combination of sound arguments and implicit statements authoritative enough to be regarded as self-evident.

We can even go a stage further: the most viable received ideas are perhaps those which are based on valid explicit reasoning and whose conclusions are contaminated by implication. Simmel's model would therefore explain why, to adapt Alfred Jarry's famous phrase, without Marx there would be no Marxism, without Darwin no Social Darwinism, and why, to quote a third example which I prefer here, without contemporary philosophy and sociology of science, relativism would not today have the influence that it has.

Although these statements may seem trite, a model which claims that false beliefs are rarely brought about by the attendant arguments is unable to account for them. Moreover, even the most recalcitrant false ideas contain a sound core of reasoning, and this fact is surely sufficient to show that theorists who claim that false ideas are exclusively the product of passion and blindness are taking a particular case for the general case.

Like Simmel, I think that false ideas are often generated by arguments which own their strength of conviction quite simply to their objective validity. Generally speaking, there is a tendency to exaggerate the scope of the type II model, according to which false ideas are only exceptionally the result of attendant arguments. Neither Third Worldism, for example, nor present-day relativism are explained *only* in terms of feelings. These ideas would not be as influential as they are if they were not *also* based on valid cores of reasoning.

I could have taken my examples at random from the huge pool of theories put forward by the human sciences. In fact, though several of them are taken from sociology, political science, economics and other disciplines, many of them revolve round theories developed by contemporary sociology and philosophy of science.

The reason for this is that one of the motives behind this book, if not its genesis, is that for many years I had been both interested and disturbed by my (very serious, I hope) study of works by the influential philosophers and sociologists of science of our time, such as Kuhn, Hübner, Feyerabend and Bloor. Their findings are rather surprising and partly, I think, questionable. However, these questionable conclusions are, in most cases, based on reasoning which it is difficult to challenge.

After today's relativist philosophers and sociologists have had their say, the notions of *truth*, *objectivity* and *progress* as far as knowledge is concerned are so devalued that they seem to be trivialities belonging to a kind of bygone prehistory of thinking about human knowledge. All these writers conclude that it is difficult to explain why science seems more effective than magic. They tell us that scientists choose between particular theories not for objective reasons, but for reasons as subjective as those which lead us to prefer, for example, one style of furniture to another.

These strange conclusions are based on arguments which are acceptable from a logical as well as from an empirical point of view. At first sight, therefore, we are justified in thinking that we are in a situation where Simmel's model applies – where valid reasoning leads to dubious conclusions.

The fact that, above and beyond my various examples, criticism of relativism – more accurately, of *modern cognitive relativism* – is one of the leitmotifs of this book, is therefore explained partly by my long-standing instinctive perplexity when faced with it. However, another reason why I have emphasized this theme is that, on the one hand, *cognitive* relativism seems to me to be one of the most typical and entrenched received ideas of our time, a notion so well established that it is hard to oppose it without immediately appearing 'retrograde'[49], as Auguste Comte would have said; and, on the other hand, it is defended, unlike *ethical* or *aesthetic* relativism, by first-rate advocates and sound arguments.

To my mind, however, the main function of relativism is to show

how important a contribution Simmel's model has made to the theory of belief.

WHAT IS 'BELIEVING'?

Finally, I need to clarify a point of vocabulary. As is doubtless apparent, what I call 'belief' is any dubious or false inference, while recognizing straightaway that, in everyday language as well as in the language of philosophy, anthropology or sociology, the word has all kinds of other meanings.[50]

If I limit myself to a few quick remarks on this subject, I would say that everyday language like philosophy also speaks of beliefs with reference to valid inferences – one can *believe* that it is raining when it is as well as when it is not. Again, one speaks of beliefs in the context of adherence to statements of fact not deriving from inferences. Thus one can believe, or not, that Tegucigalpa is the capital of Nicaragua. One can also speak of *belief* in the context of adherence to propositions which, like *normative* statements, cannot be said to be either true or false.

Although adherence to normative beliefs is a classical sociological topic, I will not deal with it here.

Generally speaking, the number of possible definitions of the notion of belief matches the number of acceptable combinations of the various *types of statement* (deriving/not deriving from the categories true/false, deriving from these categories and true/deriving from these categories and false, inferential/non-inferential statements, statements which are descriptive/not descriptive of states of affairs, and so on), and the types of adherence to these statements which can be identified (regard them as true, plausible, possible, established, unquestionable, questionable, and so on).

Therefore, compared with normal usage, it is in a deliberately very restrictive sense that I am using the words *believe* and *belief*.

Summary

Three models are used to explain belief in weak, dubious or false ideas: Weber's model, which accounts for them in terms of reasons (type I); the La Rochefoucauld – Pascal model (type IIa), according to which 'the mind is the dupe of the heart' (explanation in terms of *affective* causes); and the Lévy-Bruhl model (type IIb) which explains these beliefs in terms of *non-affective* causes.

The type II models owe their influence to their congruence with the classical philosophical theory of knowledge, to the fact that they provide easy explanations, and to the fact that the spontaneous sociocentrism of common sense has a natural tendency to regard beliefs whose meaning escapes it as determined by causes rather than reasons.

This is why there is a misuse of type II explanations (irrational explanations).

Writers such as Max Weber and Popper suggest we should start from the premise that the strangest behaviour or beliefs are explained by reasons, and abandon this premise only when no other course is possible. Similarly, Durkheim, in his best analyses – his theory of magic, for example – accounts for beliefs that lack objective foundation by reference to the reasons which social subjects have for believing in them.

In general, the human sciences – sociology, economics, cognitive psychology, philosophy of knowledge, theories of argumentation, and so on – have in recent decades extended the sphere of the *rational* explanation of beliefs.

However, as is well shown by the example of Durkheim's theory of magic, the reasons which explain why social subjects subscribe to a particular belief may be not objectively valid and, at the same time, intelligible, when social context is taken into consideration. In other words, Durkheim's subjects are here obeying reasons which are good though without valid foundation.

Simmel's model highlights an important species of 'good reasons'. He suggests that false ideas can arise from unimpeachable ideas contaminated by implication. This is a vital theoretical element in cognitive sociology: one can put forward the hypothesis that many received ideas first circulate in the small groups according to the logic of Simmel's model, then spread to other groups as a result of the kind of process associated with Perelman, Toulmin or Pareto.

The explanatory power of this model is examined using various examples from the human sciences, particularly the philosophy and sociology of science. For some time, these disciplines have contributed to the establishment of a received idea – cognitive relativism, which says that the search for objectivity and truth is illusory. Should we interpret the establishment of this cliché as a manifestation of the 'Simmel effect'?

2

Good reasons for believing in false ideas

In Flaubert's *Madame Bovary*, when Emma Bovary is given an emetic to empty her stomach, Homais the pharmacist comments by declaring very learnedly: 'As soon as the cause ceases, the effect should cease; it's obvious.'

The wry comedy of this quotation is of course that the pharmacist's scientism is incongruous in the particular situation; but also that he is applying in all innocence a generally valid principle to a situation where it is obviously not applicable. *If* the effects of the poison *were* reversible, the general principle that a good way of making an effect disappear is to eliminate its cause would apply, and Homais' comment would be legitimate. It is, however, absurd because it incorporates within formally sound reasoning an implicit statement which is of general validity but unacceptable in this particular case.

Here, Flaubert's readers smile wryly, recognizing themselves in the character of Homais, or in those of Bouvard and Pécuchet in *L'Education sentimentale*. In fact, even though we do not always take the same intellectual risks as Homais, we frequently rely, in ordinary knowledge, on systems of arguments with the same structure as the line of reasoning taken by Flaubert's character.

In effect, Homais' reasoning is a caricature of Simmel's model. His arguments are in an appropriate order; they are based on a principle whose very general validity is undeniable. Nevertheless, the conclusion is unacceptable. Simmel says, of course, that we frequently think in this way: without being aware of it, we incorporate into our reasoning statements which seem to us self-evident because they are commonplace. However, in doing so, we run the risk of taking certain dubious ideas as proved.

The quotation from Flaubert is an example of what I was stressing in Chapter 1 – the case where a belief, though false or weak, stems from reasoning based on good reasons. Obviously, Homais' certainty, clearly the effect of J. S. Mill's 'moral causes', is based *also* on his scientistic bigotry. But it is consolidated by arguments which are formally correct.

I said earlier that the importance of Simmel's model – and more generally, type I theories to which it belongs – was not fully grasped because it runs counter to the classical model that adherence to false ideas should be regarded as the result of causes and not of reasons. However, opposition to this model is greater because it appears to be based on an elusive concept – 'good reasons'. Should a reason, in order to be 'good', be true or objectively valid?

The fact that the notion of 'good reasons' is difficult to grasp is – at least partly – because of the philosophical tradition, which I mentioned, whereby reasons need to have an objective basis, otherwise they are fallacious. Durkheim's analysis of magic suggests, however, that apart from *objectively* good reasons there are reasons which, though objectively bad, are plausible and are regarded by the knowing subject as *subjectively* good.

> It is these reasons which, departing from the meaning given in some quarters, I will call 'good reasons'.[1]

The objection will obviously be that, seen like this, every reason can be 'good'. However, I would argue that this is not true – that a reason can be subjectively but not objectively good, and nevertheless not only not be arbitrary, but even – in a way which I will explain later – endowed with a certain universality. In other words, we are quite justified in going along with ordinary knowledge, which often uses 'good reasons' in this sense: it is quite normal, for example, to say 'he had good reasons for not seeing things as they really are.'

We can refer to contemporary cognitive psychology to show that this monster really exists. This branch of the human sciences is remarkably active and productive nowadays, largely because it regards the type I model as basic in the explanation of beliefs. What contemporary cognitive psychologists show us is that, contrary to the widespread conception, false beliefs often derive less from affective than from intellectual causes. Their message goes even further, in that they also tell us that ordinary knowledge has no difficulty in containing within itself falsity as well as truth.

Recourse to experimental cognitive psychology has another advantage. It means we are dealing with clear-cut cases, as in a laboratory experiment, where, unlike what happens in natural cognitive processes, there can be no doubt concerning either the relevance of the true/false categories, or the attribution of these predicates to replies given by subjects. The disadvantage is that experiments such as these are somewhat artificial. However, as I will try to show in other chapters, the processes highlighted by cognitive psychology are to be found in non-experimental situations.

At the same time, a discussion of these experiments allows us to remove a particular ambiguity. My feeling is that cognitive psychologists often tend to be much closer to Lévy-Bruhl's than to Durkheim's interpretation of distortions observed in ordinary knowledge. They are probably trying to develop, to use the phrase of Nisbett and Ross,[2] a *cold* theory of adherence to false ideas, and therefore stress the fact that beliefs often stem from the application by the knowing subject of inference procedures and reasoning, whereas tradition attributes them exclusively to affective causes. On the other hand, however, what they say seems to suggest that such beliefs indicate a kind of 'prelogical mentality' characteristic of ordinary knowledge but distinct from methodical knowledge.

In other words, there appears to be a confusion between two interpretations: do they regard the beliefs in question as the product of good reasons? Or else do they see in them the indication of a particular inductive logic followed by subjects with ordinary knowledge? To use the phraseology of Chapter 1, do they suggest replacing 'hot' models (type IIa) with type IIb models (exemplified by the theory of primitive mentality) or type I models (causes = reasons)?

Let us for a moment consider Monsieur Homais as an example – though somewhat exaggerated – of a subject with ordinary knowledge. The question then is whether we should attribute a 'prelogical mentality' to him as we would to Lévy-Bruhl's 'primitive person', or whether he is more like Durkheim's magician who is no different from scientists and is just as capable of believing, for good reasons, in false ideas.

This question gives me the opportunity to reiterate that the distinction in cognitive psychology between *cold* and *hot* theories coincides only partly with the distinction between type I and type II theories, as is seen in figure 2.1.

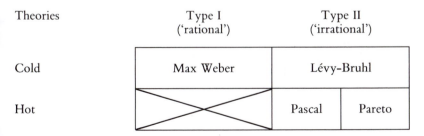

Theories	Type I ('rational')	Type II ('irrational')	
Cold	Max Weber	Lévy-Bruhl	
Hot		Pascal	Pareto

Figure 2.1

Type I theories are those which can be introduced by phrases such as 'Subject X *had good reasons* for believing Y, *because* . . .', and type II theories by 'Subject X *had no real reasons* to believe Y, *but* . . .'.

It is also possible to describe type I theories as 'rational' and type II theories as 'irrational', provided these words are given their true meaning.[3] In this case, Lévy-Bruhl-type theories, which assume that the subject – the 'primitive person' in Lévy-Bruhl, or the ordinary knowing subject in cognitive psychology – obeys particular rules of thinking, are of the *cold* type, since they minimize the role played by affective factors.

However, they are also 'irrational' (that is, type II) in that they are introduced by phrases such as 'The subject *has no real reasons* for believing that . . ., *but* . . .', rather than by an expression such as 'The subject had *good reasons* for believing that . . ., because . . .'. It would therefore be said of Lévy-Bruhl's primitives: 'They have no real *reasons* for believing that their rituals can bring rain, *but* their thinking is subject to rules of association of ideas which make them confuse symbolic relationships with causal relationships.'

I take the view that what cognitive psychology shows us can be interpreted in line with the cold-rational mode – in other words, that the distortions of natural inference are often the result of good reasons.

In summary, a close look at a few examples from this discipline will allow us to clarify the notion of good reasons, show that false beliefs can stem from sound reasoning, exemplify the 'rational' explanation of false beliefs, and at the same time highlight the mechanism present in all these examples.

CLIMBING A MOUNTAIN

A man decides to climb a mountain;[4] he sets out at eight o'clock in the morning, and follows the path to the summit, which he reaches at half past six in the evening. For the whole of this time, he has walked more or less steadily at his own pace, never leaving the path. After spending the night in a refuge, he sets off again the following morning, at the same time of eight o'clock. He goes back down into the valley, again maintaining a more or less steady pace and not leaving the path. As we might expect, he comes down from the mountain quicker than he went up, and arrives at the previous day's starting point at five o'clock in the afternoon.

The question is:

Is there a particular point on the path which he passed at exactly the same time on both days?

I was fascinated by the problem, or rather by the conclusions to which it seemed to lead. Without embarking on the kind of experiment which cognitive psychologists would undertake, I put the problem to a variety of people of different cultural levels and various groups of students. In an overwhelming majority of cases, though with varying degrees of certainty, the reply was in the negative, either unambiguously or with a degree of reservation ('it is not very likely'). 'Intuition', in other words, tends to prompt people – if we take seriously the results of my rather crude experiment – into thinking that it is impossible for the climber to pass a specific point on the path at the same time on both days.

I then tried to find out the reasons behind the replies, with varying degrees of success. This kind of comment was very frequent:

> The climber came down quicker than he went up; on both days he walked at his own pace, without trying to keep to a uniform speed. The hypothetical point which he might have passed at the same time on both days could in any case only be on a limited section of the path. This section is about half way between start and finish, though a bit nearer the valley than the summit because he walked more quickly on the way down . . . Apart from sheer coincidence, why should he have passed at the same time on both days a particular point on this ill-defined section?

We can therefore surmise that people's negative replies to the question, though 'intuitive', are based on reasoning made up of four arguments formulated with varying degrees of clarity and linked thus:

1) the point where the climber could have been at the same time on both days has to be – if it exists – in the middle section of the path;
2) in fact, *only one* point can be characterized thus: if he passed it at the same time on both days, it follows that he passed all other points above and below it *at a different time*;
3) suppose the climber passed on the first day at time t_0 a point on the central section of the path which we can call p_0. What are the chances of his passing p_0 on the following day at exactly the same time? Very small, or even non-existent, if measurement of time is accurate enough;
4) not just p_0, but *all* points on this central section have the same characteristic – the virtual improbability that the climber passed them at exactly the same time on both days;
5) *ergo*, there is no reason to suppose that the climber passed any point at exactly the same time on both days.

We will leave aside for the moment the question of whether this belief is true or false, and simply point out that this example contains a set of characteristics frequently present in the formation of beliefs:

1)   Firstly, the experiment is a good illustration of the case where belief in Y ('there is no reason to suppose that the climber passed any point at exactly the same time on both days') is the *effect* of a particular line of reasoning.

Obviously, we need to distinguish cases where the reasoning is explicit from those where it is not. In many cases, it is only when subjects go back over their reply and think about it *a posteriori* that they are able to see, with varying degrees of clarity, the reasons which led them to adopt their belief. In other words, though the reasons behind the belief may be apparent in varying degrees to subjects, they are nevertheless there. This point may raise some theoretical questions, but it is difficult to deny that in practice reasons can exist and, as here, have a causal influence on beliefs, even though they are semi-conscious.

2)   Secondly, the subject's 'reasoning' consists of two parts – an *explicit* part corresponding to the arguments just outlined, and an *implicit* part.

Thus, in the present context, subjects undertake a mental induction operation giving them a finite set of points $(p_0, p_1, \ldots p_n)$ and then ask with regard to each whether they are likely to have characteristic x, that is, whether the climber passed them at the same time on both days.

This leads them to reply in the negative: '$\sim x\ (p_1)$' ('there is no likelihood at all that any of these points has characteristic x).

They come to the conclusion that, if the statement '$\sim x\ (p_1)$' is true for points $o_0, \ldots, o_n$, it is true also for *all* points on the central section of the path, of which of course there is an infinite number.

Subjects therefore implicitly admit that the generally recognized validity of the induction process allows them to move from a (mental) analysis of a few points to a statement valid for all points in the section.

We can moreover see many other implicit statements in this reasoning: for example, that the correct approach to answering the question is to take all points o_0 to o_n and with respect to each ask oneself whether statement '$x\ (p_1)$' is true; or again that, though the method used is obviously not the only one possible, any other possible method would give the same result, and so on.

3)   The third main characteristic is that all arguments put forward by the ideal-typical subject, such as I am dealing with here – 'explicit' arguments as well as 'implicit' ones – are valid. Of course, induction is generally acceptable as a procedure. Even if it has no logical foundation, as writers such as Bochenski[5] correctly point out, not only ordinary knowledge but also all sciences are based on it. Moreover, the question we are examining is clearly whether there is one (or several) point(s) p, such that $x\ (p_1)$.

In short, since all the arguments leading to the near-unanimous negative replies are valid, we can say that the resulting belief is based on *good reasons*.

4) These reasons, however, are *good* in the sense in which I used the word earlier in this context – while perfectly valid subjectively, they lead to a conclusion which is objectively false (I ask the reader who is not convinced of this to be patient). At the same time, although these reasons are subjective, they are not arbitrary, as is shown by the fact that many subjects tend to share them.[6]

All in all, this belief on the part of subjects ('there is no point p_1 such that x (p_1)') is based on a reasonable set of arguments, in that each of its components is acceptable. Nevertheless, the conclusion is false.

In other words, we are dealing with a cold-type belief stemming from a line of argument which is reasonable yet false.

Let us be clear about the false nature of this belief: firstly by presenting it differently, using Cartesian coordinates representing time and the path from valley to mountain summit.

The climber's journey is the sequence of points indicating his location at any one time, from 0800 hours to 1830 hours; the return journey is a similar line going down from the summit to the starting point.

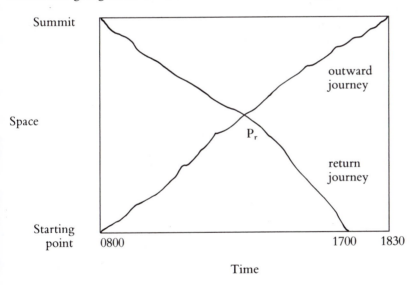

Figure 2.2

From figure 2.2, it is not difficult to see that the climber, even if his pace is not uniform, will *of necessity* pass at least *one* point on the path at the same time on both journeys; moreover, this point is unique.

I have sometimes been surprised by the reaction of some of my respondents when I indicated this solution: it appeared to be so out of keeping with what intuition showed that they were not convinced that figure 2.2 was an accurate representation of the problem. Because of this, I sought further proof by conceiving the climb in a more concrete way. This 'physical' representation was much more convincing: the climber makes his way to the summit in exactly the same way as before, but this time we assume that a *second* climber sets off down the mountain from the summit, making the journey in exactly the same conditions as the first climber will make the following day.

Obviously the first climber will of necessity meet the second at, say, point p_r. Since the second climber is simulating the first climber's return journey, it follows that on this return journey the first climber passes point p_r at exactly the same time as on the outward journey the previous day.

Why does the 'intuitive' reasoning which I tried to reconstruct above lead in this case to a false belief? Because it exaggerates the trustworthy nature of induction. As figure 2.2 shows, this is a case where the statement $\sim x$ (p_1) is true for all points, that is, for the infinite number of points in the two lines . . . apart from one! In a case where a predicate applies to an infinite number of objects except one, the application of inductive method leads necessarily to the conclusion $\sim x$ (p_i), for any i.

Expressed in words: there is no point where the climber is on both days at exactly the same time. In fact, there is no likelihood that mental sampling of points $p_0, \ldots, p_n$ will light on point p_r such that $\sim x$ (p_r) is false.

The reason why respondents end up with a false belief is quite simply because they regard it as self-evident that the best way of answering questions such as 'are all crows black?' is to refer to a sample of crows, or mental images of crows, ask oneself whether all in the sample are black and – assuming the answer to this question is positive – infer that '*all* crows are black'.

This question is of the kind 'Are all points on the path characterized by the impossibility of the climber being there on both days at the same time?'

Why, finally, do respondents regard recourse to induction as *self-evident* and why do they deal with it in an implicit way? For the simple reason that very often it is self-evident. In this sense, the respondents' reasons, though *subjective*, are not *arbitrary*.[7]

A few more examples, this time taken directly from cognitive psychology, will show that, apart from a few variations, this *same* process is found in most of the distortions of inference which are the subject of very instructive examination by the discipline.

The examples in the following chapters endeavour to show that this general process can be identified not only in ordinary thinking, the laws of which the somewhat artificial experiments of cognitive psychology try to highlight, but also in methodical and scientific thinking.

PATHS OF CROSSES AND BUS–STOPS

In one of their multiple experiments, Tversky and Kahneman[8] get subjects to look at two blocks of crosses, one of which (A) is made up of three lines of eight crosses, and the other (B) of two columns of nine crosses, or, put another way, nine lines of two crosses (see figure 2.3).

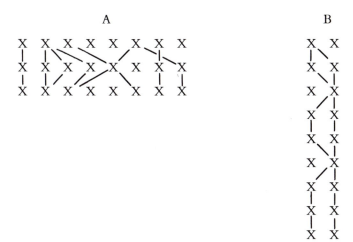

Figure 2.3

The question put to the subjects is:

Is the number of paths you can trace from the top line to the bottom line, passing through only one cross in each intermediate line, greater in A or B, or is it the same?

The question was put to 64 people. Of these, 46, that is about three-quarters, said that there were more paths of this kind in A than in B. In fact, there is exactly the same number of paths (512) in each case.[9]

To explain this error of inference, Tversky and Kahneman use a concept which figures largely in their writing – availability heuristics. The important hypothesis behind this rather clumsy concept is that, to answer the question put to them, the subjects 'looked for' (I put this in inverted commas to show that the search was probably in most cases semi-conscious rather than conscious) heuristic means, and they came up with the simplest and most natural – to try to estimate the number of paths of the kind indicated by the question. Since it is impossible mentally to do a complete count, they made do with a 'poll', trying to identify the number of paths in A and B corresponding to the definition.

However, as the reader can easily see by reference to figure 2.3, it is easier to *see* paths on A than on B. The eight paths in A which go directly down each column from the top line to the bottom line are immediately obvious. Similarly, it is easy to *see* all the paths joining the top and bottom lines by moving one, two, three, etc., crosses to the left or right on the middle line. In other words, it is easy to pick out a large number of paths in A which meet the definition in the question. With B, it is much more difficult to see a significant number of paths, mainly because paths in B, composed of seven segments instead of two, are much longer than in A. Moreover, if one tried to draw all the paths on the grid, or even an equal number on A and B, there would be a more chaotic result in B than in A.

In summary, subjects replying 'more paths in A' no doubt reached this conclusion by the following process:

1) application of a numbering heuristic by mental sampling;
2) intermediate conclusion: the sample for A is larger than the sample for B;
3) mobilization of the principle of induction;
4) final conclusion: there are more paths in A.

Therefore, what starts the crystallization of the false belief is the same as in the previous case: the subject relies on a principle – the principle of induction – introduced without thinking about it, probably without even being fully conscious of it. The mobilization of this principle allows the subject to move from the intermediate conclusion to the final conclusion. The intermediate conclusion is of course quite acceptable, since it merely describes correctly a simple state of affairs ('I have identified more paths in A than in B'). On the other hand, the final conclusion is false.

The general nature of the process used by respondents in the previous example is shown in many other examples given by Tversky and Kahneman. I will refer briefly to one of them.

Imagine a bus route which has *ten bus stops* between the two termini, and assume that the decision is to make some of them, for example, *two*, compulsory. There are several ways of doing this: make compulsory stops 1 and 2, 1 and 3, . . ., 2 and 4, . . ., 9 and 10 (we are disregarding the practical matter of the appropriateness of one place or another for a compulsory stop). The question put to subjects is the following:

Compare the situation where two stops are made compulsory with that where eight are made compulsory, and determine whether the number of possibilities is higher, lower or the same in the first case or the second case.

The same question is then repeated, changing the numbers of compulsory stops in each case.

Faced with this kind of question, respondents tend to find a greater possibility of choice in the case of *two* than in the case of *eight* compulsory stops; similarly, they think that the number of choices is higher for *two* compulsory stops as opposed to *seven* or even *six* stops.

In fact, the number of possibilities is the same in the case of *two* and *eight* stops, and – contrary to what most respondents thought – it is *greater* (more than two times greater) in the case of *seven* compulsory stops than in the case of *two*, and four times greater for *six* stops than for *two*.[10]

The distortion of intuition, therefore, is quite significant in this example. It arises because subjects apply a procedure similar to the previous one: it is easier to imagine – or to show in graphic form – a fairly large number of choices in the case of *two* stops than in the case of *seven*. When this acceptable result from mental sampling is combined with the idea that the principle of induction can be applied to the question, it gives the false conclusion that there are more ways of combining two stops than seven.[11]

A certain number of conclusions can be drawn from these three examples.

Firstly, in all cases, the false belief is the result of an identical procedure.

Secondly, this belief stems from the application of something which is not only intelligent, but also 'defensible' in that it gives objectively acceptable results in all kinds of situations which, at first sight, subjects readily regard as similar to the one they are dealing with. In other words, these experiments show, in a way which is indisputable if artificial, the case where subjects adhere to a false belief by relying on good reasons.

Thirdly, it must be stressed that these reasons, far from arbitrary, in fact have a certain *universality*. This explains why in general the wrong reply tends to be given by almost all respondents rather than a bare majority.

The origin of this 'universality' is clear: it stems from subjects' reliance on the principle of induction. Obviously, it is an incorrect application in this case. However, subjects have all the reasons in the world to rely on this crucial principle, which can in fact be regarded in all kinds of circumstances as 'self-evident'.

Moreover, it seems almost natural in the three problems to have recourse to mental induction. In the first example, the question is whether a set of points has the characteristic *x*. Why not indeed 'extract' some to see whether they have this characteristic, just as one would take a sample of balls from a container to determine the proportion of white ones to black ones? The second and third examples bring to mind the everyday case of the person fishing: on days when more fish are caught, the conclusion – a valid one – is that *there are* (no doubt) on that day more fish in the stretch of water being fished.

It is this same kind of reasoning which makes subjects conclude, for example, that there are more paths of the requisite kind in A than in B, since they are more easily seen in A than in B. Similarly, by *identifying* a larger number of ways of choosing two bus stops than seven or eight, the conclusion is that *there are* more in the first case.

Finally, it must be pointed out that these examples illustrate very clearly a situation where false beliefs stem exclusively from reasons. There is no passion or feeling here to be the cause of the false belief.

ORDINARY INFERENCE AND MAGICAL THINKING

A further example will allow us to extend the discussion on two points.

In the previous examples, the nub of the argument giving the false answer is represented by subjects' metaconscious[12] adherence to the principle of induction. Of course, the implicit *a priori* which, according to Simmel's model, can contaminate a line of reasoning are not attributable to this principle alone. This will be seen in the next example, and in all those in subsequent chapters which fall outside the field of cognitive psychology.

Above all, the example which I will now give will allow us to be absolutely clear about the interpretation of the findings of 'cold' cognitive psychology – whether it should be a *Lévy-Bruhl-type* interpretation, which claims that ordinary knowledge obeys rules that are *different* and in any case less strict than those of methodical thinking; or a *Durkheim-* (or *Simmel*)-*type* interpretation, that is, that ordinary knowledge and methodical knowledge basically follow the same rules.

Clearly, the question is a significant one, since the first interpretation leads to the notion of a proliferation of different logics and more generally of procedures of inference; the second one, on the other hand, leads to the conclusion that there is universality in the rules of functioning of thought. The first gives rise to the conclusion that natural thinking is subject to rules which condemn it to false representations of the world, and that it is in essence magical. The second, however, suggests that we should regard natural knowledge as well as controlled knowledge as more or less fragile constructs resulting from the combination of observations and conjectures. Whereas the first sees a basic discontinuity between natural and scientific thinking, the second sees continuity.

Although cognitive psychologists are not always clear on this point, there are many things which suggest that some of them veer towards a *Lévy-Bruhl-type* interpretation; by opting for a polytheist conception of thought, they are admitting that there is a multitude of thought systems, and in particular they tend to interpret ordinary knowledge as obeying principles which Lévy-Bruhl would have called *prelogical*.

This in fact is the position adopted by Shweder. In an important article in an anthropological journal, he explicitly tries to show that the ordinary thinking of modern people is thinking of a *magical* kind, as the title of the article indicates.[13] Moreover, the article is jokingly dedicated to the little boy who, convinced that spiders hear through their legs, cuts the legs from one, orders it to jump, and triumphantly concludes when it does not that it in fact hears through its legs.

The vital question of course is what conception Shweder has of magic.

As he says explicitly, he does not accept the type I theory propounded by Lévy-Strauss, that magic should be seen as an effort by subjects in traditional societies to control their environment,[14] and as being no different from science either in its functions or in its underlying motivations.[15] Shweder thinks that this theory, which is largely derived from Durkheim's, is incapable of explaining the experiences on which it is based, and which I will deal with shortly.

Shweder also rejects Malinowski's type II theory – the *hot* theory – that magic should be seen as the symbolic expression of a desire, or, more accurately, as an irrational attempt to control events so as to facilitate the fulfilment of a desire – the desire, for example, for thriving herds or a good harvest.[16]

Finally, Shweder does not agree with writers such as Tambiah (and, as might be added to Shweder's own list, Wittgenstein) who deny the existence of magical beliefs and see in them a form of rhetoric intended to evoke feelings, rather than a system of theoretical and practical beliefs about the real world.[17]

Instead of these classical theories, Shweder puts forward what he considers a more acceptable alternative:

> Magical thinking is an expression of a universal inclination of normal adults to draw correlational lessons from their experience, coupled with a universal inclination to seek symbolic and meaningful connections (likenesses) among objects and events.

And he adds:

> Magical thinking is no less characteristic of our mundane intellectual activities than it is of Zande current practices.[18]

The idea of correlation would therefore be absent from ordinary everyday thinking, which would instead apply unsound rules to diagnose the existence of a similarity between A and B in circumstances where correlational analysis would not lead to this kind of conclusion.

The phenomenon of magic would simply be the result of this lack of familiarity and affinity of ordinary thinking with the principles of inference described by statistical theory.

Therefore, according to Shweder, magical thinking should be regarded not as characteristic of societies which anthropologists call traditional, but as universal. Moreover, the argument is that this mode of thinking is the result of 'inclinations', which reveal the presence of laws of ordinary thinking having a dominant influence on the knowing subject. Finally, these laws are 'prelogical' (to use a non-Shwederian word); in any event, they contradict the theory of statistical inference.

It will be seen that here we are not far from the *primitive mentality* dear to Lévy-Bruhl.

On the other hand, however, there is a quantitative difference between the two writers. Whereas Lévy-Bruhl sees in this primitive mentality what he regarded (in his own evolutionist perspective inherited from Auguste Comte) as a stage in the mental evolution of humanity, Shweder gives magical thinking the status of an atemporal dimension of human thought.

This interpretation is contentious, as will be seen, and it begs enormous questions. However, it is based on experiments which are very instructive and where analysis is not at all straightforward. In one of them,[19] for example, students were asked to estimate the frequency of two personality traits: in a random group of a hundred people, how many would exhibit self-esteem, and how many would show qualities of leadership?

Subjective estimates by American college students always turn out, according to Shweder, more or less as indicated in table 2.1, 65 out of 100 being credited with self-esteem and 20 with leadership qualities.

When the group of students in question is then asked to estimate how many of the 20 people supposed to have leadership qualities might have self-esteem, they put the figure at 15.

Table 2.1

	Self-esteem		
	Present (A1)	Absent (A2)	Total
Leadership Present (B1)	15 (a)	5 (b)	20
Absent (B2)	50 (c)	30 (d)	80
Total	65	35	100

From table 2.1, we see that the correlation between the two variables is indeed very slight.

In fact, the probability of showing leadership when one has self-esteem is seen from the table to be 0.23 (15/65). The probability of leadership without self-esteem is 0.14 (5/35). The difference between these two figures is 0.09. In statistical terms, we would say that self-esteem *explains* leadership only slightly. The students' estimates of the frequency of the two characteristics does not in any way imply a relationship between them. In other words, the estimates in no way imply that self-esteem is a condition of leadership either necessary or sufficient or *a fortiori* necessary and sufficient.

However, the same students, when questioned, say they are certain that the former trait is a condition of the latter. The students are drawing conclusions from their estimates which are totally unwarranted. The estimates imply, once again, a quasi-independence of the two personality traits. However, most students assert that the presence of one of the two means that the presence of the other can be predicted with some degree of accuracy.[20]

This sort of observation led Shweder to say that ordinary thinking is of a magical kind, in that it actually appears to be completely impervious to contradiction. Let us ignore the objection that one very often contradicts oneself when one fails to notice the consequence of an argument. Such an interpretation is in fact completely inadequate to account for the data on which Shweder relies.

The experiment just described, in common with the whole impressive set of the author's experiments, shows in fact that normal adult subjects with a high level of education tend to draw from their observations, and even from their own estimates, unwarranted causal consequences. Like Lévy-Bruhl's or Evans-Pritchard's magician, subjects with ordinary knowledge think they see causal relationships where there are none. It goes even further: they insist on asserting causal relationships between A and B, even where their own beliefs, as here, imply the absence of a causal relationship.

In fact, I think we are in no way obliged to interpret these findings *in the way of Lévy-Bruhl*, and we can give them a type I interpretation. After all, contrary to appearances, there is no reason to believe that this new example is very different from previous ones.

The problem put to subjects can be formulated as follows:

Do you think that people exhibiting leadership qualities are people who have self-esteem?

In his analysis, Shweder's starting point is that such a question ought normally to trigger, in respondents' minds, a table such as table 2.1, but that this triggering does not actually happen: if it did, respondents would not establish a causal link between the two variables. They are therefore obeying rules of prelogical thinking.

In fact, if we look at the form of the question put to the respondents, we see that the task given to them is to determine *whether a predicate applies to a subject.* However, despite its formal simplicity, this kind of question is extremely ambiguous, because the nature of the information needed to answer such a question – affirmatively or negatively – is not derived from the *form* of the question, but can generally be determined only from the context, and can vary considerably.

In other words, an affirmative or negative reply to the question will be a function of certain information which one has, or thinks one has, about the frequency with which certain elements appear in a statistical population. To use Shweder's vocabulary, we can say that an affirmative or negative answer to a question of this kind is determined by '*correlation-relevant frequency information*'. The important point, however, is that the nature of the information relevant to a question is often conjectural.

In keeping with the conventions of logic, we will use $x(y)$ to indicate the statement that 'y is x', or, in other words, that the predicate x applies to subject y.

A small number of simple examples will show how the relationship between a question '$x(y)$?' and the nature of the *relevant frequency information* to give an affirmative or negative answer is in fact often unclear: the information can vary, depending on the question. Moreover, it is not always clear that one type of information rather than another should be linked with a particular question. There are times, therefore, where one would subscribe to the statement $x(y)$ only if $x(y)$ is true for *all* cases of y.

Taking a traditional example from philosophy, a statement such as 'crows are black' suggests that the characteristic 'black' is one of the traits which allow us to identify a bird as a crow – in other words a trait which is *distinctive* if not for zoology, at least as far as ordinary knowledge is concerned. As soon as the predicate (x) is interpreted as a distinctive trait, the statement $x(y)$ tends to be regarded as true only if all y are x, that is, if *all* crows are black. Naturally, it is impossible to verify whether all crows without exception are black. But the discovery of a yellow crow would be considered sufficient to make the statement $x(y)$ difficult to accept.

This case in point is even more clearly shown when $x(y)$ is a straightforwardly analytical definition. Here, $x(y)$ is acceptable only if absolutely all y are x. Take, for example, a statement such as 'a molecule of CO_2 is made up of one atom of carbon and two atoms of oxygen'. It would be totally impossible to reconcile this statement with the existence of a single molecule of CO_2 which was not made up in this way.

In cases of this kind, therefore, the 'relevant frequency information' can be shown in a figure with only *two* boxes, one of which contains a 'nil' (see figure 2.4).

	Black (x)	Non-black (~x)
Crows (y)	N (all)	0 (nil)

Figure 2.4

In other words, the 'relevant frequency information' normally associated with a statement such as 'all crows are black' does not give a four-box figure, as would be the case with four combinations of the two variables 'crow/non-crow' and 'black/non-black', but a two-box figure corresponding to a single variable. Moreover, the statement implies, by its very nature, that all units in the set are characterized by the same value of the variable. If we let $p[x(y)]$ be the proportion of y with the characteristic x in a set, then the relevant frequency information corresponding to the statement $x(y)$ is simply $p[\sim x(y)] = 0$. In other words, no CO_2 molecule can be made up of anything other than two atoms of oxygen and one of carbon; similarly, no bicycle can have anything other than two wheels.

On the other hand, let us look at an interpretation of $x(y)$ such as 'Beethoven's piano sonatas are played extremely well by Alfred Brendel'. As in the previous case, the question is whether a predicate x ('being played well by Brendel') applies to a set of objects y (Beethoven's 32 piano sonatas).

This statement, like the previous one, is represented by a figure with only *one* variable, and the statement $x(y)$ will be accepted if (and only if) the 'relevant frequency information' has certain characteristics. The question is therefore to determine the nature of this 'relevant frequency information', which I will call RFI.

It is easy to see that, in this case as in the previous one, the RFI is determined by a one-variable figure (see figure 2.5). However, the requirements of the parameters are different from those in the previous case: the statement will doubtless be accepted if Brendel's interpretation of *some* (or of *many*) sonatas can be regarded as good.

In this case, the condition which the RFI has to satisfy for the statement $x(y)$ to be accepted is therefore $p[x(y)] = $ 'some' (or 'many'). Let us now consider another $x(y)$-type statement: 'American trains do not run on time'. Let us assume that frequent passengers on these trains are likely to regard this statement as acceptable if they have noted, for

	A good Brendel interpretation (x)	A less good Brendel interpretation $(\sim x)$
Beethoven's sonatas (y)	'Many'	Difference between 32 and 'many'

Figure 2.5

example, a late train on two out of ten occasions. Here, an RFI can be associated with the $x(y)$-type statement, and indicated in a figure with a single variable which corresponds to the condition $x(y)$ if and only if $p[x(y)] > 0.2$ (see figure 2.6).

	Late (x)	On time $(\sim x)$
American trains	2	8

Figure 2.6

The value of the proportion to the right of the inequality can vary according to the speaker; but the latter will always have in mind an RFI corresponding to an inequality of this kind.

It should be noted, however, that the same $x(y)$ statement ('American trains do not run on time') could easily have a different meaning in a conversation on a French high-speed train, where it could mean 'American trains are less good at keeping time than French trains.'

Here, the RFI on which the statement is likely to be based has to be taken from a figure with four boxes (see figure 2.7). The statement would, for example, be accepted if $p[x(y)] - p[x(\sim y)] > 0.1$.

Many French people would be justified in summarizing the information contained in figure 2.7 by the statement: 'American trains do not run on time.' Here, the context of the conversation relies on 'frequency information' based on the comparison of two variables. Moreover, in this context, any difference – even a minor one – between the two frequencies is treated as significant. Here the difference is 0.1, and the

	Late (x)	On time ($\sim x$)
American trains	2	8
French trains	1	9

Figure 2.7

correlation is therefore very small. However, it will usually be regarded as large enough to justify the statement, since the comparison is by implication with the ideal of ten out of ten trains on time.

Of course, there will be cases where by implication a close correlation is required, just as all crows ought to be black. Consequently, before accepting that a particular factor is in fact the cause of a specific failure, we will need *all* symptoms showing this factor to be included.

These very basic remarks show in other words that the 'relevant frequency information' which allows us to regard an $x(y)$ statement as true depends critically on the semantic content of the statement and possibly on the conversational context in which it occurs. This information will belong to one of the types indicated by examples in figure 2.8.

Some types	Frequency information	Examples
Type 1	$x(y)$ if $p[\sim x(y)] = 0$	Crows
Type 2	$x(y)$ if $p[\mathrm{x(y)}] = $ 'many'	Beethoven
Type 3	$x(y)$ if $p[x(y)]$ $-p[x(\sim y)] > 0.1$	American trains
Type 4	$x(y)$ if $p[x(y)]$ 'much' bigger than $p[x(\sim y)]$	Shweder

Figure 2.8

In some cases, when an $x(y)$ statement is made, for example, in a conversation, each participant immediately and without ambiguity associates one of these *types* of frequency information with the particular statement. In a discussion about whether American trains are on time, participants will apply either a type 3 or a type 4 interpretation.

However, situations also exist where the type of frequency information which should go with an $x(y)$ statement, and which will determine whether subjects accept or reject the statement, is not clear. Here, subjects will *surmise* what the relevant information is. However, what they come up with is very likely to be already implicit and to be dictated by reasons of economy. By this I mean that, without realizing it, subjects are likely to come up with something similar to what they normally opt for in comparable situations. Because $x(y)$-type questions overwhelmingly call for type 1 or 2 frequency information, subjects will normally answer such a question by reference to this type of structure without it being their conscious 'choice'.

This uncertainty of the relevant frequency information is clear from the way in which the information is very responsive to the linguistic context. In fact, depending on the conversational context, the *same* statement can correlate with different types of RFI. For example, 'Brendel is a fine interpreter of Beethoven sonatas' can mean either that his rendering of the sonatas is particularly good (type 2), or that his interpretation of the great sonatas is better than Arrau's (type 3), or that he is better at Beethoven's sonatas than Schubert's (type 5, perhaps). In everyday conversation, we cope with this uncertainty without too much hesitation, though we continually make assumptions about what type of 'frequency information' needs to be associated with a question or statement.

Similarly, we can assume that when cognitive psychologists ask subjects about the relationship between self-esteem and leadership qualities, they come up with a metaconscious conjecture about the 'relevant frequency information' needed to answer the question, just as they do normally in relation to a wide variety of topics.

There is therefore no greater need to call on 'magical thinking' in this case than in a case where people choose an interpretation of what their hearer's understanding is of a statement that Brendel is a fine interpreter of Beethoven. In both cases, people may link irrelevant information with the statement. However, it would be going much too far to describe these distortions as *magical thinking*. I want to suggest very strongly that Shweder's example given above can provide an analysis which is exactly identical to that of the earlier ones.

In the examples taken from Tversky and Kahneman, the crucial importance of the principle of induction explained why subjects applied it even where it was inappropriate. Similarly, subjects in the Shweder example answer the question 'do people showing leadership qualities have self-esteem?' by reference first to the statement of fact contained in table 2.1: 'leaders *frequently* have self-esteem.' When they then link this statement with the *a priori* that 'the answer to the question assumes the application of a type 2 information structure', they conclude that 'leaders are people who have self-esteem.' The fact that most of them draw this conclusion does not mean that they are obeying a particular logic, but simply that most of them have followed the procedure which I have just outlined and which, as we have seen, is not particularly mysterious. In fact, it is no different from the way in which people, in an everyday context, normally become convinced of the validity of $x(y)$-type statements.[21]

Interestingly, in Shweder's analysis of the fascinating data which he collected, he himself relies, just like his subjects, on the *a priori* that the structure of the relevant frequency information to reply to *any* $x(y)$-type question is type 4.

That this is not so, and that there can be examples where this structure is in fact type 1, 2 or 3, is adequately demonstrated by the points just made. In other words, Shweder's *Lévy-Bruhl-type* interpretation derives from the metaconscious mobilization of an *a priori* which is just as questionable as those used by his respondents.[22]

Why does he use this *a priori*? Clearly because professional social scientists think that any $x(y)$-type statement has to be made on the basis of type 4 frequency information. As for ordinary respondents, my hypothesis is that they tend, in cases of uncertainty and lack of clarity, to choose everyday *a priori* by applying the principle of simplicity.

If what I say is right, we can first of all conclude that there is no noticeable difference between the case analysed by Shweder and those in the previous examples. In all of them, subjects have good reasons for believing what they do, even when their beliefs are questionable, even downright false.

There is no doubt that the findings in table 2.1 and the statement 'leaders have more self-esteem than other people' are contradictory. However, this contradiction disappears, or at least ceases to be unassailable, if the statement is formulated in a slightly different way: 'leaders are people who have self-esteem.' Here, the RFI corresponding to the statement is no longer defined in an unambiguous way.

Generally speaking, Shweder's *Lévy-Bruhl-type* interpretation is because he erroneously thinks that, in a bi-univocal manner, every question has a particular RFI. However, this is true only in the case of certain questions. In the general case, a question becomes associated with a particular RFI because of metaconscious *conjectures* with varying degrees of certainty.

Secondly, the analysis means we are again aware of the place of the implicit and of the *a priori* in ordinary reasoning, and also how *a priori* statements present in all reasoning – whether, as here, in ordinary reasoning, or, as we shall see in succeeding chapters, in methodical reasoning – can vary enormously. In the first examples given in this chapter, the implicit mobilization of the principle of induction forms the central core of the reasoning and leads to dubious responses by subjects. In the last example, the reasoning is crystallized around a 'choice' about the type of frequency information needed to deal with the question asked.

We also saw how, despite their crucial importance in the argument, subjects fail to notice these *a priori*, which are readily regarded by them as self-evident.

The final point is that the last example leads us to the hypothesis that, when there is a 'choice' between several implied statements, we can observe in certain cases a tendency on the part of subjects to go for the *simplest* 'solution', especially when it is clearly valid in the context of everyday life. This is true of the last example: we usually answer, perfectly satisfactorily, all kinds of $x(y)$-type questions by reference to frequency information of type 1 or 2. Often therefore, we simply note that in a significant number of cases two characters appear simultaneously, and conclude that there is a causal link.[23]

We could no doubt describe as 'magical' thinking these implicit conjectures that frequently appear in reasoning. We would then have to admit, however, that *all* thinking is magical.

The examples from cognitive psychology we have looked at in this chapter show that there are *cognitive* mechanisms giving rise to false ideas, and that these reveal a certain degree of generality. Although false, dubious or weak ideas can be exclusively affective in origin, they also very often have intellectual origins. On a general level, we can even say that the two types of sources combine, and that both are needed to induce conviction.

In any event, the advantage of the examples is that they show the existence of some of these mechanisms which give rise to false ideas in cases where the affective source of error is virtually absent.

More particularly, they show that false beliefs can be the *effect* of a line of reasoning, even one based on good reasons. Thus one can have good reasons for thinking that the climber will not be in the same place at exactly the same time on both days, or that leadership presupposes self-esteem. In both cases, these conclusions derive from reasoning which combines acceptable statements of fact and *a priori* statements to which the subject not surprisingly subscribes, since they are valid in an everyday context.

We will see later how this model which gives rise to false ideas, and which can be constructed from some rather artificial examples taken from cognitive psychology, applies to reasoning characteristic not only of ordinary knowledge, but also of methodical knowledge.

Summary

The contemporary human sciences have extended the domain of the *rational* explanation of beliefs; their approach is to explain in terms of good reasons many beliefs in weak, dubious or false ideas which common sense and tradition tend to explain in an irrational manner, that is, in terms of causes which are not reasons.

These *good reasons* are *objectively* bad and *subjectively* good. But they are neither arbitrary, nor dependent on the specific nature of the subject; while not objectively valid, they tend to be shared by everybody. Although paradoxical, this notion of good reasons (in the particular meaning given to this expression in this context) is the nub of the analyses used by writers such as Durkheim or Weber to explain, for example, those beliefs in false causal statements which are by definition magical beliefs.

In another field, and in the artificial but ideal conditions of a laboratory investigation, contemporary cognitive psychology has by implication come up with the same notion: from the various experiments it has undertaken, it concludes that an overwhelming majority of subjects tend to be convinced of the *same wrong* answer.

Cognitive psychologists often explain these findings in the same way as Lévy-Bruhl, by assuming that natural thinking, ordinary knowledge and 'intuition' unconsciously follow different rules of inference from those deployed and regarded as legitimate by controlled thinking.

In fact, these distortions of ordinary thinking can in many cases be interpreted as arising from *good reasons*. More particularly, the explanation of these distortions is that subjects faced with a question mobilize conjectures – *a priori* – which can readily be seen as self-evident. In this way, these experiments are a prime example of the 'Simmel effect', and experiments in cognitive psychology mean that we can be clear about what this paradoxical notion means.

3

Simmel's model

I will briefly summarize the very simple idea at the heart of what I am calling Simmel's model, of which the experiments analysed in the previous chapter are prime examples.

THE MODEL

Simmel argues that when we, whether scientists or laypersons, construct a theory to explain a phenomenon, we always introduce, as well as explicit statements to which reasoning is applied, implicit statements which do not appear directly in the field of our consciousness. Moreover, Simmel says, it may very well happen that the structure of the theory is modified as soon as these statements are made explicit. It may also happen that we regard the conclusions drawn from a theory as different as soon as the implicit statements contained in it become open to view.

This idea, the consequences of which are considerable, appears at its clearest in a passage from *The Philosophy of Money*:

> If we reflect on the huge number of presuppositions on which all defined knowledge depends for its content, it seems perfectly feasible for us to prove statement A by statement B, but that b, through the truth of C, D, E, etc., is in the end provable only by the truth of statement A. There merely needs to be a sufficiently long chain of reasoning – C, D, E, etc. – for the return to the starting point to elude our awareness, just as the size of the earth conceals its spherical shape from immediate sight, creating the illusion that we can move to infinity along a straight line.[1]

Therefore a theory – including a theory of our own – may *be* circular, but be *regarded* by us as linear because of the hidden presence of statements which are not only present in our reasoning, but are also, unknown to us, decisive in the formation of our convictions.

I realize that it may seem odd to say that at the same time we are unaware of certain statements and that they have a decisive effect. We only have to remember, however, the examples in the previous chapter to see that it is not strange at all: subjects who are asked whether the climber will be at the same point exactly at the same time on both outward and return journeys convince themselves of the validity of their reply *because* they mobilize certain statements, such as that which asserts the validity of the inductive method in the case under consideration. They introduce these statements without realizing it, but they use them *because* they regard them as valid. In any event, they need them in order to pass from the mental process provoked by the question to the conclusion drawn from it, which determines their belief and their response.

Before further analysis, we need to make it clear that the model stems directly from Simmel's theory of knowledge. I will give a detailed presentation of the theory in Chapter 10, but, for the moment, we need to look at the main points to see why Simmel regarded the model as characteristic of the basic functioning of human thought, drawing the conclusion that the discrepancy between our reasoning as it *appears* to us and what it *is* in reality applies not only to ordinary knowledge but also to scientific knowledge.

Simmel goes back to this theme in *The Problems of the Philosophy of History*,[2] which looks at the nature of historical knowledge, the importance of which was recognized by Max Weber.[3] In this book, Simmel links it more closely with the neo-Kantian theory of knowledge to which he subscribes.

He stresses the importance of the Kantian principle that knowledge is never a copy of reality but assumes active intervention by a knowing subject, but immediately rejects the content of Kantian *a priori*, or, rather, he suggests that these *a priori* are much more numerous and varied than Kant had indicated. Though all knowledge activities mobilize *a priori*, Kant deployed, says Simmel, only the *a priori* of Newtonian physics. We need to go further and, says Simmel, realize that not only physics and chemistry, but also history, psychology and, in general, all the natural and human sciences mobilize *a priori* (variable from one discipline to another). Of course, the same applies to ordinary knowledge.

Moreover, though they have a certain universality, these *a priori* must be regarded as being, to a certain degree and contrary to what Kant said, variable in time. Referring to the more general *a priori* which he sees as underpinning the work of the historian, just as other *a priori* make physics or chemistry possible, Simmel says:

However, these *a priori* should be regarded in a less rigorous way than Kantian *a priori*.[4]

Although *a priori* are a necessary ingredient of all sciences, Simmel in his book *The Problems of the Philosophy of History* is looking particularly at history and the 'social sciences' as they later came to be called.

An example of an *a priori* normally deployed by historians indicates how the Kantian theory of knowledge has been toned down, as Simmel recommended:

> The statement that for us other people are a psychological unit, that is, a coherent and comprehensible set of processes which we recognize as such and know as such, is an *a priori*. The effect of the corresponding function is the aggregation of a host of observable psychic facts. But it goes beyond these facts in that the principle of the internal unity of the personality also invites us to *complement* these observations.[5]

As a general rule, in *The Problems of the Philosophy of History*, Simmel tries, if not to draw up a list of *a priori* used by historians or sociologists, at least to suggest that this would be feasible. His examples show at the same time that these *a priori* can be identified and accurately described, and that they in fact condition historical knowledge.

However, although these *a priori* make historical or sociological knowledge possible, they do weaken it, since historians and sociologists tend, like physicists and chemists, not to recognize them for what they are, and therefore to fail to recognize the way they can influence their analyses:

> The fact that external data are thus spontaneously complemented by the observer is one of the most irrefutable demonstrations of the proposition that internal processes are not induced by observable facts, but injected into the facts on the basis of general hypotheses. In everyday life, we have many opportunities to verify the validity of this *a priori* and the particular consequences which stem from it. . . . In the case of more abstract and more complex psychic processes, these conclusions become uncertain and lead to numerous errors. But these errors show that, even in less ambiguous cases, one also resorts to hypotheses.[6]

In this way, the *a priori* which allow historians to make sense of their subject means that there is also the danger of distortion. The framework which they impose on historical analysis gives it shape; but at the same time, they cause historians to go further than what is perceived.

The effect of this ambiguity, which seems to be inherent in the *a priori* of knowledge, is that alleged 'distortions' of reality which are characteristic of statements by witnesses should be regarded as a normal phenomenon:

It is sometimes claimed that very few people are capable of recounting accurately an event they have witnessed. It is true that witness statements in legal proceedings and eye-witness accounts confirm this proposition. Even with the best will, and a desire to keep to the truth, witnesses add the missing links to what they have observed; they fill out their account to give the event the meaning they think they see in it.[7]

The importance and originality of this analysis, which anticipates the findings of modern psycholgy and sociology, are obvious: Simmel is suggesting that it is the *normal* functioning of knowledge which gives rise to mistakes.

Later on in the book, Simmel further analyses the notion of *character*, and stresses that it should not be used in circular arguments: to explain the remarkable nature of their subject's achievements, historians refer to certain *character traits*; but they can convince their readers that these are real only by pointing to the achievements which are supposed to show they exist.

It is clear how an *a priori form* – the notion of character – both makes historical analysis possible and obliges it to stamp its mark on reality.

Simmel cites the passages from *The Philosophy of Money* which I quoted at the beginning of this chapter, and suggests that this circularity is typical of knowledge in general, and not limited to either this particular *a priori* form or historical knowledge alone. This is clear from the fact that, when we interpret other people's behaviour in everyday circumstances, we are acting in the same way as historians when they attribute *character traits* to people they write about.

Simmel's view is that, far from being exceptional, this circularity is in fact what constitutes ordinary thinking:

It seems that this case in point belongs to that set of basic circles, of erroneous reasoning, which characterize the higher reaches of human knowledge.[8]

My brief outline of Simmel's theory of knowledge can be summarized as follows:
1) All knowledge – ordinary knowledge as well as scientific knowledge – assumes the mobilization of *a priori* which are more extensive than those suggested by Kant.

In fact, as has become clear, Simmel's notion of *a priori* corresponds in Kantian vocabulary to notions familiar to modern social sciences. The best way to characterize Simmel's *a priori* is perhaps to regard them as the common denominator of notions in the sociology of knowledge, cognitive psychology and the sociology or philosophy of science, all of which, quite apart from continual shifts of language and the wide variety of situations under consideration, convey the idea that knowing subjects handle the real world by stamping their mark on it. For example, we can speak of the notion of *frame* as applied by writers such as Goffman, or that of *form* (*Gestalt*) as in Gestalt psychology, or of the concepts of *paradiom* in the sense that Kuhn uses it, of *thema* as used by Holton, or again, quite simply, of the notion of *conjecture* as understood by Popper.[9]

No doubt all these notions do not coincide perfectly, just as they reflect the varied nature of the areas for which they were devised. However, what they have in common is that they all denote *a priori* of perception and cognition.

2) Even though they make knowledge possible, *a priori* can also lead to errors. Therefore distortions in, for example, statements by witnesses, but also in general terms in all the processes of perception and knowledge, have to be regarded as a normal phenomenon.

However, it does not follow – and this must be emphasized – that, because of this, knowledge is relativized so that individuals could justifiably assert *their own* thruth. The reason is that distortions arising from the *a priori* of knowledge can be identified and eliminated in the final analysis, as in the example of witness statements in a judicial context.

Therefore, the fact that the real world can be perceived and interpreted only through the spectacles of an *a priori* should not be a cause of scepticism: historical interpretations can be subjected to critical analysis in the same way as theories in physics or statements by witnesses.

3) The fact that there are *a priori* elements in all reasoning means that there may be a discrepancy between the knowing subject's reasoning as it really is, and the same reasoning as the subject perceives it. More particularly, subjects can perceive as linear a line of reasoning which is in fact circular. They may also draw unwarranted conclusions from a line of reasoning without, however, making any mistake of logic.

4) These *a priori* elements, hypotheses, frames or conjectures present in any thought process are not only *implicit*, but also generally *unconscious*.

A major reason is that the processes of knowledge, like the phenomena of perception, are subject to the phenomenon of attention. Just as, in perception, our attention is focused on what we are *looking at* rather than what we *see*, we do not give the same degree of attention to all the components of an argument:

> This act of relating, as seen in the use of *a priori* statements, generally remains unconscious, since consciousness pays more attention to the external data which it is examining, than to its own activity.[10]

I will say in passing that, because the Freudian tradition has, since the time Simmel was writing, imposed a particular meaning on the notion of unconsciouness, it may be better to replace the word, in the way Simmel uses it, with either 'subconscious' or, better still, 'metaconscious', which is understood by writers such as Hayek[11] as having a meaning identical with the one Simmel gives to 'unconscious'. This approach has the advantage of avoiding any confusion with Freudianism, which is why I will adopt it here.

Another reason, however, why the *a priori* elements of a thought process tend to remain 'unconscious' (in the Simmel sense) or 'metaconscious' is that they have a very extensive validity:

> And since these *a priori* statements apply uniformly to the most divergent contents, since they have a kind of permanence, and since they have an inherent generality, they create a familiarity effect.[12]

In short, the fact that the knowing subject is obliged to use, in a non-critical way, *a priori* which have very wide validity is one of the central features of knowledge and, at the same time and bound up with this, a major cause of its errors and its beliefs in dubious, weak or false ideas.

All these passages which I have quoted, taken from *The Philosophy of Money* and *The Problems of the Philosophy of History* give a clear indication of a theory of beliefs and knowledge which is as original as it is authoritative.

APPLICATION

Unfortunately, Simmel does not really go into the application of his theory. The most he does is to point out a devastating consequence of his observations: since in many cases – though not in all – we cannot be sure that we have made explicit all the statements implicit in a theory, we cannot be sure either that the conclusions which we draw from them are correct.

In fact, the only example which he gives of his theory ties in with the passage from *The Philosophy of Money* quoted at the beginning of this chapter. It is somewhat abstract, and it recurs in *The Problems of the Philosophy of History*.

Suppose, says Simmel, that we have developed a theory containing explicit statements such as:

1) p
2) $p \rightarrow q$ (= if p, q)
3) $q \rightarrow r$ (= if q, r)

The totally legitimate conclusion from these statements is:

4) r

Here, we will justifiably have the impression of arguing on the basis of unexceptionable rules, and we will believe with good reason in the validity of the statement *r*. Our belief in *r* will be, in other words, the natural effect of our reasoning.

However, says Simmel, what is the basis of our belief in the first statement *p*? In some cases, it arises from the fact that we have in our mind, implicitly, a set of statements such as

5) *r*
6) $r \rightarrow p$ (= if *r*, *p*)

from which the conclusion is:

7) *p*

To distinguish explicit statements from implicit statements, the latter could be indicated by an asterisk, as follows:

5*) *r**
6*) $[r \rightarrow p]*$ (= if *r*, *p*)*

To summarize, we think we are applying theory T made up of four statements:

1) *p*
2) $p \rightarrow q$
3) $q \rightarrow r$

----

4) *r*

In reality, if these explicit statements are combined with the implicit statements from the edge of our consciousness, our reasoning is made up of the following sequence of statements:

5)*   *r*
6)* $[r \rightarrow p]*$
7) and 1) *p*
2) $p \rightarrow q$
3) $q \rightarrow r$

----

4)   *r*

The explicit theory based on statements 1) to 4) is linear, but the theory which includes statements 5) to 7) as well is *circular*. Moreover, the complete theory – the one obtained by making implicit statements explicit – amounts to a reordering of the statements.

However, since the implicit statements are not present in our consciousness, we *believe*, with good reason, that we have constructed a linear theory and that statement *r* is proved by this theory. On a more general level, Simmel suggests in this example that we may well *believe* that we have come up with theory T including a set of statements P, whereas in fact what we have in our mind is theory T' containing, besides P, a set of implicit statements Q*:

$$T' = P \ \& \ Q\star$$

However, it may well be that, when Q* is made explicit, the theory:

$$T'' = P \ \& \ Q$$

has a different structure from that of T, and leads to different conclusions from those derived from T.

SIMMEL AND THE PROBLEM OF INDUCTION

One may wonder why Simmel draws from this example the spectacular conjecture that human knowledge is circular in nature and *appears* linear because of the finitude of the human mind, which prevents us from dealing simultaneously with more than a limited number of statements.

The reply to this question is perhaps to be found in the following passage:

> If we follow the demonstration of a principle to its basics, and the latter to their basics, and so on, it is a notorious fact that one often finds that the demonstration is possible, that is, demonstrable in turn, provided one assumes that the original principle, which it was supposed to demonstrate, is itself already demonstrated. If this, applied to a particular deduction, renders it illusory like a vicious circle, it is in no way unthinkable that our knowledge, taken as a whole, is the prisoner of such a form.[13]

Unfortunately, very little light is thrown on this somewhat puzzling passage by the context. It is an example of Simmel's often very allusive style.

Nevertheless, it may well be that Simmel, using this abstract example, is offering an interpretation of the problem of *induction* which, from Hume down to Popper, features so largely in the deliberations of philosophers concerning knowledge. How can universal statements be inferred from singular observations? How, in particular, can we avoid the sceptical answer which Hume gives to the problem?[14]

In any event, it is not inconceivable that Simmel, who regarded himself as much as a philosopher as a sociologist, was offering his own solution to the problem.

As soon as we postulate, as Simmel does, following on from Kant, that knowledge always includes *a priori*, we can try to formalize inductive 'reasoning' in the following way, for example:[15]

> All the beans from this bag are the same colour.
> *Some* beans in this bag are white.
> _____
> *All* the beans from the bag are white.

In the formal sense, reasoning such as this is unexceptionable. It means we can move from a singular statement (the second one) to a universal statement (the third one). But this move is possible only because of the first statement, and therefore the question is, of course, whether this statement is valid.

However, the only means of knowing this is to test the conjecture by specific observations, which, if they are consistent, will confirm it.

In other words, it may well be that the paragraph from *The Philosophy of Money* just quoted gives an interpretation of the paradox of induction, and that the reasoning outlined in it conveys in a generalized and abstract way an inductive argument such as:

1) Up to now, all the beans taken from this bag are white.
2) [(This gives rise to the *conjecture* that) all the beans from the bag are the same colour]*.
3) The beans from this bag are all the same colour.
   _____
4) *All* the beans in the bag are white.

The complete reasoning – that is, including the implicit statement – is of course circular, and therefore invalid. More particularly, since one of its premises is conjectural, its conclusion is as well. However, we see only the explicit element and are not conscious of the fact that our confidence in premise 3) ('the beans in this bag are all the same colour') is based on statements 1) and 2). Since we have no clear perception of 2), we fail to see the conjectural nature of the conclusion and in fact regard it as just as sound as statement 1).

The reason why, for two hundred years, induction has been a problem for the theory of knowledge is that, as is recognized by all philosophers of science from Peirce down to Popper himself,[16] it is reasoning which, while apparently unacceptable from the point of view of logic, forms the basis of everyday experience as well as of all sciences of observation and experimentation. For example, chemists will agree that all water molecules have the same composition; having observed each time they analysed water that it had the same molecular composition, they conclude that a molecule of water has two hydrogen atoms and one oxygen atom.

The question is, then, how we can have confidence in a form of reasoning which has been known since Hume to be theoretically invalid, since it has the appearance of a sleight of hand whereby a singular statement is transformed into a general statement or limited information into unlimited assertion.

In any event, it does seem that Simmel's abstract example refers to the 'problem of induction' and is meant to be – in a discrete way – a reply to Hume.

It is true that, just like Simmel's example, inductive 'reasoning' includes implicit and unconscious statements, but this unconscious element is vital as the basis of the *confidence* which we have in the conclusion derived from it. Moreover, this type of 'reasoning' is in fact fundamental to all sciences – natural as well as historical. This is why Simmel is able to say that the circularity which he evidences 'characterizes the higher reaches of human knowledge'.

This statement, which looks like a rhetorical hyperbole, may simply be a different way of conveying straightforward methodological remarks arising from Simmel's detailed study of historical writing.

Let us refer back to the case of biographers who want to give unity to the thought, action or career of their subject. They start with a jumble of observations, and try to establish this unity by giving their subject certain *character traits*. No doubt these traits are *inferred* from the acts and declarations of the subject. However, historians make these observations much more revealing than they in fact are. They might even think that they can justifiably speculate on what their subject might have done in imaginary situations. This process is at the same time quite common, in that it happens not only in historical analysis but in everyday life as well, and also unwarranted from the point of view of logic.

In the formal sense, what is at the heart of this process – which historians cannot really dispense with and which is therefore an *a priori* of history – is a circular argument analogous to the one which Simmel describes in the passages quoted:

Some acts of subject X reveal character trait T.
[The conjecture can be drawn from this that T is dominant in the subject]*.
Every act of X shows a dominant character trait.

All the acts of X show T.

It is in fact this kind of reasoning which we deploy when, without being conscious of the premise, we observe a set of actions by X and conclude that X is, for example, 'kind-hearted', or 'sensitive'.

Finally, it may well be that Simmel is suggesting an answer to the problem of induction which anticipates that of writers such as Peirce or Popper, and which, at the same time, is perhaps more fruitful in the sense that it explains the origins of the *confidence* which ordinary knowledge and scientific knowledge alike bestow on the conclusions of inductive 'reasoning'.

For Peirce, *induction* is, with *deduction* and *abduction*, one of the basic forms of 'reasoning' which tend to become combined in any line of argument. All three are conjectural[17] – deduction, because it starts from conjectural premises; induction and abduction, because they draw conjectural conclusions from non-conjectural premises.

For Popper, universal statements are always conjectures which can of course be suggested to us by experience, but which we cannot derive from experience.[18]

According to Simmel (and if it is indeed true, as I am arguing, that he is dealing with induction in the passages I have quoted), inductive 'reasoning' is based on *a priori*. However, Simmel's *a priori* are nearer, in their large number and varied nature, to Popper's conjectures than Kant's *a priori*. This is clear in the explicit examples presented by Simmel in the field of history. For example, the *character traits* with which historians endow their subjects could well be examples of conjecture in Popper's sense. We are therefore close to Popper's remarks on the conjectural nature of induction.

Simmel, however, has the edge in that he explains why *conjectures* which the knowing subject continually utters in everyday life or in scientific research are not *experienced* or *perceived* as such, but are seen by the knowing subject as self-evident statements, or at least as statements which appear obvious enough for there to be no thought of questioning them.

This discrepancy between the objectively *conjectural* nature of statements established by induction, and the confidence we have in them, is not well explained, either by Peirce's theory or Popper's, whereas Simmel gives a simple explanation of it.[19] He says that it stems from the fact that any argument contains *implicit* statements – perceived by subjects in a metaconscious way – side by side with the *explicit* statements on which their attention is exclusively focused.

This theory also allows us to understand why inductive reasoning, though central to the natural and human sciences, and vital not only to historical analysis but also to the conduct of everyday life, is also the source of all kinds of false beliefs.

For example, it is on the basis of reasoning of this kind that we reify the personality of other people.

Generally speaking, inductive 'reasoning' is responsible for many false interpretations and many incorrect simplifications.

It is therefore probable that Simmel was thinking of the problem of induction in the passages quoted. The reason he did not refer specifically to it was perhaps that the field he was looking at undoubtedly stretched beyond induction: inductive reasoning is not the only one which contains implicit statements or is based on metaconscious conjectures.

On the contrary, Simmel suggests – perfectly clearly this time – that every thought process contains such statements and that moreover this is an essential characteristic of human thought: there is no reasoning without what he calls *a priori* or *general hypotheses*. These very conditions of possibility of knowledge also lead to error and mean that false beliefs are based on mental processes which are unexceptionable both from the point of view of observation and from that of logic.

SIMMEL'S MODEL AND COGNITIVE PSYCHOLOGY

To conclude my presentation of Simmel's model, it is useful to refer again to what was said in the last chapter – that most distortions of inference studied by contemporary cognitive psychology can be regarded as applications of Simmel's model. The effect of this is that the model can be treated as a theory of natural inference, of its successes and its failures.

The reasoning apparent in all distortions of natural inference highlighted by cognitive psychology can easily be analysed in the terms suggested by Simmel:

- Statements based on conclusions from observation, that is, *empirical* statements appearing in a line of reasoning are often perfectly acceptable;
- Logical procedures deployed are completely valid;
- 'General hypotheses' linking empirical statements to their conclusion are characterized, as Simmel says, by having an extensive validity, that is, by 'being applicable to a wide variety of different contents';
- These 'general hypotheses' or *a priori* are moreover, as Simmel also argues, introduced in an 'unconscious' (metaconscious) way, precisely because their validity and their 'inherent generality' mean they are readily regarded as self-evident in circumstances where they are in fact irrelevant;
- Therefore, all elements of the reasoning are valid, so that subjects have good reasons for endorsing the conclusion which follows from it;
- It is a fact, however, that any 'general hypothesis', any conjecture, any 'frame' or, as one could add, any *a priori*, even one with a very extensive validity, may be inappropriate in certain circumstances, even though it is naturally suggested to the knowing subject by those very circumstances.

Therefore, from a set of correct observation protocols, one can deduce a false conclusion despite following closely the canons of logic. Conversely, a false belief can be brought about by correct reasoning based on valid empirical statements. Generally speaking, the *normal* functioning of thought gives rise at the same time to knowledge and error, to true ideas and false beliefs.

It would be easy to show that the examples analysed in the previous chapter are all derived from this pattern. However, rather than going into that, I will outline briefly an example very close in form to Shweder's example, but different from it in content. This will allow us to keep our discussion in focus.

When doctors are asked whether, for example, a particular symptom can legitimately be taken as indicating with a certain degree of probability the presence of a particular ailment, they can – in theory at least – reply in the affirmative or negative only by mobilizing 'relevant frequency information'. More specifically, the frequency with which the illness develops must be significantly greater when the symptom is present than when it is absent. In other words, a relevant answer assumes a comparison of two frequencies, each of which is determined by two sets of numerical data. We therefore need four sets of data in order to answer the question.

For example, the left-hand side of table 3.1 shows a situation where symptom *x* cannot be taken as a symptom of illness *y*. In fact, in a sample of 150 patients, the illness is present in two cases out of three, whether or not symptom *x* is observed. On the right-hand side, on the other hand, the illness is overwhelmingly present when the symptom is present (in two out of three cases when it is present; in only four out of seven when it is not).

Table 3.1

Symptom x	*Illness* y					
	Present	*Absent*	*Total*	*Present*	*Absent*	*Total*
Present	20	10	30	20	10	30
Absent	80	40	120	80	60	140
Total	100	50	150	100	70	170

In any case, to give a sound answer to the question we need to have quantitative information such as that in both sides of table 3.1.

However, many studies show that subjects, whatever their level of education or area of specialization, tend to base their approach on just *one* of the four sets of data making up the 'relevant frequency information'.

For example, psychiatrists will generally answer the question whether depression is a cause of suicide by referring to cases of attempted suicide encountered in patients who also show symptoms of depression. If their impression is that such cases are *not rare*, they tend to conclude from this that depression is in fact a major cause of attempted suicide.[20]

Clearly the inference is wrong: only if the proportion of suicides among depressives is higher than that among non-depressives can one conclude that there is a causal link between depression and suicide.

There is no reason, however, to assume that correlational analysis is intuitive, nor especially that the nature of the *relevant frequency information* which has to be mobilized to answer a question can in every case be determined in a univocal manner.

Simmel's model can in fact be applied to this case:

- The observation protocol used by the psychiatrist is correct: it is quite true that a certain number of cases have been observed where the two characteristics are linked;
- To answer the question, the psychiatrist can then make use of an initial *a priori*; or an initial general hypothesis.

This initial 'general hypothesis' would consist of a translation rule allowing the question to be reformulated as 'Does it often happen that the predicate "to attempt suicide" is linked with the subject "depressed patient"?'

Such a hypothesis can be readily introduced for the simple reason that, in very many cases, this translation rule can in fact be applied. There is no need for a contingency table with four sections to see the truth of causal statements such as 'the shoe pinches' or 'money does not bring happiness', or even of comparative-type causal statements such as 'envy is less easy to get rid of than hatred'. In all three cases, it is legitimate to reformulate the causal statement as an ordinary statement of the $x(y)$ kind linking a predicate with a subject.

- It is also conceivable that in cases of this kind, some subjects mobilize a stronger general hypothesis, namely that the statement 'often $x(y)$' is sufficient to give the conclusion 'x is the cause of y'. After all, this hypothesis is not always unwarranted.

Quite frequently we can in fact make causal inferences which are more or less reliable by merely stating that two phenomena *often* appear in a linked form. Sometimes, a mere co-occurrence is enough to suggest the existence of a link of cause and effect. For example, a single case of sunstroke would no doubt be enough to dissuade many people from exposing themselves to the sun for too long. Cases of this kind are far removed from the ideal experimental conditions described in table 3.1

above. However, nobody would suggest rejecting causal inferences of this type.

The counter-argument is that the causal relationship in question can seem certain to a particular subject because it has been established in a methodical way *elsewhere*, for example, by scientists who have verified the effects of exposure to the sun. The answer to this is that we conclude with the same degree of confidence, for example, that a particular food does not 'agree' with us, or on the other hand suits us very well, without such statements being based on anything other than the observation of a very small number of phenomena of co-occurrence.

Generally speaking, in all kinds of situations, the presence of phenomena of co-linearity or the scarcity of available data makes it impossible to draw up tables such as table 3.1. Despite this, in cases of this kind we can often make plausible causal statements.

This is true not only of ordinary knowledge, but also of scientific knowledge.

For example, Daniel Bell has argued that the average American values artistic and literary culture less than the average European *because* the immigrants who founded America belonged to religious traditions which were indifferent or hostile to art, or, in cases where this was not so, came from groups who, for social reasons, were not really able to adopt the positive attitude of their religion to art. The first case is that of the Puritans, the second that of Irish Catholics.[21] A causal statement such as this is obviously neither consistent with the ideal indicated by Table 3.1, nor lacking in validity.[22]

In short, the relationship between a causal statement and the nature of the information on which it is based is far from automatic. In many cases, 'x causes y' can be inferred from 'often $x(y)$'; in other cases, this is of course impossible.

It is not surprising therefore that psychiatrists who are asked whether depression encourages suicide seem tacitly to accept the equivalence of the two statements. This 'general hypothesis' plays a decisive role in establishing their belief, because it builds a bridge between the observation protocol and the question asked. Of course, as Simmel argues, it is at the same time 'unconscious' but nevertheless present in the 'reasoning' of the psychiatrist. In other words, it is 'metaconscious'. And it is 'metaconscious' because, being of general validity, it is readily regarded by the subject as self-evident.

To summarize, the hypothesis might be that, depending on the case, psychologists determine their belief and their answer on whether depression encourages suicide by mobilizing one of the two *a priori*, either the simple one:

[The question can be reduced to a question of form: 'often x (y)?]*, or the stronger one:

[if often $x(y)$, then x causes y]★.

Why are these *a priori* so readily used? Firstly, because a causal question is nearly always a complex question, which assumes that the person trying to answer it will make 'general hypotheses' on the nature of the information relevant to the question, or on the 'form' of the question.[23] Secondly, because information which would be ideally relevant is not always in fact accessible, for example, because of phenomena of co-linearity. Finally, because the 'general hypotheses' to which I have referred are of very wide validity and are therefore very frequently used and usable in analogous situations.

Like Shweder,[24] Nisbett and Ross comment on the distortions of inference which become apparent when they suggest that the subject with ordinary knowledge conforms to a kind of prelogical mentality:

> The logic exhibited by subjects in the fourfold table experiments is suspiciously similar to the logic shown by *poorly educated* [this author's italics] laypeople in discussing a proposition such as 'does God answer prayers?' 'Yes,' such a person may say, 'because many times I've asked God for something, and He's given it to me'.[25]

It is true that this answer follows the same logic as that applied by the psychiatrist: it takes into account only one of the sections of the contingency table. It is also true that this kind of distortion occurs frequently. The important phrase, however, is 'poorly educated', which suggests that *magical* thinking or *prelogical* thinking is natural, that it can to a certain degree be compensated by education, but that this gloss is very thin, in that even doctors are capable of reasoning like 'poorly educated laypeople'.

The writings of Nisbett and Ross suggest in a general way that these experiments reveal a logic of natural inference, obeying false rules; and that therefore there is a solution of continuity between natural inference and scientific inference. They argue that ordinary thinking turns its back on scientific thinking, with the former obeying its own 'logic' which has little to do with 'proper' logic.

Nisbett and Ross's explicit suggestion is that the 'logic' in ordinary inference is close to that of magical thinking, which characterizes prescientific cultures.[26] On this point, they refer to the famous findings of Evans-Pritchard about the Azande, and try to show that in both cases the procedures are comparable.

The proposition that inference procedures used by the Azande are similar to those used by American doctors can be readily accepted, and it confirms the intuitive insights of the major theorists of magic – that the logic of 'primitive people' is no different from our own.[27]

However, Nisbett and Ross turn this proposition round, and argue that the doctors are using a logic which is no different from that of primitive people. The result is that both these writers and the theorists of magic remove the old distinction between traditional thinking and scientific thinking and relocate it between ordinary thinking and scientific thinking.

However, the whole point of Simmel's theory is to remove this distinction by postulating that any thought process implies 'general hypotheses' or *a priori*. These *a priori* are essential to knowledge. At the same time, it often happens that knowing subjects mobilize an *a priori* valid in many situations in cases where in fact it is inappropriate. They are then subscribing to a false belief on the basis of a line of reasoning which does not deviate in any way from the rules of logic.

In fact, all experiments in cognitive psychology show that at the root of distortions of natural inference lie *general hypotheses* which are metaconscious and, like the principle of induction, of very broad inherent validity.

It is not necessary to draw the conclusion that subjects with ordinary knowledge are a prey to some kind of prelogical mentality.

In any event, the fact that it is easy to find examples of the application of Simmel's model shows that, despite its paradoxical appearance, it is in no way speculative, but is a powerful tool for the analysis of beliefs in dubious, weak or false ideas. As I tried to show in the previous chapter and in the final section of this chapter, the model means that we can interpret distortions of ordinary thinking in the area of cognitive psychology without recourse to the cumbersome hypotheses to which I have referred.

There is, however, no reason to restrict the field of application of this model to natural inference. Thinking which I call *methodical*, in an effort to avoid the pitfalls of the phrase *scientific* thinking, is also subject to the pitfalls of the *a priori*.

Reciprocally, *received ideas can also be engendered by methodical thinking.*

Summary

Georg Simmel propounded – allusively – an important model to explain beliefs in dubious, weak or false ideas: in many cases, there are the best reasons in the world for believing in dubious ideas, since they may well stem from an objectively valid line of reasoning.

How can a valid line of reasoning – a scientific one, for example – give rise to dubious beliefs? Quite simply because implicit propositions creep in which are able to distort the consequences to be drawn from the reasoning in question in the absence of the halo of implication.

Simmel finds the presence of these implicit statements characteristic of the functioning of thought. This is equivalent to saying that, in its most normal functioning, thought naturally produces true beliefs and false beliefs.

Simmel drew his inspiration for the model from Kant's philosophy of knowledge. For Simmel, all reasoning contains an implicit element, just as for Kant it contains *a priori*. The Simmelian implicit, however, has not at all the same rigidity as Kantian *a priori*.

More specifically, the model is perhaps the result of Simmel's thinking on the 'problem of induction'; we are convinced by an inductive line of reasoning because, since we do not see the implicit elements, we do not perceive its circular nature.

'Simmel's model' can be applied to the distortions of ordinary knowledge in the area of cognitive psychology, which stem from the presence of implicit propositions regarded by subjects as *self-evident*.

Generally speaking, Simmel's model is an essential element of the 'rational' theory of beliefs – the theory which attempts to explain beliefs by reference to *good reasons*, in the sense defined above.

4

Hyperbole machines

Simmel's model suggests that false or dubious ideas can stem from valid lines of reasoning. All my examples from now on are therefore in my mind, because of the constraints imposed by the theme, characterized by the fact that any weak ideas apparent in them are the product of unexceptionable arguments. My aim in analysing a particular theory is in no way polemical, nor indeed critical, but exclusively to identify and illustrate some of the typical mechanisms by which a faultless line of reasoning can, as Simmel suggests, lead to false ideas.

AN EXAMPLE FROM THE PHILOSOPHY OF SCIENCE

My first example is taken from Karl Popper's philosophy of science, probably the best known of modern times, and more specifically from one of its most fundamental and influential aspects – his theory of refutation, or, as it is still sometimes called, 'falsification'. Since Popper extended the usual meaning of the words 'falsify' and 'falsification' to make them synonymous with 'refute' and 'refutation', both pairs of words can conveniently be used.

Not only this philosophy is very interesting in itself, but the human sciences, if they took it more seriously and became more rigorous, would themselves no doubt gain in interest.[1] Moreover, it would be easy to show that in this field, writings which advance our understanding of the real world espouse, consciously or unconsciously, Popper's conception of science. Karl Popper's thought is important, therefore, from a practical as well as a theoretical viewpoint: it contains essential *regulae ad directionem ingenii*.[2]

What is more, Popper's whole approach is based on an idea which from the point of view of the analysis of the phenomena of knowledge and belief is crucial, that is, that the least clear theories tend, in the nature of things, to be the most immune to criticism.

Most important of all, I believe that *critical rationalism*, of which Popper was the analyst and champion, is the ideal foundation of all communication as well as of all knowledge.

The best theory, however, and the most rigorous reasoning can also lead, as Simmel says, to dubious ideas. The starting point for Popper's theory of falsification is a classic concept in logic – *modus tollens*.

> [I]n my view there is no such thing as induction. Thus inference to theories, from singular statements which are 'verified by experience' (whatever that may mean), is logically inadmissible. Theories are, therefore, *never* empirically verifiable.[3]

We can ignore the inverted commas in which Popper puts the phrase 'verified by experience' (a favourite expression of the Vienna Circle), in that they indicate that 'data' become 'facts' only if interpreted with the help of certain theories. To put it more simply, there are no raw observations. For example, taking a thermometer reading assumes that one accepts the validity of certain laws of physics. However, the nub of the argument lies elsewhere, and it can be restated as follows: assume there is a theory T on the basis of which one expects to observe the 'fact' q. Let us further assume that q is in fact observed. It is 'logically inadmissible' to draw from this the conclusion that T is true:

> My proposal is based upon an *asymmetry* between verifiability and falsifiability; an asymmetry which results from the logical form of universal statements. For these are never derivable from singular statements, but can be contradicted by singular statements. Consequently it is possible by means of purely deductive inferences (with the help of the *modus tollens*[4] of classical logic) to argue from the truth of singular statements to the falsity of universal statements. Such an argument to the falsity of universal statements is the only strictly deductive kind of inference that proceeds, as it were, in the 'inductive direction'; that is, from singular to universal statements.[5]

Later in the book,[6] Popper introduces the idea that the notion of the universality of a statement is relative, and speaks of 'more' or 'less' universal statements. As the context indicates, what he means is that when a theory T leads us to predict q, it may be that q is regarded as a new theory from which will be drawn, for example, the consequences q'. In this case, T will be 'more universal' than q. We can ignore the point about how this notion of degree of universality can be reconciled with the idea that Popper's asymmetry between falsifiability and verifiability derives 'from the logical form of universal statements'. In one case, the universality of a statement seems to be a matter of its place in a line of argument, in the other of its form.

In fact, the heart of Popper's argument is the asymmetry between *modus tollens*, which he calls 'the falsifying mode of inference', and what can be called 'inductive reasoning' (although Popper does not use this phrase, the passage I have just quoted does define *induction* as the 'mode of inference' from singular statements to theories): whereas the former is valid because of its very form, the latter is not.

We use the figure of *modus tollens* every time we conclude from

1) $p \rightarrow q$ (if p, then q)

and from

2) $\sim q$ (it is not true that q)

that:

3) $\sim p$ (it is not true that p)

This simple logical form is fascinating, because it is universally valid. Whatever the *content* of p and q, and whatever the nature of the entities indicated by these symbols, from 1) and 2) there will always derive 3). Whether p and q represent statements, or sets of statements, whatever subject they address, if 1) and 2) are true, then 3) necessarily is as well. In all these cases, the reasoning is valid. As Whitehead says, it is always fascinating to come across theories which are at the same time empty and true.[7] *Modus tollens* belongs to this category.

Just as Molière's Monsieur Jourdain used prose without realizing it, we use *modus tollens* in everyday life as well as in the most complex reasoning; for example, we conclude from:

1)   when it rains, the road is wet,

and from

2)   the road is not wet,

that:

3)   it is not raining.

A symmetrical figure of *modus tollens* is *modus ponens*;

1) $p \rightarrow q$
2) p
_____
3) q

Like *modus tollens, modus ponens* is universally valid; and it is as common as breathing, as, for example, when we conclude with total certainty, and no need for empirical verification, from

1)   when it is raining, the road is wet

and from

2)   it is raining

that:

3)   the road is wet.

However, there is a figure which resembles the two previous ones, which can be called 'inductive mode of inference' – or 'sophism by affirmation of the consequent' – and which is unacceptable:

1) $p \rightarrow q$
2) q
_____
3) p

This is in fact false reasoning. A doctor could not, for example, conclude from the fact that a particular patient had a fever (q), and that a particular ailment caused fever ($p \rightarrow q$), that the patient had contracted the ailment in question (p).

Let us assume now that p is any scientific theory. It would normally lead scientists to expect to observe certain states of affairs. If it is a theory in astronomy, it will mean, for example, that they can predict that a particular planet will be in a given place at a given time. One of two things can then happen – either the planet is there, or it is not. If it is, astronomers cannot conclude that the theory is true, because this would be an example of unacceptable reasoning. If, on the other hand, the planet is not there, and therefore the theory is – I might even say by good fortune – contradicted by the facts, they could rely on *modus tollens* and conclude quite calmly that the theory is false.

On the other hand, nothing could make them certain that it is true, even if it were consistent with experience a thousand times.

Since the 'inductive' mode of reasoning is defective in its very form, one cannot in fact conclude from:

1) $p \rightarrow (q_1 \ \& \ q_2 \ldots \ \& \ q_n)$
2) $q_1 \ \& \ q_2 \ \& \ldots \ \& \ q_n$

that p is true, whatever the magnitude of n. There is in fact nothing to say that theory p', which has nothing to do with p, does not also allow us to predict q_1 & q_2 . . . & q_n. All we need do moreover is to replace this conjunction of statements by a single symbol to see the unacceptable reasoning in its pure and simple form.

Before going further, we need to mention two points without discussing them in detail.

The first is that Popper introduced a significant correction into his theory of falsification: though it is impossible to regard a theory as true, one can regard it as more or less *probable*. In fact, with an increase in the number n of the consequences of the theory which seem consistent with reality, it generally becomes more and more difficult to imagine that an alternative theory which is totally removed from p can lead to the same set of consequences. This amounts to saying that, when a theory successfully undergoes an increasingly large number of tests, it can be regarded as more and more *probable*.

It is none the less important to ensure that the true and the probable are not miles apart, and that the conclusion that it cannot be shown that a theory is true remains valid. If we simply produce theories which are more and more probable, it becomes impossible to *verify* any theory.[8]

The other point which needs to be noted, and which is clear from the passages quoted above, is that Popper uses two closely related arguments to defend his theory.

The first is based on the fact that inductive reasoning is generally unacceptable by its very nature, whatever the content and nature of p.

The other argument is that a universal statement such as 'crows are black' can – by its very form – be refuted, but not verified (in the case where the statement in question is treated as 'analytical', that is, true by definition, the distinction is obviously irrelevant). The impossibility of proving this statement by any finite set of observations stems from the fact that, even if we could do the impossible and examine all existing crows, we could not observe all future ones.

The two arguments are distinct. The first one is more general, and applies to any theory, *whatever its form and content*. There are, however, all kinds of cases to which the second does not apply – for example, when theory p is made up of statements relating to finite sets. The second argument on the other hand presupposes that the continual aim of a scientific theory is to discuss universal statements of the 'crows are black' kind. However, one has only to think of theories of a 'historical' nature, such as cosmogonic theories or those about continental drift, to realize that many theories cannot be reduced to this form. Although Popper recognizes the existence of scientific theories of a 'historical' kind, as well as their verifiable nature, he clearly does not regard them as typical.

I will not go into Popper's point, referred to earlier, about *degrees* of universality. When he says that one statement is more universal than another when the former is a hypothesis for inferring the latter, one may well ask whether, by substituting the notion of degrees of universality for the universal/singular distinction, then defining degrees of universality by reference to the hypothesis/consequence distinction, Popper is not implicitly proposing to reduce the argument about the impossibility of verifying a universal statement to that of the asymmetry between *modus tollens* and the 'inductive mode of inference'.

The argument from the asymmetry between *modus tollens* and 'inductive reasoning' is in any case completely general and perfectly clear.

One can understand why a simple theory like Popper's should have aroused such interest. It comes to a conclusion that is spectacular, paradoxical and devastating. People had always thought that science allowed access to the truth. Popper showed that a theory – apart from theories which he regarded as atypical – can be proved false or be provisionally regarded as not false, but never be regarded as true: 'science can never claim to have arrived at the truth'.

We cannot dispense with the theory of falsification by putting the ball back in Popper's court and arguing that, since no theory can be proved true, his cannot be either. The problem is that his proof relates only to theories containing empirical statements, that is, statements describing states of affairs which could be verified as being observed in reality or not. Popper's theory is not itself empirical. In fact, it is based exclusively on a formal argument of universal application. It is therefore not *self-defeating*. In other words, it has sufficient stature in comparison with empirical theories to ensure that none of them could be regarded as true.

As Lakatos says,[9] Popper's theory overturned a belief which was twenty-five centuries old. During this time everybody had been more or less a *verificationist*, that is, had believed in the possibility of verifying scientific – and other – theories. Popper showed by an irrefutable argument that only the *falsificationist*[10] approach was acceptable: a theory can be shown to be false, but not true.

We have only to be aware of the conclusions Popper drew from his studies to understand the excitement which it created and still creates:

> Science is not a system of certain, or well-established statements; nor is it a system which steadily advances towards a state of finality. Our science is not knowledge (*episteme*): it can never claim to have attained truth, or even a substitute for it, such as probability. . . . *We do not know; we can only guess.* And our guesses are guided by the unscientific, the metaphysical (though biologically explainable) faith in laws, in regularities which we can uncover-discover.[11] . . . But these marvellous imaginative and bold conjectures or 'anticipations' of ours are carefully and soberly controlled by systematic tests.[12] . . . The old scientific ideal of *episteme* – of absolutely certain, demonstrable knowledge – has proved to be an idol.[13]

The unanswerable nature of Popper's proof, the total break with an age-old tradition which it represented, is enough to explain the impact it had. Apart from the reasons for this must be added that aspect of the theory of refutation which, if not nihilistic, is at least *tragic* (if I can use this expression): it implies in fact that many scientific theories are condemned in advance, and that the history of science is a series of mutually correcting failures. No doubt researchers can also – at least in principle – chance on true theories; but neither they nor anyone else will be in a position to tell whether this is in fact so, and therefore they have to carry on trying to refute all theories with no hope of determining whether any of them is true.

Followers and critics of Popper have fine-tuned the theory of refutation, for example, by stressing that it is not always easy to judge whether a theory is in fact contradicted by reality, or to decide which part of the theory can be regarded as wrong,[14] or to know when it is appropriate to abandon a theory which seems to compound failures. None of these 'objections', however, refutes Popper's central argument.[15] They are refinements and improvements rather than objections *stricto sensu*.

I would like to say parenthetically that, although Popper claimed in all sincerity to be a defender of *critical rationalism*, and his theories were inspired by the desire to distinguish truth from falsehood (or at any rate to separate the wheat of serious theories from the chaff of pseudo-theories), he in fact started in modern philosophy and sociology of science a move towards scepticism which culminated in what may be called new relativism, to which I will return later.[16]

At this point, however, appears a double difficulty and a double doubt.

Firstly, *modus tollens* on which the whole of Popper's falsificationism is based is, if not as old as the world, at least as old as logic. Why did it take twenty-five centuries to draw from it the conclusions which Popper did?

Secondly, it is clear that, at least in everyday life, we are always coming up with explanations of phenomena, some of which appear true to any sensible person. How then do we explain that scientific thinking, meticulous, fastidious, rigorous and systematic, is unable to arrive at the certainties reached by ordinary knowledge? Must we conclude that the latter is the plaything of illusions which nobody manages to spot and that the certainties are in fact pseudo-certainties?

Obviously, these two questions cannot be answered by reference to some technical difficulty or other needing twenty-five centuries before the conclusions could be drawn from *modus tollens* which Popper draws. In other words, the logical impossibility of verifying the scientific theories on which Popper's theory is based is easy to establish. But how can we then explain that, during all this time, theoretical knowledge and practical manipulation of *modus tollens* co-existed peacefully with a verificationist philosophy of knowledge, that is, with the idea that *to know* means to have *verified* one's affirmations about the real world? How were these two commonplaces able to co-exist for so long before their incompatibility was perceived?

APPLICATION OF SIMMEL'S MODEL

The answer to these paradoxes – and it will be readily agreed that they are significant ones – lies in Simmel's model. Contrary to appearances, Popper's theory contains implicit statements which help to give the theory added strength, that is, to make it assert more than it can.

Firstly, the stark contrast which Popper makes between *modus tollens* and the 'inductive mode of inference' conceals the complexity in the links that logical forms have with reality. However, this concealment is perhaps explained easily: since logical forms are sometimes interpreted as laws of pure thought, there is a normal tendency not to pay attention to the problem of the conditions in which they are applied.

As soon as attention is paid to them, we note, as Peirce does, that although 'inductive reasoning' is formally incorrect or 'fallacious' (as Simmel says) it is in fact continually applied in everyday life as well as in scientific thinking.

A fact which perhaps shows up these ambiguities is that, although the basic figures of logic are a classic, even hackneyed, theme, there remains a lack of precision in words used to describe them. We can note in passing, for example, that Peirce's suggestion was to call this kind of unacceptable reasoning *abduction* rather than *induction.*[17]

A simple example will show that this unacceptable reasoning is in fact very common. If we link together the following statements:

1) When it rains (p), the road is wet (q)
2) The road is wet (q)

3) It is raining (p),

in logic, the inference is unacceptable. However, nobody would be shocked by it; and in fact, we continually reason in this way without any negative reaction.

This contradiction between 'theory' and 'practice' is easily resolved.

The reasoning is unacceptable because the conclusion is wrongly deduced from the two premises. Formally, there is nothing to say that the road is wet *only* when it rains. In practice, however, we know that when the road is wet, this is because it is raining or has just rained, since we can in most cases discount other possible causes of this state of affairs

– for example, that the municipal street-cleaning machine has just been through.

Let us look at another example:

1) Without petrol (p), a car will not go (q) $(p \rightarrow q)$
2) My car does go $(\sim q)$
_____
3) My car is not out of petrol $(\sim p)$

This reasoning is perfectly valid: it is an illustration of *modus tollens*. Its form and the truth of its premises guarantee the unshakable soundness of the conclusion.

The same is true when the same statements are combined in *modus ponens*:

1) Without petrol (p), a car will not go (q) $(p \rightarrow q)$
2) My car is out of petrol (p)
_____
3) My car will not go (q)

On the other hand, the 'abductive' equivalent of *modus ponens* – to borrow Peirce's expression – or 'inductive' as Popper would have it, is immediately seen as so unacceptable that the reaction is a smile or a shrug of the shoulders:

1) Without petrol, a car will not go $(p \rightarrow q)$
2) My car will not go (q)
_____
3) My car is out of petrol (p)

The contrast between these two examples shows up an asymmetry between the two forms of reasoning. *Modus tollens* and *modus ponens* are always true. The abductive equivalent of *modus ponens* is always unacceptable from a formal point of view, but can of course be regarded either as acceptable or unacceptable depending on the *content* to which it is applied. It is totally acceptable in the example of the rain, and unacceptable in that of the car (since clearly a car breakdown can have many causes).

Peirce went even further, and, as we have seen, showed how essential abductive reasoning is in scientific thinking.[18]

The important thing, however, from my particular point of view here, is that these examples put us on the track of the implicit statements in Popper's theory of falsification. It is clear in fact that Popper takes no account of these complications. Instead, he maintains a purely formal stance: *modus tollens* is always formally acceptable, the 'inductive mode of inference' always unacceptable.

An initial reaction to the examples of the application of *modus tollens* which I have just given would be to suggest that ordinary thinking is more flexible, more indulgent and more open to compromise than scientific thinking. However, this reaction would be a purely verbal one, and gives no insight into how the two examples differ.

The second, more interesting, reaction is to take seriously the fact that the same reasoning seems acceptable in the rain example and absurd in the car example. Because the *form* of the reasoning is exactly the same in both cases and, moreover, a line of reasoning can be valid or invalid only from a formal point of view, the two examples must therefore correspond to reasoning which is different *in reality*, even if formally identical. In other words, the suggestion is that the two lines of reasoning contain different *implicit statements* which make them in reality different from one another.

The reasoning about the rain seems to us immediately acceptable because, apart from the municipal street-cleaning machine, rain is more or less the only reason for the road being wet. However, we can recognize when the street-cleaning machine has been past, for example, if only part of the highway is wet; moreover, it usually comes in the early morning. The abductive line of reasoning is in reality therefore the following:

1) $p \rightarrow q$ (when it rains the road is wet)
2) q (the road is wet)
3) $[p' \rightarrow q]^\star$ (the street-cleaning machine also wets the road)
4) $[q \rightarrow (p \; v \; p')]^\star$ (if the road is wet, it is because it has been raining or the street-cleaning machine has been past).

Statement 4 implies that p & p' can happen. Let us assume that this is rather improbable and that, when it rains, the street-cleaning machine does not appear. We can therefore state:

5) $[q \rightarrow \sim (p \; \& \; p')]^\star$.

Let us now assume that the cleaning machine has wet the road, which implies that the pavement is dry:

6) $p' \rightarrow r$

However, it is not dry:

7) $\sim r$

Therefore:

8) $\sim p'$

and by 4), 5) and 6),

9) p: it has been raining.

It is not true, therefore, that, in using abduction, ordinary thinking is being lax – the reasoning is perfectly rigorous, provided one is careful to put in the implicit *a priori* statements on which it is based, and which are not – thank goodness! – in fact elucidated in practice.

This formalization immediately highlights the difference between the rain example and the one with the car which will not go.

In the second case, the situation is much more complicated: when a car refuses to go, this might be because it is out of petrol, or for all kinds of other reasons. The effect of this is that statements 4) and 5) above have to be replaced by:

4') $[q \rightarrow p \; v \; p'v \ldots v \; p'']) \star$
5') $[q \rightarrow \; \sim (p \; \& \; p', p \; \& \; p'' \ldots)] \star$

Assuming that, as above:

5) $p' \rightarrow r$

one cannot obviously derive p.

In other words, in both cases there is an abductive form of inference, but it is only so as long as one fails to consider what might be called its implicit *environment*. As soon as this is made explicit, the reasoning assumes a deductive form, leading in the first case to a sound conclusion, but in the second case to no conclusion at all, which means that new statements have to be brought in if the cause of the breakdown is to be determined. We might note in passing that this is an example of the case referred to by Simmel where a line of reasoning is in reality different from how it *appears* to the consciousness of the person formulating it.

The important point, however, is the following: the fact that this environment is present in a metaconscious way explains why we readily accepted the reasoning concerning the rain, but not the second example.

We see therefore that ordinary thinking is less nebulous than one thinks. We must regard it rather as possessing a high level of virtuosity, capable of manipulating complex sets of statements of which only some are explicitly revealed to the consciousness of the subject, while many remain implicit.

Returning to Popper, we can say that the theory of falsification takes account of all the consequences of the fact that abduction is in principle – by which I mean from a purely formal point of view – an unacceptable type of inference.

However, as we have just seen, *it is in fact unacceptable only in certain environments.*

More specifically, it is always unacceptable in the environment:

$$[p \lor p'v'v \ldots \lor p''].$$

and *a fortiori* in the open environment:

$$[p \lor p' \, v \ldots].$$

In this case,

$$
\begin{array}{l}
p \to q \\
q \\
\hline
p
\end{array}
$$

is most certainly not valid, whereas in an environment such as:

1) $(p \lor p') \& \sim (p \& p')$
2) $p' \to \sim q$

the same reasoning is valid.

We need only look at some classic examples to see that the processes not only of 'ordinary' thinking, but also of scientific thinking, are often characterized by such an environment.

IS THE EARTH ROUND OR FLAT?

Since the advent of satellite observation, this question has without any doubt taken the form of a singular statement followed by a question mark, and there is hardly any difference between an interrogative statement such as 'is this ball round or oval?' and the question 'is the earth round or flat?' However, the two questions became truly identical only when it became possible to answer the second one on the basis of direct observation.

Before, the question may have been formulated in the same way, but it was simply the shorthand summary of another question: 'Do observations about the shape of the earth lead to the conclusion that it is round or flat?' In other words, before direct observation was possible, the question was essentially of a *universal* nature, that is, of the *form* 'are all crows black?'.

The new formulation, apart from expressing better the situation before the age of satellite observation, has the advantage of emphasizing the fact that the universal or singular nature of a question depends – at least in some cases – on the way in which it is formulated. This is another reason for preferring a formulation of the theory of falsification based on *modus tollens* rather than on the unprovable character of universal statements.

In any case, the two arguments converge in the example under discussion. When the question is put in this form, Popper's theory of falsification applies: one can always imagine a new observation which contradicts the previous ones.

The theory that 'all possible observations prove that the earth is round' is therefore *refutable*; but it is not *verifiable* (my standpoint is still the period before satellite observation). Even if it seems to be *corroborated* by all available observations, we cannot say it is *true*. Strictly, the theory has to be regarded as *probable* – even *infinitely probable* – but it cannot be said to be *true*. It is therefore a case of a theory which is covered by the two arguments on which the theory of falsification is based.

The question of the shape of the earth was used by Gerard Radnitzky to illustrate the theory of refutation.

At the same time, Radnitsky used this example to develop his own original idea that when scientists decide to subscribe to a theory or to reject it, they are conforming *volens nolens* to the economic principle of *cost-benefit* analysis.[19] Briefly summarized, this hypothesis suggests that scientists tend to abandon a theory as soon as a defence of it involves prohibitive costs.

From early times, as Radnitzky reminds us, arguments were available to show that the earth was round, particularly the fact that sails of boats appear on the horizon before the hull. This observation is easily explained by the hypothesis that the earth is round, but not by the competing theory.

This does not mean, of course, that the latter cannot be saved by an *ad hoc* hypothesis. Such a solution is always possible, at least in principle.

In the same way, the former theory easily explains that the shadows visible on the moon during an eclipse describe the arc of a circle. The latter explains it only if we assume that lunar eclipses are due to something other than the shadow of the earth on the moon. This hypothesis is itself credible only if we can imagine an alternative theory of eclipses. This is not impossible, but it presupposes a considerable intellectual investment with very little chance of success.

Similarly, the theory that the earth is round easily accounts for the first circumnavigation. This new observation does not prove the *truth* of the theory any more than existing ones. However, the more observations there are which are readily explained by this theory and difficult to explain by the competing theory, the more *costly* it becomes to keep the latter in contention. We had no need, therefore, to wait for satellite observations to be certain that the earth is round: well before that, it had simply become *prohibitive* to try to defend the competing theory. *That is why*, says Radnitzky, certainty was established that the earth is round, though it remained, until satellite observation, a *quasi-certainty*.

This example eloquently illustrates both Popper's theory of falsification and Radnitzky's ingenious hypothesis that one's *quasi-certainty* in some cases regarding the *truth* of a theory simply conveys the fact that the defence of alternative theories is considered to be too *costly*. As Popper says, we can arrive at the truth, but not the certainty of truth. Before satellites, the theory that the earth is round was only very *probable*; it could not be regarded as certain.

This example is interesting in that the solution makes us uneasy. Our clear feeling is that, even before satellites, the theory of the earth's roundness was seen not only as very probable, but as *certain* and *true*.

In this case, the inadequacy of the asymmetry between 'verification' and 'falsifiction' in Popper's theory arises quite simply from the fact that, at the same time that observations were destroying the theory that the earth was flat – 'falsifying' it – they were confirming *to exactly the same degree* the theory that it is round. Here, therefore, there is no asymmetry between verification and falsification – in 'falsifying' one theory, one was 'verifying' the other.

Doubtless the fact that a boat's sails appear above the horizon before its hull was not enough to verify the theory of roundness, and other arguments were needed before everybody subscribed to it. This observation, however, was not more sufficient to *falsify* the opposing theory.

Finally, the reason why there was certainty that the earth is round well before the advent of satellites is that all observations without exception *invalidated* the first theory and, in an indistinct and perfectly symmetrical way, *confirmed* the first one.

In the final analysis, this story, if not in its prominence and importance at least in its principle, comes down to ordinary observations in the phenomenology of perception. We may not be sure at dusk whether an indistinct shape is that of a tree or a person; but once the clues build up in favour of one solution, there is no further room for doubt, other than hyperbolic doubt. To say that in this case the subject has the *quasi-certainty* that the object is a tree, or that the theory that it is a tree is very *probable*, is to use a formulation which is not only complicated but also hard to accept in that it contradicts the feeling of absolute certainty in the subject.

Mutatis mutandis, it is by means of a scenario such as this that the relative certainty that the earth is round was established.

It must be added that the earth in fact is not *truly* round, being flattened at the poles. The theory that the earth is round can therefore be replaced by a better theory, and there is no limit to the precision with which its form can be described. Similarly, once one has recognized that the shape in the half-light is a person and not a tree, one can establish a whole host of details on further inspection. However, the theory that the earth is round and not flat is as indisputable as the theory that the shape is that of a person and not a tree.

In any event, if one insists that certainty is never absolute and that it is better to speak of probability rather than *truth*, the same reservation applies just as much to the *falseness* of the theory that the earth is flat as to the *truth* of the competing theory. If one of them cannot legitimately be described as *true*, the other cannot be called *false*, but only *improbable*. Similarly, if one cannot be absolutely sure that the vague shape seen in the half-light is a person, one cannot be absolutely sure either that it *is not* a tree. If the *verification* of one of the propositions is in principle conjectural, so is the *falsification* of the other to exactly the same degree.

Why does Popperian analysis leave a feeling of unease in asserting that before satellites it was impossible to be certain about the shape of the earth? Because it tries to impose an asymmetry between 'falsification' and 'verification' in a situation where the two operations are symmetrical.

This symmetry arises quite simply because the debate was limited from early on to two hypotheses which are obviously mutually exclusive. The question here is not therefore of the form 'are all crows black?', but 'is this particular object blue or red, given that it is one or the other and cannot be both at the same time?'.

In other words, there is no problem in applying Popper's theory of falsification when the question to which the answer is sought is of the type:

for every y, x (y)?

but not when it is of the form:

x (y) w x' w (y)?[20]

We can then ask whether its apparent universality is real or whether it does not assume that question asked by science are of a certain form.

I hasten to add that this question is not trying in any way to discredit the theory of falsification, but simply to specify *its degree of generality*.

There are many examples which show that the reply to the above question is in the affirmative. For it not to be, questions in the form '*x (y) w x' (y)*?' would, through some principle or other, have to be kept out of science.

In the case of the shape of the earth, the fact that the question is in the form of an alternative does not really follow any logical necessity. In principle at least, many other hypotheses could be imagined. In fact, two surfaced: either the earth is round or it is flat.

Very often, however, questions asked by science imply *by their very form* a finite number of possible answers; the most commonplace case is that in which the question implies two, and only two, exclusive answers.

However, as soon as one asks which of the two statements *x* or ~*x* is true, to prove the falsity of one of the theories ('*x* true', '~*x* true'), is *ipso facto* to prove the truth of the other. There is therefore no trace of asymmetry between *falsifiability* and *verifiability* and, consequently, no longer a theory of falsification which holds up.

The counter-argument may well be that many questions can be put in the form '*x w* ~ *x*?', but that this in no way means that the two terms of the alternative can be treated symmetrically. It is true that false alternatives of this kind are easy to imagine. For example: either Max Weber's theory in *The Protestant Ethic and the Spirit of Capitalism* puts forward an acceptable interpretation of the different correlations observable between Protestantism and capitalism, *or* it does not. If the second answer prevails, it provides no explanation of the correlations. To refute Weber's theory does not necessarily mean setting another theory against it. The counter-argument is simply saying that, among the alternatives, we must distinguish those where only one of the terms represents an authentic theory and those which set two competing theories against one another, which can be called *true* alternatives.

The battle of the electron which took place in 1910 between Millikan and Ehrenhaft is a famous historical example where the question asked takes the form of a true alternative.

Ehrenhaft claimed to have discovered 'sub-electrons':

> Drops of liquid, metal particles and other very small objects observed during various experiments were found to be carrying charges of a much lower value than that of the electron. Over time, he discovered charges of half, a fifth, a tenth, a hundredth, a thousandth that of the electron. As his

work progressed, the hypothesis that there was a lower limit to the electrical charge associated with the matter became less and less reasonable . . .' Meanwhile, Millikan and his pupils, with others, were assiduously refining and reaffirming the hypothesis of a unitary electron.[21]

The problem, therefore, was whether we could maintain an *atomistic* conception of electricity, or whether, following Ehrenhaft, a *continuist* conception had to be adopted.

The battle raged for some time, and seventeen years after it started a respected physicist was able to say: 'Neither side can claim finally to have won, in the sense of all research scientists adopting one of the two possible answers to the problem.'[22]

In the end, after many ups and downs and an acrimonious conflict between those who believed in atoms and those who did not, Millikan's atomistic thesis prevailed. Holton describes well the continual ambiguity of both sides' findings. He also says that Millikan was sustained in his fight by a profound faith – of metaphysical character – in atomism. Holton even suggests that some uncertainty remains, despite one of the theories winning the day.[23]

The debate lasted a long time and the outcome was for a long period uncertain. I must stress, however, that the battle of the electron is not covered by the falsificationist theory: any argument or finding adding grist to the mill of one of the theories necessarily took as much from the other. Each argument in the debate strengthened the position of one of the theories to the same degree as it weakened that of the other. By the very *nature* of the question they were trying to answer, the battle between Millikan and Ehrenhaft was a zero-sum game.

A likely counter-argument to what I am saying is that the notion of alternative is a logical and not an empirical one: though there exist sets of two mutually contradictory propositions, there are no realities of which it can be said that they are contradictory. Of this there is no doubt. However, knowledge of the real world is always composed of answers to questions. Of course, these questions have a *form*, and in numerous cases this form is such that it implies a finite number of answers, mutually incompatible.

This is why the theory of falsification does not apply to cases like the Millikan–Ehrenhaft debate. Perhaps the classic experiments[24] which gave Millikan victory should not be seen as a definite confirmation of his discontinuist theory, and perhaps it is better, as Holton suggests, to regard them as constructs which made an impact through their ingenuity, simplified the debate, and led people to subscribe to the theory. One thing is certain in any event: the degree of certainty which can be given to one of the theories is of necessity complementary to that given to the other. If one cannot be said to be verified, the other cannot be said to be falsified, and vice versa. *Doubts about the truth and falseness of the two theories can only be shared out in an absolutely symmetrical manner.*

Perhaps significantly, Popper mentions Millikan in his classic work *The Logic of Scientific Discovery* only to compare (on page 267) the hypothesis 'all crows are black' with the hypothesis 'the electronic charge has the value determined by Millikan', saying that the latter is better corroborated since it can be subjected to stricter tests. In this example, the theory of falsification applies: there is nothing to ensure that other observations will not modify the value of the constant in question, and therefore it cannot strictly be regarded as *true*[25] However, the theory does not apply to the main theme of the debate between Millikan and Ehrenhaft.

Must we regard these true alternatives as abnormal cases which can be ignored? In fact, many more examples could be found.

THE INHERITANCE OF ACQUIRED CHARACTERISTICS

The same remarks as before apply to the debate on the inheritance of acquired characteristics – an eminently classic example. It went on without resolution for a long time; at one point a negative answer – that there is no inheritance of acquired characteristics – was beginning to gain the upper hand, but over several decades 'new facts' were continually emerging to add weight to a positive answer.

A negative answer seemed to be emerging victorious when Weismann experimented with cutting off the tails of several generations of mice; he noted that, despite this, baby mice were always born with normal tails. This observation, however (just like the case of Millikan's drop of oil or the boat's sail which appears first above the horizon), was not enough, despite its being simple and evocative, to dispel once and for all the claims of the rival Lamarckian theory.

In his book *Histoire de la génétique et de l'évolutionnisme en France*,[26] Denis Buican painstakingly drew up a list of all the facts marshalled, until very recently, against the theory which ended up by being dominant in a large part of the world. He refers[27] to Philippe l'Héritier, who states in his memoirs:

> The idea that what might be called Morgano-Mendelism covered only a fairly small part of the area of heredity existed in France well beyond the 1920s . . . In 1937, Georges Tessier and I discovered, by pure chance, a very curious phenomenon – a certain strain of fruit fly was subject to a rather strange physiological reaction: CO_2, which for other insects only really acts through any anoxia produced, was a deadly poison for this particular strain. By using chromosomic markers, . . . it was easy to show

that the hereditary transmission of this characteristic not only did not conform to Mendel's laws, but even operated in a way which was completely independent of the chromosomes.

This fact was in reality only in *apparent* contradiction with 'Morgano-Mendelism', since, as L'Héritier says, 'the problem was solved some years later when, with various colleagues, I was able to show that the fruit fly's sensitivity to CO_2 was not strictly speaking a hereditary characteristic, but the symptom of the fly's infection by a virus which was not contagious in normal circumstances, but transmitted from generation to generation by gametes'.

Buican's point is that the fact highlighted by L'Héritier provoked jubilation in many French scientists because they saw in it a possible confirmation of the theory of the inheritance of acquired characteristics and, in any event, a serious challenge to classic genetics.

Another colourful example is also provided by Buican – the way in which certain species of moths have turned black in industrial regions of Britain:

> In the second half of the nineteenth century, the dominance of textiles in the Birmingham and Manchester regions led to a covering of soot on trees and walls. This new environment meant that the silver birch moth, the adult of which was an ash-grey colour close to the colour of the lichen on the tree trunks, adapted to their new habitat, and the black form of the moth which had been rare up to 1850 became more common until, within a few decades, it made up the vast majority of specimens.[28]

Initially, many interpreted this fact as a confirmation of Lamarckian theory, and it was only in 1937 that the British geneticist Ford cleared up the mystery: 'Before pollution, the black forms which were highly visible on the trunks of trees were eliminated mostly by natural selection – they were eaten by various insectivorous birds. Afterwards, the blackening of the tree trunks had the opposite effect – grey moths were attacked by predators, and black ones hidden by the new background colour'.

When theories are in competition, it is very rare – as these examples show – for findings to decide the issue in a straightforward way; getting at the truth is difficult, and can be interminable. A particular theory which is regarded as true can be continually thrown into question. New facts can always be found which go against it, like the black moths or the sensitivity of the fruit-fly to CO_2. Initially, these new facts are interpreted as being unfavourable to the theory, before being themselves ruled out.

Like proponents of the flatness of the earth, opponents of classical genetic theory ended up without a leg to stand on – they had either to renounce their pet theory or sustain it by mystical arguments.

What is important in the context of the present discussion, however, is that the *falsification* of one viewpoint is at the same time the *verification* of the other whenever, as here, the logical environment of the debate is that there are two, and only two, theories, which cannot both be true. In this case, the degree of confirmation of one is exactly the same as the degree of invalidation of the other.

These examples perhaps show that there is no reason to assume that questions which exercise scientists are always situated in the open logical environment which Popper's theory would imply. On the contrary, many questions, including the major ones, are of the form:

$$x \ w \ {\sim}x'$$

In this context, of course, falsification and verification are perfectly symmetrical operations.[29]

In other words, in both ordinary thinking and scientific thinking, there are all kinds of questions to which the answers can be not only not false *or very likely*, but also *true*.

By their very form, questions such as 'does a molecule of water contain two atoms of hydrogen or not?', 'did the Battle of Marignano take place in 1515?', 'did the captain kill Harry?' (see Chapter 5), 'is there continental drift?', 'is there life on Mars?', 'does unemployment always vary inversely with inflation?', 'does taxation have deflationary effects?', 'are acquired characteristics inherited?', 'is there such a thing as a minimal electrical charge?' give answers which are at the same time verifiable and falsifiable. There is no serious reason to assume that these questions are less 'typical' of scientific research than questions about, for example, the nature of light.

In other words, one could give a thousand examples of scientific theories which do not fall within Popper's inevitable asymmetry.

All that I am trying to show here is that this asymmetry implies an *a priori*, that it disappears when the *a priori* does, and that there are very many real-life situations where the operations of verification and falsification are inseparable from each other. In some cases, like the shape of the earth example, this process comes to an *end* and we can say that one of the theories is true and the other one false. In other cases (for example, the debates on the electron and the inheritance of acquired characteristics, verification and falsification are *inconclusive* processes. I am not arguing, therefore, that in the case of authentic alternatives it is always possible to determine which of the two theories is true (this may or may not be the case), but only that it is then impossible to declare oneself fallibilist rather than verificationist (or vice versa).

We can also note in passing that there are questions which, by their very form, give rise to theories – or answers – which can be neither *verifiable* nor *falsifiable* without anybody thinking that they are not worth considering, or not scientific.

Two typical cases can be mentioned in this respect. Firstly, since 'theories' which strictly speaking are statements less on reality than on ways of apprehending reality are normative rather than positive, they cannot be called true or false, only sensible or not. In the same way, an opinion or piece of advice can be sensible or not, but not true or false.

This case in point can be illustrated by as significant an example as Darwin's theory of evolution. It caused Popper a lot of problems, and he was never sure whether to regard it as falsifiable – and therefore as scientific – or not. The question is easily solved if Darwinism is taken as describing a way of analysing evolutionary processes – an attempt to make them the result of mechanisms of mutation and selection. In this form, the normative nature of the theory is clear, and one need no longer be surprised at the fact that it is at the same time *not falsifiable* and yet *scientific*. It is scientific because the explanatory programme which it proposes has shown its effectiveness many times (compare the moths in the English textile areas). It is not falsifiable because it is not very clear what kind of facts could contradict the statement 'evolution is explained by the operation of mutations and selection'. The fact that a particular phenomenon has not been explained in this way does not mean that it could not be, for example, if more data became available. Darwinism is not therefore refutable. Nevertheless, it was one of the most significant new developments in the whole history of science.

What I have said underlines another *a priori* of the theory of falsification, which is that, since scientific theories are not verifiable, they can only be falsifiable. This implies that a theory has to have one of these two characteristics. Darwinism contradicts this *a priori*.

The second case relates to theories which are very numerous, for example, in economics, of the kind: 'under general conditions, statement p is true'. As long as the conditions are not specified – and usually they cannot be fully specified – the theory in question cannot, by its very form, be either *verified* (for reasons deriving from the theory of falsification) or falsified (since a failure of the theory can always be blamed not on the theory itself but on the 'conditions' referred to in the statement which are by definition imprecise).

Hotelling's theory, which I will analyse later in this chapter, provides, I think, a sufficiently convincing illustration of the existence and the typical nature of this case in point: the human sciences contain innumerable examples of 'models' which are epistemologically comparable with Hotelling's model, in that they are neither verifiable nor strictly speaking refutable. However, there is no reason for saying that they do not belong to science in general.

For example, there are scientific theories which are, as Popper claims, refutable and non-verifiable. There are others, however, which are both refutable and verifiable, and yet others which are neither of these.[30]

Popper's theory, therefore, is valid only under certain conditions: it is true only if the logical environment which it implicitly assumes is in fact relevant.

We are now in a position to describe this implicit environment quite easily: Popper's theory assumes that *any* scientific theory is in competition with an open set of other theories:

$$p', p'' \ldots$$

In fact, if the question is in the form '$p \, v' \, p'' \ldots$?', then from

$$(p \rightarrow q) \, \& \, q,$$

one can never draw the conclusion p.

The conclusion is that Popper's theory of falsification contains the implicit statement:

[scientific questions are typically in the form $p \, v \, p' \, v \ldots$]*.[31]

This statement is crucial to show the general nature of the theory of refutation.

There is no doubt that this implicit statement is a generalization of important cases: when phenomena were observed which seemed hard to explain by either the emission theory or the wave theory of light, the *form* of the questions shifted and a question of the '$p \, w \, p''$ type moved to an open one of the Popperian kind: '$p \, v \, p' \, v \ldots$'. There is, however, no reason to regard this latter *form* as *typical*, nor to concede that any closed question should be converted into an open question. Cases of scientific questions taking the form, for example, of true alternatives are so numerous and significant that such a statement can only with difficulty be sustained in an explicit way.

It sometimes happens that a discussion takes the form of a series of alternatives resolved one after the other (for example, 'is Weber's theory of the relationship between Protestantism and capitalism acceptable or not?', 'if it is not, is the theory acceptable which says that this relationship was really a result of the Counter-Reformation?', and so on). In other words, a discussion can remain open indefinitely without this implying that it is impossible to assert, at each stage, the truth of one of the competing statements.

Since my aim here is not to conduct a systematic debate (which would belong to the philosophy of science) either of Popper's theory, or of any of the theories examined in this book, but simply to show the *implicit formal a priori* on which they are based, I will not try to list counter-arguments to the theory of falsification. I will merely repeat – since this reinforces the argument that falliblism is based on tacit *a priori* – that Carnap had already countered the notion of asymmetry between verification and falsification with the idea that both operations can imply the other, as in the case of a statement of the kind 'for any *x*, there is a *y* such that . . .'.[32]

However, what I must particularly emphasize here is that *The Logic of Scientific Discovery* is a perfect illustration of Simmel's theory; the theory of falsification seems to be stimulated by the presence of implicit statements to the extent that it gives hyperbolic conclusions: a theory can *never* be proved true (except for 'atypical' theories such as historical ones); we cannot be sure about the truth of a theory; we must abandon the age-old ideal of verification, and so on. No doubt we must recognize that Popper in no way denies the importance of the notion of truth, nor the existence of true theories: 'We do justify our preferences by an appeal to the idea of truth: truth plays the role of a regulative idea. We test for truth . . .'.[33] However, since we can never be sure of the truth of a theory, and since we cannot determine whether a theory is true when it is in fact true, we see that Popperian truth ceases to play a central role.

Popper's conclusions seem all the more inevitable in that they are based on unexceptionable reasoning: who could deny that, from a formal point of view, *modus ponens* and *modus tollens* are valid ways of reasoning, whereas the 'inductive mode of inference' is not?

In fact, Popper's *explicit* reasoning does not, in itself, allow us to draw the conclusions in question. For this, we require also the presence of an *implicit* statement which is readily accepted, regarded as self-evident and, because of this, present in the subject in a *metaconscious* rather than a conscious way. Is it not 'obvious', in fact, that scientific questions are always *open*?

However, when the crucial implicit statement in the theory of falsification (and especially its pivotal role) is perceived and made explicit, we see that the theory has to be formulated in completely different terms: *the notion of truth then takes its rightful place; in other words, there is no longer any bar to a theory being identified as true.*

Moreover, Popper's fallibilism can now be replaced by the following statement:

Depending on the case, a scientific theory can be either refutable, or verifiable, or both, or neither, and it is very difficult to regard one of these cases as more typical than the others.[34]

The same result is of course reached if we start, not from the *modus tollens*, but from Popper's argument at the beginning of *The Logic of*

Scientific Discovery in favour of the theory of falsification, that universal statements of the type 'all crows are black' can be falsified, but not verified. In fact, scientific statements are not all of this type, even assuming – which is going a long way – that science is science 'of the general'.

The circular nature which Simmel attributed to theories where the explicit statements seem to be linked in a linear way is also present in the example of the theory of falsification: the implicit statement on which it is based presupposes that scientific questions are of such a kind that the 'inductive mode of inference' cannot validly be applied to them. However, the theory itself derives from the invalid nature of this type of reasoning.

We see at the same time why it needed twenty-five centuries to draw from *modus tollens* the conclusion that scientific theories can only be falsified: far from being an immediate logical consequence of *modus tollens*, it assumes the presence of an implicit statement which is innocuous but decisive.[35]

Finally, we see the reason why the crucial role of this implicit statement has not really been studied or discussed: it seems to be 'self-evident'. Is it not 'obvious' that, when a scientific theory is formulated, it may find itself in competition not only with other theories where the content can be formulated, but also with theories not yet devised? Cartesians could perhaps conceive of no other theory of light than the one formulated by their patron, and this did not justify their assertion that there could be no others. However, any such stubbornness would have been dissipated by the wave theory or the electro-magnetic theory of light. Moreover, is anybody willing to swear that, in the future, a theory of light of which today we have no inkling is inconceivable? However, recognizing the importance of this case and showing that it occurs frequently is one thing; making it the *typical* case or reading into it the very *essence* of scientific endeavour is a different matter.

I hope it is clear that I am in no way saying that the theory of falsification is false, or that it is uninteresting. All that my analysis is suggesting is that it is *hyperbolic*: in other words, that it leads to conclusions whose extreme degree of generality is the effect not only of the explicit arguments on which it is based, but also of implicit arguments which are much less restrictive.

THE GENERALITY OF SIMMEL'S MODEL

Implicit statements like those on which Popper's theory is based tend to be present in any theory. Moreover, as Simmel suggested, these statements can be constructed on the backs of others:

[scientists should be open; therefore they must never assume that the theories currently available are the only possible ones]*;
[scientific questions therefore take the form $p \; v \; p' \; v \; . \; . \; .$]*;
[and not for example the form $p \; w \; p'$]*, etc.

Although they seem broad, these statements are in fact *restrictive* in that they assume a particular situation to be general. In this way, they fulfil the role of a hyperbole machine.

We are dealing here with a typical phenomenon. In fact: 1) any theory tends to contain implicit statements which restrict its conditions of validity; 2) highlighting these statements assumes not only good will and absence of prejudice but also a more or less thankless research programme; 3) they are generally detected only when the theory happens to suffer setbacks, which is not always the case of those which, like the theory of falsification, contain no prediction about the real world; 4) their dissemination depends in the end on all kinds of contingencies of varying degrees of improbability.

Since these conditions are fairly general, we deduce from them that:

Every theory tends to be interpreted as if it had a greater validity than it deserves.

This is not because of some liking for generalities in the human mind, but because of the hyperbolic effect of implicit hypotheses.

If we turn this theorem round, we see a basic mechanism by which false ideas can be the product of the most unexceptionable theories.

AN EXAMPLE FROM POLITICAL THEORY

Let us go down this path, using a second example taken from political theory, to confirm the argument that many received ideas in fact come from these hyperbole machines.

In the 1960s, people were convinced that two-party systems had a moderating influence on ideology. Alain Lancelot, one of the more perspicacious analysts, said[36]: 'The second [characteristic of two-party systems] is the continual drawing together of the image and policies of those parties which try to win over decisive centrist voters at election time. . . . Eventually, this drawing together may deprive party politics of all meaning and turn voters away from it towards anti-system *protest movements.*'

The idea that two-party political systems are essentially more moderate than multi-party systems was not based only on observation. It was of course easy to see the contrast between acute political conflict in multi-party systems such as in France and the ideological calm – though a relative calm – of the situation in Britain and the United States. It was quite clear also, however, that this contrast was due to the unequal implantation of Marxist thought, and the varying influence, over time and space, of intellectuals.

In fact, this received idea derived principally from considerations of theory: a particularly vivid theory had long shown that two-party systems tend to draw the two dominant parties together ideologically.

This is Hotelling's theory, and since it is as well known to political scientists as Popper's is to philosophers, it can be presented very briefly here.[37]

Assume, says Hotelling, that the political position of an elector is indicated by a point on a left – right ideological continuum and that electors are distributed in a unimodal way on this continuum; assume also that the distribution is symmetrical and that electors vote for the party nearest their own position on this segment (see figure 4.1). In this case, a party whose programme is pitched elsewhere than at the *median* point of the continuum will *ipso facto* hand over some of its electors to its opponents and will be bound to lose the election. For example, let us imagine that a right-wing party is foolish enough to locate itself not at *m*, but at *m'*: it will lose about half of the electors between *m* and *m'*. Since by the definition of the median, 50 per cent of electors are on one side and 50 per cent on the other side of *m*, it is bound to lose.

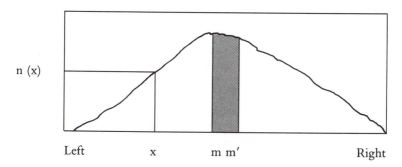

Figure 4.1

Like Popper's theory, this model is absolutely rigorous, and in no way sophistical. Moreover, it leads to consequences which are consistent with what is in fact observed in some two-party system elections. It is true that the American system has sometimes looked as if the two major parties had policies that were ideologically close. In other words, the impression is that the model does show a kind of underlying trend in two-party systems.

Obviously, it is clear that the theory is not a copy of the real world. Unlike the case of the theory of falsification, *some* of the simplifying hypotheses which it introduces are immediately perceptible: for example, can a variety of political positions be represented on a right-wing segment? Language, by using 'right' and 'left', invites this, but is itself indulging in simplification. Moreover, why assume that the distribution of the population is unimodal? It *may* be, but there is no absolute necessity which makes it so. These *visible* hypotheses mean that one can readily accept that the model expresses a *trend*, while conceding that it can on occasions not be verified.

Nevertheless, the tendency would be to endow the theory with a validity which is still excessive, because other hypotheses – this time implicit – are also contained within the model.

Time has been spent on discovering these hypotheses. Hotelling's model dates from 1929.[38] In 1936, it looked as if the model was contradicted by the facts, and the hypothesis was introduced that electors disappointed by the progamme of the party to which they nevertheless felt closest might also *abstain* from voting.[39] The hypothesis also developed that each party could try to guess its rival's reactions, and an attempt was made to deal with the implications of this.[40]

Generally speaking, objections to the model prompted by the real world, by giving rise to corrective hypotheses, at the same time revealed that the original model had crucial implicit hypotheses. Not only had Hotelling not made them explicit, but he had probably not even thought of them. Nevertheless, they were there, and in the end they gave rise to two very tenacious received ideas: that political programmes in two-party systems converged, and that it was inevitable – unless one party made a wrong move – that elections were going to be closely fought.

Hotelling convinced himself of this, and this is seen in the atemporal nature of his conclusion: 'The competition for votes between the Republican and the Democratic parties does not lead to a clear drawing of issues, an adoption of two contrasted positions between which the voter may choose. Instead, each party strives to make its platform as much like the other's as possible. Any radical departure would lose many votes.'[41]

Such a conclusion suggests that Hotelling thought he had brought into the open all the important hypotheses of his model. In other words, the conclusion assumes a implicit hypothesis such as:

[all important hypotheses have been stated]*

Hypotheses advanced by Lerner and Singer introduced the idea that parties can lose out at the margins and be subjected to centrifugal forces, whereas Hotelling considered only centripetal forces. Much later, on the other hand, Hirschman introduced an idea which revealed another of Hotelling's unspoken hypotheses. This presupposes that voters have no means of exercising pressure on party leaderships. The hypothesis, however, is that this is not the case and that voters are all the more inclined to show their discontent in that the party they support is proposing a programme further removed from their wishes. Consequently, the party leaderships can easily think that their supporters are more extremist than is in fact the case.

Hirschman came by the idea for these hypotheses when Goldwater was crushed in 1964 and Nixon was overwhelmingly victorious in 1972: because of external pressures, in 1964 the Republicans chose a candidate who was too right-wing, and in 1972 the Democrats had a candidate who was too left-wing. In both cases, the influence of extremists was boosted by the general ideological climate – favourable to the right in the early 1960s and to the left at the beginning of the 1970s.

Lerner and Singer showed that Hotelling's original model assumed that voters were incapable of voting with their feet, and that Hirschman assumed they were incapable of voicing their dissatisfaction.

As soon as these hypotheses are made explicit, the validity of the theory shrinks like the ass's skin. We become aware that all kinds of conditions have to be present for its conclusions to be consistent with the facts. The more these hypotheses are totally explicit, the less we are led to think that the theory describes an inevitable trend. Conversely, as long as these hypotheses are not made explicit, they give the theory an exaggerated validity.

This inevitable hyperbole effect can be expressed in a different way. A theory generally includes a certain number of visible hypotheses which it is agreed can be unsatisfied. This is not always the case, and it is clear from Popper's example that it may look as though a theory contains *no* particular hypothesis. In fact it is easy to have the impression that the asymmetry between falsification and verification is an absolute given deriving from the laws of thought themselves. However, even in the case where a theory contains visible hypotheses, like Hotelling's, it is difficult to conceive that others can be invisible. If we accept that they are there without managing to make them explicit, the theory remains unexpressed and it yields nothing. If we do not recognize their existence, we deduce from the theory conclusions which in fact it may very well not contain.

This amounts to saying that we cannot really avoid positing the implicit hypothesis which artificial intelligence experts call 'the closed world assumption': whereas the theory contains the visible hypotheses $H_1, H_2 . . ., H_n$, but also other invisible hypotheses $H_{n+1}, H_{n+2} . . .$, then the body of hypotheses H will be implicitly defined as:

$[H = H_1 \text{ \& } H_2 \text{ \& } \ldots \text{ \& } H_n]^\star,$

whereas, in reality, it is:

$H = H_1 \text{ \& } H_2 \text{ \& } \ldots \text{ \& } H_n \text{ \& } H_{n+1} \text{ \& } H_{n+2} \text{ \& } \ldots$

We need to make clear in passing that Hotelling himself of course drew from his theory fewer hyperbolic conclusions than people who later used it.[42] It is true that in his article (page 54) he said:

> So general is this tendency [to find the golden mean, that is, that which gains maximum support] that it appears in the most diverse fields of competitive activity.

Convinced that the law he deduces from his model is of very general scope, he gives various examples of its application, quoting particularly the tendency for furniture and other consumer goods to be uniform. He explains that this may perhaps be a matter of imitation, but it is a good example of the general tendency whose logic his model tries to analyse. As the above extract from his article shows, his suggestion is of course to apply this *law* to politics as well; political competition also involves a move towards uniformity.

It is interesting, however, to note that, although he identifies a trend to uniformity in political supply, he does not really dwell on the idea that election results are of necessity close; this is a conclusion which others drew for him.

Why was this? Hotelling's article appeared in 1929. Harding's 1920 presidential victory was of course overwhelming – one of the largest majorities ever achieved. Vice President Coolidge, who succeeded him in 1922, was elected in 1924 with almost as great a margin as Harding. When Coolidge did not stand in 1928, Hoover, flushed with success as Commerce Secretary during the Coolidge boom years, stood against the Governor of New York, who had against him the fact that he belonged to the Catholic minority and was 'wet'. Hoover had one of the biggest Republican margins ever and carried forty states, including some in the 'solid South'.

It was therefore difficult for Hotelling to deduce from his model the corollary which it in fact contained – that elections *tend* to be close in a two-party system.

In any event, these two examples – Popper's and Hotelling's – illustrate a general process: they show that it is quite normal to draw distorted conclusions from many theories.

To put it another way, it is normal not to see exactly to which part of reality a theory applies, and to what extent it applies.

The almost inevitable nature of these hyperbole effects (and I hope I am not slipping into hyperbole himself here!) means that one of the essential forms of scientific progress is *negative*, as it were: it consists of making clear, and in most cases *limiting* – often severely – the extent of validity of scientific theories.

These two are therefore a good illustration of Simmel's programme: our beliefs often stem from the fact that we see only a part of our reasoning. If the full argument is considered, it may be that the conclusions and the structure are thereby changed. This is of course what we are looking at here: in the case of Popper's theory of falsification as in that of Hotelling's theory of a tendency to uniformity, by making explicit the implicit environment of the line of reasoning, we move from a strong to a weak conclusion. Moreover, we note that the structure of the former theory is not linear but circular.

It needs, however, to be emphasized once more that the two theories described are unexceptionable: they contain no mistake of logic, no confusion of terms, no empirical proposition which is arguably totally wrong. They are theories which are not only perfectly acceptable and rigorous but also significant contributions to science.

Nevertheless, they have given rise to dubious ideas. And their potential to legitimate these ideas is on a par with their quality.

It is easy to understand why a false theory which is not identified as false gives rise to false ideas. It is much more difficult to understand why valid theories generate false ideas. Most theories of beliefs come under the first heading, which clearly is important. Simmel of course also suggests another case, more paradoxical at first sight, but which my two examples show does in fact exist.

A final point which I would like to stress is that the implicit statements of Popper and Hotelling are mainly *empirical* in nature. For example, Popper assumes – without realizing the importance of this *a priori* – that 'scientific questions are *always* of the kind $p \lor p' \lor \ldots$', that is, they are always *open*. Hotelling unconsciously conjures up passive electors, with neither feet nor voices.

Of course, implication can take on other forms and also include, apart from these *empirical* statements, ones which are *non-empirical*, relating, for example, to the theory itself, its relationship with reality or the language it uses.

A perfectly ordinary example of this: every theory presupposes that the words in which it is expressed have a meaning and, moreover, a meaning which is unchanging and univocal from one statement to the next. Of course implicit statements of this kind are rarely made explicit. As we will see, although such implicit statements usually have no effect on the structure of the argument and its conclusions, they can nevertheless give rise to hyperbole or distortion effects.

Any number of examples could be given which are similar to the ones I have looked at. I showed in a previous book[43] that models derived from the neo-Marxist theory of dependency, as well as those stemming from what has been called developmentalism, are often perfectly *scientific*. In other words they are based on reasoning and statements of fact which are unexceptionable. However, hyperbolic conclusions, even *false* conclusions, are often drawn from them by mechanisms such as those I have analysed. All these examples have in common an *a priori*, that is, the assimilation of the hypotheses *in fact* contained in a line of reasoning with the hypotheses which the knowing subject perceives:

$$[H \ldots = H]^\star.$$

In the same way (I will not develop this point in detail), many received ideas are legitimated by theories which are acceptable but which introduce the *a priori* that all facts relevant to the theory have been identified and considered:

$$[F \ldots = F]^\star.$$

For example, Marcel Granet tried to show that the representation of space varies according to culture. On the basis of this argument, space appropriate to science and Western thought constitutes only one of these possible visions, and Chinese civilization, for example, would come up with a completely different one. In fact, as Robert Merton points out[44], Granet was looking in the Chinese case at *ordinary* representations of space (ones pertinent to everyday life), and in the Western case at its scientific representations.

Here, the *a priori* $[F \ldots = F]^\star$ has significant consequences, since Granet's theory of a cultural variation of representations of space is based entirely on it. We have to be aware, however, that, like the *a priori* $[H \ldots = H]^\star$, it is almost inevitable because it is only when these *a priori* are implicitly introduced into a line of reasoning that it is possible to draw conclusions from it.

In no way do I deny that false ideas in the field of development – ideas of which the consequences have sometimes been incalculable – or that the *cultural relativism* to which a theory such as Granet's leads, *also* came about as a result of *feelings* in the Pareto sense. I am simply saying that these ideas did not spread from an anonymous collective source. On the contrary, their origin is totally identifiable: it is to be found in a set of theories which are scientific and *valid*, but which give rise to Simmel effects.

In the same way, though the idea that the *truth* is inaccessible to methodical thinking is so widespread as to be one of the most deep-seated received ideas of our time, this is most certainly the result of a whole variety of factors (and no doubt partly of collective feelings of irrational origin), but also of the perfectly legitimate authority with which authentically scientific theories such as Karl Popper's have been endowed.

As suggested by my examples from the philosophy of science and political science, what I call Simmel effects are apparent in all fields. Reciprocally, many *received ideas* stem from valid scientific theories into which *a priori*, apparently totally innocuous, have stolen. Since these ideas are likely to be very resistant, we can appreciate the importance of Simmel's model for the sociology of knowledge: it describes a fundamental mechanism of adherence to dubious, weak and false ideas.

The following chapters will try more specifically to show that anodyne *a priori* statements, of a *non-empirical* kind, like those referred to just now, are in fact the cause of many distortions and the origin of many received ideas.

Summary

The 'Simmel model' tells us that belief in dubious or false ideas often stems from the fact that, into a perfectly valid line of reasoning, there slip *a priori* or implicit statements which subjects treat as self-evident, and which they therefore perceive metaconsciously.

One can in fact, in keeping with Simmel's intuition, find examples of perfectly valid arguments which give rise to dubious ideas because *a priori* which distort the consequences slip into them.

The first example is taken from the philosophy of science, and more specifically from one of the most significant parts of Karl Popper's philosophy. His theory of 'falsification' is based on arguments of unshakeable soundness. However, the conclusions he draws from these arguments are hyperbolic to the extent that there creep into them apparently innocuous *a priori* which seem at first sight to be self-evident, such as the idea that any scientific question always contains – in its very essence, as it were – an infinite number of possible answers. It is only on the basis of this *a priori* that one can deduce from *modus tollens* that it is by definition impossible to be convinced of the truth of a scientific theory.

The second example is taken from political theory: Hotelling's theorem is based on an unexceptionable line of reasoning, but it gave rise to a hyperbolic belief: the parties in a two-party system will tend to be indistinguishable from each other. Once more, the hyperbole is because of implicit statements.

Since there is implication in all reasoning, scientific reasoning usually gives rise to hyperbolic beliefs, which are all the more tenacious in that they are legitimated by faultless reasoning.

Simmel's model is particularly important from the point of view of the sociology of knowledge: in fact, although adherence to ideas can come about through all kinds of processes, an idea based on valid reasoning is more likely to establish itself than one which has no basis or only a flimsy basis.

Part II

5

Questions and answers

WHO KILLED HARRY?

Cinema-goers, after being introduced to the characters of Hitchcock's famous film, ask themselves 'Who killed Harry?' The question, however, is very likely to be associated in their minds with a set of statements that are *implicit* and unconscious, or to use a better word, *metaconscious*.

Some of these statements are of a *factual* nature (for example, x is a sympathetic character; it is unlikely that y or z is guilty, and so on). Other statements, those in which we are interested here, are of a *formal* nature, that is, the question is situated in what we will call a *logical context*.[1] At the beginning of the 'investigation', when Hitchcock's art has established maximum uncertainty, this context can be described by the statement:

$$[x \, v \, y \, v \ldots]^{\star}.$$

This statement is simply an *open* list of suspects x, y, z, etc. Since some of the suspects may well have acted together, the conjunction 'v' (=or) has of course the usual meaning in logic: or = *vel* in Latin, sometimes written in English as 'and/or'. Put simply, the film-goers cannot be certain that the crime was committed by just one person. Moreover, during this period of maximum uncertainty, they cannot be sure that the murderer belongs to the group of people who have already made their appearance: the list is open, as shown by the dots at the end. Some suspects are identified, but the possibility that the crime was committed by an unidentified person cannot be ruled out.

Hitchcock then leads his audience to modify their *a priori* without realizing it, by hinting first that a particular suspect should be struck off the list, then that they should be reinstated and a different person eliminated. There comes a time when the audience is half certain that the suspect is on a list which is closed.

The new logical context for its 'investigation' can then be represented by the following statement:

$[x \ v \ y \ v \ z]^\star.$

If they further learn – provided it has been suggested to them – that the crime could not have been committed by two people and that only one of the three suspects is the criminal, the audience will modify once more the logical framework of their investigation:

$[(x \ v \ y \ v \ z) \ \& \sim (x \ \& \ y) \ \& \sim (x \ \& \ z) \ \& \sim (y \ \& \ z)]^\star.$

This rather cumbersome formula can be shortened to:

$[x \ w \ y \ w \ z]^\star.$

In this formula, the symbol w is used in the sense of the Latin *aut* (the 'exclusive *or*': x or y, but not both).

Any further trimming of the logical framework could be described by the *a priori*:

$[x \ w \ y]^\star.$

A question such as 'Who killed Harry?', therefore, can be set in different logical contexts. Despite its apparent clarity and simplicity, it is ambiguous in the extreme: its meaning changes as the audience's 'investigation' unfolds; and at the same moment in time, it may well be different for any two members of the audience taken at random. In any event, the question has an exact meaning only when its *logical context* is clear.

This example, in its simplicity, throws light on a fundamental point – that people conducting the 'investigation' can make a mistake when, in a metaconscious way, they locate the question in a set logical framework.

The whole secret of detective films or fiction lies in suggesting to audience or readers, for the longest time possible, logical contexts within which there can be no satisfactory solution to the puzzle, that is, no theory which allows them to tie up the *facts*.

Clouzot's genius, in the film *The Murderer Lives at Number 21*, is in the fact that he manages to impose on his audience, throughout virtually the whole of the film, a logical context of the type:

$[x \ w \ y \ w \ z]^\star.$

– in other words, a finite list of mutually exclusive suspects, in which the audience has no chance of finding the answer. The story suggests that any one of the characters under scrutiny could be the murderer. Since the plot focuses on the inhabitants of Number 21, the audience thinks that the murder cannot have been done by somebody from outside. The logical context of the context of the question, therefore, takes the form of a closed list. The peculiar character and psychological isolation of each tenant in the boarding house gives rise moreover to the *conjecture* that one and only one of them is the murderer. Towards the end, when the boarding house keeper organizes a performance of Beethoven's trio op.1 no. 3, the audience, still guided by the subtle hand of the director, is induced into having grave doubts about the logical context of their 'investigation' up to that point. The psychological tension throughout the film falls away as soon as they see that the answer is not in the framework

$$[x \ w \ y \ w \ z]^\star.$$

but in the framework

$$[(x \ v \ y \ v \ z)^\star.$$

The conclusion is that the logical framework in which subjects implicitly locate a question can be suggested to them by the nature of things. In the present example, it is the skill of the scriptwriter that puts a particular framework into the mind of people watching the film. However, this framework *may* not correspond to reality. People watching *The Murderer Lives at Number 21* do not see – except at the end – that the puzzle cannot be solved in the logical framework which they have metaconsciously accepted as obvious.

This is an example of a phenomenon studied in detail by sociologists and social psychologists, such as Rokeach or Goffman: they showed that in problem-solving situations and in cases of social perception, subjects – or actors, as they tend to be called – mobilize *a priori* frameworks. Similarly, Tversky and Kahneman, in their work on ordinary inference, stressed the fact that it is through a frame, or framework, that subjects perceive problems put to them.[2]

For my part, I am interested here in the *logical* frameworks which guide cognitive activity, and would like particularly to emphasize that, as Kant and later Simmel indicated, these *formal a priori* condition scientific activity.

However, just as people watching films opt for inappropriate *a priori*, scientists can 'choose' *formal a priori* which lead them down false paths. This is why, as Simmel clearly saw, the most ordinary cognitive procedures so readily harbour both the true and the false.

Another comment is suggested by the examples from Hitchcock and Clouzot – that the logical frameworks associated with a question can be put in an order of complexity. In the Hitchcock example, people watching the film are taken through a series of *frameworks* corresponding to a partial order represented by the 'tree' shown in figure 5.1, from the most open to the most closed:

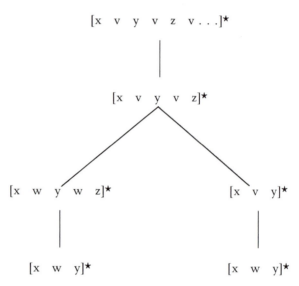

Figure 5.1

The branches of this tree could in principle be infinitely complicated. I have limited myself to a few only, but there could be others, such as:

[x w y w z w . . .]*, [x w y v z)]*, etc.

Another point that needs to be made – we will encounter it several times, and it appeared in the last chapter – is that, in cases of doubt, the most restrictive framework is the most advantageous.

For example, in the case of frameworks [x w y]* and [x v y v z]*, with the first, if one manages to exclude y, x will have been proved to be the murderer:

x w y
~ y
_____

x

In the second, one will simply have proved a vaguer statement (x v z) while not yet answering the question 'Who is the murderer?'. In the open frame [x v y v z v . . .]*, the truth of the statement '$\sim y$' means that nothing else can be proved except itself.

All Dr Watsons in detective fiction are cast in the same mould: they always limit themselves to logical contexts which are too restricted, but which scriptwriters try to impose on the audience using the tricks of their trade.

Finally, it is clear that these logical frameworks remain implicit, and are not the object of the audience's attention. At the same time, it is impossible for them not to be at the edge of their consciousness, since they structure their acts and emotions.

If the scriptwriter did not play on logical frameworks, Sherlock Holmes would not be seen as a hero with superior intelligence, and there would be no need for the suspense or heightened tension which good detective fiction or films create.

To summarize:

1) A question is always located in a logical framework;
2) Reality can suggest an inappropriate logical framework to persons asking themselves the question or persons to whom the question is put;
3) The possible logical frameworks associated with a question may be hierarchized, some being more restrictive than others;
4) The more restrictive the framework, the easier the answer to the question;
5) These logical frameworks are usually implicit and metaconscious.

The *relevance* of a logical framework is the degree to which it corresponds with reality. For example, in the case of *The murderer Lives at Number 21*, the framework [x w y w z]* is not relevant, in so far as the problem cannot be solved within this framework.

Of course, problems of criminal detection are not the only ones where the answer is sought in a logical framework. This characteristic is at the heart of any question, particularly those raised in the course of scientific research.

A situation which is particularly interesting in this respect is the following: it often happens that question Q is asked within a logical framework F_1, that an answer A_1 can be produced within this framework, and that, unlike what happens in the case of a detective film (where by definition there is only one correct answer to the question and where wrong answers can be seen as such), one is not in a position to define the criteria for accepting or rejecting A_1. Assuming that A_1 is acceptable, that is, that this answer is the result of an empirically and logically valid process, then A_1 could easily be regarded as endowed with the authority of science. Moreover, since F_1 is generally metaconscious, one will not be aware that A_1 depends on the validity of F_1. The logical framework will not receive any attention, nor *a fortiori* be the object of any debate.

In other cases, F_1 is the wrong one, but not *perceived* as such. The impression (and a justified one) is therefore that, from totally valid reasoning, only one conclusion was possible, whereas that conclusion, determined not only by the reasoning but also by an irrelevant logical framework, is itself wrong.

I will now move away from the cases of criminal detection which I have been using as examples.

GOING BACK TO POPPER

We saw in Chapter 4 how Popper's theory of falsification and, in fact, his whole idea of science are based on an *a priori*, that a scientific theory always has to cope with a set of other theories of which some are known and others are yet to appear.

The theory of falsification, in other words, is based wholly on the *a priori* statement:

[Any question about the validity of p is in the form: '$p \vee p' \vee p'' \vee \ldots$?']*

Paradoxically, it is because he adopts a very *liberal* hypothesis about the logical environment of questions asked by scientists that Popper himself brings in a logical framework which is too restrictive and inappropriate as far as reality is concerned. This framework no doubt means that he can reach a very powerful conclusion: 'any scientific theory can be proved false, but never proved true'. However, because this conclusion stems from a logical framework that is too closed, it is hyperbolic.

The paradox comes about because the *open* conception which Popper has of science leads to a *restrictive* simplification of reality. In reality, questions asked by scientists appear in logical environments of varying types:

$$p \ w \sim p$$
$$p \vee p'$$
$$p \vee p' \vee p''$$
$$p \vee p' \vee p'' \vee \ldots$$

These different environments, and other conceivable ones, are in fact present in the real world of research, and they can easily be illustrated by numerous examples.[3] However, Popper's point is that only the last one corresponds, as it were, to the *essence* of science. In fact, scientific activity is *open* enough *also* to ask itself *closed* questions.

We must again make the important point that the logical environment of a question can, by the very *form* of the question, be determinate or indeterminate. For example, the logical environment of the question 'Who killed Harry?' is indeterminate. On the other hand, for the question 'Did the captain kill Harry?', it is determinate – the answer is positive or negative and cannot be anything else. In the former case, the question can in fact be placed in various logical frameworks; in the latter, the framework is given.

Popper's example suggests an initial conjecture – that, in cases where the logical environment of a question is *indeterminate*, it often happens that a restrictive logical framework tends to be imposed *by default*. Assume that the question is 'Is p true?' This question can be placed in various implicit logical frameworks, for example:

1) $[p \lor p' \lor p'' \ldots]^\star$
2) $[p \lor p' \lor p'']^\star$
3) $[p \lor p']^\star$
4) $[p \, w \, p']^\star$

These frameworks are increasingly restrictive. The third one is an application to the pair p, p' the principle of the excluded middle; the fourth applies to it the principle of contradiction.

Very often, where there is doubt as to the framework in which to place an 'is p true?' question, one may be tempted metaconsciously by the most restrictive framework. However, the central hypothesis of Simmel's model shows that the consequences and the structure of the theory can be affected by this.

A second conjecture is that scientific thinking follows in this respect the same rules as ordinary thinking.

In everyday life, when we ask ourselves certain questions and the logical environment of these questions is *indeterminate*, we tend to use *by default* logical frameworks which are as restrictive as possible and which will be abandoned reluctantly, and only where failure is repeated or prolonged.

In this way, it is usual for logical frameworks of type 3 or 4 to be implicitly introduced, whereas reality would call for a more open framework.

When we start looking for a lost bunch of keys, we often initially place the question 'where are my keys?' in a type 2 logical environment: 'I lost my keys in place x, or it might have been in y, or there again in z.' It is only after a fruitless search that we will open up the logical framework and move to a type 1 framework.

Similarly, somebody trying to repair a boiler will often resort initially to a type 4 framework: the breakdown is due to a single cause from a finite set of possible causes which are mutually exclusive. Only if this fails will the repair person admit that the breakdown could be the combined result of several causes, or, if nothing is found inside the boiler, that the cause could be an electricity supply failure.

These observations from everyday life coincide with the findings of social psychology.

When people are asked to construct four triangles with six matches (without breaking, crossing or slicing them), they will try to solve the problem by moving the matches around interminably on the table without managing to construct more than two triangles. By doing this, they are unconsciously working on an *a priori* hypothesis: that the answer to the problem is to be found in *two-dimensional* space. Only after repeated failure do they realize that there is no solution in this (geometric) framework and that they have to consider *three-dimensional* space. In fact, the change of *a priori* in their minds hardly impinges on their consciousness: as soon as they realize that their first framework is inapplicable, the answer becomes obvious: 'Of course, I've got it. What I'm being asked to do is *quite simply* to construct a tetrahedron.'

In this example, the subjects tend to resort to the simplest *geometrical* framework. Similarly, when a question does not immediately call for a determinate *logical* framework, the tendency is often to choose the simplest and the most restrictive.

A few typical examples will allow me to back up these conjectures and to show that they apply to scientific reasoning as well as to ordinary reasoning. As in the rest of this book, I have chosen to look at theories which are as classic as possible.

THE EXAMPLE OF DURKHEIM'S THEORY OF RELIGION

In *The Elementary Forms of the Religious Life*, Durkheim examines the origins of religion. Analysing previous writing on the subject, he notes that, leaving aside 'those theories which, in whole or in part, make use of supra-experimental data',[4] there are two theories: the *animist* theory and the *naturist* theory. The starting point of both is that in all religions there is worship of spirits, souls, genies and demons, and worship directed at 'either great cosmic forces such as winds, rivers, stars, the sky, or objects of all kinds on the earth's surface – plants, animals, rocks, etc.'. The former theory makes animism into primitive religion, the latter the worship of nature.

Durkheim then proceeds to criticize the two theories. The *animist* theory, he says, has tried, through Tylor and then Spencer, to show that the idea of the soul, central to religion, came about 'without taking any of its elements from an existing religion', that it gave rise to the idea of spirit, and that the worship of nature is derived from it. As for the idea of soul itself, Tylor tries to show that it stems from the experience of dreams, arguing that it is imbued with the properties of subjects as they see themselves in dreams. As the body's double, the soul can move about during sleep; it is more mobile than the body and takes no account of physical obstacles. Tylor then tries to show how the soul becomes the spirit: since primitive people analyse death as a separation of body and soul, liberated souls take the form of *spirits* which make up a whole battery of causes available to explain physical phenomena.

Durkheim notes that this theory contradicts what is said by the people involved. Primitive people do not regard the soul as the body's double: 'here are organs which are not only its appointed seat, but also its outward form and natural manifestation.'[5] Secondly, the hypothesis of the 'double' is neither the simplest nor the most economical to account for the phenomenon of dreams, and therefore there is no reason to regard it as a hypothesis to which 'primitive people' would have had to resort: 'Why, for example, should sleepers not have imagined themselves able to see at a distance?' A 'double' moreover cannot account for the movement of the subject over time. Why should primitive people believe that their senses are more infallible at night than in the daytime? What is more, why should subjects look for an explanation for the phenomenon of dreams? Durkheim, in other words, sets objections of fact against the arguments of Tylor and Spencer: Melanesians attribute only their forceful dreams to the wanderings of the soul.[6]

Above all, the animist theory offers no satisfactory explanation either of the soul's transformation into spirit, or of ancestor worship.[7] How does death make the soul into a sacred thing when its fate is conceived by primitive people as linked to that of the wounded body? The fact that the soul is disturbing is not enough to explain why it is sacred, since the sacred inspires respect rather than fright. Among Melanesians, only important men have *mana* and are regarded as having a soul worthy of being held as sacred after death.[8] This ancestor worship moreover is important only in developed societies. For example, Australian peoples have no worship of the dead of this kind, though they have other very complex forms of worship. The latter could not therefore stem from the former.

Durkheim has no difficulty in then showing that primitive people's confusion of the animate and the inanimate is a hypothesis which is too strong. Finally, the animist theory gives rise to an unacceptable conclusion:[9] that religious life, which has such a significant place in society, originates in hallucinatory phenomena.

Let us note firstly that, though all Durkheim's arguments have interest and validity, none of them is really decisive. This is no doubt because he feels he needs to counter with a long list. In the language of dialectics, Durkheim produces a set of arguments whose function is to *support* his rejection of animist theory. They have a *backing* function in the Toulmin sense, rather than *falsification* in the Popper sense.

It also needs to be said that Durkheim congratulates Tylor on having recognized the historical nature of the idea of soul, instead of following philosophers and making it a simple and immediate object of consciousness.[10]

He then attacks the second theory – *naturism*. It was put forward not by anthropologists but by philologists such as the Grimm brothers or Max Müller, who came by it from a comparison of the great civilizations. Based on his study of the Vedas, Max Müller shows that Dyaus in Sanskrit means 'bright sky'. He deduces from this the idea that the function of gods for primitive people was to remove the terror caused by nature.[11] He then develops an interesting theory of language which says that words are not a simple reflection of things, but a pragmatically induced crystallization. This pragmatic origin of vocabulary explains why the Vedas have six different ways of indicating 'sun'. Based on this theory of language, Max Müller explains the whole range of mythological characters representing the various natural elements, as well as their family histories. As for Müller's theory of the soul, Durkheim asserts that it is little different from that of Tylor.[12]

Durkheim gives a list of objections to naturism, as he had done for animism:[13] the reason we have a need to get to know things is to control them. However, knowledge of religious things has little practical significance: an error system is not viable.[14] Naturism also regards religion as a hallucinatory phenomenon by conceiving it as a disease of language. Why should nature generate a feeling of marvel rather than monotony?[15] Why should fictions as disappointing as mythological fictions have this capacity for survival?

Most important of all, naturism, like animism, tries to produce from experience something which transcends it – the idea which the Sioux describe as *wakan*, the Iroquois as *orenda* and the Melanesians as *mana*, and which Durkheim suggests is present in all religions.[16] This notion evokes the idea of an impersonal force which becomes concretized in particular beings.[17] The impersonal nature of this force means that it cannot be interpreted in a sensualist way,[18] that is, it cannot arise through the senses. However, both naturist and animist theory are theories of a sensualist kind.[19] Since it does not come from the senses, this impersonal force which provokes a feeling of respect in fact reflects, argues Durkheim, the feeling of respect which society inspires in us.[20]

I said in Chapter 2 how much I admired Durkheim's theory of magic in *The Elementary Forms of the Religious Life*, and I tried to give my reason, for this. In the same way, it is not difficult to express my enthusiasm for his theory in the same book on the origin of the idea of soul. I have no problems either in reminding the reader that this famous theory of the origin of religion always provoked a good deal of scepticism. I will not deal with all the arguments mounted against Durkheim, since I feel that the unease brought about by the main thesis of Durkheim's book (which I have just outlined) comes from elsewhere.[21]

It stems from the fact that Durkheim's reasoning contains an implicit statement – one neither discussed nor even mentioned by Durkheim – which is extremely powerful.

This *a priori* consists of placing the bold question at the heart of the book – the origin of religion – in a logical frame of the kind:

$[x \ w \ y \ w \ z]^{\star}$.

To make it clearer, let us call the animist theory T_1, the naturist theory T_2, and Durkheim's sociologist theory T_3. The whole of Durkheim's reasoning, as my curt summary has doubtless shown, is based on the implicit statement:

$[T_1 \ w \ T_2 \ w \ T_3]^{\star}$.

More specifically, the general structure of this reasoning is:

1) $[T_1 \ w \ T_2 \ w \ T_3]^{\star}$
2) $\sim T_1$
3) $\sim T_2$
___
4) $\sim T_3$.

In other words, Durkheim arrives at the conclusion (T_3) by presupposing implicitly that there are only three possible theories. Then, by deploying a lot of *backing arguments*, he 'shows' that the first two are unacceptable and concludes that the third is true.

As is immediately apparent, this reasoning needs to be modified only slightly – by evoking the readily acceptable idea that there are other theories, even if unformulated, than the three envisaged by Durkheim – for T_3 to have no foundation. In fact, by adding suspension dots after T_3 in the implicit statement, there is strictly *nothing* to be inferred about the validity of T_3 from refuting T_1 and T_2:

5) $[T_1 \ w \ T_2 \ w \ T_3 \ w \ . . .]^{\star}$
6) $\sim T_1$
7) $\sim T_2$
___
8) ?

The fact that Durkheim devoted so much time and thought to refuting T_1 and T_2 shows therefore *a contrario* that he regarded the implicit statement in question as more or less self-evident.

To use the language of artificial intelligence, Durkheim never considers for one moment that he is introducing – as is frequent in ordinary thought and as is often indispensable – the so-called closed world hypothesis.

How did Durkheim *persuade himself* of the validity of this hypothesis in the example we are examining? It is difficult to find an answer and one can only indulge in conjectures on the matter.

Firstly, we must remember that the hypothesis of the closed world has an intrinsic *efficiency/effectiveness*. Even assuming that the backing arguments used by Durkheim against theories T_1 and T_2 are acceptable, without the implicit statement 1) they do not in the slightest strengthen confidence in T_3. On the other hand, if the closed world hypothesis is accepted, the validity of T_3 is *proved* by the refutation of T_1 and T_2.

Secondly, the closed world hypothesis is extremely *ordinary*. Its power and the huge cost incurred by its non-acceptance explain why it is such a vital recourse of ordinary thought: the person repairing the boiler, or the doctor seeing a patient for the first time, will generally start from an *a priori* of the kind $[x \ w \ y \ w \ z]^\star$. This *a priori* will be chosen *naturally* because of its pragmatic efficiency/effectiveness. Conversely, an *a priori* of the open kind gives rise to a feeling of uncertainty and doubt, and has a paralysing effect.

However, that is not all. There are in fact circumstances where we readily persuade ourselves that we *are* in a 'closed world', particularly when we feel we have to choose between two *contradictory* theories.

It is true that there are theories which are in fact contradictory and that these theories can exhaust the range of possibilities. In this case, the validity of the closed world hypothesis is verified almost mechanically.

A statement such as 'A causes B' contradicts 'A does not cause B'. Here, the very form of question x ('Does A cause B?') ensures the validity of the closed world hypothesis. One can then argue in all certainty, for example:

9) $[x \ w \sim x]^\star$
10) $\sim (\sim x)$

─────────────

11) x

In this case, there is no problem with the *a priori* 9) – the excluded third and the contradiction principle apply mechanically. There is no need therefore for suspension dots at the end of statement 9), and one can simply use the 'exclusive or' ('*w*' = *aut*) rather than the 'non-exclusive or' ('*v*' = vel).

However, this case must be distinguished from others where the same *a priori* is, to use classical vocabulary, no longer *analytical* (imposed by the very form of the question) but *synthetic* in nature (containing, in other words, a judgement of fact devoid of any element of necessity)[22].

In this way, by setting *sensualist* theories of religion against *non-sensualist* theories, or, expressed in another way, theories which claim that religious feeling is derived from a sensory experience against theories which say that this causal link is totally invalid, Durkheim gives the impression – and no doubt had the impression – that he is placing himself in the first of these cases:[23]

12) x: 'A causes B' ('sensualist' hypothesis)
13) $\sim x$: 'A does not cause B' (anti-sensualist hypothesis).

In fact, Durkheim's reasoning proves only that sensualist theories have weaknesses, not that sensory experience has no part in the creation of religious feeling, nor that this cannot arise from a non-sensory experience. Self-evidently, the statement $[x \ w \sim x]\star$ is no way *analytical* when the symbols x, A and B in 12) and 13) are interpreted as in Durkheim's theory. Despite this, 12) and 13) allow us to understand one of the reasons why Durkheim was persuaded that his theory was valid.

His reasoning can be reconstructed finally as follows:

14) $[x \ w \sim w]\star$
15) The animist theory T_1 accepts x
16) The naturist theory T_2 accepts x
17) The sociological theory T_3 rejects x
18) $[(T_1 \ v \ T_2) \ w \ T_3]\star$
19) $\sim x$
20) $\sim T_1$
21) $\sim T_2(\sim x)$

___

22) T_3.

Durkheim perhaps persuaded himself of the legitimacy of 18), that is, the implicit hypothesis supporting the full weight of his proof, on the basis of statements 15) and 16), which are perfectly acceptable, but also on the basis of 14), which interprets the *opposition* between sensualist and non-sensualist theories as having *contradictive* value and as making the mobilization of the excluded third *analytically* valid.

If one removes the logical frame – defined by statement 14) – in which Durkheim places his discussion, the latter becomes the series of backing arguments, quite relevant and interesting in themselves, on which he bases his rejection of the two dominant theories of the time.

In this case, however, his reasoning no longer supports the conclusion which he drew from it, and the main thesis of the book becomes a mere *assertion*.

Put another way, the opposition between *sensualist* and *non-sensualist theories* is not of the same *analytically contradictory* nature as, for example, the difference seen in the last chapter between Ehrenhaft and Millikan, or between the Lamarckians and the supporters of Mendel and Darwin. Either the elementary electric charge has a lower limit, or it has not. Either the acquired characteristic is genetically transmitted, or it is not. However, a theory can be both *sensualist* and *non-sensualist* in origin.

There may be another reason why Durkheim persuaded himself that there were only three theories on the origin of religion: the fact that these theories relate to three classical ontological areas: *nature* (naturist theories), the *soul* (animist theories), and the area which Comte added to traditional ontology – *society*.

I will not insist on this point, which suggests that the art of self-persuasion also mobilizes, very often, *substantive a priori*. In other words, theories often introduce implicit statements which have the status of *statements about reality*. Undoubtedly Durkheim, following the precedent of Comte, gave to *society* the kind of primacy which explains certain of his conclusion.[24] However, it is a point which is referred to so often that all we need to do here is mention it. Moreover, I am not interested here in the criticisms of Durkheim's theory. I chose his theory of religion because it is widely known and it provides a good illustration of the role of formal *a priori* – the only ones to which I will refer here – in the cognitive processes that give rise to dubious ideas.

A final point is to note that Durkheim's theory is a perfectly scientific one: all the statements in it are acceptable. Durkheim's backing arguments are always relevant, even though they can be the subject of debate. The conclusions drawn from these arguments are relevant according to the most canonical logical rules.

However, the main point of our discussion is the following: the feeling of weakness which the theory gives – contrasting with the authoritative nature of, for example, his theory of magic or theory of the origin of the soul in the same book – is perhaps explained above all by the formal *a priori* which creep into it. Nevertheless, it is easy to see why Durkheim adopted them: it is their very *ordinariness*.

The preceding analysis of Durkheim's theory of religion could equally apply to another major thesis in *The Elementary Forms of the Religious Life* – that basic categories of human thought are social in origin. For example, people took their inspiration for the idea of *force* from the fact that they are normally exposed to *social constraints*. Durkheim's whole reasoning, in this case as well, rests on the *a priori* of the 'closed world': the idea of force comes from experience *or not*. If it does, it can be *either* the psychic experience of will (T_1), *or* the physical experience of the resistance of matter (T_2), *or* the experience of social constraints (T_3). As in the example which I looked at in detail just now, the reasoning takes the form:

$$T_1 \ w \ T_2 \ w \ T_3$$
$$\sim T_1$$
$$\underline{\sim T_2(\sim x)}$$
$$T_3.$$

RELATIVISM

Certain key texts in modern cognitive *relativism* will provide a second example of the effects of these formal *a priori*, which are as destructive in their consequences as they are innocent in appearance.[25]

The concept of relativism is one of the most ambiguous there is. However, we must differentiate the two ways, both current and often confused, in which the word is used.

In the way it was used in Germany in the nineteenth and early twentieth centuries, the idea of relativism retains its Kantian origins. The relativist theory of knowledge, according to this usage, affirms the presence and the indispensable nature of *a priori* in any knowledge process. A neo-Kantian such as Simmel argues that there cannot be knowledge unless it is based on what he calls a *viewpoint*, and which I would call a *paradigm* or *frame*.[26] Relativism, however, is in no way incompatible with the notions of *objectivity* and *truth*. It merely rejects the idea that truth should be seen as a copy of reality in the mind of the knowing subject.

In modern English usage, on the other hand, relativism has become a kind of alternative to *scepticism*: since knowledge depends on the viewpoint where one is situated, the concepts of truth and objectivity cannot have very precise meaning. At the most, they can have a vague regulative function.

Relativism in this latter sense is no doubt one of the most accepted received ideas of our time. It is not easy to trace the way in which this came about, but I do not intend to pursue this here.

One point, however, seems to me undeniable. Like all persistent and influential received ideas, this one was, if not brought about, at least confirmed and legitimated by all kinds of analyses of indisputably scientific quality. I am thinking, for example, of those by Kuhn, Feyerabend, Hübner or Bloor. Their work has meant that relativism in the modern sense – what will be called *sceptical relativism*, to distinguish it from *neo-Kantian relativism* – assumed the dimensions of a *scientifically* confirmed received idea.

As in the case of Durkheim's sociology of religion, my aim is in no way to criticize the *explicit* arguments for relativism. This has been done, often brilliantly, by several writers.[27] On another level, several critics have focused on the historical point that arguments produced by contemporary philosophy, sociology or history of science, and which have sustained present-day sceptical relativism, are not always new. F.Isambert rightly stresses the undeniable family resemblance between contemporary theorists of relativism and the conventionalists of the beginning of this century.[28]

However, what must, I repeat, be emphasized is the scientific soundness of work by writers such as Kuhn, Bloor or Hübner.[29] Although their arguments can be debated and refined, it is hard to refute them. It is even more difficult to show that there are dubious interconnections between them. In other words, they satisfy the requirements of any scientific theory – to consist of propositions acceptable in principle to a universal audience, and properly linked to each other. The question then is how an unexceptionable line of reasoning can give doubtful conclusions.

My argument is that sceptical relativism is a remarkable illustration of Simmel's model: the conclusions it reaches stem not only from the explicit arguments on which it is based, but also from the *implicit logical frame* in which it is situated.

In other words, for me, these texts no more imply sceptical relativism than Durkheim's reasoning in *The Elementary Forms of the Religious Life* proves his sociological theory of religion.

In fact, the principal arguments on which sceptical relativism is based are very few – they simply vary between authors.[30] The main one is the argument that any scientific theory not only contains, but *is necessarily based on* unfounded and unjustifiable beliefs. In different forms, this idea was developed by Kuhn[31], Feyerabend[32] and Bloor.[33]

However, Hübner[34] is perhaps the one who treats it in the most circumspect, most analytical and most convincing way, so that his book *Die Wahrheit des Mythos* can be regarded as the methodical formulization of a line of reasoning presented more impressionistically by the other authors mentioned.

HÜBNER'S ARGUMENT

What makes Hübner's book both enchanting and confusing is the quality of his reasoning, but also the boldness of his conclusions: there can be no more a grain of truth in a scientific theory of whatever kind than in any myth – hence the title of his book.

This conclusion of course reminds one of the argument previously advanced by writers such as Feyerabend. However, wheras the latter had written in the style of a brilliant, disjointed, allusive, deliberately chaotic essay, mixing detailed analyses from the history of science and moral, even political, pleas, Hübner set about methodically proving the validity of this disturbing conclusion: not only can scientific theories not be truer than myths, but

> even the greatest successes of [scientific] theories say absolutely nothing about their truth.[35]

Hübner's starting point is that all explanation now regarded as scientific can be reduced to the following *minimal* form (the author's original notation is preserved):

22) *a* is F (F*a*)
23) always, if F, then G
24) *a* is G (G*a*).

To show that this logical outline sustains any theory, Hübner uses examples from various fields of scientific activity, mostly classic ones.

He considers first an example taken from *physics*, where the three propositions 22) to 24) become respectively the three statements: a body (*a*) falls in time *t* from height *h* (F*a*);[36] when a body falls from this height, it reaches the ground in time $t + \Delta t$ (if F, G). As a consequence, the body (*a*) reaches the ground in $t + \Delta t$ (G*a*).

An example from *history* tries to show that there is no distinction between the structure of explanation in history – if historical reasoning is reduced to its minimal form – and explanation in physics. The only difference is that in the latter case the proposition as in 23) corresponds to laws of nature, and in the former case to laws in the juridical sense, rules, norms or moral constraints. Proposition 23) has therefore to be seen as formalizing the notion of *law* in the very general sense in which a writer such as Montesquieu would use the word, although Hübner does not specifically quote him.

For example, the explanation of the defeat of the Teutonic knights at Tannenberg lies in reasoning of the 22) to 24) kind: Ulrich von Jungingen, the grand master of chivalry, encountered in 1410, in certain circumstances, the Polish-Lithusanian army (F*a*). The circumstances were of the kind where it was understood that battle would not be engaged (if F, G). This was why he refused to engage battle (G*a*).

Hübner's example from *sociology* – Malthus's Law – reveals the same minimal structure: in a particular country, birth control is not practised (F*a*). In all countries of this kind, increase in population is geometric, and increase in resources arithmetic (if F, G). Therefore, in the country in question, scarcity of resources will lead, in time *t*, to a stable population.

Finally, the same minimal structure of reasoning is shown in an example from *psychology* which is as classic as the preceding ones: one of Pavlov's dogs hears a bell at time *t* (F*a*). Every time a dog conditioned by Pavlov's methods hears a bell, it salivates (if F, G). Therefore the dog (*a*) salivates at time *t* (G*a*).

These examples are of course simplified. Scientific reasoning trying to explain phenomenon G*a* generally contains a larger number of propositions. The outline should therefore be seen as a kind of basic atom of the logical molecules of varying complexity which scientific theories are.

Without dwelling on the matter, we can note in passing that Hübner seems to be adopting the nomological theory of explanation in human sciences propounded by Hempel.[37] According to this theory, all explanation, in human sciences as well as natural sciences, is based on conditional laws of the kind 'if F, G'. This has been attacked by many writers, and particularly by W. H. Dray,[38] who argued that the laws in question often proved on closer examination to be merely tautological. The counter-argument is that, although they sometimes are, they can also not be tautological. As shown by the simple example of the battle of Tannenberg, this second case must be regarded as very frequent, even typical: it is clear that, though some 'laws' are trivial, others are the result of complex social and historical processes and can easily be seen by the observer as just as far from tautological as the laws of nature.

The other objection[39] is that in the human sciences the need for information is in general not satisfied if one keeps to the atomic level described by statements 22) to 24). We must try to reach the sub-atomic level, as it were – in other words, explain the laws themselves, instead of regarding them as simple factual data. That is, we must try to answer the question 'Why "if F, then G"?'. To do this, we must find the 'individual causes' which lead actors in a given social system to come up with the pattern 'if F, then G'. In definitive terms, we must find the reasons why actors produce this pattern, or, to use Max Weber's words, to *understand* these sub-atomic actions.

This objection applies to the Hübner example: the reader who is not well versed in medieval German history is likely to find the 'laws' governing the behaviour of Teutonic knights strange, and to react to the suggested explanation by a new question of the type: 'Why "if F, then G"?'. For this reason, sociologists with an allegiance to this type of tradition tend to regard the nomological theory of explanation as incomplete.[40]

In any event, Hübner does not take the debate so far. Perhaps he thinks that the answer to the question 'Why "if F, then G"?' would be provided by a theory also capable of being reduced to the 22) to 24) structure and including a new law, for example, 'if M, then P'. He simply emphasizes, as we shall see, the fact that statements of the type 'if F, then G' are in general derived from theories.

Hübner then comes to the decisive stage of his demonstration – the one which in the end leads him to reject notions such as truth or objectivity.

This is the stage showing that the three statements 22) to 24), identifiable in any scientific theory, whether in the natural sciences or social sciences, always contain *a priori*. We are already familiar with this; but it is interesting to follow Hübner in the finer points of his demonstration.

Let us first consider type 23) statements (if F, then G). Belief in the truth of such statements generally stems from the fact that they are based on theories regarded as valid. For example, 23) assumes that we accept, respectively, the theory of gravitation in Hübner's example from physics, the theory of conditioned reflex in his example from psychology, the system of the rules of chivalry from history, or the theory whereby Malthus concluded that resources increase arithmetically and population size geometrically.

However, says Hübner, one can verify empirically only basic statements (*Basissätze*), that is, statements describing singular events localized in time and space. One cannot therefore empirically verify statement 23). Although he does not say so, Hübner is here restating the classic argument, constantly propounded by writers from Hume to Popper, about the impossibility of induction: it is logically impossible to verify a universal statement. There is nevertheless a difficulty stemming from the fact that a statement such as 'the rules of chivalry required that . . .' does not put the same obstacles in the way of verification as the statement 'all crows are black'.

In any event, it is true that a statement of the type 'if F, then G' is generally valid only if the theory T on which it is based is itself valid.

Similar remarks could be made about the verification of statements of type F*a* and G*a*: this is often problematical, though it does not encounter the same difficulties as the verification of 'if F, then G'. One has only to think of the complexity and often exorbitant cost of instruments used by physicists, chemists or astronomers to verify their basic statements. However, even in historical or social sciences, it can be very hard to establish a statement of fact. Verification is often established indirectly on the basis of cross-checks of varying complexity, the only objective of which is to arrive at a plausible conclusion. Basic statements in historical or social science can also require the deployment of powerful means of observation.

That is not all, however: in Hübner's example from psychology, although the statement G*a* ('the dog salivates') appears to be based on the simplest of observations, we see that 'the dog' in question (*a*) is not really an ordinary dog, but 'one of Pavlov's dogs', an 'experimental dog'. The subject (*a*) does not therefore correspond to an immediately identifiable subject, but represents a second degree entity, existing only in Popper's 'third world' rather than the first one.

Therefore, statements of type 22) to 24) are valid only under a set of conditions T_1 of varying complexity. The same is true of statements of type 24) (G*a*); one can rely on them only if one accepts a system of conditions T_2.

In fact, the system of conditions T_1 and T_2 constitutes a set of axiomatic presuppositions (*axiomatische Voraussetzungen*); when using them to explain the 'phenomenon' G*a*, we treat them as statements which we are not trying to validate. If we wanted to validate them, we would have to deploy statements whose validity would itself depend on conditions T'_1, T'_2. We would then be launching into an infinite regression.

Hübner is then able to conclude on this point: 'Scientific facts contained in basic statements are never pure empirical data', since the validity of these statements depends on conditions (T_1 and T_2) which are not themselves empirical statements.[41]

That is still not all: statements 22) to 24) imply in particular that F*a* is not always accompanied by G*a*. In reality, this is not strictly true – Pavlov's dog may be stricken by as yet undetected food poisoning, and not salivate when it hears the bell. Generally speaking, under the influence of factors not always identified, 'F*a* & G*a*' will not be observed in all cases, but in certain circumstances only. When, despite these failures, the validity of the statement 'F*a* & G*a*' is accepted, this has to be on the assurance of certain procedural rules regarded as acceptable. These rules allow us to determine whether we have to keep a type 22) to 24) explanation even where 'F*a* & ~G*a*' has been observed with some frequency.

No doubt generally these procedural rules (T_3) (*judicale Festsetzungen*) are not arbitrary, and may well be valid; but their validity is necessarily based on other rules and theories themselves dependent on a set of conditions.

Our problems are not yet at an end. The validity of a type 22) to 24) line of reasoning also depends on axioms at a higher level (T_4), that is, rules which are more or less difficult to state, but which it is impossible to do without, and which define the very notion of science: 'These axioms generally define art and the way in which reality is considered from a scientific viewpoint.'[42]

Therefore, one cannot say of a scientific explanation that it conforms to reality.

All that can be said is that, under conditions T, T_1, T_2, T_3 and T_4, that is, under the set of conditions ST^1, several of which are (might be tempted to add) partly undefinable and invisible, there occurs a set of phenomena such as F*a* and G*a*.[43]

To summarize:

1) Type 21) statements (F*a*) depend on type T, *a priori*. For example, psychologists introduce all kinds of assumptions when they treat a dog as a Pavlov dog. The same applies to historians when, for instance, they decide to regard Ulrich von Jungingen as a historical actor rather than as a mythical hero;

2) Type 22) statements (if F, then G) depend on a set of theories (for example, the theory of conditioned reflex) but also on procedural rules;

3) Type 24) statements (G*a*) depend on the observation procedures used and the considerations on which their validity is based. For example, the determination of the authenticity of documents depends on rules which themselves depend on principles. Similarly, techniques to establish dates and places depend on theories which themselves depend on a variety of conditions;

4) Further back in the chain, loose systems of rules define scientific activity and its objectives, methods and means. For example, these rules tell us about whether delayed action over time (*hysteresis*) or in space is acceptable and, in general, whether to accept any of those *a priori* which Hübner calls ontological.[44]

Therefore, one cannot say of an explanation that it is true or objective, or even that it is the best one, or even that the facts which one claims to observe *correspond* to reality.

Once more, one can only say that if one accepts the complex and partly undefined set of conditions ST^1, the system of statements 22) to 24) has a meaning. Science is therefore always located in the realm of the provisional and the uncertain.

From Popper to Hübner is therefore a giant step towards relativism. According to Popper, a theory can never be regarded as verified. Hübner goes much further: not only can a theory not be verified, but it cannot be refuted either. In fact, this refutation is itself dependent on certain empirical conclusions. However, as has been established, these *basic statements* themselves depend on a variety of conditions which can be accepted or not. Moreover, any judgement of the type 'this basic statement refutes this theory' is itself dependent on all kinds of procedural rules.

Therefore, says Hübner, there is no reason to establish any asymmetry between verification and falsification. Not that Hübner is proposing a return to the verificationist conception of knowledge which, as Lakatos rightly says, dominated for twenty-five centuries; its demonstration leads rather to the conclusion that a scientific theory is never either verifiable or refutable.

In this sense, a scientific theory cannot be said to be more objective, more true or even more acceptable than a myth.[45]

Why therefore does one *believe* in the value of a particular sociological, historical or physical explanation?

Hübner rejects the *conventionalist* answer that science is the product of arbitrary tacit agreement between members of the scientific community: the frameworks within which scientific research develops, he explains, are in fact *historical* products which are no more arbitrary, for example, than the state of manners in a society at a given time.

He also rejects not just *rationalism* as such, but the critical rationalism of Popper. Since knowledge depends on the historical framework in which it appears and cannot be analysed other than as an effect of this context, it is futile to try to understand its development by interpreting it, like most philosophers and even certain historians of science, as a game defined by formal rules and played mainly by scientists.[46]

Of course, Hübner also rejects *realism*: knowledge cannot be conceived as highlighting real mechanisms.

However, he also rejects the external forms of *relativism* since, in the context which scientists create, their proof can be perfectly rigorous, logically sound and consistent with experience. This is why he does not go along with Feyerabend's *anarchism*, which sees the only possible approach as being through imagination, fantasy and the saying 'anything goes'.

Finally, it is the adjective *historical* – a *leitmotif* in Hübner's work – which is closest to his conception: scientific 'truths' are neither more arbitrary nor in any way more certain or more sound than moral and political 'truths'. Our scientific 'ideas' about the world must be regarded as products of history, just as our 'ideas' about what is proper, for example. The history of science cannot claim to be any different from other kinds of history.

Hübner's theory is important from the point of view of the history of ideas about science. This, as he himself says, undeniably keeps itself within its own aim, which is to draw conclusions from the wide-ranging debate within not only philosophy but also the history and sociology of science since the era of logical positivism.[47]

Hübner introduces refinements to modify his theory on one point, to which he does not attach particular importance: he agrees to consider the point that there are degrees of relativity of 'facts' to theories (*Theorie-abhängigkeit*, or theory dependence). Thus, for Hübner, the fact that Napoleon marched on Moscow in 1812 is less 'relative' (*theorieabhängig*) than the statement 'in *t*, a cloud of electrons is observed in a particular place'.

However, this modification, in the form in which Hübner makes it, does not change his conclusion – that science never takes over reality itself, it always presents a particular interpretation of it. The answers that it gives us depend on our question.[48] However, Hübner repeats that this does not imply 'that science has to be given over to a boundless relativism'.[49] Therefore science is not arbitrary – with the result that conventionalism's view of it is unacceptable. At the same time, however, none of the answers which it gives can be *objective*, since it is obliged to provide at the same time both questions and answers.

We should beware of interpreting these remarks as a neo-Kantian profession of faith. They show in fact that there can be no inevitable link between reality and the theories which help us to understand it.

There is one image, taken from Hübner himself, which allows us to concretize the confusion of the knowing subject. Supposing I have an electronic watch; even if my representation of it is totally wrong, which it would be if I thought it was a mechanical watch, my predictions about its functioning would be perfectly acceptable. My representation – that is, my theory – of the watch is at the same time purely mythical and entirely reliable. It is therefore only *by chance* that, in certain cases at least, our conception of reality is as it in fact is. This, however, is no consolation, since we have no way of deciding whether there is consistency between the two or not.

Truth and objectivity are therefore in a word notions devoid of content.

I have presented this reasoning in detail because I find it fascinating: all Hübner's arguments have a sound basis. His theory is interesting in that it is general and formal, covering every scientific activity, whatever its nature and object. Moreover, Hübner's standpoint is original. He cannot be accused of purely and simply falling back on traditional conventionalism, for example. Of course he says that the intersubjective confidence in systems of conditions such as ST, cannot be interpreted as the product of intersubjective historical conditioning. In this sense, he is defending a modern form – Durkheimian, as it were – of conventionalism.

Why therefore does his conclusion create a feeling of unease? What should we make of the feeling of tension which many readers will no doubt have when they compare the quality of Hübner's arguments with the paradoxical nature of his theory?

After all, though it is true that *some* scientists and *many* philosophers of science share Hübner's doubts about the objectivity of science, what is most striking is the confidence with which *most* scientists are naturally *realistic* – by which I mean that they seem to be easily convinced that a scientific discussion comes to an end because the truth has been identified and it can be assumed that reality has been described *as it is*. No doubt scientists readily introduce into their theories concepts corresponding to realities which they have had no opportunity of observing. For instance, the existence of viruses was originally a hypothesis, but we ended up by being able to see them; similarly, in the end we came up with the means to observe directly that the earth is round. It is not surprising that realism and verificationism are the spontaneous philosophy of the scientist and that this metaphysics constitutes, as it were, scientific activity.

Nevertheless, doubts which philosophy and sociology of science have about science in the end became a received idea and conferred on this spontaneous philosophy the attributes of naivety. Conversely, the idea that modern science is no more able to arrive at the truth than are archaic myths became commonplace as a result of the kind of work of which Hübner's is a shining example.

In fact, Hübner's premises in no way make his conclusions inevitable; they are simply the product of Simmel's hyperbole machine.

It must be stressed that, although Hübner's theory leads to something quite original, the *arguments* on which it is based had already been propounded for some time. Without going back to Kant, Peirce (in a passage very close to the ones by Simmel given in Chapter 3) sees in all knowledge a discursive process: 'But the beginning and the end of this chain are not distinctly perceived.'[50] As Jürgen Habermas notes, for Peirce,

> there are neither fundamental principles which, without being founded on other principles, are valid once and for all, nor latter elements of perception which, not being affected by our interpretations, are immediately certain.[51]

For the neo-Kantians, or for writers such as Simmel or Cassirer, it is clear that knowledge assumes *a priori*. Popper, for his part, maintained that there is no 'fact' free of any interpretation. All these writers are against the contemplative theory which sees knowledge as a simple copy of reality.

But neither Peirce, nor Simmel, nor Cassirer, nor Popper, nor of course Kant before them, infers from this disqualification of the 'copy' theory sufficient reason to abandon the notion of objectivity.

In fact Hübner's reasoning reproduces, while making its content much more specific, Hans Albert's *Müchhausen's trilemma*:[52] for any deductive theory, it is true that its premises are necessarily either 1) without foundation, 2) based on other propositions themselves based on other propositions which in turn need a basis, or 3) based in a circular fashion on their own conclusions. The only theories which would arguably not be covered by this trilemma are those with strictly empirical premises. Thus from two propositions such as 'snow is white' and 'if something is white, it is not black', one concludes that 'snow is not black'. It will be generally agreed, however, that such trivial cases are of no great interest.

Hübner does not mention Albert's trilemma, but he draws from a line of reasoning which is in essence close to Albert's a conclusion which Albert does not draw. Here therefore is a case similar to Popper's: for twenty-five centuries, nobody had imagined that the *modus tollens* implied the theory of falsification.[53]

Albert draws *no* sceptical conclusion from Münchhausen's trilemma, for a very simple reason highlighted by Popper:[54] assume that Theory T is made up of a set of propositions S; and that from S can be drawn a set of conclusions Q. If these are inconsistent with observation, the propositions S have to be amended in some way. In the contrary case, they may be regarded as provisionally acceptable. As Popper says, it is a *myth* to believe that a theory cannot be objective because it is based on unfounded premises. That deductive theories are based on *principles*, that they are constructed from *frameworks* and *paradigms* is one thing; that this *framework* cannot be challenged is another. These *frameworks* are merely a special case of the *conjectures* which we use in all kinds of situations. And who would seriously claim that a conjecture cannot in principle be criticized?

The idea that a *framework*, far from being an iron cage, can be challenged and replaced by a better one, is commonplace in psychology. I have already referred to the experiment where subjects are asked to make three triangles from six matches without overlapping or breaking them. They usually look for the answer in a two-dimensional *frame*, then move to a three-dimensional *frame*.

Why does Hübner draw from well-founded arguments a conclusion which many people who have developed the same arguments do not draw? Ironically, the solution to this paradox lies in the fact that Hübner himself metaconsciously uses a *framework* which might very well not be accepted.

In fact, Hübner starts from the idea that one, and only one, of the following statements is true:

[either 1) *all* the propositions of a scientific theory have either a logical or an empirical foundation, and the theory is *objective*,
or 2) this is not the case, and the theory is not objective]*.

To appreciate the rigidity of this frame, we can use a simple example of the most elementary judicial investigation, where an attempt at explanation can initially be inspired by beliefs which have no empirical or logical foundation. Nevertheless, the same investigation can very well lead, in its final stage, to complete certainty on the part of all participants – the certainty of having reconstructed *reality as it is*, or at least of being in a position to give an objective answer to the question of whether, for example, Dupont is guilty. At the beginning, all the propositions constituting the attempt at explanation by the person conducting the investigation are hamstrung by unfounded beliefs; later, this prop is removed to allow for a description of reality as it is.

As elementary as this example is, it is impossible to apply to it *either* of Hübner's alternatives. *A contrario* it shows their excessive rigidity.

Moreover, this impossibility arises not because the example is peculiar in any way. On the contrary, it is clearly characteristic of any investigation, whether judicial, scientific or ordinary (like the one we conduct when we are looking for a bunch of keys). In all these cases, at the beginning the investigation is based quite naturally on more or less well-founded beliefs. The function of the ensuing investigation is to sort these beliefs, until a point is reached when the person conducting the investigation feels that reality as it is has been grasped.

The dose of *subjectivity* and *arbitrariness* in the theory of the enquiring person is in other words extremely variable, depending on the stage of the investigation.

For example, *in antiquity*, the theory that the earth is round was *dependent* on all kinds of *a priori*. Clearly this is not the case today, and nobody doubts the validity of the assertion that that the earth is round.[55]

Hübner's conclusion stems therefore from an argument in two parts. The nub of the first one is constitued by the irrefutable Münchhausen trilemma. The second is the simple implicit logical *framework* on which I have just been focusing.

Since there is no obligation to adopt this logical *framework*, there is no obligation either to endorse Hübner's conclusion. On the contrary, there is every reason to reject it as soon as we see that it cannot be applied to such an ordinary case as the judicial investigation, or that it does not allow us to distinguish between a theory based entirely on arbitrary principles and a hypothesis based on principles which are provisionally unconfirmed, but open to criticism, refutable and confirmable – a situation obviously characteristic of scientific activity, and nothing less than exceptional.

Hübner's theory is therefore a perfect illustration of Simmel's model.

In particular, it *is* circular, though it appears linear and well founded in the detail of its arguments: in fact, it tacitly introduces the idea that the notions of truth or objectivity imply the absence of *a priori*, or again that a true theory can only be one which can be shown to give a faithful reproduction of reality. He has therefore no difficulty in showing that these conditions are never satisfied.

Even a question as simple as 'Is Dupont guilty?' has an *a priori*, if only because the concept of guilt is meaningful only in the context of the Criminal Code and because its content varies with changes in law and custom. The answer to this question is therefore *dependent* on these *a priori*. However, once this point has been recognized, who can doubt 1) that one of the two possible answers to the question is necessarily true and the other false, 2) that it is – at least in principle – possible to show that the one considered true at the end of the investigation is in fact the right one?[56]

As Mary Hesse has shown, even the concept of 'tree' assumes a theoretical construction and is meaningful only in relation to this context. It does not follow from this that the proposition 'this is a tree' cannot be – in an absolute way – true or false.[57]

More generally, the *frame* in which Hübner's conclusion is situated is incapable of accounting for crucial distinctions; a theory can either not contain any *a priori* (though this is uncommon) or contain provisional and revocable *a priori*, like Clouzot's frame in *The murderer Lives at Number 21*, or in fact contain *a priori* which are non-revocable except by a socially explicable movement of certain intersubjective beliefs. It is no doubt this movement which led to the appearance of that singular phenomenon called science. However, this origin in no way implies that science is not capable of truth. A *passion* can also lead to *objectively* valid discoveries.

It must also be noted that, though the surreptitious intervention of an excessively closed *a priori* makes Popper's theory *hyperbolic*, it makes Hübner's theory *false*.

Before concluding our examination, let us again say that it has a devastating corollary. Since answers to one's own questions *depend*, according to Hübner, on the nature of these questions, there can be as many truths and 'realities' as ST, systems. On any subject, there can therefore in principle be developed thousands of truths between which it would be futile to try to choose on objective criteria.

This conclusion was also reached by Kuhn, Feyerabend and more or less all relativists, in the modern sense of the term.[58]

It is therefore true that Hübner, as he says, goes to the very limits (*zu Ende denken*, he says) of the thought of these writers.

THOMAS KUHN'S ARGUMENT

Kuhn's *The Structure of Scientific Thought* is certainly one of the most remarkable books of recent times in the philosophy, sociology and history of science.

However, as in the case of Hübner and Popper, some of Kuhn's conclusions – often the most important ones – derive not from his arguments themselves, which are strong and unexceptionable, but from their implicit contamination by restrictive logical principles.

It is interesting to observe that in *The Structure of Scientific Thought*, as in his reply to his critics ten years after the book's publication, Kuhn keeps his reasoning within a very narrow logical framework.[59] The choice between theories and scientific paradigms, he said, is based

> on techniques of persuasion or on an exchange of arguments in a situation where neither proof nor error is at issue. The transfer of allegiance from a paradigm to a paradigm is a conversion experience that cannot be forced. Lifelong resistance . . . is not a violation of scientific standards, but an index to the nature of scientific research itself. . . . Though the historian can always find men – Priestley for example – who were unreasonable to resist for as long as they did, he will not find a point at which resistance becomes illogical or unscientific.[60]

As Kuhn says, it is wrong to see in this passage, as some of his critics have done, the idea that scientists can believe in anything, that might is right, or that choice between theories is based on irrational, even mystical, considerations.

He maintains, however, that decisions about rejecting or endorsing a theory are never based on entirely *objective* criteria.

In fact, unlike what happens in mathematics, Kuhn argues that, in experimental sciences, there are no objective criteria *obliging* the researcher to accept or reject a particular theory, but only *good reasons* based, for example, on the relative precision, scope, simplicity, productiveness or indeed elegance of the theory compared to another. These reasons are not strictly speaking *aesthetic* – at least not wholly – though they have an element of subjectivity in their evaluation. A further point is that, since these decisions are generally based not on one but on several reasons, they are given different weightings by the researcher; and of course this operation can itself be based only on subjective criteria.[61]

Kuhn supports his argument by various examples from the history of science, particularly that of Priestley, who figures largely in *The Structure of Scientific Revolutions*:[62]

> When Lavoisier saw oxygen as 'the air itself entire', his new theory could cope not at all with the problems presented by the proliferation of new gases, a point that Priestley made with great success in his counterattack. . . . Until the discovery of the composition of water, the combustion of hydrogen was a strong argument for the phlogiston theory and against Lavoisier. And after the oxygen theory had triumphed, it could still not explain the preparation of a combustible gas from carbon, a phenomenon to which the phlogistonists had pointed as strong support for their view.[63]

For example, the theory of phlogiston was regarded by many as 'neater', 'more appropriate', 'simpler':

> [It] gave order to a large number of physical and chemical phenomena. It

explained why bodies burned – they were rich in phlogiston – and why metals had so many more properties in common than did their ores. The metals were all compounded from different elementary earths combined with phlogiston, and the latter, common to all metals, produced common properties. In addition, the phlogiston theory accounted for a number of reactions in which acids were formed by the combustion of substances like carbon and sulphur. Also, it explained the decrease of volume when combustion occurs in a confined volume of air – the phlogiston released by combustion 'spoils' the elasticity of the air that absorbed it, just as fire 'spoils' the elasticity of a steel spring.[64]

On the other hand, there were also phenomena which the phlogiston theory did not explain: whereas, in accordance with the phlogiston theory, '[m]ost natural bodies (e.g., wood) lose weight on roasting', some metals become heavier.[65]

This example shows that *for some time*, Priestley's reasons were as *good* as those of Lavoisier: the choice between them could not be made on decisive grounds. Adherence to each was therefore based on criteria which were subjective but not arbitrary. (This shows, incidentally, that it is vital to include in a theory of action a category such as *subjective rationality*. In fact, the reasons for the belief of Lavoisier and Priestley were *good* in the sense discussed in Chapter 2.)[66] Both theories were quite simply based on the fact that they could explain a significant number of phenomena.

Afterwards, but only afterwards, everybody had to agree that Lavoisier's theory was *objectively* better. When the debate was underway, however, there were equally good reasons for believing in the two competing theories. Neither *had* to be accepted by chemists on objective criteria; moreover it was because the reasons for both were good that the two theories had supporters.

Kuhn concludes his argument by stressing that, in an ambiguous case like this, adherence to a particular theory is based on *value judgements*.

What tips the scales is that a particular fact is regarded as *more important* than another, a particular theory *more neatly* ties up the phenomena, and so on.

Since Kuhn's argument is accepted as sound, it is surprising that his opponents can still

compare theories as representations of nature, as statements about 'what is really out there'. Granting that neither theory of a historical pair is true,[67] they nonetheless seek a sense in which the latter is a better approximation to the truth. I believe nothing of the sort can be found.

How can they say of a theory that it approximates to reality?
In the end, Kuhn's argument comes down to these two statements:

1) An *objectively* based choice between two theories T and T′ implies total elimination of value judgements and, generally, *subjective* decision-making criteria;
2) However, in the Priestley–Lavoisier debate – and in the other examples from the history of science quoted in Kuhn's book – it is clear that the protagonists take position on the basis of subjective criteria.

These two points are indisputable, but from these arguments Kuhn draws some stark conclusions, since he suggests at the end of his book that the scientist, like the philosopher or sociologist of science, can and indeed must learn to do without the notions of *truth* and *objectivity*:

> It is now time to notice that until the last very few pages the term 'truth' had entered this essay only in a quotation from Francis Bacon.

And, later on:

> Does it really help to imagine that there is some one full, *objective, true* [my italics] account of nature . . .[68]

Statements 1) and 2) above (or similar ones readily available in Kuhn's book) do not in themselves lead to this conclusion. For it to be deduced from them, there would also have to be a statement such as:

[either the choice between T and T′ is always (alternative: often or most often) based on objective criteria, or there are examples to show that 'it is not generally the case']★.

The whole question is therefore whether one can apply to most pairs (T, T′) of competing scientific theories the predicate x indicating that one of them is preferable for *objective* reasons. This question is therefore:

generally x (T, T′)?

If moreover we write:

[the notions of truth and objectivity imply: in general x (T, T′)]★,

we can deduce from this implicit statement and from the explicit statement

in general x (T, T′)

the conclusion, which Kuhn in fact draws, that the notions of *truth* and *objectivity* have no real meaning.

There is no need to emphasize the great strength of this implicit statement. As soon as it is elucidated, it does seem hard to accept. If there are examples, like those quoted by Kuhn, where it is in fact difficult to choose between two theories on the basis of objective criteria, there is nothing to say that these cases are more typical or more frequent than those where it is not. However, statements of this kind have to be included to draw from 1) and 2) the conclusions which Kuhn draws.

Kuhn introduces these implicit statements because he is convinced that his examples are typical; but this is an illusion whose mechanism is readily apparent.

It is true that, in any debate, the protagonists generally have good reasons for choosing their viewpoint, and their adherence is based on criteria at least in part subjective. This is why we can easily see that the example of the Lavoisier–Priestley debate is not unique. The example in Chapter 4 of the debate between Millikan and Ehrenhaft, or the one between supporters and opponents of the inheritance of acquired characteristics, could also have been used, since they point in the same direction. Like the Millikan–Ehrenhaft debate, the one on the theory of evolution was also long-running. 'New facts' were continually appearing, where 1) proponents of the classical theory of evolution did not see *immediately* that they did not contradict it, and which 2) could be interpreted on Lamarckian lines. We can go even further than Kuhn and argue that, in a case like this, the adherence of the protagonists to each viewpoint was for *metaphysical* reasons.[69]

However, the vicissitudes of a scientific debate such as this are – once again – no different from those of a judicial investigation. *As long as the investigation is continuing,* supporters of both theories T and T' – assuming there are two – very often have *good* reasons, that is, reasons which are neither objective nor yet arbitrary, for subscribing to one of them. However, it can obviously happen that the debate ends because one side has to yield to the other's reasons.

No doubt it also happens that an investigation – scientific as well as judical – has no conclusion, or it comes to an abrupt end when one side is worn out or is eliminated. There is no reason to think, however, that these are typical occurrences; if they were the rule rather than the exception, the very concept of scientific or judicial investigation would lose its purpose.[70]

As in Hübner's case, the implicit logical framework of Kuhn's conclusions means that he cannot account for the ordinary case where the scientist's preference for theory T seems to be based in t on subjective reasons, and in t+k on objective reasons.

However, that is not all: Kuhn has no difficulty in showing that *all debates* in the history of science involve protagonists whose convictions are based on *subjective* reasons, since as soon as the reasons of one side become *objective*, the object of the *debate* disappears. Therefore, it is almost true, by *definition* as it were, that there is no debate – neither scientific nor judicial – which does not involve protagonists prompted by *subjective* reasons.[71]

This does not mean – except if one accepts Kuhn's implicit logical framework – that one of the two theories cannot in the end be regarded as true for objective reasons.

This is a particularly interesting case of the 'paradox of composition': what is true *at the time* or in the short term can become false *in time* or in the long term. Similarly, what is true *locally* may be false *globally*, and vice versa. For example, mechanization can cause unemployment in each specific firm, but be a factor in reducing unemployment in the economy as a whole.[72] Similarly, convictions may appear at a particular time to be based on subjective reasons, yet be based in the long term on objective reasons.

This is why the history of science is like other histories – for example, the history of morals – only for an observer who tries to decipher it on the basis of 'instantaneous' observations.

The rigour of Kuhn's logical framework leads him to regard adherence to a theory as a *conversion* phenomenon. This expression is itself also appropriate at a particular time, but not over time. It is true that in the light of a particular 'new fact', one can suddenly have a 'sneaking feeling', that is, a conviction based on subjective reasons, that 'Dupont is not guilty'. However, the investigation will end, and the 'sneaking feeling' will become a conviction only when it has become *objectively* impossible to believe another hypothesis.

If one removes Kuhn's implicit logical framework ([do scientists decide on the basis of *objective* or *subjective* reasons?]), Priestley's resistance to Lavoisier's ideas proves only that one cannot always determine the truth *immediately*, not that there is no truth, nor that one cannot decide in favour of a theory for *objective* reasons.

It is clear that there is a significant difference between the two conclusions. The fact that Kuhn endorses the second one is because of the *form* of the questions asked.

'One can doubt', said Nietzsche, 'the very existence of alternatives.'[73] Niels Bohr said that profound truths can be recognised for the fact that they are contradictory.[74]

These aphorisms, paradoxical as they seem, are easily applied to the examples referred to here. We are justified in doubting whether we can ask ourselves questions such as: 'Are scientific beliefs generally based on *subjective* or *objective* reasons?' They also apply to other examples; for instance, one *cannot* have a *realistic* view of knowledge (it is always construct, never copy); but, on the other hand, one *cannot not* have a realistic view of it (it deserves its name only when it really tells us about reality as it is).

Summary

The questions asked by ordinary knowledge as well as scientific knowledge are generally associated with a logical framework. For example, in the detective's mind, at a particular moment in an investigation, the question 'Who is the culprit?' can be associated with either a short closed list or an open list of possible culprits.

However, reality can suggest an inappropriate logical framework to persons who ask themselves, or to whom is asked, a particular question.

This happens in particular because, by default, we often tend to adopt a restrictive logical framework, which means we can more readily come up with an answer to the question. However, a critical analysis of these logical frameworks shows, on the one hand, that they are usually metaconscious, and on the other, that it is often difficult to determine the relevant framework.

These logical frameworks define one kind of application of Simmel's model. The implicit *a priori* which distort the conclusions of a valid line of the reasoning in fact often take the form of logical frameworks.

The fact that these distortions are a characteristic of scientific thinking as well as ordinary thinking can be clearly illustrated by numerous examples. The first one is taken from Durkheim: the whole reasoning behind his theory of religion is guided by an implicit logical framework which he neither discusses nor even perhaps perceives. My analysis is no way intended to be a methodical criticism of this theory; it aims merely to show how it is dependent on the implicit logical framework in which it is located.

The other example in this chapter is taken from present-day relativist philosophy of science. From an unimpeachable line of reasoning, Hübner concludes that scientific thinking can say goodbye to the notions of truth and objectivity, and that a scientific theory cannot be said to be truer than any myth. These hyperbolic conclusions stem from the fact that Hübner's reasoning is located in an implicit logical framework which one can accept but which it is probably better to reject.

Certain of Kuhn's conclusions can be subjected to the same kind of analysis. His theory that choice between scientific theories is always based on subjective considerations implies recourse to implicit 'logical' statements.

6

No effect without cause

In everyday life, we constantly practice logic without realizing it. For example, we decide whether two predicates are compatible or contradictory. We consider whether or not some other set of predicates exhausts the world of possibilities.

Generally speaking, when we come up with a theory, without realizing it we put into it all kinds of *a priori* about the relationship between the theory in question and the world, about the words it contains, about the notion of truth, and many other points of epistemology, linguistics or 'methodology'. A theory therefore is surrounded by a halo of *a priori*, aspects of which are described in figure 6.1.

It should be made clear that figure 6.1 indicates essentially *a priori* of a *formal* kind – the ones I am dealing with in this book. There are of course others: empirical *a priori* which Durkheim follows Bacon in calling *prenotions*, and *ethical a priori*. For example, symbolist theories of magic – those which deny the existence of magical beliefs – can be analysed as interpretations allowing us to reconcile the existence of magical rituals with the observer's concern (of an *ethical* nature) to safeguard the dignity of the person carrying it out.[1]

Obviously *epistemology* is a scholarly word; but we indulge in the activity it describes all the time, by which I mean that we accommodate and use in all thinking, most often metaconsciously, all kinds of ideas, principles, notions or statements corresponding to the main questions in epistemology: what is the truth? is it always unique? what tells us that a theory is acceptable? In truth, it is hard to imagine a statement, even the most ordinary, which does not involve an epistemology. For example, the fact that we are ready to defend stoutly, against any person contradicting it, the statement 'this book is on the table' as soon as we have noted that the book in question is in fact on the table, implies that we subscribe to Tarski's theory of truth: the statement 'the book is on the table' is true if and only if the book is on the table. Without our being

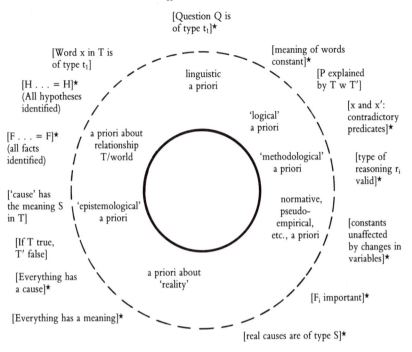

[Question Q is
of type t_1]*

[Word x in T is
of type t_1]

[H . . . = H]*
(All hypotheses
identified)

[F . . . = F]*
(all facts
identified)

['cause' has
the meaning S
in T]

[If T true,
T' false]

[Everything has
a cause]*

[Everything has a meaning]*

[meaning of words
constant]*

[P explained
by T w T']

[x and x':
contradictory
predicates]*

[type of
reasoning r_i
valid]*

[constants
unaffected
by changes in
variables]*

[F_i important]*

[real causes are of type S]*

linguistic
a priori

'logical'
a priori

'methodological'
a priori

normative,
pseudo-
empirical,
etc., a priori

a priori about
relationship
T/world

'epistemological'
a priori

a priori about
'reality'

Figure 6.1

aware of it, this theory, called the *correspondence* theory, lies behind many of the statements we make.

Generally speaking, all our statements imply that we subscribe to various epistemological propositions. For example, 'everything has a cause', 'there is no effect without cause', 'truth is unique', 'knowledge is the mirror of nature', 'everything has a meaning'. We can speak of 'ordinary epistemology' to indicate this implicit, prereflexive epistemology which is present in all discourse, thus setting it against the epistemology produced by philosophers.

Just as in the case of logic, this ordinary epistemology is made up of a set of propositions and principles whose strength lies in their soundness and which help us crucially in everyday life. Let us take the case of Tarski's correspondence theory. Clearly, if we were not all Tarskians, even metaconsciously, we would not get through the day, or have any serious communication with anybody. What dialogue could one have with somebody who did not accept that the statement 'this book is on the table' is true if and only if the book is on the table?

The soundness and validity of the principles of ordinary epistemology explain why we trust them unquestioningly and why we use them without realizing, because we regard them as 'self-evident'. We regard the principles of contradiction or excluded middle as absolute rules, even as laws of thought, because they are of vital importance in everyday life. Similarly, we regard the correspondence theory as obvious and self-evident. However, as in the case of *ordinary logic*, this *ordinary epistemology* can, in certain cases, be an inappropriate framework, and consequently lead to distortions of inference.

If my car has broken down, I expect the garage mechanic to find out what is wrong. My expectation therefore implies that I mobilize the principle 'truth is unique': if the breakdown is because the distributor is not working, then it is not because of something else. In this case, I am right to use the principle in question and I would probably cause mirth if I tried to discuss its validity. My conversation with the garage mechanic assumes that we both take as self-evident the fact that, out of the many causes or combinations of causes which can lead to a car breaking down, only one applies.

Similarly, we apply Tarski's principle in everyday life: where have I left my keys? In the bank? – perhaps I left them on the counter when I was signing my cheque? In my car? – as I was getting out, I heard a metallic noise which I did not identify at the time. Somewhere else? – somewhere that I am not thinking about at the moment? In any event, I am sure of one thing – that one and only one of these hypotheses is true. Which one? The one which *corresponds* to reality as it in fact is. If, for example, the second one is true, it corresponds to a state of affairs – that my keys are on the floor of my car – which I could easily check to see if it was real or not.

The same applies to another principle: 'every event has a cause'. This vital principle, a classic discussion topic for philosophers, seems to us so natural that it is difficult to imagine a case where it is not valid. I tripped *because* I did not see the electric wire on the floor. I sneeze *because* I have caught a cold.

The important point is that these principles and, in general, all principles of the same kind that one can imagine are not *in reality* of universal validity. They can easily be regarded as such in most everyday situations. However, even here they are not necessarily valid. There are many examples in cognitive psychology of experiments where subjects tend to see causal relationships where there are none, because they attribute excessive validity to the principle that 'everything has a cause'.[2]

These distortions, however, are not confined to ordinary knowledge. The widespread validity of these principles means that, even in methodical knowledge, we tend – metaconsciously – to endow them with more validity than they deserve. The fact that they are perceived as *self-evident* is hardly an inducement to the researcher to challenge them, even when they help to confer weak or false conclusions on otherwise perfectly acceptable reasoning.

In fact, we are well aware that these epistemological principles – just like logical principles – are not *in fact* of universal validity. We recognize, for example, that there are situations where the truth depends on the viewpoint in which the knowing subject is located. For instance, we accept, to quote an example from Morton White, that a doctor can justifiably say that the patient is in pain from a stomach ulcer, whereas the patient's wife attributes it to the food she has served up. However, we would also tend to accept that, of these two truths, one from the doctor and the other from the patient's wife, one must be superior to the other by virtue of the principle that *truth is unique*.

Similarly, we readily acknowledge that some phenomena are *accidents* and that, in this regard, they are – in a sense which I will go into later – *without* cause. However, we will tend to accept this only restrictively.

In a given investigation situation, one can introduce epistemological *a priori* of varying complexity, in the same way that one introduces logical *a priori* of varying complexity. When one asks oneself a question of the kind 'why X?', one can accept that the possible answers constitute a set which is either open or closed. Similarly, for a question about the causality of phenomenon X, one can start from the principle either that X has *one* cause, or that the causes of X are *several*, or that X is *without* cause. *Like logical a priori*, these epistemological *a priori* can be seen as of varying *complexity* and *power*, the most complex being the least powerful, and vice versa. Therefore, the *a priori* 'X has a cause' means the investigation can be concluded more easily than with more complex *a priori*.

In this chapter and the next one, I will look at two cases – the *a priori* 'everything has a cause' and 'truth is unique'. It would of course be possible to look at others. The *a priori* 'everything has a meaning' is also of great importance; it is on the basis of this *a priori* that Job asserts that his suffering is part of the order of things, that Freudians claim they can interpret any slip, and that Marxist sociologists claim that all social phenomena are the expression of the class struggle.[3]

I must again stress one point: Simmel's model, the subject of this book, emphasizes the *cognitive* causes of belief in weak or false ideas; but it in no way implies that the *affective* causes of these beliefs should be ignored. On the contrary, even when beliefs are legitimated by perfectly valid arguments, they can *also* be accepted under the influence of affective causes. Popper's theory of falsification proposes a perfectly rigorous line of reasoning; but this does not mean that, through it, Popper did not *also* want to express the *aversion* he had to certain modes of thought.[4]

THE PRINCIPLE OF 'EVERYTHING HAS A CAUSE'

Since logical principles (principles of identity, contradiction or excluded middle) are of widespread application in everyday life, we have the impression that we are dealing with laws of thought, whereas they are postulates, applicable to certain statements but not to others. For example, the 'idealist' and 'materialist' predicates are contradictory only if I decide so. Similarly, the principles of contradiction or excluded middle apply to statements such as 'beliefs have affective causes'/'beliefs have cognitive causes' only if I want them to.

Of course, there are also circumstances where the predicates p and p' are in fact contradictory, as when p$'$ = $\sim p$. In this kind of case, the principles of contradiction and excluded middle are indeed universal. In other words, they apply whatever the content and concrete meaning of p and p'. However, there is often a tendency to accept too readily $[p' = \sim p]$* and, consequently, to use a logical context which is too closed.

The same applies to the principles related to the notion of cause, Kant treats the principle that every event has a cause as an '*a priori* synthetic judgement'.[5] This judgement is *a priori*, because it is not dictated by experience, but on the contrary allows us to organize our experience. It is *synthetic*, because it tells us about the world. On the other hand, *analytical* statements – for example 'a centimetre is a hundredth part of a metre' – tell us not about the world, but about the meaning of the words we use to talk about it. According to Kant, in the same way that we cannot think of physical phenomena outside space and time, we cannot conceive of an event without a cause. I accept that this is a summary of Kant's thought, but it serves my purpose here.

In reality, the lively debate which grew up concerning this proposition of Kant virtually concluded that this famous *a priori* synthetic judgement is above all an idealization of the procedures of ordinary knowledge.

It is true that it is very often to our advantage to start from the conjecture that every event has a cause, and that this principle has great potential for organizing everyday experience. However, it is also true that it is ambiguous, that the very notion of cause can have several meanings, and that, in ordinary experience itself, we sometimes also see more or less vaguely that it is preferable not to use this principle.

In other words, we get from this debate the impression that, like the excluded middle, for example, the principle of 'every event has a cause' is a *conjecture*. Often, we can apply it with every confidence and assurance. In other cases, we would not even dream of using it. However, in intermediate situations, the knowing subject will tend to accept its validity as self-evident, whereas it may well not be relevant. In these cases, distortions of inference may result and false beliefs may develop on the basis of otherwise sound reasoning.

THE AMBIGUITY OF THE PRINCIPLE

The ambiguity of the principle has been emphasized many times; its identity and even its very nature have been questioned.[6]

It is true that 'every event has a cause' is not an *analytical* judgement. We do not deduce the principle from the very notion of event, as we conclude from an examination of the notion of bicycle that a machine has to have two wheels to deserve this name. On the other hand, it is true, as Kant argues, that it is not an *a posteriori* proposition, that is, a proposition derived from experience, since experience could not convince us that *all* events have a cause. In the case of past and present events, we could not note or have noted all of them; in the case of future events, even if we could comprehend them, we could not claim to know them all in advance with certainty.

If the principle is neither *a posteriori* nor *analytical*, does this mean that it is *synthetic* and *a priori*? This would be to apply too hastily the great logical principles and accept too quickly that these adjectives describe two contradictory pairs.

In fact, though the assertion 'every event has a cause' is not analytical, it is not synthetic either. If it was, it would tell us something about the world. After all, by definition, a synthetic statement has to tell us that the world is made up in a particular way and not in another. The statement 'the bicycle has two wheels' does not tell us anything about the world, only about the meaning of the word 'bicycle'. This is why the statement is *analytical*. Conversely, the statement 'an unsupported bicycle does not stand up unless it is moving' is a *synthetic* statement. For a statement to be synthetic, we have to be able to imagine a state of affairs which is different from the one it describes and where we are assured by the statement that it corresponds to reality. For example, 'a bicycle falls over if it is not moving and if it is not being held' is a synthetic statement, because one can imagine a state of affairs where this statement is not true. Conversely, we cannot imagine a state of affairs which refutes the statement 'a bicycle has two wheels'.

Similarly, it is impossible to imagine a state of affairs which refutes the statement 'every event has a cause'.

Let us assume in fact that I think I have proved the proposition 'A causes B' because I have observed repeated cases where A does cause B. If I encounter a case where A is not the cause of B, I may still assume that invisible causes or causes which are at any rate not known to me are responsible for the fact that reality has refused the statement 'A causes B'.

The principle 'everything has a cause' would not thereby be contradicted, or even weakened.

I may also, despite my efforts, not manage to identify the causes of a phenomenon. This failure gives me no reason to doubt in any way the validity of the principle. Generally speaking, no observation which I may make on the world can refute the statement 'everything has a cause'. It is even totally impossible to imagine what kind of observation could contradict this statement.

The statement 'every event has a cause' is therefore compatible with any state of affairs. It follows that it could tell us nothing about the world, and that it cannot therefore be regarded as a synthetic statement.

In other words, the famous principle is in fact *neither analytical, nor synthetic*. It tells us nothing either about the world, or about what is in our minds when we refer to the idea of 'event'.

It would be premature to conclude from this that a statement which tells us nothing either about the world or about the words we use to think about the world is a statement that could only be 'vacuous and totally uniformative'.[7] If this were the case, how could such an empty principle figure as largely as it has done among the *a priori* of ordinary thinking as well as scientific thinking?

After all, for all that it is empty and silent about the world, this principle is at the same time essential: it is in fact a heuristic principle, or, if one prefers, a *conjecture* which guides our thinking in the explanation of all sorts of phenomena. If I fall ill, I consult a doctor, thereby assuming that my illness has a cause and that this can be eliminated. All sorts of social roles – the doctor or the garage mechanic, for example – prove that there is, as it were, an institutionalization of this type of question. People go to the mechanic or the doctor only to ask them questions of the type 'what is the cause of P?', to which they think they can give a competent answer. One cannot therefore say that a principle which from time immemorial has been the guiding spirit behind all sorts of professions and actions is an empty one. However, like all conjectures, this one may be valid or not.

THE AMBIGUITY OF THE NOTION OF CAUSE

However, that is not all. Not only is the statement 'every event has a cause' a conjecture rather than an *a priori synthetic judgement* whose validity is universal and certain, but the notion of *cause* is, despite appearances, an inexorably obscure notion.

Not only does the principle in question not tell us anything about the world, but its meaning – like that of the notion of cause itself – is vague. For both these reasons, though it is an essential guide, it is not always trustworthy and can on the contrary give rise to many dubious ideas about the causes of phenomena.

The ambiguity of the notion of cause has long been noted. As John Stuart Mill rightly says,[8] one cannot strictly say of patients who have caught a cold that they caught it *because* they went out. The going out is not, by itself, the cause of the cold. It can arise also from the patients' proneness to external attacks and, beyond that, to their general state of health.

It is only the sum of these factors – only the *whole* causes[9] – which deserves, says Mill, to be considered as the true cause of the cold. Mill therefore suggests that the notion of *cause* should be assimilated to that of *the whole cause*. Of course he acknowledges that the notion of cause has other meanings and that in everyday speech one says things like 'So and so has caught a cold *because* she went out'. However, these are, says Mill, loose expressions typical of 'common parlance', which have to be kept out of methodical thinking.

In fact, Mill's distinction reveals an excessive optimism, since it is impossible to attach an objective definition to the notion of cause.

This is because, firstly, the meaning of the notion depends, to use Habermas's phrase, on our 'cognitive interests'. This is clear in the dialogue between the doctor and the patient's wife referred to above: the patient's wife says that her husband's illness was caused by the food she gave him; the doctor says it is due to a stomach ulcer which has been diagnosed in the patient. Their causal theories are inspired by their cognitive interests: the doctor by the desire to cure the patient; the patient's wife by the wish to avoid a repetition of the illness. Both are right.

The presence of these cognitive interests is not only clear in ordinary usage of the notion of cause, but also in its *scientific* uses.

For example, according to their interests, historians will attribute different meanings to the notion of cause. The definitions – tacit or metaconscious – by which they give a particular meaning to it are the magic wand which means that they see, in a *particular* cause of phenomenon A, *the cause* of the phenomenon.

When a historian such as Pirenne says that the Muslim invasion was a cause of the decline of Mediterranean civilization, he is proceeding, according to Morton White,[10] like the patient's wife. He is seeing the decline as an *abnormal* event which disturbs a *normal* state of affairs, just as eating food which has gone off makes a person in good health ill.

In many cases, therefore, the cause of a phenomenon is the accident which upsets a state of affairs regarded as normal.

In other cases, the same notion of cause is defined as describing an underlying state. For example, though Marx does not deny that the character of Louis-Napoleon played a part in the success of the coup d'état of 2 December 1851, he suggests that it was really because 'the situation created by *"the class struggle"* in France [Marx's italics] made it possible for a grotesque and mediocre person to play the part of a hero.' In this second case, the definition of the notion of cause is nearer to that of the doctor than that of the patient's wife.

The presence of cognitive interests is of course not the only factor which makes it difficult to arrive at an objective definition of the notion of cause. Another reason for the uncertainty, usually more widely acknowledged, and possibly overlapping the first one, lies in the fact that it is rarely possible to put precise limits on the networks of causality which give rise to an event or a state of affairs, and that it is not always possible to go back all the way along the causal chain: the result is that any imputation of cause implies a choice, which itself may be based on principles with a varying degree of soundness and which are very likely to remain unarticulated.

It was thought that these ambiguities could be removed by defining the notion of cause on the basis of the concepts of necesssary condition, sufficient condition, or necessary and sufficient condition.

Oswald Ducrot[11] has suggested that the statement 'A causes B', as used for example, in history, is equivalent in fact, in certain cases, to the assertion that 'one could not have had A without B'. Inversely, denying the truth of the statement 'A causes B' amounts in this case to saying that one could have had A but not B. For example, historians who claim that the annexation of Alsace-Lorraine was not the cause of the First World War will emphasize factors leading France to accept the annexation. In this type of use, the notion of cause is in fact close to the idea of *sufficient condition*.

In other cases, the assertion 'A causes B' amounts to denying that one can have B without A. In this case, the notion of cause is close to the idea of *necessary condition*. Historians trying to prove the falsity of the statement 'A cause B' would aim to show that B could happen without A. Therefore, the statement 'the Sarajevo assassination was the cause of the First World War' would be refuted by proving that, even without the Sarajevo assassination, the war would have occured.

'A causes B' can indicate the existence of a general link between A and B of the type 'if A, then (often, sometimes) B': a particular party lost the election because it was involved in scandals. In this case, A is neither the necessary condition nor the sufficient condition of B, but a condition likely to lead to B. For example, historians who argue that the annexation of Alsace-Lorraine was the cause of the First World War are likely to have in their minds a statement such as: 'a nation which is humiliated and/or has lost part of its territory will try (often, sometimes, if this is plausible, and so on) to wipe away the humiliation.'

However, the notion of cause has further meanings: the grain of sand in Cromwell's bladder, or Cleopatra's nose, were neither the necessary condition nor the sufficient condition, nor *a fortiori* the necessary and sufficient condition of anything, even though these causes are supposed to have had enormous effects. Therefore, 'A causes B' might also mean 'A gave rise to B'. This meaning is not the same thing as the previous ones.

It is clear therefore that there are examples where the notion of cause is close to one of these definitions. At the same time, however, it is easy to see that none of them can claim universal validity. For example, it is true that oxygen is a necessary condition for a fire and that, in certain circumstances, it will be natural to say that the presence of oxygen was the cause of a particular fire. However, in other cases it will be normal to attribute the cause of the fire more to carelessness than to the presence of oxygen. Even if the presence of oxygen is a necessary condition for a fire, to say that it is the cause of the fire would in certain circumstances be patently absurd. This shows that one cannot define the notion of cause by reference to that of necessary condition. It would of course be possible to come up with a similar proof for the other cases.

In other words, it is only in certain contexts that the notion of cause can be identified with the notions of necessary condition and sufficient condition, or with any other particular definition.

Following John Stuart Mill, numerous writers such as White or Ducrot[12] stressed, directly or indirectly, the ambiguities inherent in the notion of cause. Mill's approach was indirect, since he thought he could produce an *objective* definition by assimilating it to the notion of *whole cause*. White to a certain extent entertains the same hope, and suggests that one can speak of cause in an objectively well-defined sense in one case at least; where one can be certain that, without A, B would not have happened (for example, without the spark, the dynamite would not have exploded). However, he emphasizes that even in the most considered historical research, when one speaks of the cause of an event, one inevitably mobilizes cognitive interests. Passmore[13] clearly showed that the ambiguity in the notion of cause was just as great in scientific knowledge as in ordinary knowledge.

A fortiori, the principle that 'every event has a cause' cannot itself be anything but ambiguous.

Put another way, in many cases, the statement 'A is the cause of B' stems from a line of reasoning which includes implicit statements; and it is these implicit statements which mean that we can move, for example, from the statement 'A is *a* cause of B' to the very different and much more powerful statement 'A is *the* cause of B'.

For example, the statement

[A causes B if and only if A is the necessary condition of B]* allows us to regard A as *the* cause of B as soon as A has the characteristic of a necessary condition, even if numerous other causes contributed to the production of B.

DIVERSITY OF THE *A PRIORI* UNDERLYING CASUAL STATEMENTS

Conversely, the ambiguity of the notion of cause, as well as the principle that everything has a cause, means that underlying every causal statement there is a set of *a priori* which, like the logical *a priori* analysed in the last chapter, can on the one hand be of varying complexity and on the other be more or less appropriate in relation to reality.

These *a priori* relate above all to the nature of the causal network which allows us to account for phenomenon P. After all, despite our confidence in the principle 'everything has a cause', we are well aware that in reality the causality of a phenomenon can be of varying complexity; if, in the most simple case, phenomenon P can be regarded as stemming from a single cause, in other cases one cannot bring in the *a priori* [x has *one* cause]*. One would then go for more complex *a priori* which allowed the existence of multiple causality, even of circular causality, or even the absence of causality.

What needs to be realized, however, is that the knowing subject has a wide 'choice' of these *a priori* and that very often they are not dictated by reality.

In some cases, we are certain that a particular *a priori*, for example, the *a priori* of single causality, is the right one. This is what White is thinking of when he suggests that 'A causes B' means that, without A, B would not have happened: if the match had not come into contact with the barrel of gunpowder, there would have been no fire. In other cases, the relevance of the *a priori* [x has a cause]* is less obvious. The decline of Mediterranean culture is at least as complex an event as the First World War. Nevertheless a writer such as Pirenne argues that the Muslim invasions were *the* cause of it. Other historians resort to the *a priori* of the single cause because they tend to consider only underlying causes. Others argue that the true cause is the factor which, like oxygen in fires, is always present.[14]

Therefore, even in a case where complex historical phenomena have to be explained, we often see a tendency to reduce this complexity in such a way as to keep the explanation within the framework of the single cause. These examples show how much freedom the knowing subject has: the intrinsic *complexity* of a phenomenon does not necessarily deter him or her from explaining on the basis of simple *a priori*.

In other cases, we use *a priori* which acknowledge the existence of multiple causes, even of phenomena with circular causality. That this kind of case exists and is even quite common is shown by the fact that it is easy to find examples: an increase in the value of a particular currency makes it attractive and leads to a further rise. The severity of courts makes certain types of crime rare, which leads to courts cracking down on it. Deviance leads to social exclusion, which reinforces unsocial behaviour and increases social exclusion.

However it often happens that the knowing subject decides to analyse phenomena with circular causality on the basis of *a priori* which do not recognize them.

Similarly, there are cases where, contradicting the principle that 'every event has a cause', a phenomenon *is* contingent, that is, has no cause. Very often, however, these phenomena are analysed on the basis of *a priori* which endow them with a cause or causes. This is so not only in thinking officially acknowledged as magic, but also in scientific thinking; the principle that every event has a cause looms so large that it is hard to envisage and *a fortiori* to introduce the *a priori* of contingency.

I will develop this point further at a later stage; but for the moment I would like to stress the points of similarity between these *epistemological a priori* and the logical *a priori* of the last chapter. Just as one can put questions of varying complexity and openness from a logical point of view ('*p w q?*', '*p v q?*', . . ., '*p v q v r v* . . .?'), one can ask oneself in relation to phenomenon Q causal questions of varying openness:

– What is *the cause* of Q?
– What are *the causes* of Q?
– What are *some* of the causes of Q?
– What are *the causes* of Q (it being understood that these causes can themselves be an effect of Q)?
– What are *some* of the causes of Q (ditto)?
– Has Q *no* cause?

As in the case analysed in the previous chapter, these questions are of different degrees of complexity; secondly, it is clear that they have significant implications: for example, the first question assumes that Q has a single cause; thirdly it is difficult to tell in advance whether a type T question is relevant to Q; fourthly, the irrelevance of an *a priori* is not always immediately revealed. The epistemological *a priori* included in these questions can, in other words, give rise to answers which, though possibly very weak, will convince subjects that their conclusions are sound.

We are back again with the example of 'Who killed Harry?'. Before this question is investigated, there is nothing to say whether it should be put in the framework [*p w q*]★ rather than [*p v q*]★. Similarly, very often there is nothing to tell us, when faced with a phenomenon Q, whether we have to look for the *cause* or the *causes*, or whether we have to try to explain it by assuming that it has *no* cause. In some cases, the apparent complexity of a phenomenon will lead us to steer clear of types of question which are too simple. However, in reality this protection is very limited. For example, a phenomenon such as the development of capitalism is undoubtedly complex. Nevertheless, many people do not think it odd to speak of *the* cause of this development. Similarly, some psychic phenomena are 'obviously' complex; but this does not prevent questions like 'what caused this person's confused state or neurosis?' from appearing to be meaningful.

The consequence of this indeterminate nature of the relevant *a priori* is that the knowing subject has to *take* a chance; but what makes things more difficult is that taking a chance does not always work out. In the example of *The murderer Lives in Number 21*, the person conducting the investigation uses a framework which is too restrictive and ends up with a feeling of failure that leads to replacing a simple *a priori* by a more complex *a priori*. However, it does not always happen like this. Popper[15] rightly argued that the existence of an *a priori* in no way harms the cause of truth, and he rejected the myth that the existence of *frameworks* implies the impossibility of objective knowledge; wrong *a priori*, he explains, often lead to impasses; when they prevent knowing subjects from solving problems which they pose, they thereby condemn themselves.

It sometimes happens like that – but not *necessarily*. There are many examples, and I will give some in a moment, showing why we must not put too much faith in the effectiveness of criticism directed at *frameworks*. I must again stress, however, that, since *a priori* – what Popper calls *frameworks* – cannot be deduced, it is a matter of taking a chance or making conjectures. Because reality does not always oblige them to avoid a particular *framework*, knowing subjects tend to succumb to the influence of common sense *a priori*, and be sensitive to the fact that the simplest of them, apart from allowing economy of thought, are more powerful. All this tends to make them choose *by default* restrictive *a priori*.

It is clear therefore that causal thinking usually gives rise to Simmel effects. If, as in normal usage, the distortions of causal analysis are called *magical thinking*, the conclusion is that magical thinking is so natural that it usually permeates not only ordinary causal thinking, but also methodical causal analysis.

Since I cannot go into all the ramifications of this topic, I will confine myself to two examples – that where the knowing subject under-estimates the complexity of the causal network underlying a particular *explanandum* (phenomenon to be explained), and the particularly important case where the investigator tries to attribute causes to a contingent phenomenon, that is, to a phenomenon which has no cause.

FIRST EXAMPLE: WHY THE COMPLEXITY OF CAUSAL NETWORK IS SO READILY UNDERESTIMATED

Subjects can persuade themselves that P is *the* cause of Q by reasoning which can be formulated as follows:

1) [Q has a cause]*
2) What is the cause of Q?
3) [a *true* cause has the property S]*
4) P has the property S
5) P is a cause, and a *true* cause of Q

---

6) P is *the* cause of Q

We see that the introduction of the two implicit statements 1) and 3) is able to transform

'P is *a* cause of Q'

into

'P is *the* cause of Q'

The first implicit statement 1) legitimates for subjects the form of their question in 2). The second implicit statement 3) is a definition of the notion of cause. Since the word 'cause' is extremely ambiguous, every causal question implies *a priori* statements not only about the form of the causal network underlying an *explanandum*, but also about the notion of cause. In our present example, the combination of the two kinds of implicit statements means in fact that the status of a *single* cause can be given to a particular cause – a cause having the property S.

This reasoning is of very general application and it is characteristic of many weak causal assertions. As for what I call the 'property S', it covers a small number of typical cases which could be specified through a few examples, some of which have already been given.

1)Firstly, the property S is attributed to an explanatory factor which thereby receives, following 1) to 6) above, the status of single cause if this factor can be said to have been able to activate an inert system. In this case, the reasoning in 1) to 6) includes a statement 3') in a 3'a) form:

3'a): [S = ability to activate an inert system]*.

This interpretation of S is the common one, since the notion of cause is very close to some mechanical representations. On a billiard table, the balls are usually at rest, unless I set one of them moving with the help of a billiard cue. *The* cause of this transition from being at rest to moving is in the initial nudge which I have administered to the system. The influence of these mechanical representations no doubt explains the frequency of a type $3'a$) interpretation of S and why, by means of this *a priori*, one can attribute to a particular complex phenomenon a *single* cause.

For example, Leslie White, in his famous, brilliant and enlightening book,[16] tried to show that phenomena which were clearly complex, such as the social, political and economic upheavals in the Western world in late medieval times, could be attributed to *one* main, even single, cause – technological change.

The attraction of White's book lies in his excellent examples and his rigorous and precise analysis. There is no doubt that the inventions he quotes – for example, the metal ploughshare and the horse's bit – in fact produced a series of chain reactions, and that in the end they revolutionized the social and political, as well as the economic, system of medieval societies.

The metal ploughshare allowed the cultivation of land which was wetter and heavier, but also more fertile. Since this land is generally located in valleys, this technological innovation led to huge population transfers. Since metal ploughs need much more energy than swing ploughs, demand for draught animals rose sharply, entailing the organization of supply to meet it. Since the cost of this animal energy was beyond the means of the average peasant, new forms of cooperation were promoted. Because of this, the social organization of medieval society underwent a fundamental change: not only was new land occupied and put to use, but old land divisions were redrawn, since a holding needed to be of a particular size before it was profitable. Naturally this significantly complicated financial management of the new holdings. In the end, these changes led to a complete upheaval in social stratification, and were bound to affect political institutions significantly.

This example, like others quoted by White, shows that a technological change which at first sight is of little importance can lead to a fundamental reform of the social system in which it occurs.

However, the important point is that White's book is rarely regarded as concluding that technological change *can* lead to significant social change, or that it is *one* of the causes of social change. It is seen as proof that technological change is *the* cause of the continual social upheavals in Western society since the Middle Ages.

From the Marxist point of view, White brought grist to the mill of the theory that a change in the *forces* of production leads to upheaval in the relations of production.

This 'interpretation' – which to a certain extent is also White's – is no doubt based on a mistake of logic. The fact that X (here, technological change) is *one* cause of Y (here, the move to modernity) does not prove that X is *the* cause of Y. In other words, the conclusion usually drawn from White's book in no way flows from his analyses.

How does it happen therefore that this conclusion seems *natural* to the reader? Why did it have to be adopted by White and by writers of textbooks on social change when they refer to the book? My hypothesis is that its power to convince arises from the fact that it is seen as deriving from type 1) to 6) reasoning, with a 3') statement in a 3'a) form. If one thinks about it, each of the statements 1) to 6) is acceptable. Statement 1) because, at the beginning of a piece of research, there is nothing to prevent the thought that every event has a cause; statement 3) because it is necessary to specify what one means by the notion of cause; statement 3'a) because it is normal to speak of cause in relation to a phenomenon which activates a system, by changing rest into movement. These statements are of course only implicit in White's argument, and remain so because there is nothing extraordinary about them. This is why they are readily accepted as self-evident statements on which there is no need to spend any time.

However, once statements 1) and 3'a) are accepted, all the elements of the process transforming the statement:

'A is *one* cause of B'

into

'A is *the* cause of B'

are in place.

The first statement has only to be confirmed by the facts – and here White's argument is unexceptionable – for it to be *believed* that the second one is *ipso facto* proved. Once again, the substitution is all the easier for being dependent on metaconscious statements regarded as self-evident.

White's example, far from being unique, is in fact typical. For instance, it would be easy to show that a line of reasoning consisting, apart from statements 1) to 6), of statement 3) in the form 3'a), is characteristic of much writing in sociology as well as development economics.[17] Despite the 'obvious' complexity of, for example, economic 'take-off', many examples could be given of theories which literally illustrate this framework of reasoning.

Indeed, virtually all theories appearing at the time when research into development was booming are based on this model, purporting to see *the cause* of development in education, the setting up of a pilot industry, the establishment of an adequate transport infrastructure, the injection of capital, the dominant collective ethic, the 'need for achievement', the establishment of means of communication the 'basic personality', the stimulus provided by marginalized minorities, the end of foreign exploitation, the 'dependence' on the developed world, or any other phenomenon.

There is a remarkable degree of agreement between theorists belonging to intellectual traditions and national contexts which are so divergent. It is clear in retrospect that the reasoning of both Marxists and reformists, despite their disagreement on basics, is located within an identical framework. However strange it may seem when one considers the complexity of the phenomena in question, both sides were for a long time convinced that development and under-development had a single cause. They defined 'cause' in the same way (as in $3'a$), though they differed on the *content* of this cause. The same *framework* crossed not only ideological boundaries but also disciplines – economists used it as well as sociologists.

I find it hard to understand the attraction and the influence of these theories, as well as the revelatory effect of a writer such as Hirschman,[18] who drew the attention of development theorists to the significance of its complexity, unless this is an example of a cognitive procedure which has a certain degree of universality. There is no other way of explaining why, when the complexity of the subject is so obvious, single-factor theories were so prevalent.

2) In a further case, equally typical, a factor is regarded as causal if it has the property S defined as follows:

$3'b$): [S = the ability to put a system into an *abnormal* state]★

Clearly, as in the previous case, this definition is based on the normal usage of the notion of cause. When speaking of the cause of a case of poisoning, we use a type $3'b$ implicit definition of the notion of cause. In fact, this definition is a mirror image of the previous one. In the $3'a$ case, *the* cause is the nudge which activates an immobile system. In the $3'b$ case, it is the obstacle which the moving object meets. The role attributed by Pirenne to the Muslim conquest as the cause of the decline of the Mediterranean world is an example which I have already given of this type of cause. As in the previous case, it is surprising that a historian tries to explain such a complex phenomenon by *one* cause.

The same can be said of many other examples. For instance, it is at first sight surprising that we should so readily accept Weber's argument in *The Protestant Ethic and the Spirit of Capitalism* that the Calvinist ethic played a decisive role in the development of modern capitalism. Obviously Weber carefully phrased his argument to suggest that there was a *family likeness* rather than a causal relationship between the Calvinist ethic and the development of capitalism. However, everybody took it that an elective affinity between the Protestant ethic and the spirit of capitalism implies an influence of the former on the latter. Therefore Weber did indeed propose a theory of the *origin* of modern capitalism as a break with the traditional world. This theory consists of endowing the phenomenon with *one* cause – if not a single cause, at least one of decisive importance.

Despite Weber's caveats, his framework of reasoning is of the same kind as Pirenne's. The reason why it was convincing is no doubt that the theory, deploys a lot of factual data in an original and convincing way. However, if only this aspect is taken into account, the conclusion is that the Protestant ethic is *one of the causes* of the development of capitalism.

The subtle intervention of two type 1) and 3'*b*) statements is therefore needed to move from this *weak* conclusion to the *strong* conclusion usually drawn from Weber's book. The *weak* conclusion is perhaps debatable; but it is certainly defensible.[19] The *strong* conclusion is nowadays unacceptable.[20] However, it is the one on which people usually focus.

It would be easy to show – though I do not want to dwell on the point at this stage – that criticisms of Weber's theory have usually suggested its replacement by another unicausal theory.

3) In a third case in point, S is defined as:

3'*c*): [S = the property of always being present when effect Q is evident]★

This third meaning of the word 'cause' is also in current use in ordinary causal inference: 'nothing ventured, nothing gained', 'genius is an infinite capacity for taking pains', 'virtue is always rewarded', and hundreds of other sayings show how important this meaning is.

It is because he uses an approach of this kind that Popper attributes a decisive importance to the *falsification* of scientific theories. *The* main cause of the cumulative nature of science lies in the systematic effort by scientists to subject to critical tasting theories as they appear.

Popper's theory of the 'growth of knowledge' is therefore another example of a theory whose conclusions go far beyond what its *explicit* arguments allow. In fact, these arguments lead only to the conclusion that a theory which is contradicted too often by reality will end up by being dropped, and not that the institutionalization of critical debate is *the* cause of the cumulative nature of science.

Modern history and sociology of science have abundantly shown this factor was indeed only one of the causes of scientific progress.[21]

4) A factor which can be regarded as a *necessary condition* is also a good candidate for the role of *single* cause. In this case, if Q is the phenomenon to explain and P the factor claiming to be single cause, then property S is defined as:

$3'd$): [S = a factor P has the property S if the statement 'if Q, then P' is true]★.[22]

This meaning of the word 'cause' is very frequent in everyday causal inference: 'lazy people will not succeed', 'a court decision will depend on whether you are rich or poor', and so on.

The famous scientific example of Durkheim's main argument in *The Elementary Forms of the Religious Life*, quoted in the last chapter in a different perspective, is relevant to this case in point. Durkheim's main question is about the origins of, and reasons for, the universality of religion. Although the content of religions varies, there is no society without religion; the origin of religion is indeed a complex phenomenon. However, and here Durkheim is no different from other writers, he does not hesitate to start from the *a priori* of a single or main cause. Moreover, he implicitly introduces the statement that this single cause has the status of a necessary condition.

It is in fact these two implicit statements which prop up his whole theory: Durkheim starts from the principle that religious feeling is a feeling of respect. He then moves to a series of analytical statements: respect is always respect for something, and of necessity respect for an entity regarded as *superior*, by which one feels dominated. If this something cannot be *unreal*, even if *homo religiosus* thinks of it as such, the only serious possibility is, as Durkheim argues, 'society'.

Strong criticism has been levelled at Durkheim's argument[23], and justifiably. However, the question which interests me here is how Durkheim was able so easily to persuade himself and persuade his readers of the truth of a theory as weak as this.

In fact, Durkheim's reasoning is valid as much in the detail of its propositions (for example, it is true that religious feeling is a feeling of respect and that one can only have *respect* for something perceived as *superior*, and so on) as in their relationships. Like all reasoning on which I am focusing here, it is not a matter of a sophistical argument. The weakness of the conclusion stems rather from the presence of implicit statements, particularly of the *a priori* of a single cause and the assimilation of the notion of cause with that of necessary condition.

5) The notion of cause can also be defined by the notion of *sufficient condition*. In this case, the property S is defined as:

$3'e$): [S = a factor P has the property S if the statement 'if P, then Q' can be regarded as true]★.

There is no need to say that in everyday life we are often led, almost without thinking (so self-evident is it) to put the following interpretation on the notion of cause: 'I did not sleep well because I drank too much coffee.' There is no need to quote again the examples from history which I gave earlier; and it would be easy to find a large number to go with them.

6) The notion of cause can also be defined in many other ways. In one of the earlier cases in point, it was associated with the idea of an accident which upsets a state of affairs regarded as normal. It can on the contrary be associated with the philosophical idea of *essence*: a particular phenomenon happens because it is of the nature or of the *essence* of the system in which it appears that it happens. In this case, property S is defined as:

3'*f*): [S = a factor P has property S if it is an essential property of the system in which the phenomenon Q to be explained is located]*.

The point can be illustrated by reference to an extremely interesting book by J. Q. Wilson, *Thinking about Crime*.[24] The author is an expert in crime prevention policy, and states that sociologists and criminologists are interested only in the causes of crime about which very little can be done.

Writers such as Sutherland have found, for example, that family breakdown plays a decisive role in crime. They also stress the status problems of young people given to crime. Classic works on adolescent gangs have indeed shown that juvenile crime was often a sign of a wish to assert oneself, a need to be recognized and, in the final analysis, the desire to be integrated rather than the desire to be hostile – when one cannot get oneself noticed or recognized in a positive way, the temptation is to deploy one's nuisance value.[25] In this way, some theorists of crime profoundly changed our view of crime by showing that it should be seen not as a 'revolt against society' or a 'rejection of society', but as the expression of a wish to be integrated.

However, in developing these theories, Wilson tells us, criminologists and sociologists reveal a particular view of the notion of cause. Their professional activities lead them to accept as worthy of the name of 'cause' only those factors at the level of 'social structures', or very basic social mechanisms. In doing this, they introduce an *a priori* which has an important consequence, that is, that a *cause* is a factor which is not amenable to action.

The fatalism for which the social sciences are often criticized frequently derives from these professional *a priori*.

In any event, it is interesting to note that, although sociologists are not always in agreement on which characteristics of a system should be called *structural*, they are agreed on one point, that the *true* causes of phenomena are in fact to be found in this kind of characteristic.

Sociologists or criminologists are here simply adopting, in order to make it an implicit norm in their research, a definition also commonly used by ordinary knowledge: 'Everybody has a fault, to which they always return', 'Once a wolf, always a wolf' (La Fontaine), and so on.

This tendency to accord the status of cause only to what might be *structural* is not of course confined to criminology. On the contrary, it is often in this way that 'scientific' explanations are distinguished from 'anecdotal' explanations.

The fact that present-day criminologists emphasize social factors – just as a previous generation stressed genetic factors – shows the influence of the *a priori* [causal = structural]*. Similarly, the attraction of a writer such as Marx, and the fact that in regard to him people speak of 'scientific' history, is largely a result of his efforts to find 'profound', 'structural' causes of developments: for Marx, Louis-Napoleon's 1851 coup is not explained only and primarily in terms of contingent and 'anecdotal' causes, but by the *profound* causes of the class struggle in France in the second half of the nineteenth century.[26]

7) Of course, the opposite 'choice' may also be observed. In everyday life, cause is often assimilated not with *structural* factors, but with *contingent* factors which one can legitimately try to eliminate.

In this case, the property S is defined as:

3'g): [S = a factor P has the property S if it can be modified]*.

For example, a car breakdown has a cause which needs to be eliminated. It is of no use to me to know that my car has broken down *because* it is old: what I want to know is whether the clutch can be repaired. In other words, in everyday life, the factor which can be regarded as relevant from a praxeological point of view is often regarded as causal.

Specialists in applied sciences and experts in public policy, whose ethos is directed towards action rather than knowledge and theory, often reject – implicitly – the idea that true causes are structural, and look for factors which it is possible to influence.

It is on the basis of this *a priori* that we have the *so-called opportunity theory* and the view that criminals are not following deep 'impulses', but in a calculated way attack the weakest victims and, generally speaking, try to maximize their *benefits* while minimizing *costs* and *risks*.

According to this theory, the *true cause* of crime lies in the 'opportunities' which are offered to criminals, and that 'opportunity makes the thief'. After all, these could easily be reduced, at least in principle, by increasing the costs of lawbreaking.

This theory is of course partly correct and can explain many facts, such as different crime rates in different places or over time.[27]

Naturally, it is impossible to mediate in this debate among criminologists: their respective *a priori* mean that they can see *the* cause of crime in what is only *one* cause. This transformation – tacit and metaconscious – in the nature of things then leads each side to discredit *the* cause propounded by the other.

Here we can also see that the spirit is not always 'the dupe of the heart' (La Rochefoucauld): even something which can readily be seen as an example of intellectual 'intolerance' does not always have purely affective causes.

Of course, one could identify other typical definitions of the notion of cause. I will merely note the existence of what may be called the *ontological* definitions of this notion, those which suggest that the true causes are always located in a certain part of reality. For example, for some people it is ideas which make the world go round; for others, interests, relationships of production, and so on.

In any event, it is easy to find all kinds of examples where the *a priori* used by knowing subjects seem to be out of phase with reality. In situations where one would expect to see them adopting *a priori* which reflect the complexity of the real world, methodical thinking and ordinary thinking quite commonly explain complex phenomena on the basis of simple *a priori*.

This fact is surprising, unless we see in it a Simmel effect. As soon as the patient's wife in Morton White's example adopts – tacitly – a 'practical' meaning of the notion of cause, it is understandable that she regards the meal given to her husband as *the* cause of the stomach pain. Conversely, when only the structural characteristics of a system are considered worthy of the status of cause, the living conditions of the worse-off are usually seen as the cause of the link between social standing and crime rate.

At the same time, these Simmel effects lead to the formation of belief in causal relationships which have no counterpart in reality, or which are a caricature of reality. In other words, 'magical thinking' is never far away: it preys on methodical thinking just as it does on ordinary thinking.

What further complicates things is that, although causal beliefs can often be set against reality, there are cases where this is impossible. It is only in the first category that one can speak of magical thinking. Unfortunately there is no adequate word to describe these beliefs – so characteristic not only of ordinary thinking, but also of scientific thinking in its most normal functioning – which see A as *the* cause of B when A is only one of the factors responsible for B.

These examples serve to illustrate the main point in this section: the application of the principle of the single cause is made plausible by adopting a restrictive and particular definition of the notion of cause. At the same time, the process allowing the indefinite article (*a* cause) to be replaced by the definite article (*the* cause) is possible only if the choice is regarded as self-evident and therefore if it remains implicit.

SECOND EXAMPLE: SEEING CAUSES WHERE THERE ARE NONE

We speak of magical thinking in two cases: firstly when cause X, which the subject attributes to Y, belongs to a part of reality which the observer cannot see as capable of including the cause of Y. For example, we generally reject the hypothesis of *hysteresis*, where X can, without mediation, act on Y at some distance in time.

Another typical case in point is that in which the subject believes in a causal link where there is none and where it is in fact a matter of a contingent phenomenon.

A phenomenon is contingent when it is due to the coincidence of independent causal sequences – put simply, when it is a question of an accident.

There are of course cases where we unhesitatingly accept that a phenomenon *is* an accident. For example, to say that a particular event could easily not have happened if a particular person had not been there at precisely that time is tantamount to acknowledging the accidental nature of the event. However, even everyday events can appear ambiguous in this respect. Of the same road accident, one can say 'it happened because the driver was going too fast', or 'that would not have happened if, just at that moment, the driver . . .'. The first quote attributes a cause to the event in question. The second makes it a pure coincidence of causal sequences. Despite this ambiguity, the contingent nature of this type of event is nevertheless generally recognized. This is why the word 'accident' has lost its original link with the idea of chance in the phrase 'road accident'.

In many other cases, it is difficult to decide *a priori* whether an event or a state of affairs should be interpreted as a Cournot effect, that is, as the accidental product of a meeting of independent causal sequences, or whether it should be seen as the result of identifiable *causes*.

This ambiguity, by leaving the knowing subject a large freedom of choice, can easily produce distortions of inference. In a case of this kind, the person interpreting will apply – without realizing it – the principle of 'everything has a cause', whereas in fact it is a matter of a contingent event or state of affairs. This choice is all the more likely to happen the less the event or state of affairs in question has the external appearance of the accident, or the less it is expected, or, generally speaking, the less easily it evokes the idea of *chance*.

In the same way, according to Evans-Pritchard,[28] when an Azande encounters an exposed root, the tendency is to see this as the manifestation of an invisible force.

This type of interpretation is characteristic neither of the Azande alone, nor of magical thinking *as a whole*, and there are many examples to be found in ordinary thinking as well as in scientific thinking.

AN EXAMPLE FROM SOCIOLOGY

This case can be illustrated by an example. In a fine study of American teachers, the sociologist Steinberg[29] shows spectacular correlations between university teachers' specialisms and their religion. They are presented in table 6.1. More than the figure 1 indicates an over-representation, less than 1 an under-representation of each of the main religious denominations in each discipline.

Protestants are over-represented particularly in several classic scientific disciplines: earth sciences, chemistry, botany, zoology. Conversely, they are significantly under-represented in human sciences and the humanities. The latter seem particularly to attract *Catholics*. As for *Judaism*, this has the major share of all the human sciences, from anthropology through economics, political science, law and social work, to psychology. Medicine also has a strong Jewish over-representation, as do some of the natural sciences – physics, physiology, biochemistry and bacteriology.

The least that can be said is that this data does not readily evoke the idea of chance; on the contrary it gives the impression that there are elective relationships between disciplines chosen by the three denominations: *cultural* disciplines seem particularly to attract Catholics, whereas Jews opt for all the disciplines which, from psychology to medicine, include directly or indirectly a strong 'human relations' dimension. As for Protestants, they figure particularly in science.[30]

Obviously some data is harder to put into simple categories, such as the fact that Protestants seem to dominate in music and Catholics in fine arts; or that Jews seem to be attracted by certain natural sciences and not others. However it is clear that *statistical correlations* are never perfect, since major factors are always affected by minor ones. In other words, just as there are exceptions to every rule, there are peculiarities in every correlation.

Like most readers, no doubt, I concluded that these correlations were due to *real* causes: Protestants, Catholics and Jews were all guided in their professional choice by the characteristic ethic of the three religions. In other words their choice is explained by the fact that they subscribe to

Table 6.1

Disciplines	Representation		
	Protestant	*Catholic*	*Jewish*
Protestant			
Agriculture	1,42	0.50	0,05
Arts and crafts	1,18	1,05	0,22
Physical education	1,15	1,00	0,22
Journalism	1,12	0.61	0,55
Education	1,12	0.94	0,55
Commercial studies	1,05	1,00	0,89
Earth sciences	1,11	0,72	0,44
Chemistry	1,03	1,00	0,78
Botany	1,17	0,61	0,55
Zoology	1,12	0,61	0,78
Biology	1,05	0,89	0,78
Geography	1,20	0,72	0,22
Music	1,28	0,61	0,67
Catholic			
Art	0,97	1,22	0,67
Fine Arts	0,94	1,05	1,00
History	0,98	1,17	1,00
English	0,97	1,22	0,78
Religion	0,97	1,78	0,22
German	0,94	1,39	0,55
Foreign languages	0,77	1,78	0,89
Spanish	0,76	2,28	0,33
Philosophy	0,74	2,00	1,00
French	0,73	1,94	1,11
Jewish			
Engineering	0,97	0,89	1,11
Architecture	0,97	1,00	1,11
Medicine	0,88	0,78	2,55
Social work	0,88	0,94	1,89
Law	0,76	1,05	3,00
Physics	0,89	0,78	1,55
Physiology	1,00	0,67	1,33
Biochemistry	0,85	0,72	2,44
Bacteriology	0,89	0,77	2,00
Anthropology	1,00	0,44	1,44
Political science	0,97	0,89	1,78
Sociology	0,92	1,00	1,33
Psychology	0,92	0,94	1,55
Economics	0,91	0,89	1,78
Experimental psychology	0,88	0,72	2,33
Social psychology	0,74	0,94	2,22
Clinical psychology	0,70	0,78	4,00

different value systems. The humanities are generally more in keeping with the value-oriented nature of Catholicism; science and technology, with their ascetic dimension, fit in better with the values to which Protestants subscribe; Jews are attracted more to disciplines with a significant human relations element because of values inculcated in childhood and adolescence.

This interpretation could be called *cultural*, since it locates the causes of the correlations in the highest values characteristic of each religion.

An interpretation of this kind is easy to accept, for three reasons. Firstly, the *correlations* are close. They are also readily interpreted in the sense that one can easily see resemblances, if not between all the disciplines attracting the respective preferences of the three groups, at least between a large number of them.

Secondly, it is well known that there are correlations of the same kind in many other research projects. For example, the influence on the behaviour of Protestants of the ascetic values characteristic of their religion has been a constant theme since Weber's famous book *The Protestant Ethic and the Spirit of Capitalism*. Weber showed, for example, that schoolchildren in the Duchy of Baden tended to choose different subjects at school according to their religious denomination, with Protestants leaning more to scientific and technological subjects and Catholics to literary studies.[31] Taking up Weber's torch, Merton, in a classic study,[32] stressed the central role of Puritanism in the development of the ascetic ethic which for him characterized scientific life.

However, the credibility of this cultural interpretation is due to a third reason – that it is not easy to find an alternative interpretation for the correlations. In particular, the idea that they are due to Cournot effects, that is, to the chance encounter of independent causal sequences, is hard to swallow. In fact, the idea of chance seems to contradict the fact that similar correlations have been repeatedly observed. Although one sometimes accepts that an isolated and unexpected event is the product of chance, one is less ready to introduce this *a priori* about a *correlation*, especially when the latter tends to be present in various contexts.

In other words, one usually expects that a *correlation* is the result of *real causes*, even if the action of the latter is disrupted by adventitious circumstances. We also accept that these causes are *hidden* and that they can only be rediscovered by reconstruction or deduction. However, once again, it is hard for us to conceive that they might not be real.

When investigators have to interpret a recurrent *correlation*, they are likely to provide themselves straightaway with an *a priori* that the correlation must be interpreted as the effect of real causes.

Finally, the cultural interpretation of correlations has the advantage of introducing a *similarity* of nature between the cause and the effect.[33]

However, the best interpretation of this data is the one where they are seen as the product of Cournot effects, that is, of the coincidence of causal sequences totally independent from each other.[34]

Presented in summary form, this interpretation is as follows:

The time when it became conceivable for a child from a Jewish background – because of the increased social mobility of the American Jewish community – to go to university and think of becoming a university teacher coincided with a huge expansion in social sciences, human sciences, law and medicine. A fairly large number of teaching posts were therefore created in these disciplines.

No doubt the fact that the social mobility of the Jewish community increased at that time is not in itself a matter a chance, but the result of a process which is easy to analyse. Similarly, it is easy to explain why the human sciences, law and medicine expanded more at certain times than others.

However, the fact that the two causal sequences came together, that demand on the part of Jews grew at exactly the same time as the supply of posts expanded in certain disciplines and remained steady in others is purely *contingent*. In this sense, strange as this statement may seem at first sight, the over-representation of Jews in human sciences is purely and simply because of chance.

Choices by Protestants can in large measure be explained in the same way. Originally, when university teachers were virtually all Protestant, the disciplines in which there were the most teaching posts were those which met the most immediate economic, social and also religious needs. This is why teaching staff in agriculture, but also music, were principally Protestant. Generally speaking, disciplines which were established first tended to have over-representation of Protestants: for example, of the sciences, it was the oldest established – zoology, botany and chemistry, for example – which show Protestant over-representation, while newer ones like biochemistry and bacteriology are characterized by an over-representation of Jews.

In this way, a large part of the correlations thrown up by the findings can easily be explained on the basis of variations in the *structure of opportunities* over time.

Similarly, there are very strong arguments against the competing theory, the *cultural* interpretation. Firstly, correlations between disciplines and religious denominations are not stable over time. In tables similar to table 6.1 covering 1944, 1944–53, 1954–63 and post-1963, out of 73 disciplines, only twelve show the same structure in all three coefficients of representativity for two successive periods. Of the disciplines, only two show no change over the four periods in question – music and agriculture. It is one thing to try to explain the continued over-representation of Protestants in music on the basis of the Protestant ethic; but it seems unlikely that this applies to agriculture. In any event, the fact that there are changes over time in the correlations between disciplines and denominations runs counter to the idea of established cultural choices.

Secondly, the structure of over-and under-representation in table 6.1 is easier to piece together when account is taken not of the *content* of the different disciplines, but of *the history of their expansion*. For example, a simple guide[35] shows that those disciplines which expanded rapidly for three of the four years 1930, 1940, 1950 and 1960 (psychology, political science, anthropology and sociology) were also those with Jewish over-representation. The other disciplines reached a plateau before the influx of Jews and Catholics. This does indicate that increased opportunities played a particularly important part. The reason why Jews were not followed by Catholics is probably that there were other opportunities in Catholic institutions, and that Catholic entry into university teaching came later.

Overall, what emerges from table 6.1 is that Jews and Catholics hardly figure in slow growth disciplines, but are conspicuous in rapidly expanding disciplines *from the time when the two groups* experienced significant collective mobility.

We see therefore that a specialism/religion correlation on the basis of the coming together of independent causal sequences accounts for the data much more satisfactorily than a cultural explanation.

Nevertheless, this explanation is often grudgingly accepted: how can *chance*, an unreal, impalpable, imaginary factor, explain correlations, and moreover, correlations which are replicated in differing contexts? The unreal nature of chance usually leads investigators in this kind of situation to 'give themselves' a different *a priori*:

[the correlations in question have a cause]*

We must also emphasize that this *a priori* tends to guide investigators to a *cause* rather than to *causes*, for the reasons outlined in the previous section of this chapter. To explain why a particular discipline is chosen, investigators in fact start from the idea that such a crucial choice must indicate the basic values of the subject's personality. They will therefore find it quite plausible that values inculcated by a religious or philosophical upbringing will form the reservoir in which *the* cause of the choice must be sought, and interpret the notion of cause in the way indicated by case 7 of the previous section (see p. 162).

I have analysed this example in detail for two reasons. Firstly because it illustrates a particular, but significant, type of Simmel effect. Secondly, because it does not provoke too much affective resistance.

There is much more resistance – at least in my experience – when these effects of chance are illustrated by Schelling's models of segregation phenomena, for example, or by the various applications of opportunity theory.[36] The reasons for this resistance are the same as those which aroused, and still arouse, hostility to Darwinism and neo-Darwinism: how can *chance* explain a phenomenon as significant as the evolution of species?[37] Generally speaking, people find it hard to see why effects seen as significant should not be imputed to causes of the same degree of importance.

Conversely, there is very little resistance, for example, to explaining professional choice by reference to religion. Moreover, it is possible to argue that the success of Weber's *The Protestant Ethic and the Spirit of Capitalism* derives largely from its explanation of the most spectacular development of modern times by reference to a momentous cause.[38]

Kant unintentionally gives a reason for the proliferation of this particular – but important – type of Simmel effect. By making (in the *second analogy*) the 'everything has a cause' principle into a component principle of human thinking, that is, a kind of 'law of thought' analogous to the great principles of logic, he showed the decisive importance of this *a priori* in ordinary knowledge as well as in scientific knowledge. However, this *a priori*, like the principle of contradiction, is only a conjecture, valid in some cases but not in others.

Summary

Every theory produced by ordinary knowledge as well as scientific knowledge is surrounded by a halo of *a priori* of various kinds; logical, but also epistemological, ontological, linguistic, and so on.

This chapter looks at epistemological *a priori* linked with the way in which the notion of cause is used. Just as with logical *a priori*, these *a priori* can be of varying complexity. However, the tendency, by default, is to have the most restrictive *a priori* possible.

One *a priori* often regarded as self-evident is the principle that 'everything has a cause'. It is often seen as just as vital to the functioning of thinking as the great principles of logic. However, it is a principle of great obscurity; moreover, its status is not clear; 'analytical' or 'synthetic', *a priori* or *a posteriori*, of universal validity or not? Furthermore, the notion of cause can, according to context, have widely divergent meanings.

Theories of the kind 'A is the cause of B' are often the product of valid reasoning and implicit *a priori*. These *a priori* consist on the one hand of accepting that B has to have a cause, and on the other hand of conferring on the notion of cause a particular meaning. Thanks to these *a priori*, we can conclude that 'A is the cause of B' when the reasoning on which this statement is based allows us only to conclude – when it does not have these *a priori* – that 'A is the cause of B'.

Examples taken from sociology in particular, but also from history, illustrate this particular kind of Simmel effect.

These *a priori* can also make us see causes where there are none, that is, where chance and contingency give rise to regular patterns which have no cause, as illustrated by a detailed example taken from sociology.

Generally speaking, distortions of causal inference are not characteristic of magical thinking. They are also to be seen in scientific thinking. In neither case should we interpret these distortions irrationally. They stem from the interference of implicit *a priori* whose presence is vital to the normal everyday functioning of thought.

7

Truth is unique

One happiness is the whole of happiness; two is as if it no longer existed.

Ramuz

THE TWO TRAINS AND THE FLY

Two imaginary trains set off simultaneously, one from point O and the other from point P, and travel towards each other at constant speed. An equally imaginary insect – for example, a fly – faster than the trains, sets off at the same time as the first one from point O and flies continually between the two trains. The trains meet at point R. Since they are imaginary trains, there is no collision (see figure 7.1).

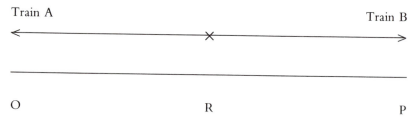

Figure 7.1

Most people who are asked where the fly is when the trains meet give the correct answer: at point R.

Without stopping at point R, the two trains then set off again for their starting point: train A towards O, and train B towards P. The fly continues to go backwards and forwards between the two trains.

Question:

Where will it be at the precise moment when the two trains arrive back at their starting point?

Most people reply either that the fly will be at O on train A, or at P on train B, or that it will be at point R, halfway between O and P. Others say they do not know.

Position of
trains

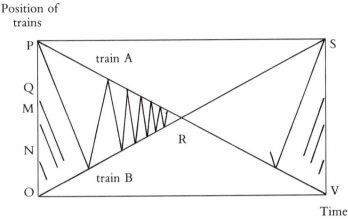

Figure 7.2

In fact, it is impossible to determine where it is: it could be *anywhere*.

To understand this, we need to refer to figure 7.2. Time is shown on the *x*-axis, and space – the line OP – on the *y*-axis. The broken line represents the movement of the fly: if it goes continually from one train to the other, it is in fact at point R when the two trains meet. They then immediately set off again for their starting point; this journey is shown by RS for train A and RV for train B. The movement of the fly could have been shown in triangle RSV by a broken line like the one in triangle OPR. This has not been drawn because it would have been necessary to show not one but an infinity of broken lines ending at all possible points on SV. If the fly had set off, not from P, but from O, Q, M, N . . . or from any other point on OP, it would in all cases have ended up at point R when the trains met. Its movement when setting off from R is therefore the mirror image in triangle RSV not only of the particular broken line shown in OPR, but of any line of this kind beginning at any point on OP. *The movement of the fly is predictable when the trains are going towards each other, but unpredictable when they are going away from each other.*

Truth is therefore unique in the first case, *multiple* in the second case.

The fact that the correct answer is so hard to arrive at through intuition shows the importance, for ordinary knowledge, but also as we shall see, for methodical knowledge, of an essential epistemological *a priori*:

[*truth is unique*]*.

From this principle we deduce, for example, that, when two answers to a question seem possible, either one of the two is wrong, or both are wrong. But we usually reject the idea that both can be true.

The surprise and curiosity aroused by the riddle of the trains and the fly come about because it violates this principle in a spectacular way: *all possible replies – and there is an infinity of them – are correct*; there is no reason why one should be preferable to the others. This discrediting of the principle of the uniqueness of truth, and the appearance of a world (triangle RSV) where *everything* is correct in the literal sense of the phrase, leads not to a feeling of relief, but one of unease.

Of course, the example is very artificial; it is located in an imaginary world, and the notion of truth can in this case have only a *formal* meaning. But it has the advantage of bringing out an important point – the difficulty we have in accepting that truth can be other than unique.

ORDINARY KNOWLEDGE AND PHILOSOPHICAL TRADITION

Philosophical tradition and common sense join forces to corroborate this principle of the uniqueness of truth. Not only is it essential to ordinary knowledge, but it is *implicitly* present in many theories and, generally speaking, in lines of argument, including those which try to deny its importance. In fact, as we will see in an example from Montaigne – or Rorty – it is the nub of all sceptical reasoning. However, since it usually appears only in a latent state, it can, unknown to the knowing subject, twist or distort the conclusions which the latter draws in all good faith from arguments which are totally unexceptionable in their explicit part.

The implication of this principle is that, when several solutions to a problem or several different answers to the same question are possible, we must pare them down. In its strong version, it implies that when it seems impossible to choose between several solutions or answers, the reason is in fact that there is no truth. In the case of the riddle of the trains and the fly, this strong version would lead us to conclude – wrongly – that the question is impossible to answer.

The respect we have for this principle derives mainly from the crucial part it plays in everyday life. For example, it is used – metaconsciously, of course – in perception. Depending on my location in a room, I can perceive a cylinder as a parallelepiped, as a disc, or . . . as a cylinder. However, one thing I am sure of is that all these hypotheses cannot be valid at the same time; while there are in reality discs, parallelepipeds and cylinders, there is nothing which can be characterized in these three ways at the same time. I must therefore make a choice, and the correct label to give it is that which will consider the object in question *as it is in reality*.

In other words, the principle of the uniqueness of truth is of virtually universal validity in everyday life. I may have various ideas about what a particular object *is*; but I am sure that in reality it can correspond to only one of these hypotheses.

This *a priori* principle, like others, is therefore of crucial importance, which is why it is generally used in an implicit way and is only metaconsciously perceived by the subject. However, like many other *a priori* principles of the same kind, it is not really of universal validity. In fact it often happens that several different explanations of the same phenomenon can be regarded as true. In the case of perception itself, a picture taken at ground level is no less true than one taken from an aeroplane.

Here we have a familiar situation: often the principle of the uniqueness of truth applies in an obvious way, for example, when we hesitate over the geometrical nature of an object which is visible only from a particular viewpoint. Sometimes it does not apply at all. However, there are ambiguous situations. In this case, as in the riddle of the trains and the fly, the subject often tends to choose *by default* the simplest solution and to regard the principle as valid. In the same way, the principle of contradiction or that of the excluded middle are readily accepted in ambiguous situations.

However, *in reality*, all situations are possible: far from being reduced to being *either* unique *or* non-existent, truth can also be multiple.

Ordinary knowledge is not the only source of our trust in the principle of the uniqueness of truth. It has also been sanctioned by an ancient philosophical tradition. As Perelman points out, the Ancients tradition-ally gave the name *colour* to interpretations favourable to one side in court proceedings. The term had a pejorative meaning; it indicates that they saw it as self-evident that there is always *one* truth about facts. Quintilian thought that this truth was known to lawyers, who tended to give it a *colour* which altered it.[1]

These visual images in fact reveal a traditional conception of know-ledge, which writers such as Richard Rorty carefully analysed. Accord-ing to this conception, knowledge is a *mirror of nature*, a reflection in the mind of reality as it is.[2] In this tradition, it is clearly difficult to avoid the principle of the uniqueness of truth.

Rorty argues[3] that, in Descartes and Locke, knowledge is conceived not as '*knowledge that*', but as '*knowledge of*': we model 'knowing' on 'seeing'. The aporia to which this theory leads were clearly recognized by Kant, who saw that, if we cling to this assimilation of knowledge and perception, it is impossible to account for the ability of the knowing subject to come up with *propositions* – and not just *images* – and to subscribe to them. The genius of Kant was to replace the traditional '*knowledge of*' by '*knowledge that*'.

Rorty concludes, however, that Kant did not go far enough: maintaining the Cartesian approach of a distinction between internal and external space, he too sees knowledge as a mental reflection of external reality. No doubt this reflection is no longer a mere copy of reality, but is given *form* by understanding. Nevertheless, Kant's faithfulness to Cartesian ideas still leads him – and a large part of modern philosophy with him – to the conclusion that truth must be nothing if not unique.[4]

In other words, Descartes and Locke, and also Kant and those after him, adopt the principle of the uniqueness of truth.

Moreover, this principle is so incontrovertibly self-evident that the main argument of scepticism is to show that, in regard to all kinds of subjects, including the most weighty, it is impossible to decide between divergent opinions. The simple fact that one cannot arrive at a unique truth is enough to prove that in no way can one arrive at the truth. The whole history of scepticism shows that uniqueness is generally seen as an essential – or more precisely *analytical* – attribute of truth. Truth is by definition unique, just as bicycles have two wheels.

Underlying the whole of one of the most important works of scepticism, *In Defence of Raymond Sebond*, is the principle that truth is nothing if not unique: *two* truths can only be two *opinions*. Simply by accumulating and juxtaposing a host of extremely divergent opinions on all kinds of topics, Montaigne tries to imbue the reader with the certainty that there is no truth. He is well aware that he has only to pile up 'truths' for them to assume, simply because of their multiplicity, the status of ineffectual opinions.

It is difficult to say what Montaigne's final objective is. Perhaps it was to show that, since the understanding is unable to choose for certain between divergent opinions, there is no reason to believe that the Protestant interpretation of the Bible is superior.[5] This is of no consequence. What is clear is that the nub of his reasoning lies in the principle that truth *is* unique and assumes that the reader is also convinced of this principle.

The pattern of reasoning which Montaigne so brilliantly used has often been adopted since his time. The simple fact that there can be several equally respectable theories about the same subject is often used as an argument in favour of scepticism – an argument all the more effective for its remaining implicit.

For example, the unremarkable statement that on many subjects historians cannot choose between divergent interpretations has led to the conclusion that their aim should therefore not be to establish historical truth – a task assumed to be impossible – but to 'create the existing'.[6] Beneath this 'modern' phrase lies a classical theory – that, since historians cannot claim, because of their duty to *interpret* facts, to present anything other than *their* interpretation of them, their activity cannot be *cognitive* in nature.[7]

Although this view is worth while and appealing, it is significant, on the one hand, that the nub of the argument on which it is based lies once more in the postulate of the uniqueness of truth; and, on the other hand, that the principle is seen as so glaringly self-evident that it is not necessary to discuss it, or even to be aware of it.

The same line of reasoning is found in all sceptical proof:

1) Phenomenon P can give rise to various interpretations;
2) It is impossible to tell which of these interpretations is objectively preferable to the others;
3) [Truth is unique]*;
4) It is futile to speak of truth in relation to the interpretations of P;
5) The importance of a particular interpretation of P cannot, in this case, be based on its truth value;
6) It must therefore derive from the fact that it expresses other values, for example, *aesthetic* values.

Conclusion 6) has an *ad libitum* character, and one can stop at scepticism without going as far as aestheticism; but it is frequent enough to deserve a mention.

One can also draw from statements 1) to 5) another typical conclusion, which could be called *Durkheimian*: that, since no objective criterion allows us to choose between the interpretations of P, the reason why a particular one is chosen is that it has the force characteristic of collective *representations* – in other words, because it is *socially* accepted. The 'conventionalist' position, a classic one in the philosophy of science, is also based on type 1) to 5) reasoning. More particularly, the move from a 1) to 5) pattern to the conventionalist position is because of an extra implicit statement:

5') [A statement is regarded as true *either* because it can be proved *or* because it is considered as such by virtue of convention or of collective representations]*.

Rorty of course, after convincing himself that the very notion of truth is meaningful only in the philosophy of Descartes and Locke (which made knowledge a mirror of nature and which Kant, according to Rorty, did not go far enough in changing), arrives at a conventionalist position by means of reasoning, the logical skeleton of which is statements 1) to 5') above:

The True and the Right are matters of social practice.[8]

As with all conventionalists, this conclusion is wholly based on two implicit statements – on statement 5'), which starkly sets (exploiting the principle of the excluded middle) *objectively* based beliefs against *socially* based beliefs;[9] and on statement 3), that 'truth is unique'.

My reason for making this point is in no way to 'refute' Rorty, but to give another example of the way in which it is difficult to divest oneself of the principle of the uniqueness of truth. Although it is not universally valid, it is of such decisive importance in ordinary knowledge that it is very hard to escape from it, even when, like Rorty, one is trying to *break* with philosophical tradition and launch into *post-modernity*.

Its weight is such that it is useful to show by means of several simple examples that it is possible for truth not to be unique, without having to draw from this statement a sceptical or conventionalist conclusion.

TWO EXAMPLES

That truth can be the opposite of unique can be seen in various examples, and there are two particularly important cases in point where the notion of truth is not discredited by being multiple.

As Henri Atlan says, a computer can be described in two ways: either based on the *intentions* of the engineer who built it as a machine designed to perform certain functions and constructed so as to do this best; or based on the *mechanisms* located in it. In other words, the machine can be described in a *teleological* way or in a *mechanical* way.

This familiar example shows that an object can sometimes be described in different *languages*, with all these descriptions being relevant and correct. The difficulty arises because one does not always know *a priori* whether a particular language is appropriate for a given phenomenon. In the case of a watch, one can easily introduce the hypothesis that it was designed by a watchmaker and made in order to fulfil a clearly defined function; but this teleogical language is of doubtful significance in other circumstances.

Truth can be not unique in another example – when it is a matter of a reality so complex that it cannot be apprehended except by means of simplifications. In other words, it is often impossible to identify all the causes of a phenomenon. In this case, certain causal chains will be selected within a network which is too complex to apprehend. Each of these chains could 'correspond to reality' and, in this sense, be regarded as *true*. However, the same phenomenon could be explained by several, even many, causal chains of this type, with all of them having claims to be regarded as *true*. Similarly, one can generally associate several accounts with the same events. Among these accounts, several could give the feeling that they are *correct*. In any event, plurality is not seen here as implying that the notion of truth is discredited.

According to Simmel,[10] the fact that the knowing subject encounters situations where truth is multiple is an example of what he calls the *freedom of the spirit*. This is apparent, for example, in the sometimes surprising and unpredictable nature of paradigms used in sciences. Before Ricardo, nobody thought that one could speak of international trade *in this way*. The operation of the *freedom of the mind* is responsible for the appearance of theories which are mutually incommensurate, that is, representing non-convergent *viewpoints*, each of which corresponds to a truth.

It is easier to recognize that one is in a 'multiple truth' situation when the various truths relative to a phenomenon convey institutionalized viewpoints. For example, one accepts that two *recognized* disciplines have different *viewpoints* regarding the same phenomenon, or that they approach it through different *paradigms*. However, in many ambiguous situations, particularly when viewpoints are not institutionalized, one applies *by default* the principle of the uniqueness of truth.

It is a common phenomenon in ordinary knowledge – 'intuition' reveals such a strong tendency (as shown by the example of the trains and the fly)[11] to apply *by default* the principle of the uniqueness of truth that it is baffled when it encounters cases such as this.[12] However, this is true also of scientific knowledge. There will be no difficulty in identifying numerous episodes in the history of human sciences (examples could be found in the natural sciences as well) indicating the adherence of the whole of the scientific community to the principle of the uniqueness of truth in situations of 'multiple truth'.

A 'multiple truth' situation is created therefore either when the same subject can be dealt with in different languages which cannot be translated into each other, or when its complexity means a choice has to be made. The two following sets of examples illustrate this distinction; moreover, the two can be combined.

THE CASE OF MULTIPLE PARADIGMS: THE EXAMPLE OF THE GENETIC PARADIGM AND THE FUNCTIONAL PARADIGM

To understand the nature of the distinction between *genetic* paradigm and *functional* paradigm, I will use an example from Max Weber as a starting point.

In his article on Protestant sects in the United States,[13] written on his return from a visit there at the beginning of this century, Weber asked himself the following question: whereas industrialization and modernization seem to have been accompanied in most Western societies by a decline of traditional religions, this is not the case in the United States. In this, the most modern of all societies, religiosity remains very strong. Why?

The question is in fact enigmatic and the answer far from obvious. It shows Weber's idea of the function of sociology: to make intelligible phenomena which are not immediately so.

His answer can be formalized as follows:

1) The United States is distinguished from the older European nations such as France and Germany by certain characteristics. For example, the symbols of social stratification are less marked in the United States. The reason is that it never experienced the system of legal stratification which left its mark in the other two countries (the *états* in France, the *Stände* in Germany), and another factor was the egalitarian ideology with which the young nation was imbued. Similarly, social mobility is easier in the United States than in the old European societies. In any event, the myth of the equality of opportunity is strong in the United States, whereas in France and Germany there is a widespread idea that there is a natural social order and that people should stay in their allotted place in it.

2) From the religious point of view, whereas France and Germany are characterized by the existence of a dominant Church, the United States has a proliferation of sects. This difference is itself easily explained by historical factors.

3) Despite the power of the egalitarian myth in the United States, it is clearly a stratified society. For historical reasons easy to explain, elites tend to be Protestant, the main reason being that the first immigrants were Protestant.

4) The importance in the United States of impersonal social contact is an essential characteristic of modern societies: all day long, people who do not know each other make contact with each other, enter into reciprocal commitments, and get involved in relationships based on strength or power.

5) Impersonal social contact – and more generally impersonal inter-actions – call for, on the part of each protagonist, an assessment of how far the other is trustworthy and will resist pressure, and all kinds of other traits. In traditional societies, where interaction is more personal, actors can take their cue from the actual knowledge which they have of each other before they decide on mutual commitments or how their inter-action will be conducted. In modern societies, the impersonal nature of contact means that interactors need recourse to indirect methods. In France and Germany (we are speaking of course about the beginning of this century), it is stratification symbols which are natural candidates for this role. In the United States these symbols (symbols relating to dress, language, level of education, lifestyle, property ownership, and so on) are less marked, less immediately interpreted. There is therefore a need for something else: for the reasons given above, in the United States the 'Protestant' character plays the role of 'functional substitute' – to borrow Merton's phrase[14] – for the stratification symbols used in Europe.

6) The 'sectarian' nature of American Protestantism leads to sharp competition between the sects. The latter are well aware that they can give out certificates of worthiness or social standing to ease the social life of their recipients. They therefore try to outbid each other and end up by playing a crucial part in everyday life.

In essence, Weber's theory consists in listing the differences between the United States and France and Germany, and in showing that they involve behaviour: for the former, it is religious symbols, for the latter, stratification symbols, which catalyse the myriad interactions constituting society. Weber also gives meaning to these behaviour patterns by means of psychological statements which are simple and readily acceptable: protagonists in an interaction want to be able to assess the credibility and standing of each other; leaders of sects exploit their position to distribute certificates of worthiness and social respectability, and try to tax their members at the highest level so that they can rise on the prestige scale.

This brilliant analysis is interesting in more than one respect. It helps to solve an enigma. Moreover, it illustrates in a telling manner the procedures and principles of a *language*.

The first characteristic of this language is the total absence of recourse to historical data. Weber in no way tries to show that the *present* religiosity of Americans derives from that nation's *past*. The analysis is on the contrary entirely synchronic: it is the *present* American system of *stratification* which explains the exceptional level of religiosity in a highly industrialized nation. Furthermore, Weber establishes the plausible nature of this relationship between the two synchronic variables by aggregating them. In other words, he analyses it as the result of a multitude of individual attitudes and actions. He describes individual behaviour patterns as conforming to a simple principle: determine one's trust in others on the basis of signals that are reasonably trustworthy.

To be clear about it, we can call this language *functional*,[15] in keeping with current usage.

This theory is certainly valid. In fact, all its propositions are readily acceptable; moreover, they are internally consistent. There does not seem to be any possible serious objection to Weber's theory. In this sense, we can therefore say it is *true*.[16]

Obviously, other explanations could be given of the same phenomenon, particularly the usual one that religion has always played an important role in the United States. It is in this way that historians would no doubt answer Weber's question. They would explain why, at the time of English colonization, religion loomed large, and why this remained so afterwards. Ideally, their analysis would consist in showing how past events or states of affairs are linked over time to explain *present* religiosity in the United States.

If this is so, the historians' analysis would be conducted in a language different from that of the sociologist: the language traditionally called *genetic*. The *explanandum* is the same in both cases: to elucidate a striking *present-day* difference between *industrial* societies which are in many ways very similar.

Both these languages – *genetic* and *functional* – have been successfully applied to all kinds of subjects.

For example, either of them can be used to account for the nature and form of institutions. The explanation of the widespread use of the simple majority rule in determining collective preferences can be either by the *genetic* method, by analysing the circumstances in which this technique first appeared and the factors in its development,[17] or by the *functional* method, by showing that individuals would be likely to choose it if they had to devise the least bad possible rule for determining the collective will from individual wills.[18]

Similarly, classical theories have explained, in *functional* language, why in 'archaic' societies the unanimity rule was as widely used as the majority rule in modern societies,[19] or why marrying one's maternal cross-cousin is much more common than marrying one's paternal cross-cousin.[20]

With sufficient data, it would be natural to try to explain the extent of these institutions in archaic societies *genetically*.

In all these examples, the logical skeleton of *functional* analysis is indeed the same as that used in Weber's case.

For example, Samuel Popkin's explanation is that the unanimity rule is normal in archaic societies because, in a society near subsistence level – as is usually the case in this kind of society – any collective decision can have extremely serious repercussions on certain groups within that society. Popkin cites the example of the modernization of harvesting, which can threaten the very lives of those dependent on gathering. This kind of development can claim to be legitimate only if it gives everyone the chance to oppose a decision which could be fatal to them. The endless debates leading to a collective decision in a unanimity rule regime are no disadvantage in a subsistence economy where, as observation confirms, working time is much shorter than time available.

As in the Weber example, this analysis does not use historical data. It does not try to explain the spread of the rule by a chain of events or states of affairs in the past. It deduces the existence of the institution in question from the services which it renders to members of the particular society, in other words, from the *functions* which it performs in the particular social system.

The two *truths* determined by the genetic method and the functional method are sometimes complementary. Very often, when both are available, they are *juxtaposed* in the same way as the opinions described in

In Defence of Raymond Sebond. The language, data and mode of demonstration used in the two cases are in fact so different that it is difficult, contrary to the advice of people such as Durkheim, to keep the two kinds of analysis together.

As is readily deduced from the history of human sciences, the two languages are rather perceived as deeply *antithetical*: only *one* of them is regarded as likely to give rise to *true* theories.

FUNCTIONALISM VERSUS HERMENEUTICS

This point can be illustrated by reference to attempts by the major writers to prove the superiority either of *functional* language (Malinowski, for example) or of *genetic* language (Ricoeur or Habermas, for example).

Ernest Gellner has argued that to understand Malinowski, one of the pioneers of functional analysis, we must not underestimate the influence which Ernst Mach had on him, as on many other writers of the same generation:[21] a measure of Mach's influence as physicist and philosopher of sciences is seen in the fact that his ideas were debated in the works of both Lenin and Einstein.

Mach's *empirio-criticism* represented the wish to rid physics of all *unobservable* elements. In other words, his grand idea was that science should limit itself to determining the relationships between observable phenomena. In this way, Mach is demonstrating, in a particularly brilliant way, a classical position (Gellner says that Lenin was right to compare Mach with Berkeley) which at various times has been propounded in virtually all areas of scientific activity.

It is the same doctrine which led for example to *behaviourism* in psychology, or *positivism* in sociology. For example, *positivist* sociologists[22] have tried to eliminate all references to the motives of the social actor on the grounds that they are not observable.

Malinowski is not content passively to follow these principles, and in fact has good reasons for endorsing them. As Gellner says, Malinowski as a Pole – perhaps influenced by the turbulent history of his country – reflects on whether historical knowledge is sound and trustworthy, and very quickly reaches the same conclusions as the proponents of *Historismus*: there can be no objective truth in history; one cannot *explain* historical phenomena, only *interpret* them; the sensitivity and perspective of historians are inevitably affected by the period and the social context in which they live; they cannot ignore the interests and preoccupations of their time; they must use available means to reconstruct all kinds of invisible data, such as the moods of historical characters; and there is no objective means of verifying this kind of reconstruction.

The arguments of 'historism' are based on remarks which are not only perfectly acceptable, but are in no way cut of the ordinary.

For example, it is clear that the history of 1802 cannot be told in the same way in 1815 as in 1885. For observers in 1885, but not those in 1815, 1802 is the year when Victor Hugo was born. Similarly, the appearance and decline of certain concepts mean that the same events cannot be analysed in the same way at different times. For instance, the history of literature at the beginning of the nineteenth century cannot be written in the same way before and after the appearance of *romanticism*;[23] and there are a host of reasons – which have nothing to do with advances in documentation – why the history of the French Revolution will be different today from yesterday. It is therefore incontrovertible that the answer to certain historical questions cannot fail to be affected by the status and perspective of the observer.

However, Malinowski's treatment of this conclusion is hyperbolic. Having convinced himself that it was fundamentally impossible to reconstruct the past objectively, he concludes that it is impossible for history to attain the cognitive objectives which it claims to set itself.[24] Just as behaviourists and positivists exclude the subjectivity of the social actor from their purview, Malinowski decides to banish the *past* and to create a resolutely synchronic science devoted to studying the relationships between observable variables here and now.

Malinowski's conclusion therefore is that *diachronic* truths – those which use the *genetic* method – are mere pseudo-truths: only findings from *synchronic* or *functional* analysis deserve the name 'truth'.

Several decades later, Malinowski's hyperboles reappeared in another guise. The *structuralists* of the 1960s – who had rediscovered how important and productive functional analysis was – were convinced that they had replaced once and for all the uncertainties of the *genetic* method by a language allowing scientific certainty.

In both cases, the argument is as follows:

1) A social or historical phenomenon can be explained in two ways: functionally or genetically;
2) [Truth is unique]*;
3) [Only one of the two types of explanation is acceptable];
4) Genetic type explanations are dubious because . . .
5) Only functional analysis is acceptable.

However, one has only to change round the words 'genetic' and 'functional' wherever they occur to come up with the alternative position.

For example, Ricoeur conducts a long analysis, in his remarkable work on the philosophy of history, of the essence of historical explanation, and concludes that it lies in *narrative*: to explain a particular phenomenon is to produce a correct and therefore acceptable narrative which shows the phenomenon in question as resulting from the events and states of affairs which preceded it; a successful historical narrative is therefore in effect one which allows us to understand how state of affairs X_{t+1} arose from the immediately preceding state of affairs X_t.[25] In other words, historical method is the *genetic* method: it unravels the meaning of the past.

The mere fact of asking the question about the *essence* of historical explanation obviously in itself implies that only one *mode* of historical explanation can be regarded as acceptable.[26]

Ricoeur's main thesis – assimilating historical explanation to narrative – is proved by a line of reasoning whose outline consists of the same statements, apart from changing round the words *genetic* and *functional*.[27]

In effect, on the basis of the *historist* tradition and contemporary American writing on the philosophy of history, Ricoeur develops the idea that there can be no historical interpretation which dispenses with the observer: it always derives from the coming together of a historical theme and a person, the latter seeing it inevitably through his or her interests – in the intellectual meaning of the word – and those of the time. The idea that there can be an objective truth independent of the observer is therefore of necessity an *illusion*.

The basic outline of Habermas's reasoning in *Knowledge and Human Interests* is virtually identical to that of Ricoeur, though it is dressed up completely differently: he suggests that Dilthey was not far from the mark when he rejected objectivism in history. Every historical analysis which claims to be *objective* and independent of the characteristics of the observer is of necessity false, since it contradicts the very essence of explanation in history, which is always *interpretation*.

For Habermas, therefore, the idea that one can put oneself in the shoes of other people or make oneself into a contemporary of social actors in the past is an illusion arising from the theory of truth-as-a-copy-of-reality and from the worship of objectivity. Habermas therefore fundamentally disagrees with Dilthey's aim – which was also Weber's – to 'elevate the understanding of the singular to universal validity'.[28]

In short, the proponents of functional analysis, and those of genetic analysis, implicitly use an identical pattern of reasoning – one which encapsulates statements 1) to 5) above. The difference between the two lies in the suspension dots at the end of 4). For Malinowski, *genetic* explanations are dubious for the reasons indicated by the historists, principally because they cannot be objective. For *hermeneuticians, functional*[29] explanations are dubious because they fail to see that historical truths are always a matter of interpretation and that they lay claim to an objectivity which is purely illusory.

Finally, the principle of the uniqueness of truth has had the effect of creating a double truth, and it seems as if everybody has subscribed to one of the two vague sets of concepts outlined in the following lists:

Positivism	Anti-positivism
Rejection of hermeneutics	Hermeneutics
Explanation	Interpretation
Synchronic analysis	Diachronic analysis
Functional analysis	Genetic analysis
Truth = objectivity	'Meaning' versus objectivity

These lists are not very precise and the meaning of the terms can vary according to context or author: for example, there are variants of positivism and hermeneutics. The important thing, however, is the permanence of these 'truths' over time, and the fact that they are generally regarded as mutually exclusive. Moreover – but it is not my intention to look at this point – this situation tends to give rise to what Pareto called *oscillations*, with one truth tending to dominate the other, and vice versa.

THE OBJECTIVE MULTIPLICITY OF PARADIGMS AND LANGUAGES

In *reality*, and as the example from Weber at the beginning of this section adequately demonstrates, there are situations where a particular phenomenon seems capable of being explained equally convincingly in completely different languages – for example, in synchronic functional language and diachronic genetic language.

There are also situations where only genetic language seems to apply. In this respect, Passmore mentions the matter of the sudden disappearance of witchcraft in the eighteenth century.[30] A question such as this, he says, calls for an answer in terms of *narrative*; and he argues that the only way to answer it is to *describe* in as great a detail as possible changes in attitudes to witchcraft revealed in documents of the time. It is rather difficult to accept that Passmore's example is a particularly good one.[31] It is true, however, that very often one is right in thinking that the best way of *explaining* a state of affairs is to describe in the most factual way possible the changes which led to it. Nevertheless there are subjects where *functional* type explanations seem to be desperately weak.[32]

Conversely, there are cases where it is difficult to use genetic language. For example, when Popkin looks at the reason for the unanimity rule in traditional societies, he offers a convincing *functional* explanation which is summarized as follows: in a society close to subsistence level, individuals want to be able to veto collective decisions which might endanger their very survival; in this kind of society, there is plenty of time available, so that people can easily participate in the long discussions leading to unanimous collective decisions. It is much more difficult to give a *historical* explanation of this, since we have no evidence on the origin and development of the institution. Even assuming that this practical difficulty was removed, the genetic method – because by its very nature it emphasizes the *particular* conditions which led in specific cases to the appearance of the institution in question – would have difficulty in explaining its virtually universal presence in traditional societies.

The same could be said about the functional explanations suggested by Lévi-Strauss as to why marriage with a maternal cross-cousin is preferred: it means that there is a greater movement of women between the basic units of society and therefore a better group integration. There is no really convincing *genetic* alternative to this theory.

Historical arguments – which writers such as Malinowski or Habermas use to reach different conclusions – are also valid only in particular situations. There are in fact historical questions which, by their very nature, are based on *interpretation* and to which it is futile to try to give a single objective answer. There are others, however, which are meaningful only if an attempt is made to find a single answer to them and if one thinks as a consequence that this can be done.

The second case in point is illustrated by the post-Weber debate on *The Protestant Ethic and the Spirit of Capitalism*. It established once and for all that Weber's theory was *objectively* unacceptable and that what was needed was a *different* explanation of the correlations between Protestantism and capitalism.[33]

The example given in the previous chapter also illustrates a question with a single answer; of the two possible explanations (*cultural* explanation and explanation by the theory of opportunity) of correlations between religion and specialization among American university teachers, one is acceptable and the other not.

In these two examples, the very nature of the debate implies a single objective answer. In other words, it is hard to see how, in such cases, one could come up with an acceptable answer which did not entirely ignore the subjectivity of the analyst.

Conversely, on a question such as the causes of the French Revolution, it is difficult to see how one could move towards a *single* answer which *was not affected* by the historian's subjectivity.

Similarly, we saw in the previous chapter that an objective answer could be given to questions of the kind 'is X *a* cause of Y?', but not those of the kind 'what is *the* cause of Y?'. The former imply in principle a single answer whose validity must be capable of being verified objectively. The latter, however, exclude the possibility of a single decisive answer: they can be answered only if the observer comes up with an *interpretation* of them, which is of necessity affected by his or her subjectivity.

In reality, therefore, the explanation of historical and social phenomena has varying characteristics. *To some questions, a single objective answer can be given; to others, not.* Some questions can receive and have received multiple answers of equal validity deriving from different *modes of explanation* and *languages*. In other cases, one language may give a convincing answer to a question, while another seems unable to produce an acceptable answer.

The varied nature of these situations – of which an exhaustive description is impossible – provides arguments for both sides; for *hermeneuticians*, the fact that there are questions without an objective answer; for *objectivists*, the fact that there are questions with a single answer.

However, the unilateral nature of the conclusions of both sides is less the result of bias than of the reasoning in statements 1) to 5). The reason why the vague concepts in the lists on page 00 seem unchanging over time is that they emanate less from the passions (very problematical) they are capable of arousing, than from a simple innocuous principle which can easily claim to be *self-evident*; the principle that [truth is unique]*.

THE DISTINCTION BETWEEN CAUSAL EXPLANATION AND TELEOLOGICAL EXPLANATION

The example of the distinction between genetic explanation and functional explanation is not unique; on the contrary, it is typical. As soon as it is possible to explain a phenomenon in two different languages, it often happens that reasons are adduced to show that one of the explanations is *the* correct one. The pattern of reasoning is always the one which I looked at above, where the principle of unique truth plays a central role.

It is also to be found in the distinction between causal explanation and teleological explanation. The possibility of accounting for certain phenomena in a *causal* way or a *teleological* way does not only apply to watches and computers, but also to 'natural' phenomena. No doubt teleological language is generally regarded as inappropriate for physical or chemical phenomena, but competition between the two languages is evident when it comes to biological, psychological or social phenomena, being particularly fierce in the latter two. However, it very often happens that, because of the principle of the uniqueness of truth, one of the languages is credited with the desire to be monopolistic.

Marxist tradition provides a classic example of this kind of process; it is an example so well known that a brief survey will suffice. In a famous passage, Engels argues that ideas can be explained by their social *causes* and condemns as *ideology* the practice of explaining them *teleologically* on the basis of the questions which they try to answer and the problems which they try to solve:

> [Ideologues] work with purely intellectual material which they unthinkingly regard as produced by thought and which they do not try to explore further by comparing it with a more distant process independent of thought. And this seems self-evident to them.[34]

In retrospect, this short extract can be said to be one of the most influential of modern times, since it propounds the basic principle of Marxist materialism. Ideas – political, ethical or philosophical, for example – must not be understood, says Engels, as an attempt by those who enunciate them to resolve particular questions. To adopt this kind of perspective would be to deploy *ideology*. If we want to explain ideas *scientifically*, we must on the contrary relate them to 'a more distant process, independent of thought'. In other words, ideas must be explained not in a *teleological*, but in a *causal* way; not on the basis of the *objectives* which they seem to address, but of the social context in which they find themselves.

No more productive Pandora's box than this was ever opened. Perhaps for the first time in the history of human thought, it was proposed to consider ideas as things.

If one thinks about it, the novelty of this argument, formulated moreover in a careful way, is in fact truly astounding, since at the stroke of a pen it discredits an age-old intellectual activity. Without ever questioning it, historians of ideas try to explain ideas by means of ideas. For example, historians of philosophy will naturally analyse Kant's thought as an answer to certain questions. Similarly, historians of painting or music will normally try to explain the works they are dealing with on the basis of the painter's or musician's aims and their reaction to other works of the period. Engels argues that all that is derived from *ideological* analysis; a *scientific* analysis of ideas should be *causal* and not *teleological*.

Here again, I think it is less a matter of prejudice than the application of an epistemological principle which Engels regards as self-evident – that one cannot *really* explain a phenomenon in two radically different ways.

What leads me to this hypothesis is that Engels's argument, far from being characteristic of Marxism, is to be found in a wide variety of writers.

For example, there are observations in Durkheim which are very close to those of Engels. He also propounds the principle that explaining ideas is a matter of showing that they are the effects of social factors: moral ideas must therefore be explained on the basis of 'moral life'. As for ethics, Durkheim disagrees that it can explain for us anything about moral life, since 'all the questions normally asked by ethics have a bearing . . . not on things, but on ideas.'[35] Moreover, Durkheim also speaks of *ideological* analysis in relation to the mode of analysis which tries to explain ideas by means of ideas. As with Engels, there is for Durkheim a scientific way (*causal*) and a misleading way (*teleological*) of explaining ideas.

This dogmatism nowadays seems very disconcerting. If there is an example where two languages are complementary rather than exclusive, it is this one. In analysing Kant's thought, one cannot ignore the problems posed by Hume. One cannot therefore ignore the teleological dimension of the explanation of ideas. On the other hand, it is obvious that the social 'context' in which writers live can also help to explain their work. Engels is right to suggest that Calvin does not merely 'rethink' Luther, but that his ideas stem from a different situation and context.

Despite this, under the influence of the axiom of the uniqueness of truth, the two languages are still regarded as contradictory.

DAVID BLOOR'S QUESTION

The works of David Bloor provide an interesting contemporary illustration of the wish to give a *causal* interpretation of phenomena which seem more appropriate to a *teleological* analysis. In this, they confirm one of the points I looked at in previous chapters – that very often it is more difficult than one thinks to determine whether a particular *a priori* is relevant to account for a phenomenon.[36]

Roughly, Bloor's main thesis is that the sociology of science must analyse *scientific* ideas in a way which is not teleological but causal. It is normal to explain *false* ideas in a causal way, by referring to the intervention of psychic or social factors. However, says Bloor, we must also analyse true ideas – or rather those which are regarded as such by the scientific community – in a causal way. In fact, there is no basic difference between scientific beliefs and moral beliefs. Both, like Durkheim's collective representations, must be analysed on the basis of the state of society.

Bloor's argument can be illustrated by an interesting example. In a particularly provocative article,[37] Bloor argues that adherence to mathematical propositions must itself be interpreted in a causal way. The task of the sociologist is to show that mathematical 'truths' are based on collective *beliefs* current in the scientific community, and that they derive their potential for *constraint* from this collective characteristic.

Bloor probably owes a lot here to a passage from Peter Winch,[38] who himself is directly influenced by the later Wittgenstein.[39]

Let us assume that we are asked to continue the sequence 1, 2, 3 . . . The answer is easy: '4, 5, 6 . . .'. The *teleological* interpretation of this answer is simple: we examine in our thought the *reality* of the sequence of numbers and draw from it the answer to the question. Since this analysis assumes the existence of an invisible mathematical reality, Bloor calls it 'Platonic'. He argues that the difficulty derives from the fact that one can speak of mathematical reality only metaphorically. Is it plausible that a mathematical reality precedes the construction of the mathematical edifice? Is not mathematics invention rather than discovery? If it is, however, how can we explain that we feel *constrained* to give the answer '4, 5, 6 . . .'? In this way, Bloor suggests (and I am condensing his argument to the main points), teleological analysis leads to insurmountable difficulties.

No doubt Bloor was not the first to ask what is the *true* counterpart, as it were, of mathematical truths. He is well aware of this, since he discusses in great detail the two main classical answers to the question – by J. S. Mill and Frege.

However, he is not happy with Mill's answer – that mathematical notions are based on experience ($2 + 1 = 3$ *because* two pebbles and one pebble make three pebbles); and he acknowledges that Frege's objections to Mill's thesis are serious: it is not from experience that the notion of *zero* is derived; neither is it experience which tells us that $99,999 + 1 = 100,000$. On the other hand, explains Bloor, it is impossible to accept Frege's Platonic conception of mathematical *reality*.

Like the *equator*, the *realities* revealed by mathematicians are therefore neither pure products of fantasy nor realities discernible by the senses. What are they?

Bloor answers this question by a series of often very telling examples taken from the history of mathematics. In one of these case studies, he looks at history of $\sqrt{2}$.

Aristotle had already been able to show the *irrationality* of $\sqrt{2}$: assume that $\sqrt{2} = p/q$, and that the fraction p/q cannot be simplified. The previous equation is recast as $2 = p^2/q^2$, or again $2q^2 = p^2$. Therefore, P is even and q is odd, because if q was even, the fraction could be simplified. But if p is even, this implies $p = 2n$ and $p^2 = 4n^2 = 2q^2$. Hence $q^2 = 2n^2$. Therefore q is both odd and even.

Bloor notes that this finding was *interpreted* by Greek mathematicians in a way which seems strange to us today: they concluded that the number $\sqrt{2}$ does not exist. Since the unit square is not the least imaginary, and the length of its diagonal equals $\sqrt{2}$, they solved the contradiction by deciding that *numbers* and *magnitudes* represented different orders of reality. We, who regard $\sqrt{2}$ as a *number of a certain type*, find this answer strange: is it not as incomprehensible and opaque to the *external* observers that we are as the religious beliefs of the Nambikwara and the Azande?

Bloor draws from this example the conclusion that mathematical truths are not of a different order from truths imposed by custom: the Greeks *believed* that numbers and magnitudes represented two different realities. But the *constraining* nature of this belief derived not from some mathematical reality, but from the fact that it was the solution commonly adopted by the Greek scientific community to resolve the contradictions raised by the case of $\sqrt{2}$.

This example certainly does not prove, as Bloor recognizes, that the proposition 'there are no whole p and q such that $p/q = \sqrt{2}$' is an unshakeable truth. Conclusion: there are, as well as socially based mathematical truths (such as the *Greek* proposition '$\sqrt{2}$ is not a number' or the *modern* proposition that, on the contrary, '$\sqrt{2}$ is a number'), propositions (such as the proposition 'there are no whole p and q such that $p/q = \sqrt{2}$') whose truth is absolute and, *for this reason*, meet with universal agreement, from Aristotle to modern times.

It is therefore only about the *interpretation* of this truth that there is a difference between the Greeks and us. In the same way, one can be absolutely certain that Smith killed Jones, but hesitate about the reasons for the murder. These hesitations do not prove that truths in detective work cannot be absolute.

In other words, there are mathematical propositions in which we believe because they are true, and others which we endorse *for other reasons*. However, if there in fact are, as Bloor argues, mathematical propositions which can justifiably be called *Greek* or *modern*, the example in no way shows that *all* mathematical truths are in essence condemned to be different depending on which side of Mount Athos they are.

In fact, it is not necessary to refer to 'social factors' to explain belief in the truth of 'there are no whole p and q such that $p/q = \sqrt{2}$'. It is simply *because* it is true that we believe this statement. 'Logical necessity' is not here the product of any 'moral obligation'.

On the other hand, neither is the *Greek* interpretation of the proposition '$\sqrt{2}$ is not a number' the result of some social constraint or other. It is simply a natural interpretation, by which I mean an interpretation which allowed the Greeks an easy solution of the perplexities that $\sqrt{2}$ was giving them: for them, the idea of number referred only to our whole numbers and our rational numbers. On the basis of this definition, it is true that $\sqrt{2}$ is *not* a number. To be able to conclude otherwise, they would have had to anticipate twenty centuries of the history of mathematical thought.

In other words, rather than looking for a culturally inspired incommensurability between the meaning of the idea of number in Greece and that current in the modern world, it is simpler to note that the Greeks had a narrower definition than we do of the idea of number.

To this we must add that a definition cannot be said to be true or false. It is therefore not surprising that definitions current in a particular discipline are recast over time, and that they are not as immutable as theorems. This does not mean that changes need to be explained in the same way that one would explain the development of law, for example. Although it is possible to fail to recognize that law is a reflection of morality, changes in mathematical definitions are explained above all – *teleologically* rather than *causally* – by the fact that they have to be adapted to the evolution of the discipline.[40]

This conclusion – expressed in a different way – is consistent with that of Bloor, whose view is that mathematics is no less 'arbitrary' than any other cultural product – law, manners or tastes, for example. However, it is not more 'arbitrary' either:

> There is thus a similarity between logical and moral authority. Now authority is a social category and it was therefore of great significance to find that Frege's definition of objectivity was completely satisfied by social institutions.[41]

> [T]he theoretical component of knowledge is precisely the social component.[42]

> Logical necessity is a form of moral obligation, and (. . .) objectivity is a social phenomenon.[43]

In other words, mathematical truths must be analysed as collective representations in the Durkheim sense: for Bloor, there is no difference in kind between, let us say, the moral beliefs of the Greeks and their belief in the proposition '$\sqrt{2}$ is not a number'.

As with Hübner's argument,[44] Bloor's conclusion is drawn from a line of reasoning with *two components*: a series of acceptable *explicit* statements and a narrow *implicit* framework.

One can in fact try to reconstruct his reasoning in the following way:

1) [Of two explanations of a phenomenon, only one can be true]*;
2) Adherence to mathematical propositions is usually explained *teleologically*;
3) Other beliefs are explained *causally*;
4) Should adherence to mathematical propositions be explained *teleologically* or *causally*?
5) The former implies that one believes mathematical statements because they are objectively valid;
6) An objectively valid statement is constant over time and in space;[45]

7) [Either *all* mathematical propositions are independent of the context or not]*;
8) [A statement may be valid *objectively* or *socially*]*;
9) There are mathematical propositions such as '$\sqrt{2}$ is not a number' which appear to be dependent on the context;

---

10) Therefore, adherence to mathematical statements is explained *causally*; they have a social basis.

Once one has divested oneself of this framework, the history of $\sqrt{2}$ can be told simply: the Greeks did not have the same definition of numbers as we do, and they had good reasons for having a different one. Despite this, they established absolute truths, such as that concerning $\sqrt{2}$.[46] Because of this definition, they naturally interpreted the irrationality of $\sqrt{2}$ in a different way from us.

In other words, it is easier to recount this history using the language of *reasons* rather than that of *causes*, which does not rule out the possibility that, as Bloor argues, a definition may be socially constraining.

However, the narrowness of his *framework* is shown in the fact that he eliminates all distinction between *socially* based propositions. It is true that the definition of the idea of number is socially based; but it is not socially based in the same way as a rule of etiquette. The latter must indeed be regarded as the product of the state of society; the former is explained rather by the reasons which mathematicians have for holding to it.

What must be said, however, is that one observes today on all kinds of subjects – educational choice or crime,[47] but also adherence to ideas, even mathematical ideas – a more or less permanent conflict between *teleological* and *causal* explanation. The relevance of the two languages varies according to the subject being dealt with: we adhere to certain ideas under the influence of convention, and to others under that of truth. Neither of these languages, however, can lay claim to exclusivity, unless on the strength of metaconscious *a priori*.

SECOND EXAMPLE: VIEWPOINT

Another significant example of multiple truth is where a description is made on the basis of distinct *viewpoints*. Here again, the principle of the uniqueness of truth often gives rise to reasoning which tends to discredit the *other* viewpoints.

This point can be illustrated by yet another example from the sociology of science, which also shows the influence of the 'strong programme' that Bloor speaks about: the attempt to explain adherence to scientific beliefs by an exclusively causal model.

Bruno Latour and Steve Woolgar[48] develop a simple thesis based on

research inspired by anthropology and carried out in scientific laborator-
ies: it is the scientific community itself which creates the split between
reality and statements by scientists about reality. The effect of this split is
the idea – common to both realists and conventionalists – that scientific
truths need some kind of backing. The very notion of objectivity, the
idea of the existence of an external reality corresponding to a scientific
statement, are therefore neither glaringly obvious, nor postulates guiding scientific activity, but the *consequences* of this activity:

> We do not wish to say that facts do not exist nor that there is no such thing
> as reality. In this simple sense our position is not relativist. Our point is
> that 'out-there-ness' is the *consequence* of scientific work rather than its
> *cause*.[49]

When one observes a laboratory as an anthropologist, as Latour and
Woolgar do, one concludes in fact that scientists often hesitate about
whether there is a reality corresponding to a particular statement or not.

> Sometimes the status of statements changed from day to day, even from
> one hour to the next. The factual status of one substance, for instance,
> varied dramatically over a period of a few days. On Tuesday, a peak was
> thought to be the sign of a real substance. But on Wednesday the peak was
> regarded as resulting from an unreliable physiograph. On Thursday, the
> use of another pool of extracts gave rise to another peak which was taken
> to be 'the same'. At this point, the existence of a new *object* was slowly
> solidifying, only to be dissolved again the following day.[50]

Thus it must be admitted that to stamp 'made', 'made undeniable' on a
(basic) statement is the result of a clarification process in the laboratory
which is hesitant, uncertain and sometimes long. It is unintelligible if one
fails to see it as the product of '*laboratory life*'.

Latour and Woolgar draw from their analysis significant philosophical
consequences. The problem of correspondence between reality and the
statements of science, or even that of the effectiveness of science, in other
words, all the problems making up 'the stock in trade of philosophers
since Hume's radical treatment of the problem',[51] are dissipated, since it
is science which gives a statement the status of fact and which, therefore,
creates external facts. There is therefore no chance of not seeing a close
correspondence between reality and the statements by which scientists
express themselves: once these statements have received the scientific
stamp, they have the status of an official image of reality.

> Our contention is that the strength of correspondence between objects and
> statements about these objects *stems from the splitting and inversion of a
> statement within the laboratory context*.[52]

In fact, neither realism nor operationalism is acceptable. The truth is,
according to Latour and Woolgar, that

it is important to eschew arguments about the external reality and outside efficacy of scientific products to account for the stabilisation of facts, because such reality and efficacy are the consequence rather than the cause of scientific activity.[53]

We should therefore abandon the idea that *external reality* is the inspiration of the scientist. Science, *as it is*, is a power game within a system of norms. Facts are constructed. Their construction is deployed within a set of rules, so that a fact is always a social product. Reality is therefore in itself totally unknowable.

Latour and Woolgar support neither conventionalists nor realists. Conventionalists are, according to them, called on to rescue science in times of crisis for realism: when *external reality* can no longer be regarded as providing a guarantee of scientific beliefs, collective conventions provide the necessary backing.

Latour and Woolgar's descriptions are interesting and there is no reason to doubt their accuracy. Their intermediate conclusions – the ones which synthesize their descriptions – are credible. It is true that it is often only after long hesitation that the status of fact is given to a mental entity: phlogiston was for a long time imbued with reality; it became a product of the imagination; viruses existed in the mind before becoming realities. In a certain way, what Latour and Woolgar are saying – until they give the epistemological conclusions of their research – is part of the rudimentary knowledge of the history of science.

However, here as elsewhere, the question is how, from acceptable data and arguments, such disconcerting conclusions can be drawn.

Again, the *nub* of the proof is made up of subtle *a priori*.

What Latour and Woolgar are suggesting under the guise of 'anthropological method' is in fact nothing other than a *description* (of a particular kind) of science in action[54] or laboratory life. However, a description, by the very nature of this mental operation, can always be made in a thousand ways. The description chosen by Latour and Woolgar is, as they say, of an *anthropological* kind. It consists of lovingly focusing on the small details of laboratory life, on the hesitations of the scientists, their moments of doubt or false certainty, the uncertain and reversible character of their consensus, the fluidity of their opinions, the illogicality of their reactions, passions, jealousies, ambitions, desire for power. In other words, they watch the unfolding of scientific activity like Fabrizio del Dongo at the Battle of Waterloo.

In the end, when a consensus appears on a particular subject in the laboratory, Latour and Woolgar give the impression that it is not reality, but 'laboratory life', which is responsible. How could it be otherwise, when consensus is presented like the 'happy ending' to a story?

Similarly, a police investigation could be told from an *anthropological* viewpoint, by stressing relationships between the actors, their passions and desire for power; it could be shown that facts are 'constructed', that from Monday to Tuesday entities such as 'a particular suspect committed the crime' exist, then cease to exist. Finally, 'judicial life' would explain that when the curtain falls a reality corresponds to the statement 'So-and-so killed so-and-so'; and both realists and conventionalists could be proved wrong.

> Scientists themselves constantly raise questions as to whether a particular statement 'actually' relates to something 'out there', or whether it is a mere figment of the imagination, or an artefact of the procedures employed. It is therefore unrealistic to portray scientists busily occupying themselves with scientific activity while leaving debates between realism and relativism to the philosophers. Depending on the argument, the laboratory, the time of year, and the currency of the controversy, investigators will variously take the stand of realist, relativist, idealist, transcendental relativist, sceptic, and so on.[55]

Of course, a scientific investigation could be described in another way, as a process directed towards an end: 'to establish the truth'.

In this other kind of description, the hesitations and passions of the protagonists become secondary, and the essential thing is that scientists – whatever their passions – cannot, by their very role, continue to support a hypothesis which seems so inconsistent with the data that it would be futile to try to save it. In other words, it is indeed *external* reality that will be decisive. If not, *scientific life* would have no meaning and it would be impossible to see how or why this kind of activity could continue.

We can therefore *describe* scientific life as do Latour and Woolgar, but we can also describe it *in other ways*, unless we want *truth always to be unique* and a description to be acceptable only when it describes *reality as it is*. (I leave aside the question, since it does not interest me, of why *anthropological life* should be so different from other forms of *scientific life* that it is able to apprehend *external reality as it is* . . .)

Clearly, Latour and Woolgar are convinced that an accurate *description* (we ought to say '*the* accurate description') is *one which hides nothing*: one which has as its aim to note in a neutral way, at each successive moment, the psychological and intellectual states of the protagonists. However, a *hyper-realist* description of this type has no more claim to represent *the* truth of its object and to discredit other types of descriptions than a hyper-realist portrait can claim to discredit Frans Hals. Even a James Joyce-type description is made up of choices and *a priori*. More than that; it is loaded with value judgements (for example, of the kind: 'this is *important*, that is not', and so on). The impression of anarchy in Joyce's writing derives not from the absence of such judgements but from the freedom he gives himself in relation to what is commonly regarded as important or not important 'to say'.

Above all, far from apprehending the material reality of science, the type of description which Latour and Woolgar call *anthropological* ignores an essential dimension of it: the 'distant' objectives which structure scientists' work and which are *visible* neither for the actors, in whose consciousness they lurk, nor for the anthropologists who have decided to restrict their purview to the here and now. The whole approach of Latour and Woolgar is in the final analysis based on the reification of the *passing* moods of scientists.

It is because the earth is in fact round that we believe in the truth of the statement 'the earth is round'. However, that should not stop us describing *also* the history leading up to this statement in the greatest detail, and ending it just before the suspense stops. This story is no less full of passions, hesitations, tergiversations and doubts than that of thyrotrophin.

In any event, it is difficult to accept that virtually any scientific debate cannot be reported in several ways: in Latour and Woolgar's *anthropological* style, but also, for example, in the *economical* or – as perhaps we should say – *pragmatic* style of Radnitzky (a hypothesis is abandoned when it becomes much too costly to defend). In the former case, the ideal – in reality unattainable – will be to *tell all*. In the latter, it will be acknowledged that scientific activity is guided by a fundamental principle: defend only those hypotheses which can be defended at a cost which is not prohibitive.

The idea that the gestation of scientific truths can be described in different ways is moreover far from new. It appears in Reichenbach's classical distinction between the context of justification and the context of discovery,[56] a distinction which itself follows the medieval one between *via inventionis* and *via judicii*, or the idea of analysis and synthesis,[57] taken from Greek mathematicians and reinstated by Galileo and Descartes.

In any event, the conclusions of Latour and Woolgar assume that the description which they call anthropological is the only possible one, or is superior to others. However, by glorifying *material* aspects, their methods find it difficult to apprehend scientists' guiding aims and overall strategies, and even more so to explain the *teleonomic* dimension of their activity.

Summary

Another epistemological *a priori* is that of the uniqueness of truth, Vital to everyday life, it tends to be applied in conditions where it is not relevant.

There are many examples in the natural sciences, as well as in the human sciences, where questions, for example, of the kind 'why does a particular institution exist?', 'why does a particular phenomenon appear in a particular context?' can be answered in various ways that are equally valid and acceptable. To call them 'complementary' is merely, in a circular way, to say that one believes in the absolute universality of the principle of the uniqueness of truth.

As with the other *a priori*, the principle of the uniqueness of truth tends to impose itself by default.

Many demonstrations rely on this principle, beginning with arguments for scepticism. From Montaigne to modern times, they are constructed on the same pattern of reasoning – a pattern where the principle of the uniqueness of truth plays a crucial part.

Similarly, some of the major recurring debates in human sciences (can the past be explained or must it be interpreted? Should the explanation of historical phenomena be regarded as of a genetic or functional nature? Should a particular class of phenomena be explained causally or teleologically? and so on), as well as answers by various writers, are within the framework of the implicit *a priori* that truth is unique.

Contemporary sociology of science provides interesting examples of this; Bloor's argument that adherence to scientific statements is based on mechanisms analogous to those by which, for example, one subscribes to the rules of etiquette is wholly based on the *a priori* that truth is unique. The same is true of the work of Latour and Woolgar. The devastating nature of their conclusions derives from valid reasoning and the *a priori* that truth is unique.

8

Words and things

Every theory contains implicit statements which can significantly affect conclusions drawn from it.

These *a priori* vary in nature. Some can be described as *logical*. For example, they determine whether the principle of contradiction applies to a question of the kind '*x v y?*'. Others are *epistemological* in nature: they involve a certain conception of truth or of the relationships between the theory and reality. For instance, one often introduces the *a priori* that every phenomenon has a cause, or the *a priori* that truth is unique.

Other *a priori* are *linguistic* in nature. Their presence is in fact inevitable, and is explained by the simple fact that a question or a theory is expressed in words, which take on meaning only through implicit *a priori*. Some are innocuous, like the statement that the words used have a meaning. Others are less so and can involve the conclusions which one draws from a theory or the answers which one gives to a question.

Therefore, all kinds of arguments are based on semantic drift of which speaker and hearer may not in all good faith be aware, because they normally use the *a priori* that, in the same line of argument, the meaning of words can be assumed to be the same from one statement to the next.

Pareto[1] showed, for example, that theories of natural law were usually made up of statements acceptable, or at least defensible, in themselves and, moreover, internally consistent. However, they derived an undeserved power of conviction from the fact that both the person who makes them and the person to whom they are made tend to accept without hesitation that the meaning of words stays the same within any reasoning. The arguments conveyed by the words may therefore seem to be proof, whereas they are not. This is a classic example of the Simmel effect: knowing subjects think they are constructing a particular reasoning but in reality are following a different one, because their conclusions rely on implicit statements which exist only at the edge of their consciousness.

Like all the *a priori* which interest me here, this one is *natural* in the sense that, in any communication process, whether scientific communication or 'ordinary' communication, it is normal to think of words keeping the same meaning in a series of statements linked together in a line of reasoning. The very ordinariness of this *a priori* explains why it is normally used in a metaconscious way. At the same time, it can of course give rise to distortions of inference and lead one to persuade oneself of conclusions based on reasoning which is apparently demonstrative, but in reality not.

In the following pages, I will look at some of these ordinary linguistic *a priori* and try to show that they may in fact play an essential part in generating beliefs in weak or false ideas.

An example of a linguistic *a priori*: the allocation of a word to a type of word

These linguistic *a priori* are extremely numerous, and one cannot hope to deal with the full extent of the subject. I will leave aside the *a priori* about the consistency of the meaning of words, on which there is not much to add to what Pareto said, apart from giving further examples.

Instead, I will concentrate on another point – that the ideas and concepts in a line of reasoning are perceived as belonging to what I will call specific *types*. By this I mean that a concept can be seen as being, for example, *metaphorical* or not. To take Max Black's famous example,[2] the expression 'to purse one's lips' is usually taken to be metaphorical. However, though there are cases where the *type* of word or phrase is immediately recognized, there are others which are more ambiguous; and categorizing an idea as one type or another can affect the conclusions.[3]

For instance, Marxist theory is interpreted differently depending on whether the concept of *class struggle* is taken metaphorically or not. Depending on the text, Marx takes it in both senses. However, it is not certain that either he or his readers always distinguish clearly between them (unlike a writer such as Tocqueville, who always uses the term in a non-metaphorical way). As I have tried to show elsewhere, the play – deliberate or not – that Marx makes of this ambiguity goes a long way to explain the persuasive power of his arguments.[4]

Similarly, 'structuralism' takes on a completely different dimension depending on whether the notion of *structure* is perceived in a metaphorical mode – the correct one – or whether one sees in *structures* a 'profound' reality which is more true than visible reality.[5]

Of course, words are distinguished from each other, not just on a metaphorical/non-metaphorical basis, but on many other criteria. For example, certain concepts have a fixed referent. Others designate a reality known to be non-existent. Yet others refer to a reality about the reality of which it is impossible to make a statement (Frege). The word 'chair' belongs to the first category; the word 'unicorn' to the second; a concept such as 'the highest prime number' to the third (or at least until it was shown that the sequence of prime numbers is infinite).

Some words are 'success words' (Ryle) and cannot be qualified negatively; others are not. For example, one can speak of false coinage, but not a false theorem.

Some words represent visible phenomena, others phenomena which are in essence invisible (for example 'strength', 'intelligence', 'frame of mind').

Another point is that there are notions which can easily be defined, others which cannot. Among those which cannot, the meaning of some is immediately apprehended, of others it is not. For example, the word 'bicycle' can easily be defined by a definition (by means of 'type' and distinctive features') such as is found in all dictionaries: a bicycle is a 'machine for riding, with two wheels'. The word 'speed' cannot be defined in this way, but there is no problem in defining it as the relationship between the distance covered by a moving object and the time taken to cover this distance.

Conversely, there are families of words – between which further distinctions need to be made – where the meaning is clear and where definition is difficult.

As Pareto again says, it is impossible to give precise definitions of words such as 'old', 'young', 'many', 'big', 'rich', 'intelligent' and so on. These nevertheless are examples of a whole host of words which we use in everyday life and which cause us no problems.

If these words can be defined satisfactorily, at least they can be given definitions which, though they have to contain an element of arbitrariness, can nevertheless meet with general agreement. Nobody would be surprised if a woman 1.90 metres tall was described as *very tall*; and we would have no difficulty, even if it seems a little arbitrary, in agreeing in these circumstances to relate the idea of 'very tall' to a mathematical definition ('x' is 'very tall' if $x > x_{TG}$').

However, there are also concepts which cannot even be given an arbitrary definition of this type and which, like the previous ones, we have absolutely no problem in using in everyday life.

As Gilbert Ryle said, statements of the type 'yellow is a colour which . . .' do not exist. In other words, no definition is possible of the word 'yellow.'[6] Of course, yellow can be defined as 'one of the colours of the solar spectrum' (*Robert* dictionary), but this does not help us to visualize what yellow is. No doubt the colour yellow can be defined on the basis of its *physical* properties, since it has a specific wavelength; but it cannot be defined on the basis of its *phenomenological* characteristics. However, before physicists were able to explain the nature of colours, we were as perfectly able as we are today of *perceiving* a yellow object as yellow, or of *distinguishing* between a yellow apple and a red apple; but we were unable to put definitions on this difference in perception.

The impossibility of defining colours is clear from the fact that there is no satisfactory way of completing the gaps in a sentence such as 'a red apple is an apple which . . ., whereas a yellow apple is an apple which . . .'.

Most philosophers – but also linguists, and sociologists and anthropologists as well – who have looked at linguistic phenomena in their work have been fully aware of these distinctions between types of words.

Well before Ryle, Kant saw that certain words are indispensable and have a perfectly clear meaning, yet are undefinable. In his *Critique of Pure Reason*, he says of those who claim to establish the criteria of *truth* that they remind him of the two mad people, one of whom pretends to milk a goat while the other holds a pail underneath.[7] Kant is the opposite of a sceptic, so it is not because he considered it empty and futile that he regarded the cardinal notion of truth as undefinable.

Since we are speaking of Kant, we might also mention his comments on those words such as 'chance', which are neither a matter of the *understanding* (unlike a word such as 'cause') nor of the *sensibility* (unlike words such as 'blue' or 'hare'). Goffman's thoughts on this notion of 'chance' are – though in a different language – close to those of Kant.[8]

There is no need to give a long list of examples of classical writers' awareness of the importance of distinctions between *types* of words or ideas. I will, however, mention that, through his famous concept of 'ideal type', Max Weber tried to express the fact that concepts such as 'capitalism' or 'absolute monarchy' belong, simply by indicating a singular historical reality, to a different type from those indicated by the words 'chair', 'speed', 'yellow' or 'big'. When a writer such as Lazarsfeld speaks of 'matrix formulation', he is also denoting a type of original conceptualization, close to Max Weber's 'ideal types'. For example, he speaks of 'matrix formulation' to indicate classic distinctions such as that between 'Dionysian civilization' and 'Apollonian civilization' (R. Benedict) or between 'community' and 'society' (Tönnies).[9]

Another classical sociologist, Durkheim, argued – in his debate with Max Müller – that the relationships between words and things can vary, and that one cannot be at all satisfied with a theory of language which saw words as symbolic reproductions of reality: this would be to reduce all words to the same type as the word 'chair', for example.[10]

I could quote many other writers who seem to have reflected on the statement in Plato's *Theaetetus* that it may be inappropriate to try to be too specific about the meaning of words and to imagine that there is always a simple relationship between words and things. However, I will give only two further examples.

First of all, Wittgenstein: in a famous passage, he develops the idea that words which are clearest and apparently most concrete can be undefinable. Is this the rule or the exception? The former, says Wittgenstein:[11]

> Consider for example the proceedings which we call 'games'. I mean board games, card games, ball games, Olympic games, and so on. What is common to them all? – Don't say: 'There *must* be something common, or they would not be called "games" ' – but *look and see* whether there is anything common to all. For if you look at them you will not see something which is common to *all*, but similarities, relationships, and a whole series of them at that.[12]

Wittgenstein goes on to say that there are games with winners and losers, but there are also others, such as patience, where this is not the case. There are games of skill, games of chance, and so on. There is therefore no point in trying to identify the hypothetical characteristic common to all games: there is none. There are only *resemblances* between games; and resemblances which are not themselves always definable: 'I can do no better than characterize these resemblances by the words 'family likeness'.[13]

Wittgenstein's conception of a word such as 'game' can be shown in figure 8.1.

Each of the circles in figure 8.1 has sub-set of games with a shared characteristic (for example, they are games of chance) and therefore a 'resemblance' or a 'family likeness'. Of course, the circles overlap imperfectly: not all games of chance can be played alone; only some are card games, and so on. What this representation shows, as Wittgenstein points out, is that if the *entirety* of games is considered, there is in fact *nothing* which is *common* to all. There are also families of games, for example G_1 and G_8, which have no characteristic in common. Finally, the relationship of 'resemblance' is generally not transitive. It *is* transitive, of course, within the same circle: there is a 'resemblance' or a 'family likeness' between G_1 and G_2, G_2 and G_3, G_1 and G_3. It ceases to be transitive when one moves from one circle to another: there is a resemblance between G_1 and G_2, G_2 and G_4, but not between G_1 and G_4. Similarly, there is a resemblance between G_1 and G_3, G_3 and G_6, G_6 and G_8, G_8 and G_9, but not, for example, between G_1 and G_6, G_1 and G_8 or G_6 and G_9.

Above all, figure 8.1 is useful in indicating that, when the meaning of a word can be represented in this way, it can show itself perfectly clearly even though the word cannot be defined. For example, we can associate with each of the circles a perfectly defined characteristic (*card* games,

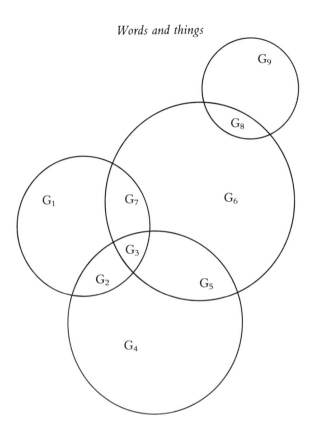

Figure 8.1

games *of chance*, and so on). There is, however, no characteristic or set of characteristics which can be associated with the totality of games and which can define the very notion of game. In other words, it is impossible to express the structure of figure 8.1 by locating it in one of the known types of definition. This is why one cannot describe *what there is in common* between all games.

In other words, the clarity and precision of a word and the certainty with which we handle it have nothing to do with its ability to be defined.

I would like to end this survey by mentioning the notion, devised by the anthropologist Rodney Needham, of *polythetic* words.[14] Wittgenstein was Needham's direct inspiration for this notion, which indicates those words referred to by Wittgenstein where the meaning is determined by the family likeness among their various usages. Needham's invention of the adjective '*polythetic*' meant that a name could be given to the type of words identified by Wittgenstein. The reason why Wittgenstein did not name them himself was perhaps that he tended to think that *all* notions we deal with are usually, as Needham says, *polythetic*.

The distinctions which I have considered up to now are obviously not exhaustive, but they are sufficient for my purpose, which is to suggest that the implicit attachment of a particular word to a particular type can be a significant source of Simmel effects.

Although the allocation of a word to a type is sometimes imperative ('to purse the lips'), this is not always so. It often happens that, in cases of ambiguity, one attributes *by default* a particular word to a simpler type than the one to which it in fact belongs. This is so when a metaphorical expression is taken as non-metaphorical, or when a polythetic word is taken as non-polythetic.

In linguistic *a priori* we therefore find mechanisms similar to those highlighted in the case of other types of *a priori*.

I will confine my examples to the case of the distinction between polythetic and non-polythetic. First, however, I will look at two questions implicity raised by an imaginary debate between Wittgenstein and Needham.

The first question concerns the extent to which words of the same type as 'game' are *frequent*, as Needham seems to argue, or whether they are, as is often thought, an anomaly or *exception* to the usual case of a word such as 'chair', or whether, as Wittgenstein seems to think, they represent the *normal case*.

The other question, obviously crucial, is whether scientific language can, without being false to itself, contain *polythetic* words, that is, words having the properties of the word 'game' in Wittgenstein's example. This question usually provokes a negative answer. *Polythetic* words are typical of 'ordinary' language, it is often argued, whereas non-polythetic words – such as 'chair' or 'speed' – are characteristics of scientific language.

Put more simply, it is usually required of concepts which are admitted into scientific discourse that they should be defined or definable. Even if a term comes from 'ordinary' language, it is usually required, before it can be accepted into scientific language, to show that it can belong to the non-polythetic type.

POLYTHETIC TERMS/NON-POLYTHETIC TERMS

In fact, many terms have the appearance of being polythetic, not only in 'ordinary' language, but also in 'scientific' language.

In Chapter 6, we saw that a word as fundamental as 'cause' is in fact of this type. There is no need to state that it occurs as frequently in the natural sciences as in the human sciences. Generally speaking, it is a necessary ingredient not only of 'natural' inference, but also of scientific inference.

However, in the case of a statement of the 'X causes Y' type, the meaning of the word 'causes' can vary considerably. According to context, the statement may indicate that X is the *necessary* condition, the *sufficient* condition or the *necessary and sufficient* condition of Y. However, the statement may also mean that X has been the 'trigger' of Y, or that X is neither a necessary condition, nor a sufficient condition, nor even a trigger, but only a circumstance partly responsible for Y, and on which influence can be brought to bear. Every combination of these criteria is possible: in other cases, we could say that 'X is a cause of Y' if X is a sufficient condition *and* a condition which can be influenced. However, 'X causes Y' may also mean, conversely, that X is a *necessary* condition (or a *sufficient* condition) *and at the same time* a condition which *cannot easily be acted upon.*

That is not the end of the matter: it may be that one agrees with the statement 'X causes Y' only if one of the links between X and Y just referred to is actually observed *and if, moreover*, X belongs to a certain area of reality. One may also agree that 'X causes Y' when X has been the 'trigger', the necessary (or sufficient, etc.) condition of phenomenon Y, *and that* Y is regarded as an *abnormal* phenomenon. Conversely, one may want Y to be *normal*.

Again, 'X causes Y' may mean that X is *the only* element always present when Y is present. But this meaning will normally be regarded as unacceptable in different contexts.

We must also add that, when the statement 'X causes Y' is associated with the notion that X is the *necessary condition* of Y, the word *necessary* is in fact being used as an approximation. In all logic, 'X is the necessary condition of Y' means that we cannot at the same time observe Y and not observe X. However, it often happens that this type of situation appears without our concluding that 'X causes Y'. In other words, even when the notion of cause is associated with a logical relationship of this type, the former 'extends beyond' the latter.

As in the case of the *games* referred to by Wittgenstein, there is not much in common among the elements of the huge number of 'X causes Y' statements, and in fact we have to speak of *resemblances* or *family likenesses* (as in Wittgenstein, it is better to put these in the plural, despite usage, since the resemblances are defined over a range of sub-sets, as we saw in the diagram above).

This catalogue *à la Borges* helps explain why some people have tried to eliminate the word 'cause' from the vocabulary of science. However, it soon became clear that this solution was just as unrealistic as Esperanto in another context. The elimination of the notion of *cause* on the pretext of purifying the language merely leads to paralysis.

Probably just as frequent as the word *cause* in the human sciences, from history through demography or sociology to economics, is the word *reason*.

I will exclude from consideration Reason with a capital R, or even 'rationalization' in Weber's sense, and confine myself to the everyday use of the words 'reason' and 'rationality', that is, to statements of the type 'subject X had *reasons* for doing Y (or believing Z)'.

Even confining oneself to this simple meaning, it is possible to draw up a list as diverse as the previous one. Having *good reasons* for doing Y may, in certain cases, mean 'having established Y as the most expeditious, least costly and most accessible way of achieving a particular aim'; but it may also mean 'having *moral* reasons for doing Y'; or again 'believing (*wrongly*), for example, on the basis of previous experience, that Y is a good way of achieving a particular aim'; or else 'believing (*rightly*), for example, on the basis of previous experience, that Y is a good way of achieving a particular aim', and so on.[15]

Of course, the word 'rationality', which is only the abstract noun describing these various meanings of 'reasons' or 'good reasons', could not itself be more simple to define, and this is no doubt why much has been written about the concept of 'rationality'. However, it is just as futile to claim to find *something in common* in these different uses of the word 'reasons' (in the context of 'reasons for doing' or 'reasons for believing') as it is illusory to look for the common denominator in all the uses of 'game' or 'cause'.

Only to allow non-polythetic words into scientific language is usually regarded as a scientific imperative. However, it is true that the word 'reasons' *is* polythetic.[16]

This is why we cannot hope for agreement on any definition of rationality which implicitly assumes the non-polythetic term.

As in the case of the word 'cause', sceptics suggested straightforward elimination: since the word 'cause' in fact 'means nothing', it should be abandoned. Similarly, this 'obscure' notion of rationality should be relinquished. However, the solution is just as naive and impracticable in both cases. In the former case, a refusal to use the notion of cause would be equivalent to suicide, since it is impossible to survive long without making statements based on causality. In the latter case, as Weber clearly saw, to relinquish the word 'reasons' – and its derivations such as 'rationality' – would be to renounce understanding oneself and others, since to 'understand' the behaviour, attitudes and beliefs of somebody is in large part to find 'reasons' for them.[17]

It is clear that, *socially*, strange or deviant behaviour is not dealt with in the same way depending on whether or not one can determine the reasons for it.

To try to abolish the notion of 'reasons', and that of 'cause', would be equivalent to trying to legislate to abolish gravity.

The other solution is to agree that scientific terms can *also* be polythetic. This solution is commonly accepted in relation to 'cause', but less so when it comes to 'reasons'.

The objection is that the ambiguity of the words 'cause' and 'reason' has long been recognized, and that they are exceptions; moreover, that most terms used in scientific language are of a *non-polythetic* type.

In fact, the opposite is true.

Let us take a notion as simple as that of *equality* – not Equality with a capital E, but equality defined in relation to a criterion, for example, equality of income. At first sight, there would seem to be no problem in defining it.

However, it is a *polythetic*-type word, not of the *Wittgenstein* kind, but of the *Pareto* kind. By this I mean that it is a term of the same type as 'big' or 'rich' – that is, a notion which one can only hope to define in a more or less *arbitrary* way.

If the term gives the impression of being non-polythetic, this is because it has a *mathematical* meaning, which is clearly univocal. The word 'equality', as used by sociologists or economists in an expression such as 'equality of income', has only a metaphorical relationship with the mathematical term; but this relationship is usually forgotten. As theorists of rhetoric would say, the metaphor is 'sleeping' (as in, for example, *sheet* of paper): by moving from metaphorical to non-metaphorical type, it has become a 'catachresis',[18] that is, a metaphor not perceived as such.

The polythetic character of the notion is clear when one tries to fix a measure to it, which has to be done to answer simple questions: whether, for example, equality of income is greater or less at one time than another, or more or less pronounced in one society than in another.

To simplify the discussion, let us consider the case of the incomes of two groups of people – group A consisting of four people, and group B containing five – and find out which group has the most equal distribution of income.

We then see that there are several ways of answering the question, and that it is difficult to choose between them.

The idea of equality can be approached, for example, by considering whether, on average, each person's income tends to deviate further in one case than in another from the overall average. Let us assume that the figures in table 8.1 refer to income in pounds. The income of people in group A deviates on average by 10 pounds, and in group B by 12 pounds, from the overall average. Group A is therefore more *egalitarian* than group B.

However, we can see that the average income in the two groups is not

The Art of Self-Persuasion

Table 8.1

Group A		Group B	
	Income		Income
Individual 1	10	Individual 1	20
2	20	2	30
3	25	3	40
4	45	4	50
		5	60

the same – 25 pounds in group A and 40 pounds in group B. An identical average deviation therefore does not mean the same in both cases: for a person earning 1,000 pounds, an average deviation of 10 pounds has a totally different meaning from somebody earning on average 20 pounds, for example. No matter, we merely bring back the average deviations to the norm to eliminate this effect. This gives 0.4 for group A and 0.3 for group B. A is therefore more *unequal* than B.[19]

At this point, one perhaps asks whether it is normal to consider all deviations from the norm in the same way. What counts above all is whether a significant number of individuals deviate *a great deal* from the norm. What one has in one's mind when considering the notion of *equality* is in fact a criterion of this kind: inequality is the greater when more people deviate *a lot* from the average. The idea can be developed further by looking not at deviations from the norm in absolute values, but the *square* of these deviations. In this way, a deviation will be all the greater the further it is from the norm.[20] Here, the measure of inequality for group A is 0.5, and for group B 0.35. A is again more *unequal* than B. But the contrast here is more marked than in the previous case.

There is another approach: to say that *inequality* is where many people own little and a few people own a lot. The classic formalization of this idea is a curve whose points indicate the share of total income of, for example, the 5 per cent least well-off, the 10 per cent least well-off, the 15 per cent, the 20 per cent, and so on. A line joining these points is more rounded the greater the inequality. Various manipulations which need not concern us here will allow us to define a measure giving 0.275 in the case of group A, and 0.2 in the case of group B. Once again, group A wins the contest for inequality, but the contrast is more marked than in the second case and less than in the third case.[21]

There is nothing to say, therefore, that these different measures, corresponding to acceptable interpretations of the *idea* of equality, have to give an identical result when they are applied to a specific situation. In other words, there is only a family likeness among the various possible meanings of the idea. The statement 'this distribution is more unequal than that one' is of the same type as 'this man is tall', not 'this man is *taller* than that one': it is impossible to give it a definition both precise and devoid of arbitrariness.

An identical demonstration could be made in relation to a whole range of instances, but I will give just one further example – that of *social mobility* – in order to show that the 'equality' example is not an isolated case and that even concepts where reasonable *measures* apply are *normally* polythetic.

Table 8.2 shows two imaginary examples of mobility.

Table 8.2

Example A				Example B			
Social class at birth	Social class now			Social class at birth	Social class now		
	I	II	Total		I	II	Total
I	60	40	100	I	70	30	100
II	20	280	300	II	30	270	300
Total	80	320	400	Total	100	300	400

In example A, 60 people change class between one generation and the next, that is, the 40 people of Class I at birth and Class II now, and the 20 people of Class II at birth and Class I now. The total is the same in example B (30 people changing from Class I to Class II, and 30 from Class II to Class I). Since the overall total is the same in both case, the *proportion* of persons belonging to a class different from that into which they were born is also the same. On this measure of social mobility, the two 'societies' A and B are therefore *equally* *mobile*. The ease (or the difficulty) with which people can change class is identical in both cases.

If that is so, does this mean that the influence of status at birth on subsequent status is the same in both cases? There is no reason for this to be so, and in fact it is not the case. This new interpretation of mobility can be approached by asking whether changing class is easier, or not, than staying in the same class. In example A, 60 per cent of people stay in Class I, and 6.7 per cent move into it. In example B, 70 per cent stay in Class I, and 10 per cent move into it. Since the difference between the two figures is greater in the second case than the first, society B this time seems *less mobile* than A.[22]

The question can, however, be put in a different way. Since the number of people in each class can vary over time (for example, social change has led to a reduction in the number of people in agriculture), there is a minimum and a maximum mobility. If, for example, the number of people in agriculture falls from one generation to the next, it follows that some of the children of farmers have moved to another sector. In example A, the total in Class I is 100 in one generation and 80 in the next, which implies a *minimum movement* of 20 (another way of putting it is to say that the *structural mobility* is 20). Similarly, since there are more people in Class II than in Class I, not everyone can change class from one generation to the next: we can readily see that there cannot be more than 180 changes of class.

Here, we are measuring mobility by asking ourselves where *real* mobility is in relation to this maximum and minimum. The figures from this new interpretation of the *idea* of mobility are 0.25 for A and 0.3 for B, and this time B is a more mobile society than A.[23]

Developing the same idea, we can also look at whether the influence of class at birth on class now tends to be nearer the minimum possible or the maximum possible. Here, the measure of mobility for A is 0.33, and for B 0.4. Again, B is more mobile than A, but the contrast is more marked than in the previous case.[24]

We can probably stop the demonstration at this point. The polythetic 'empire' is larger than is often thought. Not only are words such as 'causes' or 'reasons', 'big' or 'game' polythetic, but so are words such as 'equality' or 'mobility', even though they have given rise to a whole range of *measures*.

Terms which define *concrete* realities can themselves be polythetic in nature.

As Waismann says,[25] even a concept such as 'gold', which seems to indicate a *well-defined* matter (as we say), does not correspond to an immutably fixed definition, even in scientific usage:

> . . . we define gold in contrast to some other metals such as alloys. This suffices for our present needs, and we do not probe any farther. We tend to *overlook* the fact that there are always other directions in which the concept has not been defined. And if we did, we could easily imagine conditions which would necessitate new limitations. In short, it is not possible to define a concept like gold with absolute precision.[26]

If the definition of 'gold' can vary, how can there be an immutable definition of vital concepts such as 'anomic', attitude', 'paradigm' and a whole host of others which could be mentioned? I quote these examples simply because they have all been shown by research to have a large number of uses, linked to each other by simple *family likenesses*.[27]

Similarly, one can only see family *likenesses* between the myriad objects put into fairly watertight compartments during drawing-room conversations or scientific debates. The notions of 'novel', 'tragedy', 'drama', 'Wagnerian opera', 'sociology', 'economics', 'Romanticism', 'function' or 'structure' are polythetic words. Like the words for colours, *in many cases* we can use them with complete certainty, *even though* they are polythetic. For example, there is usually no problem in putting a piece of music into the category of either 'classical music' or 'popular music'; but nobody is in a position to decide *what there is in common* in pieces of classical music *and* which is not to be found in popular music.

A solution is sometimes suggested to the 'problem' supposedly raised by this 'contradiction' between the certainty with which we handle some categories and their indefinable quality: since there is in fact nothing in common between *all* the elements in the two compartments of 'popular music' and 'classical music', the distinction is arguably not *objective*, but *intersubjective*; 'classical' music has a function of social identification. In fact, there is no more reason to consider certain indefinable categories as social illusions than there is to regard colours as illusions because one cannot define them.

In other words, there is no reason to deny the reality and objective nature of a distinction such as that between 'classical music' and 'popular music'. Moreover, the *vagueness* of the distinction is neither more unhelpful nor more mysterious than the vagueness of terms such as 'big', 'game', inequality', 'paradigm' and so on. All the false problems, and all the false solutions to them, usually disappear if one realizes that these words *are* polythetic.

In other words, the *vagueness* to these terms is a mystery only if all words are regarded as non-polythetic, and if, as in the case of words such as 'chair' or 'bicycle', they can be given a dictionary-type definition which exclusively designates the object in question with sufficient precision to identify as such all chairs and all bicycles in Creation. Even the dictionary cannot satisfy these requirements with regard, for example, to words designating colours. No definition can indicate what a yellow object might look like if one has never seen one.

In some cases, it is easy to recognize that a word is polythetic in nature. In other cases, as is readily seen from the examples just given, a category *is* polythetic, but it is commonly interpreted by means of the opposite *a priori* (the usual notation is used here to indicate a metaconscious *a priori*):

'[this term is non-polythetic in character]★'

Therefore, those who try to find *the* right definition of terms such as 'paradigm' or 'anomie', those who are surprised that a notion can play such an important role in scientific discourse though it cannot be defined precisely, or who seek the social basis of the difference between 'classical music' and 'popular music', cannot fail to be aware of this *a priori*. On the other hand, however, they are not necessarily *consciously* aware of it.

We see that this process is analogous to that regarding other types of *a priori*: in case of doubt, the tendency is to choose metaconsciously the simplest *a priori*. In the present example, it will be accepted as self-evident that '[this term is non-polythetic]★'. The reason why this 'Augustinian' *a priori* (as Wittgenstein would say) is so common is that it constantly imposes itself on us in everyday life: in very many cases, 'words name things'.[28]

Ordinary knowledge is therefore right to make words non-polythetic. Methodical knowledge, for its part, is often right in trying to convert *notions* of a polythetic type into *concepts* of a non-polythetic type.[29] This kind of refinement can even be said to characterize scientific knowledge. For example, the term 'movement', which is polythetic in Aristotelian physics, ceases to be so with Galileo.[30] In the same way, many notions change from being polythetic to being non-polythetic when they move from ordinary knowledge to scientific knowledge: this applies, for example, to the concept of *speed*.

In other cases, such a conversion has been tried, but without success. This can be seen in the case of a notion such as *rationality*: a non-polythetic definition restricts its meaning to such an extent that we are forced to invent new concepts – *subjective rationality*, for example – to identify its content.

What interests me here, however, is that many *received ideas* are at least partly the result of linguistic *a priori* which, like the one I chose to examine, consist of attributing a term to a *type* which is not its own.

To illustrate this point, I will again quote examples from influential writing in contemporary philosophy and sociology of science.

QUESTIONS OF DEMARCATION

The Augustinian *a priori*, whereby words are regarded as non-polythetic when they appear to designate clearly distinct entities, can be illustrated by reference to debates aimed at establishing lines of *demarcation* between these entities: how do we distinguish scientific knowledge from other forms of knowledge, science from magic, or modern societies from traditional societies, and so on?

I am interested here in the first of these distinctions.

I use the term *demarcation* because it refers to one of the most famous aspects of Popper's philosophy. His theory of *demarcation* tries to define the criteria for distinguishing, in particular, science from metaphysics, but also, more generally, from intellectual products which cannot claim to belong to the category of science. Of course, Popper paid great attention to this question for several reasons. Though he always steadfastly refused to allow himself to be grouped with the positivists, he nevertheless inherited a problem which greatly exercised the Vienna

Circle. Secondly, he quickly began to harbour grave doubts – which his later collaboration with Alfred Adler in no way dissipated – about the scientific nature of psychoanalysis, another thing to come out of Vienna. Of course, he also did a lot of work analysing the soundness of Marxism. However, the only way we can prove that these two disciplines do not deserve the distinction of being called *sciences* is to establish a criterion or criteria for distinguishing science from non-science.

Let me make it clear that in no way should 'non-science' and metaphysics be assimilated – this would be completely counter to Popper's intentions – nor should we regard products which cannot be classed as scientific as being devoid of meaning, significance or interest. On the contrary, Popper insists on the importance of metaphysics. Moreover, he agrees with those who, like Holton, want metaphysical ideas to play a large part in generating scientific ideas, and he would not in any way object to the view that the main ideas of, for example, Niels Bohr are explained – at least partly – by the fact that he was an avid reader of Kierkegaard. On the other hand, however, he says that it is important not to confuse science and metaphysics. What interests Popper is not judging metaphysics and science, but saying precisely how they are different.[31]

The reader is aware of the rest of the story. Popper proposes the famous criterion of *falsification* to fulfil the function of *demarcation*.

This criterion has always provoked lively debate – firstly because it poses a fascinating problem, and then because it does not provide any solution to it.

The first difficulty concerning Popper's criterion is that many theories are falsifiable without being scientific. For example, 'the train to Caen departs at 8.47' is a falsifiable statement which could hardly be claimed to be scientific. In everyday life, we are constantly coming up with theories and making predictions which, though falsifiable, are nevertheless not scientific. Falsifiability is not therefore a *sufficient* condition of scientificity.

It is, however, not a *necessary* condition either. All kinds of scientific theories, and significant ones at that, are not falsifiable. Popper was well aware of this point; it is the main reason for the difficulties he always had in categorizing Darwin's theory. It is of course hard not to regard as scientific a theory which has played and still plays a particularly significant role in the history of life sciences; but it is true that this theory is not falsifiable. Assuming that one observes a phenomenon of evolution where one cannot explain how, *in fact*, it is the result of a process of mutation and selection,[32] one can always plead ignorance and say – without in most cases raising objections – that the information available is not enough to reconstitute effectively the process in question. Unless one was privileged to witness a demiurge create a new species of being, it is hard to see what fact or what kind of fact could *falsify* – that is, in Popper's language, *refute* – Darwin's theory or the neo-Darwinian theory of evolution.

In reality, Darwin's theory cannot be falsified for a very simple reason – it consists less of statements about reality than of statements about the *ways* of apprehending reality. Reduced to its simplest expression, Darwin's message (in its neo-Darwinian form) is; if a particular species is observed in a particular ecological niche, *try* to explain this by reference to mechanisms of mutation and selection. It is true that this *advice* is often good advice. For example, the ash-grey moths in the Birmingham and Manchester regions which I mentioned earlier[33] turned into black moths through mutation and selection. Generally speaking, one does not count cases where the advice turned out to be sound.

However, though advice can be regarded as sound or not, it cannot be said to be true or false.

This semantic distinction explains the difficulty in applying the attributes of true and false to Darwin's theory.[34] At the same time, the example of Darwin shows that some scientific theories relate to the real world, whereas others put forward general frameworks of thought within which theories will be developed. For example, Darwin's theory equips us better to come up with a theory explaining the change of colour in moths in the British textile districts.

However, these frameworks of thought, these 'paradigms' – since it is indeed a distinction of this kind which Kuhn's word *paradigm* tries to express – are not true or false, but more or less useful or sound, like *advice*.

My point in stressing this is to argue that the case of Darwinism is not an isolated one, and that it is not an *exception* to Popper's demarcation theory. The difficulties which Darwinism creates for this theory stem from its very nature. This case covers a category of intellectual products – Kuhn's *paradigms* – which is absolutely vital for the functioning of scientific thinking. Popper's demarcation criterion did not therefore hit the Darwin case as the exception which proves the rule, but as if it was an iceberg . . .

The conclusion in any event is that there are all sorts of theories which are scientific, judging by their decisive role in the history and functioning of scientific thinking, but which are not falsifiable.

On the other hand, after Popper had convinced everybody that science cannot be defined by the capacity which it had been given for centuries to *verify* the statements it propounds, and after he had destroyed *verification-ism* and replaced it by *falsificationism*, the wreck of this demarcation criterion meant that there was a void: how can one define the specificity of science among all the intellectual products which set out to explain the world?

Other writers, such as Merton, argued that science should be characterized by the criterion of *openness*: the institutionalization of the spirit of method is the *distinctive trait* of science. This conception of the boundary is all the more attractive in that it coincides with a superb explanation of the origins of modern science: Merton argued that the scientific explosion of the seventeenth and eighteenth centuries should be explained by reference to the influence of the Puritan *ethic* and its stress on analysis and critique.

Against this proposition is the argument that there are many episodes showing that scientists – and famous ones at that – can cling indefinitely to moribund theories; Lakatos even suggested, in a kind of apologue,[35] that this scientific relentlessness is normal. I have already alluded to this point when I was discussing Durkheim's theory of magic:[36] when a theory is proved wrong, there are generally as many reasons to keep it as to reject it.

Therefore science is not defined by its openness either, nor is it defined by the obligation to 'accept the verdict of the facts'. Is it not well known, moreover, that every fact is 'constructed'? Popper himself pointed out that, when we read a thermometer, we are projecting theoretical learning on to a column of mercury. Needless to say, science is not defined by a desire for truth on the part of scientists. It would be an insult to metaphysicians to suggest that they do not have this desire. Scientists also have other passions, and it is hard to tell what criterion could distinguish scientific activity from other kinds of intellectual activity.

In the final analysis, it was Paul Feyerabend who drew the moral of this long debate on the boundary between science and non-science, which I admit I am recounting in a somewhat informal way. Perhaps the very success, which was well deserved, of *Against Method*[37] was due to the fact that Feyerbend was the first to give full expression to what people were beginning to formulate in their thoughts. For years, philosophers and sociologists, implicitly and indirectly like Merton, or explicitly and directly like Popper, had been suggesting criteria of *demarcation*, though all these had collapsed one after the other. When Feyerabend said that there was no basic difference between science, magic and fairy stories, he was expressing in a provocative way a conclusion which nobody had dared to draw, but which everybody was expecting.

Chapters 15 (which contains a critique of Popper) and 16 (which discusses Lakatos) of *Against Method* show that my summary is not fictitious. Feyerabend rejects Popper's argument that science is essentially about solving problems. His main point is that the big divide when science appeared had the effect not of *solving* more satisfactorily those problems which existed before, but rather of reshaping completely the list of questions which one could, and above all which one *had to*, ask oneself – and not ask oneself. For example, says Feyerabend, with the appearance of science, one no longer tested the hypothesis that stars have an effect on the psyche. On the other hand, scientific research is often motivated not by the desire to solve a problem, but, for example, to chance one's arm.

In other words, the aims of science are not as straightforward as Popperians claim.

Secondly, science is not defined, says Feyerabend, by a measurable increase in the 'content of knowledge'. No doubt each new theory dearly wants to stress those points which it tackles better than the old ones, but it keeps quiet about what it does less well, and also what it throws away. The impression is then that, when one theory replaces another, there is generally an increase in knowledge. This, however, is merely an 'epistemological illusion'. In reality, the relationship between two successive theories is better represented by overlapping circles. The epistemological illusion of the *progress* of knowledge stems from the fact that reference is always exclusively to the *overlap* of these circles. Of course, Feyerabend agrees with Kuhn and, he says, Lakatos (whose argument he somewhat distorts on this point) in asserting that the choice between alternative theories cannot be based on objective principles. Popper's falsificationism must therefore be spurned.

Similarly, Feyerabend says that Lakatos's *cautious rationalism* has to be rejected.

Lakatos argued that *the continuous growth* or otherwise, of 'research programmes' was the objective basis guiding scientists in their work. As is shown by the resurgence of atomic theory, research programmes may very well degenerate, then reappear. Of course, there are times when some programmes seem to stagnate, but it is just as rational to abandon them as it is to become enmeshed in them. As for the reasons why a theory is accepted, these are infinitely variable in nature. They can even stem from manipulations; it was less because of the fertility of his theory that Galileo attracted the attention of some people, than that he impressed them with his telescope.[38] To summarize starkly Feyerabend's chief objection to Lakatos: the decision to back or abandon a research programme is not made on objective grounds. On the contrary,

> research programs disappear not because they are killed off by debate, but because their defenders are killed off in the struggle for survival.[39]

I note in passing that, throughout his analysis, Feyerabend's reasoning is in a narrow *framework*:

> [either *in any scientific debate* one is right because one is the stronger *or* one is the stronger because one is right]*.

He opts for the first alternative, and does not consider that the causality might be circular, going in *t* from A to B and in *t*+1 from B to A: however, if it is true, as Feyerabend argues, that Galileo was – *initially* – regarded by some people as right because he was cleverer, that does not stop us thinking that, *afterwards*, it was because he was right that he received acclaim.

However, the main conclusion of this analysis is that science is not definable: 'Everyone agrees that Corpernicus' theory was a great step forward, but hardly anyone can present it properly, and even less list the reasons for its excellence . . .'[40] In other words, very often one cannot say why one endorses a theory. The result is that Lakatos is wrong in thinking that science has a 'nature' and an 'integrity'.[41]

In short, science has no essence, because one cannot *define* it. Consequently, one cannot say that it is superior to magic. Lakatos is therefore wrong in preferring it to magic and in thinking that he has the slightest objective reason for doing so, 'as if it was established that modern science is superior to magic or the Aristotelian science, and that its findings are not illusory'.[42] Look at 'the Aristotelians': they 'manage very well',[43] and there is no objective means of proving that the knowledge content of Aristotelian theory was lower than that of modern science.[44]

Let us note in passing that Feyerabend reproduces an idea which Benjamin Whorf had propounded very intelligently and successfully.[45] Every 'theory', 'paradigm' or 'research programme', for Feyerabend, assumes the status of a sort of small hermetic *culture*, and it is impossible to say whether it is superior, equal or inferior to any other.[46] Scientific paradigms can thus be compared to artistic styles, which *similarly* constitute, argues Feyerabend, *incommensurable* totalities.[47] They can also be compared to the *cultures* about which anthropologists speak. For example, says Feyerabend, the archaic world is dominated by a *juxta-positive* conception of things (shown, for instance, in the parathetic nature of Homeric style). This conception differs from ours exactly as Einstein's physics from Newton's.

In the end, thinking about science is based on anthropological method: 'The anthropological method is the correct method of studying the structure of science (and, while we are about it, any other form of life)'.[48]

Conclusions apart, all the statements on which Feyerabend's argument is based are perfectly acceptable.

All these empirical statements stem from observable situations. Why did Galileo not in fact try to bluff with his telescope? To take another example: how can we seriously deny that scientists sometimes proceed as much on the basis of a desire for power as a concern to discover the truth, or that they often decide in favour of a particular theory for subjective reasons?[49]

Nevertheless, these conclusions are based not only on these statements but also on innocuous *a priori*:

'[only what is defined or definable exists]★';
'[two entities are distinct only when one can say in what respect they are distinct]★';
'[of two things, one can be said to be superior to the other only if one can explain in what respect it is superior]★'.

These principles are the core of Feyerabend's proof. Although they may appear ordinary, they are far from anodyne, and on the contrary presuppose a great deal. To appreciate this, one has only to think of a simple example – it is easy to say with great certainty that a particular literary work or piece of music is superior to another one, but nevertheless not be able to say why. Yet this perfectly ordinary fact is incompatible with the *a priori* mentioned above.

In any event, if these *a priori* are set aside or thrown into doubt, Feyerabend's conclusions immediately vanish.

His conclusions are provocative in appearance only. If they were nothing but provocation, they would perhaps have attracted attention, but they would not have been endorsed. The reason why they were is that they articulated *what everybody was thinking*, even though nobody dared say it. And the reason why nobody dared say it was that, if science is not superior to magic, it becomes impossible to explain its success. Feyerabend himself moreover recognizes that he has no means to explain the success of this fairy tale which is science.

In reality, the story, with actors from all kinds of backgrounds – philosophy, sociology or history – who often appear incapable of communicating with each other, is incomprehensible if one fails to see that, behind their differences, they agree on one vital point. I mean the *a priori* that a distinction in reality must correspond to a linguistic difference and vice versa: either science is *in reality* different from metaphysics or magic, and in this case the distinction has to be capable of being stated, or the distinction is incapable of definition and the conclusion is that it is an illusion.

Popper is convinced of the validity of this *a priori* and sees the falsifiablity of scientific theories as their distinctive attribute. Merton does not pitch the debate on this ground, but implicitly makes *openness* and a critical mind the distinctive characteristics of science. Feyerabend concludes that all candidates for the function of distinctive attribute fail, and that, *in consequence*, there is no *real* difference between science and the other interpretations of reality – magic, metaphysics, even children's stories.

Efforts to establish the distinctive trait of science, as well as Feyerabend's relativist conclusions, are all based on a supreme *a priori*:

[the word 'science' is a non–polythetic–type word]★.

The reason for this concurrence is that, in everyday life, this linguistic *a priori* is common. Here is another case of the influence of the *frameworks* of ordinary knowledge on methodical reasoning. The idea that one ought to be able to say *how* two distinct things are in fact distinct is rarely regarded as out of the ordinary in everyday life. It is certainly considered in scientific life as a postulate which it is difficult not to accept. Scientists perhaps accept that the postulate can be rejected in the artistic sphere, for example, but they will find it much harder not to accept it in the scientific field.

The reason therefore why the postulate in question seemed so natural to Feyerabend is also, ironically, that he regarded the basic principles of scientific activity as self-evident. Being an anarchist takes more than wanting to be one.

The same also applies to being Wittgensteinian, in that Feyerabend does not see that the key notions in *Against Method* (progress, science, and so on) are polythetic notions, and that his whole argument revolves round the opposite implied postulate – the 'Augustinian' postulate to the criticism of which a great deal of *Philosophical Investigations* is devoted.

We have only to replace the above *a priori* by the correct one, that is:

[the word 'science' is a polythetic word]*

for the whole of the argument launched by Popper and Merton and concluded by Feyerabend to crumble.

Why is this *a priori* the 'correct one'? Because 'science' covers complex and varied activities, and it is no easier to distinguish it from metaphysics than it is to distinguish classical music from popular music. The result is not that science and metaphysics *are* not distinct. However, in a case such as this, it is the wrong *a priori* which is very likely to appear *by default*.

No doubt there are cases where one recognizes, without being aware of it, that certain terms are polythetic. When one reads, for example, that Debussy's *Pelléas* is a *Wagnerian* opera,[50] one immediately takes the word 'Wagnerian' as polythetic: it does not challenge Debussy's originality, but indicates that the theme of adultery, the symbolism of night and day and of water, the mythical nature of the characters and locations, the (discreet) presence of leitmotifs, and other characteristics 'remind one' of *Tristan*. Here the differences and similarities are seen for what they are – vague and capable of being suggested rather than expressed in an entirely distinct way. The term 'Wagnerian' does not imply that there is any more than a *family likeness* between the two works.

Similarly, the *non-polythetic* nature of a term can of course be recognized as such without hesitation in many cases.

There is, however, an intermediate category of situations where – like the examples analysed in previous chapters – a hesitation appears about the appropriate *a priori* to be applied, and where one tends to adopt *by default* the simplest *a priori*. The distinction between science and magic or between science and metaphysics seems so 'obvious' that one easily perceives these terms in a non-polythetic mode.[51]

Perhaps this mode also imposes itself more easily when entities – here science, magic[52] or metaphysics – are solidly institutionalized and correspond to clear social differences. In other words, perhaps institutionalization favours reification.[53]

PROGRESS, TRUTH, OBJECTIVITY

In this analysis of the boundary between science and non-science, I have been trying less to discuss the fundamentals of the question than to bring out the linguistic *a priori* of the debate. The same applies to this final section where, again referring to an example from the philosophy of science, I return to a writer already mentioned in Chapter 5 – Thomas Kuhn.

The reason I have not referred to Kuhn in previous sections of this chapter is that he is aware of the polythetic nature of the term 'science'. In his book *The Structure of Scientific Revolutions* he says that he doubts whether a definition of science is possible:[54] science cannot be defined, or easily distinguished from other activities on the basis of objective distinctive traits, in the way in which the activity of a carpenter can be differentiated from that of a baker, for example.

Kuhn says in this respect that debates on the meaning of the word 'science', so frequent in the human sciences, do not occur in the natural sciences:

> Men argue that psychology, for example, is a science because it possesses such and such characteristics. Others counter that those characteristics are either unnecessary or not sufficient to make a field a science. Often great energy is invested, great passion aroused, and the outsider is at a loss to know why. Can very much depend on a *definition* of 'science'? Can a definition tell a man whether he is a scientist or not? If so, why do not natural scientists or artists worry about the definition of the term?[55]

In this passage, it seems that Kuhn is aware of the fact that the notion of science is polythetic in nature. He clearly recognizes that there can be no cut and dried definition of this complex activity.

How does it happen, he then asks, that some people think they are indulging in science, and others do not? On what reality is this impression based? Kuhn's hypothesis is that the notions of science and progress are indissolubly linked:

we tend to see as science any field in which progress is marked.[56]

But how can *progress* be defined? Once again it is a matter of the status of the word. Kuhn rejects the idea that progress can be defined as moving closer to reality as it is, and claims not to see what other definition could be given to this notion. Nevertheless, it is clear that certain disciplines give the impression of making progress, while others do not. What is the basis of this feeling?

Kuhn's reply is that the necessary and sufficient condition for a feeling of progress is for members of a scientific community to agree on a *paradigm* or, put another way, on the *framework* of their activities.

The same can happen with theologians, who have the feeling that their discussions are making progress as soon as they are in agreement on a certain number of principles. Painters also, says Kuhn, at certain times – when for example they were in agreement that painting should try to reproduce reality as faithfully as possible – had the feeling that their activity was making progress. Conversely, the idea that painting can make progress is regarded today as unacceptable, because there is no longer general agreement on the *rules* of art.

Similarly, economics is perhaps no more scientific than other social sciences, but it is different from the others in that economists are more or less in agreement on the rules of their discipline, and therefore they more readily have the impression that their discipline is capable of *progress*.

In the case of philosophy itself, the reason why it does not really give the feeling of being capable of making progress is that it is split into tendencies or schools. However, within these schools, a feeling of progress can arise. For example, a philosopher who develops Aristotelian or Kantian philosophy can readily have a feeling of making progress:

> Scientific progress is not different in kind from progress in other fields, but the absence at most times of competing schools that question each other's aims and standards makes the progress of a normal-scientific community far easier to see.[57]

To these examples, Kuhn adds that the autonomy in relation to the external world which characterizes natural sciences facilitates the appearance of those communities characteristic of *normal science*.

This argument is ingenious and interesting. We might try to put a form to it as follows:

1) science is not definable;
2) nevertheless, certain disciplines give the feeling of being scientific, while others do not;
3) [this feeling has a correlate]*

4) [which must be able to be defined]★;
5) by 1), there is no objective distinctive trait to science;
6) to the feeling in question, there must therefore correspond a non-objective correlate;
7) the feeling of 'indulging in science' appears when the feeling of progress appears;
8) [the correlate of the feeling of progress must be able to be defined]★;
9) progress is not definable in objective terms, for example, as coming closer to truth;
10) [if the distinctive trait of progress is not objective, it is social]★;
11) in any discipline, the feeling of progress appears when there is agreement on basic rules;

---

12) it is agreement on rules which determines that the nature of a discipline is scientific (or not).

Let us leave aside possible objections to the *explicit* statements in this line of reasoning, and merely note that at first sight they are acceptable.

After all, the important thing is that the reasoning is based on two main points: firstly, the idea that, though the notion of science is not itself definable, as soon as a particular community has the impression of 'indulging in science' or has the feeling of progress, there must correspond to these subjective or intersubjective facts *definable* distinctions; secondly, the proposition that what cannot be defined by reference to objective distinctive criteria has to be defined on social criteria. Science cannot be defined by its ends, unlike the activities of the baker. However, on the feeling 'my discipline is/is not scientific' can be put a *social* distinction: *agreement/non-agreement* between members of the community in question.

In other words, there is in this reasoning the conception that:

[to a psychological distinction, there must correspond a linguistic distinction]★.

The other *a priori* in Kuhn is that a distinctive trait which is not *objective* is *social*.

This theory gives rise to spectacular consequences, since it ends up by depriving the idea of *progress*, like that of truth, of all substance.[58] Let us recall a passage already quoted on page 000: 'It is now time to notice that until the last very few pages the term "truth" had entered this essay only in a quotation from Francis Bacon.'[59] Kuhn then explains why he has avoided the word 'truth': the definition usually given to it is unacceptable:

Can we not account for both science's existence and its success in terms of evolution from the community's state of knowledge at any given time? Does it really help to imagine that there is some one full, objective, true account of nature and that the proper measure of scientific achievement is the extent to which it brings us closer to that ultimate goal?

Later, Kuhn compares his proposed radical changes to the Darwinian revolution, while hastening to add that it is a matter of a comparison which must be seen as limited in scope. Despite this warning, the comparison allows us to gauge the significance of the Kuhnian revolution: scientific evolution is lacking finality.[60]

There are other spectacular consequences: Since the feeling of progress assumes a feeling of agreement, there can be no progess between either competing paradigms or successive paradigms. Galilean physics is not superior to Aristotelian physics; it is simply another way of seeing the world. Why is it more effective? Kuhn recognizes that this is a difficult puzzle to solve and that in fact there is no way, within the framework of his theory, of solving it.

However, these conclusions hold good only thanks to the *a priori* that for any feeling that there is a distinction there must be a distinction which is either *objective* or *social*.

On the other hand, they do not stand up as soon as it is agreed that the notions of 'progress', 'objectivity', 'truth', and 'science' are *polythetic*; in other words, if it is seen that there is a corresponding reality, even though they do not have the same relationship with it as the word 'chair' has with the thing it designates.

The word 'progress' is concretized in many ways, and between them there are only *family likenesses*. Progress occurs when a new language – 'functional' or 'synchronic', as I described it earlier[61] – is used for subjects such as international trade relations (by Ricardo) or religious phenomena (by Weber) which up to then were approached in the 'genetic' mode. Neither language is inherently superior to the other; but *together* they embrace a wider range of phenomena. Moreover, by limiting each other, they allow us better to evaluate the validity of the theories to which they give rise.

However, *progress* in the general sense can amount to elucidating a question of fact, clarifying a technique for testing a hypothesis, inventing a new theory, discrediting an existing theory, or bringing one phenomenon closer to another, as when epidemiological methods are used to analyse rumours, or Darwinism or micro-economics is applied to intellectual production, and so on.

It can also consist of limiting the scope of a theory, of clarifying, as we saw in the case of Hotelling's model,[62] the conditions in which a theory is valid; in other words, of correctly locating a theory.

This latter form of progress has significant consequences: every theory tends to attract a validity which initially is too broad but which then goes on reducing; and since the number of *points of view* and *languages* increases, the result is that knowledge takes on more and more the appearance of an archipelago. Paradoxically, the progress of knowledge may also promote scepticism, in that theories which are overarching and lacking in competition become rarer and rarer, and in that the general level of incommensurability increases because of the greater number of languages.

We must also note that the appearance of a new paradigm complicates reality; it constitutes progress but, at the same time, complicates the notion of progress. For example, Ricardo's paradigm or Malinowski's functionalist paradigm allow the explanation of certain phenomena not only *genetically*, but also *functionally*. They therefore create a situation of double truth and double language which can easily appear to be in contradiction to the very notion of truth. A 'complication' such as this can encourage a sceptical conception of science.

This sceptical conclusion, however, is based on a very specific view of the relationship between words and things.

That is not all, however. In certain cases, the geometric metaphor associated with the notions of truth or progress – and which Kuhn rejects – rings true: *progress* does indeed consist, in many circumstances, of 'getting closer to reality'. The theory that the earth is round – even if this is only an approximation, since the earth is not a perfect sphere – is obviously closer to reality than the theory that the earth is flat. Similarly, it is hard to see how scientists researching continental drift could go on pursuing their favourite activity if they were not convinced that their efforts were directed to 'getting closer to reality'.

In all examples *of this type* – and there are many of them – the visual metaphors which assimilate truth to an accurate copy of reality, and progress to the various improvements which can be made to this copy, are perfectly correct and acceptable.

However, there are also cases where this is not so, but where one can nevertheless speak of progress and truth.

When a writer such as Ricardo propounded his theory of international trade and his law of comparative advantage, this was an example of progress which Samuelson later suggested should be regarded as one of the most spectacular in the history of economics. However, the theory cannot be regarded as closer to reality than, for example, the work of historians of international trade.

Progress in the general sense can therefore consist of getting closer to reality. It can also consist of something totally different. Similarly, in a 'game' there can be an opponent or not be an opponent, but it can nevertheless be a game in both cases.

Laudan[63] showed the polymorphous nature of the notion of progress in the case of the natural sciences.

For example, Ptolemy was criticized from ancient times not because of the inability of his theory to account for certain phenomena, but because the mechanism it used – which included eccentrics as well as epicycles – seemed very *complicated*. There are therefore cases where progress consists in getting rid of a convoluted theory.

As Whewell showed, Laudan goes on, *conceptual clarification* is, together with falsification and a host of other processes, one of the most remarkable ways to progress.[64] The special theory of relativity, the development of behaviourist psychology and many other episodes in the history of science were initially inspired by a desire for conceptual clarity much more than by the wish to resolve an *anomaly* in Kuhn's sense.

It was in fact a *critique* of the notion of simultaneity (under what conditions can one say that two events occuring on two objects moving away from each other at a speed not insignificant in relation to that of light are simultaneous?) which led Einstein to the special theory of relativity.

One might add conversely that the reason why a discipline seems to be faltering is sometimes that the *ethos* behind it does not set great value by conceptual clarity.

Problems of a *methodological* nature – in the widest meaning of the term – have also played a large part in the progress of the natural sciences: can one accept in scientific language terms referring to phenomena which do not correspond to any tangible reality? Can one accept notions such as that of 'action at a distance' in time and space?[65]

Moreover, the importance of *ontological* problems is now recognized: Leibniz and Huygens had difficulty in accepting the idea of action at a distance by one body on another, since this contradicted the very idea of substance. How can one in fact accept that a substance can have properties detached from itself?

We might also stress that the notion of *theory* is itself vague: besides narrow theories (for example, continental drift, the Oedipus complex), there are broad theories (for example, atomic theory). Besides theories which are subject by their very nature to the criterion of truth, others, such as the synthetic theory of evolution, are not directly based on it.[66]

We have only to start making a list of the possible meanings of the notion of *progress* to see straightaway that it can never be completed, and that it is difficult to list these meanings in any kind of order – indications which do not detract from the polythetic nature of the notion.

As soon as this polythetic nature is recognized, it becomes clear that it is impossible to define progress by reference to a specific process such as *falsification*. However, other 'obviousnesses' also emerge just as clearly:

the fact that one cannot always choose between two theories or paradigms for objective reasons is enough to reject the existence of progress only if one fails to recognize the polythetic nature of the notion.

This polythetic character no more allows us to doubt the existence of the corresponding reality when it comes to 'progress' than it does in the case of the term 'game'.

Kuhn's failure to recognize the polythetic character of the notion of progress is apparent also in the fact that he never refers to the conceptual, methodological and ontological problems which play a decisive part in scientific life. Since he conceives of progress in a purely empirical way, he never manages to encounter it.[67]

Similar remarks to these on *progress* can be made about the notion of *truth*: Kant's sarcastic remarks about people who try to define truth deserve to be taken literally; they indicate that the notion of *truth* is also polythetic in nature.

One observation will suffice to suggest that the word *true*, applied to a theory or a statement, can have *at least* two meanings which have between them only a *family likeness*.

In fact, certain theories are true in the sense that they reconstitute reality as it is ('the earth is round').

Conversely, a theory such as that propounded by Max Weber to explain the proliferation and vitality of Protestant sects in the United States is in no way a reconstitution of reality as it is.[68] The metaphor of the copy is in this case completely misplaced, and it is not even certain that the notion of *correspondence* (in the Tarski sense) can be applied to it. Nevertheless, the theory is true; and nobody has ever seriously challenged it (unlike his theory in *The Protestant Ethic*).

It is true in the sense that all its statements can be regarded as valid; all its 'empirical' propositions, considered one by one, correctly describe traits readily observable in American, German or French society; its 'psychological' propositions, analysing the reasons why actors behave as they do, are 'obvious'[69] in a way which makes them difficult to reject.

This set of propositions, all readily acceptable, is enough to explain the vitality of sects and the religiosity of the general population; but however meaningful this concept is, their *correspondence* with reality is by nature infinitely more complex than that between the statement 'snow is white' and the reality of the whiteness of snow.

Similarly, Durkheim's theory of magic gives a feeling of truth, and Lévy-Bruhl's one of falsity.[70] This is not, however, because the former is closer to the real world than the latter. Moreover it is hard to see how the notion of truth could have this meaning in the present context, since the question of the *raisons d'être* of magic in no way implies the idea of a comparison between a statement and a tangible reality. As in the previous case, Durkheim's theory is true in the sense that it contains only propositions which are readily acceptable; and this is not so for Lévy-Bruhl's.

Just because the notion of truth is in many cases incompatible with the visual metaphors of a *copy*, *closeness* to reality, and so on, does not mean that it is an impractical concept. Clearly it is not by convention that Durkheim's theory of magic is preferable to Levy-Bruhl's, but because the former is true and the latter doubtful.

Similarly, a geographical map is based on the criteria of truth and objectivity, even though it is not a copy of the real world in the sense that a photograph is. Moreover, the *correspondence* theory cannot be applied to this case, unless *ad hoc* changes and complications are made.[71]

Finally, I will simply say that one could apply the previous remarks to a third notion central to all my analyses in this book; the notion of *objectivity*. This also is polythetic in nature: we speak of objectivity in relation to the description of a visible reality as well as in relation to an invisible or abstract reality (for example, the *raisons d'être* of magic).

Traditionally, the conventionalist view of science of which Kuhn is a particularly interesting example is based on the surprising fact that scientists very often do not hesitate to introduce invisible realities (for example, the particles, forces and action at a distance of the physicist, or the microbes and viruses of the biologist). This gives the impression that science could detach itself from reality with the same ease as the 'prelogical' theories which Lévy-Bruhl speaks about and which see invisible forces behind observable phenomena. This is one of the reasons for the unease provoked by the notions of objectivity and truth. As soon as the invisible plays a significant role, we can no longer relate simple representations to these notions. There is then the temptation to see, in the *consensus* which they enjoy, the basis of scientific 'beliefs'. In reality, this distancing from the real world is sometimes temporary, as in the case of microbes, viruses or the planet Neptune.

In other cases, such as Ricardo's theory of international trade or the theory of magic, it is more definitive, in that it stems from the very nature of the questions asked; all things being equal, moreover, the validity of an answer to a question *how* and a question *why* is not measured by the same yardstick, and it is particularly in the case of the former that the metaphor of closeness to reality is relevant. However, the notion of objectivity is not discredited when this metaphor is less readily applicable. This is seen once again in the fact that there are *objective* reasons for preferring, for example, Durkheim's theory of magic to Lévy-Bruhl's.

The 'deconstruction' of Kuhn's theory which I have attempted here allows us finally to disconnect totally his arguments from his conclusions. It is no longer a matter of rejecting the notions of progress, truth or objectivity, merely of recognizing their polythetic nature.

A FINAL POINT ON COGNITIVE RELATIVISM

My analyses in Chapters 4, 5, 6, 7 and 8 contain several examples taken from contemporary sociology and philosophy of science.[72] There is a general conclusion to be drawn from these influential sources:[73] that the notions of *truth, progress of knowledge* or *objectivity* are pure illusion. The most we can do, as Bloor says, is to confer on them the status of regulative concepts.

These hyperbolic conclusions are a remarkable illustration of what I call 'Simmel effects'.

As soon as one sees that they are made possible only by the introduction of *implicit formal a priori* which one *may* accept but whose validity could also perhaps be questioned, one is justified in putting, to the full debate ranging from Popper to Bloor or Barnes, a final point (*zu Ende denken* as Hübner would say) which is different from the one Hübner suggests, and argue that modern cognitive relativism, though an entrenched received idea, far from being a well established doctrine, actually rests on weak foundations.

This is why these studies in cognitive sociology reach a sceptical conclusion on the essential manifestation of contemporary scepticism which is represented by currently dominant philosophy and sociology of science. Contrary to the statement of one of the high priests of modern relativism, there is no need to say farewell to reason.[74]

Summary

Linguistic *a priori* are present, for the most part, implicitly, in all theories. Some are innocuous. Others may significantly affect the conclusions which can be drawn from a line of reasoning, and therefore may explain why valid reasoning can give rise to doubtful, weak or false ideas.

This point was clearly seen by Pareto, the pioneer of the sociology of knowledge – cognitive sociology. Since I could not deal fully with the subject of linguistic *a priori*, I preferred to analyse extensively a specific point; some of these *a priori* consist of consigning a particular word (used in a theory) to a particular type of word. (For example, the word 'chair' is not of the same type as the word 'force' or the word 'intelligence').

As in the case of other kinds of *a priori*, there is a tendency to 'choose' (metaconsciously) by default the simplest *a priori*.

For example, one is often led, in case of doubt, to classify terms found in a theory as of the 'non-polythetic' type. However, many concepts, including those which are vital components of scientific language, and including those with which measures can be associated, are polythetic in nature. This implicit inclusion of polythetic terms in the less complex category of the non-polythetic can profoundly affect a valid line of reasoning in its explicit part.

Feyerabend's theory in *Against Method* is used as an example of this. Here again, my aim is not to present a critical analysis of this theory, merely to identify the part played by implication – that is, by linguistic-type *a priori* – in the genesis of the conclusion of the line of argument propounded in this book.

Similarly, Kuhn's scepticism about the notions of *truth, objectivity* and *progress* (of scientific knowledge) is analysed as the product of valid arguments and linguistic *a priori*. As these examples show, the effects of these *a priori* can be considerable.

Chapters 4 to 8 contain many examples taken from contemporary philosophy and sociology of science and knowledge. The *relativist* conclusions from the theories in question are always obtained by the metaconscious mobilization of *a priori* which one can accept, but which it is perhaps more appropriate to reject. Despite the convergence of these theories, it is by no means necessary to allow oneself to be persuaded by them.

Contemporary relativism therefore provides a good illustration of the *Simmel effect* – an essential mechanism from the point of view of cognitive sociology – which is the main theme of this book.

Part III

9

Reason with a small r

The aim of this chapter is fourfold: to emphasize the importance of the notion of *subjective rationality* established by Herbert Simon; to clarify its definition and meaning; to show that the intuition behind it restates a problem which is present in latent form in all social sciences; and finally to suggest that this idea is crucial for the analysis of all sorts of social phenomena, and particularly phenomena of belief.[1]

WHAT SUBJECTIVE RATIONALITY IS

Simon suggested several definitions of the idea of *subjective rationality*. One of them is:

> In a broad sense, *rationality* denotes a style of behavior that is appropriate to the achievement of given goals, within the limits imposed by certain limits and constraints. . . . The conditions and constraints referred to in the general definition may be *objective characteristics* of the environment of the choosing organism, they may be *perceived characteristics*, or they may be *characteristics of the organism* itself that it takes as fixed and not subject to its own control. The line between the first case and the other two is sometimes drawn by distinguishing *objective rationality*, on the one hand, from *subjective* or *bounded rationality*, on the other.[2]

I am not sure that this definition is entirely satisfactory. However, rather than analysing it, I will introduce the idea of subjective definition by means of an example[3] taken from Simon himself,[4] who in turn took it from one of Feldman's studies of cognitive psychology.[5]

Subjects are asked to predict the results when a coin is tossed. They are informed, however, that the odds are stacked and that the probability of the coin falling heads or tails is respectively 0.2 and 0.8.

By a large majority, the subjects choose the wrong answer: they try to produce a random set of results governed by the same rules as the set which they are supposed to predict.[6] In other words, they predict, randomly, tails eight times out of ten and heads two times out of ten. By doing this they have 68 chances out of a hundred of guessing each throw correctly.[7] This is a mediocre achievement compared with the result they would get by predicting tails for each throw, since in this case their probability of success would be eight times out of ten.

This example seems to me very important for several reasons.

Firstly, it illustrates those situations where behaviour is governed by reasons which, although *objectively* debatable or even totally wrong, are nevertheless perceived as *good*. We very often fail to recognize the importance of this situation, because it runs counter to an everyday viewpoint based on the trusted philosophical tradition which assimilates the idea of *good reason* with that of *objectively sound reason*.

At the same time, the example raises an important question: how to determine the criteria for saying that reasons can be *subjectively right*, yet *objectively wrong*. The answer to this question is not obvious, but it is easy to see that common sense recognizes the existence of reasons of this kind. We have only to look at certain linguistic contexts where the expression 'good reasons' is regarded as acceptable. For example, it is probable that everybody would explain the behaviour of the subjects in our example by saying, for example, 'they did badly, but they had *good reasons* for choosing a particular answer, however wrong it was, *because* . . .'. On the other hand, it would probably be regarded as misplaced and mischievous to say 'they had in fact *no reason* to choose the wrong answer, *but* . . .'.

If we agree that the difference between these two comments can be summed up by the usual distinction between 'rational' and 'irrational', we can say that the casual observer would tend to regard the subjects' behaviour as 'rational' even though it is inspired by reasons which are objectively wrong.

Why are the subjects' reasons perceived in this case as right? Because they tried to answer the question by coming up with a *conjecture*: not *any* conjecture, of the kind which would give the observer the impression of arbitrariness or pure chance, but a conjecture based on a principle which is sound and in any event of very general validity – quite simply that the best way to reproduce something exactly is to find out the rules on which it was constructed and then to apply them exactly.

This principle is so important that it underlies every learning process imaginable: to do something as well as one's master, one needs to follow the rules and procedures which the master applied. This is why it is easy to imagine situations very close to our example where this principle would be perfectly relevant and would give the right answer. Let us assume, for example, that the person conducting the experiment asks subjects to predict the terms of a mathematical set governed by rules such as:

> rule 1: *y* is the value of the first term in the set;
> rule 2: add *x* to the *n*th term to get the next one.

If subjects decided to apply these rules literally, they would obviously 'guess' with total accuracy all the terms in the set.

Or else let us assume that subjects are asked to guess the results where a proper coin is tossed, that is, one where the odds are not stacked. Here, the strategy which before was a bad one becomes the best possible. If one were to toss a coin and predict whether it would fall heads or tails, one has exactly one chance in two of predicting accurately each throw.[8] The subjects in our example cannot improve on this – the strategy of choosing either heads or tails for each throw would also give them one chance in two of guessing correctly. It is no better than the other one.

Simon's subjects have therefore made the conjecture that, to replicate a model, a good strategy is to produce a copy by applying the same rules as those by which the model was made. This conjecture is valid in many situations. It is easy to regard it as *universally* valid, even though in fact it is not. It is valid in situations very close to the one faced by the subjects in our example. It is valid when the model to be replicated is a mathematical set. It is also valid for guessing the results when a normal coin is tossed. It can *also* be irrelevant, as Simon's example shows. Overall however, it is much easier to imagine situations where it is valid than those where it is not.

This is why few people would probably accept the idea that the subjects in our example were guilty of irrationality, even though their reasons were objectively unsound. These reasons are perceived as *good* because they are universal in the sense that most subjects in the same position – having no particular training in probability calculus – would quite naturally adopt the conjecture that it is relevant to use the rules which applied in the construction of a model to make a copy of it.

We see that one virtue of this example is to clarify the Simonian notion of *subjective rationality*, perhaps better than could be done by any definition as such. The example in fact suggests that we tend to regard objectively unsound reasons as *good* when these reasons are endowed with what I will call *quasi-universality*.

Another important lesson from the example is that *subjective rationality* is the normal result of the discrepancy between the complexity of situations in which subjects find themselves and the limitations of their cognitive ability. This is why Simon speaks both of 'subjective rationality' and '*bounded* rationality'.

The general conclusion from this example, however, is that, with the exception of certain simple and marginal cases, action always implies the application of *theories, conjectures, principles* or *a priori*. The upshot is that human sciences, and particularly economics and sociology, should try to develop a theory of action which takes greater account of these cognitive aspects.

Finally – and this point will be the *leitmotif* of this chapter as it was to previous ones – although these conjectures, theories, principles or *a priori* may be relevant, true or valid, they can also have the opposite qualities and still have the status of *good reasons*.

WHY THE IDEA OF SUBJECTIVE RATIONALITY IS CRUCIAL IN THE ANALYSIS OF SOCIAL PHENOMENA

The idea of *subjective rationality* is fundamental for social science because, as writers such as Max Weber and Karl Popper have shown, the attempt to substitute a rational explanation (in the sense which I suggested above) of particular behaviour, or a particular belief for the 'irrational' explanation which common sense is likely to come up with, is one of the crucial tasks of social science and one of the main sources of its legitimacy.[9]

The source for the intuition in the case of both Weber and Popper is perhaps the fact that common sense tends to find a rational explanation for behaviour where the meaning is clear, and an irrational explanation for behaviour where the meaning escapes it. In the former case, the human sciences have nothing to add to 'ordinary' sociology or psychology. Conversely, it is in the latter case that they can show how effective they are, since it is often possible and desirable to transform – by further analysis – the irrational explanations of common sense into rational explanations.

Of course, this does not mean that irrational explanations of behaviour and beliefs are *always* wrong – such a claim would be absurd – but only that common sense (as well as the human sciences, which on this point find it hard to escape from its influence) often tends to make wrong use of irrational explanations.

However, for the replacement of irrational explanation by rational explanation to be possible, we need a definition of the notion of rationality which is not too narrow. Otherwise, when we require rational behaviour to be based on reasons which are *objectively good*, we are inevitably led to regard as irrational beliefs and behaviour which – as shown by the example from Feldman and Simon – are apparently inspired by reasons that are readily understood and endowed with what I call *quasi-universality*.

This is why human sciences which use too narrow a definition of rationality are no improvement on common sense.

In other words, because it invites the observer to reject as unintelligible any belief or behaviour not based on *objectively valid* reasons, the equation:

good reasons = objectively sound reasons

is unproductive.

To take a classical example, it is partly because Pareto had a narrow conception of rationality (see, for example, his definition of the distinction between *logical actions* and *non-logical actions*) that he regarded most acts as irrational, that is, governed by invisible feelings rather than by reasons.

This narrow conception also explains why modern social science is just as ready to regard actions or beliefs that are not immediately intelligible as irrational, inspired not by reasons but by causes of a different kind, whether passions (in the moralists' sense), *feelings* (in Pareto's sense), affects, instincts or socially determined psychic constructs, which impose themselves on subjects without their realising it, and in any event are not amenable to their control.

By this I do not mean that causes of this type do not play a part, and sometimes a major part. I simply mean that it is wrong to give them an exclusive role, and arbitrary to suppose that any behaviour or belief which is not explained by objectively sound reasons is not explained by reasons at all. To do so would be to take the exaggerated view that, when reasons are not *objectively* valid, they have to be treated as covering reasons.[10]

By introducing the idea of *subjective rationality*, we are introducing a crucial element which completely alters the explanation of behaviour and beliefs: instead of trying to find causes (which are not reasons) for any behaviour that is not readily intelligible, it makes us look for the *subjective* reasons.

This is precisely what Weber is saying when he proposes that beliefs and actions should be regarded as *comprehensible*, and Popper when he suggests they should be regarded as *rational* (until the contrary has been proved). In both cases, the postulate is the same: that the crucial task of social science is to come up with reasons – *objective and subjective* – for behaviour and beliefs which common sense tends to see as devoid of reasons, and to renounce the category of *reasons* in favour of other kinds of *causes* only when we have convinced ourselves by methical analysis that it is impossible to do otherwise.

The hypothesis of Weber and Popper is, in other words, that both the move away from common sense and the legitimacy of the human sciences depend largely on their ability to replace spontaneously irrational explanations by rational explanations.

I would now like to suggest that, in keeping with this hypothesis, what are regarded as major contributions to the human sciences – those which give the impression of making intelligible phenomena not readily amenable to understanding – are in fact those which substitute a 'rational' explanation for a spontaneously 'irrational' explanation.

I will refer to some classic examples to illustrate this important point, which has been somewhat paradoxical ever since, under the influence of Freudianism in particular, the opposite received idea became established – that progress in the explanation of behaviour consists in finding its latent causes rather than its patent reasons.

AN IMAGINARY DIALOGUE BETWEEN HUME AND DOWNS

In a fascinating work of political theory, Hume develops the hypothesis that political parties are based on three fundamental mechanisms – common interest, group solidarity and mobilization around principles.[11]

In the first case, people are drawn together because they have common social positions and therefore interests in common. To use Dahrendorf's phrase, the function of political parties under this first heading is to give political expression to *latent groups*.

The second mechanism, what Hume calls *affection* but which nowadays we would call *solidarity*, is equally straightforward: individuals normally have a social sense which leads them to prefer people from the group to which they belong or to which they feel close, rather than members of groups from which they are socially or morally distant. This second mechanism is a strong factor in the maintenance of groups over and above the constant turnover of members.

Hume notes that there is absolutely no difficulty in understanding these first two mechanisms. In other words, one could argue *cum grano salis* that he would have had no problem in accepting either the Marxist idea of class consciousness – when, for example, Marx says that soldiers or artisans have interests in common and it is understandable that they should want to defend them – or Durkheim's notion of collective consciousness.

However, since Hume is a skilled political observer, he also notes that parties can be built around ideas or principles; and he goes on to say that not only has he no precise explanation for this phenomenon, but also that he sees the existence of political parties based on principles as the most difficult problem which the human sciences have to deal with:

> Parties *from principle*, especially abstract speculative principle . . . are,

perhaps, the most extraordinary and unaccountable *phenomenon* that has yet appeared in human affairs.[12]

At this point, Hume gives the reader the impression that he has discovered in the area of moral science a problem as insoluble as that of induction in the philosophy of knowledge. Why does Hume seem to be so intrigued by the existence of political parties based on principles, or, put another way, parties with ideological foundations?

The question could certainly be discussed at length, and the political situation in Britain in Hume's day partly explains the viewpoint revealed in the passage quoted above.[13] I think, however, that the fundamental reason for his surprise and expression of powerlessness when faced with the need to explain the *phenomenon* stems above all from the fact that his view of rationality is a narrow one, which is not surprising given the intellectual situation at the time. According to this narrow view, there is only one way to know whether a political programme is good or bad, acceptable or not: see what its effects are and decide whether these are acceptable, or at least whether, on criteria which themselves can be regarded as admissible, they give rise to more desirable consequences than alternative programmes.

Hume finds it very strange that a party can also be attractive in terms of its *principles*, and it is no surprise that he suggests an explanation of an inexorably irrational kind, namely 'people who vote for this kind of party have no reasons for supporting it, but a sort of instinct pushes them into it.' People are such, says Hume in effect, that they need to see that their neighbours are thinking like them:

> such is the nature of the human mind, that it always lays hold on every human mind that approaches it: and as it is wonderfully fortified by a unanimity of sentiments, so it is shocked and disturbed by any contrariety. Hence the eagerness with which most people discover in a dispute: and hence their impatience of opposition, even in the most speculative and indifferent opinions.[14]

This fine passage sensitively analyses psychological mechanisms whose existence is not in doubt. However, like Hume himself – who seems from his own comments to be so dissatisfied with this explanation that he comes close to regarding it as *ad hoc* – one may doubt whether these mechanisms are enough to explain the existence of ideological parties.

The paradox with which Hume was confronted was resolved by Downs in his classical book on political theory.[15]

The choice between, say, two political programmes can never be rational in the narrow sense of the word, says Downs. Firstly, because it is always impossible to determine with precision the consequences of a policy, and because, where such a determination is possible, it may in fact modify the consequences. Secondly, because it is naturally imposs-ible to anticipate improvements and changes to a particular programme before it is applied. On the assumption that all the uncertainties are removed, voters can still have doubts about their own preferences. And even if this is not the case, it very often happens that they prefer a particular bit of one programme, and other bits of another, so that they find it hard to decide between contending aspects.

Overall, what would be irrational for voters – because it would be impossible to achieve, given the information effectively at their disposal – would be to try their hardest to decide exclusively on the basis of the consequences of the programmes or theories put to them.

Conversely, it is reasonable to start from the *conjecture* that a pro-gramme based on principles which one regards as good will have fortunate consequences. No doubt it will not always be the case, but there are many other examples of decisions in situations of uncertainty where one has to rely on more or less weak conjectures.

On this point, Downs uses the word *ideology*: voters, if they are rational, have to go on *ideological* principles. This sentence summarizes the central theorem of Downs's book, which ensured his influence. This finding, which may seem very ordinary, shows that the *phenomenon* that seemed so mysterious to Hume in fact derives from mechanisms which are simple, but which cannot be perceived so long as one thinks, as Hume implicitly did, that behaviour which is not rational in the narrow sense is irrational.

It is not certain that, by using the word *ideology* here, Downs helped to clarify the theory of rationality. His main argument can be described more simply by saying that, like the subjects in the Feldman–Simon example, voters try to deal with the decision-making situation with which they are faced by using – more or less implicitly – reasonable conjectures or theories.

This imaginary debate between Hume and Downs can be regarded as paradigmatic for several reasons.

Firstly, it shows the strength of the classical conception of rationality. Secondly, it shows that, as soon as a less rigid conception is adopted, and space is given to what Simon called *subjective rationality*, many obscure *phenomena* become readily intelligible. By implicitly using this notion, Downs cleared up the deep mystery, for Hume, of ideologically based parties. This example also shows that the initial impression of irrationa-lity given by particular behaviour or a particular phenomenon can afterwards be profitably replaced by analysis showing it to be the result of *good reasons*. It also reveals that the reasons in question are often simply conjectures, theories or principles which most subjects in an identical situation would be likely to adopt.

THE EXPLANATION OF MAGIC

Another example – more paradoxical perhaps, but equally classic – illustrates the crucial importance of the notion of *subjective rationality* in the analysis of social behaviour; I refer to the debate on the explanation of magic.[16] I dealt with it in Chapter 1, and need therefore only refer to it again briefly, in order to add some further points.

In fact, magic is a phenomenon which has to be looked at in any discussion on rationality. Magical beliefs are usually regarded as a canonical example of irrationality where the incredulous observer tends to wonder how it is possible to believe in causal relationships which are 'so absurd'.

Nevertheless, in this example like the previous one, the substitution of an explanation based on subjective rationality for this spontaneously irrational one arouses an undoubted feeling of progress.

Adopting the common-sense approach, many writers have interpreted magical beliefs as irrational ('there is really no reason to believe that A causes B, but . . .'). For example, according to Lévy-Bruhl, they show that 'primitive people' have a different mental make-up from us. This, he says, explains, for example, why magicians confuse verbal similarities with real similarities and, generally speaking, relationships between words and relationships between things. The famous theory of 'primitive mentality' typically illustrates irrational interpretations of magical beliefs: the latter are analysed as the effect of *causes* over which individuals have no control.[17]

This theory aroused much interest, but was very soon subjected to criticism, because *causal* explanations of behaviour readily give the impression of being *ad hoc*. There are no doubt many cases where an explanation of this kind is quite legitimate: when, for example, a change in mood is attributed to a particular chemical substance. However, in a case of this kind, the causal relationship can be proved by the usual methods of causal analysis. In the case of a theory such as Lévy-Bruhl's, the situation is not the same. Here, the explanatory cause is inferred in a circular way from the effects which it is supposed to explain.

It is interesting to note that, often, those who are not satisfied with Lévy-Bruhl's *causal* theory (or theories of the same type) were seeking not a rational explanation of these beliefs (that is, an explanation of the *kind* 'however absurd the belief that "A causes B" may seem, the magician has good reasons for believing in it, because . . .'), but a denial of the very existence of the beliefs. Of course, when I speak here of 'rational', I am thinking of Simon's *subjective rationality*. After all, if one agrees to define magical beliefs as beliefs in *false* causal relationships, there is no question of explaining them in terms of *objective* reasons.

The theory that magical beliefs are a mere mirage was supported not only by, for example, Wittgenstein,[18] but also by many sociologists and anthropologists, among whom Beattie is perhaps the best known.[19] The argument of all these writers is that what are seen as magical beliefs are not, contrary to appearances, statements about the real world; they should rather be seen as the symbolic expression of a wish. Primitive people, it is argued, do not really believe that a particular ritual produces rain; they are merely expressing through the ritual their wish to see rain fall.[20]

Although a theory of this type has the advantage of preserving the dignity of 'primitive people', who are held in little regard by theories of the Lévy-Bruhl type, it is nevertheless just as *ad hoc*. As Horton showed, it contradicts the beliefs of 'primitive people' themselves, since they are seen as totally convinced of the effectiveness of their rituals,[21] even though they realize perfectly well that the latter are only complementary to technical processes without which, as they are well aware, no plant would grow.

Horton, however, not only showed, in contrast to the symbolist or expressive theory of magic, that 'primitive people' really *believe* in magic; he also came up with an indirect – and weighty – argument against this interpretation by explaining why Christianity, despite its success in many parts of English-speaking black Africa, rarely managed to eradicate local beliefs: for many Africans, it did not offer the equivalent of this 'toolbox' which magic was, and which was crucial in solving the host of problems encountered in everyday life.

In fact, the correct theory was a different one – the *rational* (in the *subjective* sense) theory propounded in more or less identical terms by Durkheim and Weber.[22]

According to this theory, we need to recognize firstly that the knowledge of 'primitive people' is not that of Westerners. Like the latter, they have not been initiated into the methodology of causal inference, and they have no reason to master the principles of biology or physics. Since the conduct of everyday life, as well as agriculture, fishing and stockrearing, calls for a whole range of skills, in traditional societies these are not only drawn from experience, but also from the corpus of knowledge which religious doctrines represent. Durkheim's hypothesis, like Weber's, is therefore that these doctrines fulfil in traditional societies the role which science plays in our own.

Durkheim interprets the fact that magical beliefs are not jeopardized by the negative verdict of experience by deploying a series of effective arguments: criticism of a causal relationship is not always easy. It assumes quasi-experimental conditions, which is not always possible. Moreover, beyond a certain stage, it needs to be supported by statistics. Finally, when a theory is contradicted by facts, it is rarely rejected immediately.

If Durkheim's theory can be illustrated by a modern example, we see that the magical beliefs that surprise observers so much are no more difficult to understand than the conviction of some people that industrial pollution has an effect on the climate. In both cases, the proof – or the refutation – of the causal relationship is objectively difficult, given the resources at the subject's disposal. There is therefore no decisive reason to reject it. The modern belief which I have just quoted is different in content, but not in form or mechanisms, from the magical beliefs of 'primitive people'.[23]

Durkheim's argument is that the magical beliefs observed in traditional societies are not essentially different from ours. The main difference is that the development of science has made some beliefs clearly obsolescent. When we see that somebody is still subscribing to them, we have the impression of an irrational adherence to nonsense. In fact, suggests Durkheim, these magical beliefs are conjectures established by 'primitive people' on the basis of knowledge which they regard as legitimate, just as we ourselves uphold, on the basis of our knowledge, all kinds of causal relationships, some of which are sound, while others are just weak or illusory.

This example shows that the substitution of a 'rational' (in the *subjective* sense) theory for an 'irrational' one can be accompanied by a feeling of progress which it is hard not to experience. In contrast with the two other types of theory, Durkheim's theory has in no way the characteristic of an *ad hoc* theory.

It is not my aim here to examine Durkheim's book. I will merely refer briefly to another example taken from his work to suggest how he is often concerned, like Weber, to give an interpretation, in terms of *subjective rationality*, of phenomena which, like magic, can give the impression of an *obvious* rationality.[24]

In a famous passage in *On Suicide*, he tries to explain why suicide rates seem to correlate with economic cycles; and to explain this fact – surprising in that suicide rates increase in the 'euphoric' phase of the economic cycle – he puts forward a theory in terms of subjective rationality. His basic hypothesis is that the expectations of economic actors are based on good reasons. In a stable economic situation, their expectations are stable. In a shifting economic situation, they produce other hypotheses and tend, *with good reason*, to formulate expectations which, through exaggeration or lack of optimism, have little to do with reality.

Here, Durkheim introduces the brilliant idea that they then tend to get to grips with uncertainty about the future by extrapolating from the tangent of the curve describing the economic cycle (see figure 9.1). For example, in the first part of the rising curve (before the mid-point of the rise), they are lacking in optimism, and therefore their expectations are too modest in relation to emerging reality. Conversely, in the second half of the rising curve, still extrapolating from the tangent of the curve, economic actors tend to show excessive optimism, which will not be borne out by reality.

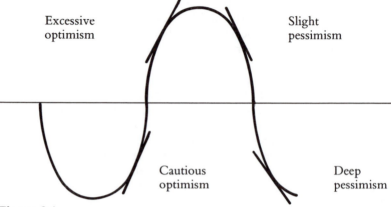

Excessive
optimism

Slight
pessimism

Cautious
optimism

Deep
pessimism

Figure 9.1

Here, I am not describing things exactly as Durkheim did, but it is the nub of his argument: and it allows him to explain why suicide rates seem, from the statistics at his disposal, to be particularly high in the second half of the rising curve of the economic cycle – a phenomenon which is not readily intelligible but which Durkheim's theory makes clear, since it is particularly in this phase that reality takes it upon itself to disappoint the actors concerned.[25]

What must be stressed, however, in this example is that the actors' excessive optimism in the second part of the rising curve, like the cautious optimism of their expectations in the first part, is explained according to Durkheim by *good reasons*: extrapolation is in fact the simplest and most natural way of reducing uncertainty.

SUBJECTIVE RATIONALITY AND THE EXPLANATION OF BELIEFS

The examples just discussed lead me to a final point: the great importance of subjective rationality in the explanation of beliefs.

Beliefs – and particularly false beliefs – are commonly interpreted as the product of causes which are not under the control of actors, rather than as the product of reasons. Among the classical writers on the human sciences, Marx – at least in his theoretical work – Freud and Pareto are a clear illustration of this paradigm. In the same way, the sociologists of present-day knowledge tend to see beliefs as the product of psychic forces, whose existence is sometimes difficult to prove. Alternatively, they limit themselves to examining the correlation between certain 'explanatory' variables such as age, sex, level of education, and a particular belief, thus tacitly revealing a naturalistic view of beliefs.

The notion of subjective rationality also outlines – in my view at least – another paradigm which is potentially more productive. This paradigm derives immediately from the fact that reasons may be good ones but nevertheless not objectively valid. This is why the actor can have good reasons for believing in false ideas.

Therefore a major task of cognitive sociology is to try to identify and clarify typical situations where the mental processes characteristic of subjective rationality lead to false beliefs. Naturally I cannot undertake this task here, and will merely give a few examples to show the importance of the phenomenon.

More specifically, I will look at three cases where sound principles of method (first case), sound ideas or theories (second case) and sound intellectual procedures (third case) give rise to false ideas.

a) Where valid methodological principles lead to false ideas

The example from Feldman and Simon at the beginning of this chapter is a good illustration of this first case. Subjects start from the conjecture that, to replicate a model accurately, the simplest thing is to apply scrupulously the rules by which the original was made. It is hard to imagine a principle of method at the same time more useful and more innocuous. However, it can give rise to false ideas.

Another principle equally innocuous and just as crucial as the previous one, which we constantly apply in a perfectly proper way, is the following: when we have to make up our minds about an empirical question of the kind 'is this x, y?', we usually start from the principle that the best way of deciding is in fact to see whether or not 'x is y'. If I am asked whether a book is on the table, the best way of answering the question is to check whether in fact it is there.

This principle, innocuous as it is, can also give rise to false beliefs.

To illustrate this point, I will take as my first example a recurrent debate: does educational achievement rise or fall with an increase in the average number of years spent in education? I will ignore the fact that it is obviously more difficult to tell whether educational achievement is rising than it is to say whether a book is on the table or not. Even if the level of achievement could be readily observed and measured, people could still have problems about the meaning of any changes.

Let us build a simple model. Let us assume that the 'learning ability' is an indisputable variable, and that the spread corresponding to this variable is identical between cohorts of pupils. Let us assume further that each year the number of pupils in a given class (second year of secondary education, or third year of secondary education, for example) increases and that this increase is due to the fact that, every year, more and more pupils from the lower end of the spread are admitted to the class. This model, though simplistic, is clearly not totally removed from the real world.

Let us assume now that a teacher (who for the sake of argument has the same class each year) is asked whether educational achievement of secondary schoolchildren is rising or falling. To answer the question, the teacher will doubtless call on his or her experience. The hypotheses of the model demand that the conclusion be totally free of ambiguity: the teacher can *see* directly that the achievement of the pupils is falling from year to year since, by definition, each year there is an intake whose average is located lower down on the 'learning capacity' variable. Moreover, the teacher can verify his or her conclusion with colleagues: for the same reason, all of them will have the same impression.

Overall, all teachers – apart from those who are new, those who do not have the same classes, those who have distorting lenses in their spectacles, or those who base their opinion less on what they see than on what they hear – ought, in the circumstances of the model, to end up with the same conclusions for the same reasons.

This pessimistic finding on the part of most teachers is in no way incompatible with the fact that 'the level is rising'. It may very well be, in fact, that the average level of knowledge in *adolescents* (say, 15 to 20-year-olds) is rising. The model is in no way incompatible with such a development. After all, unless one accepts – a totally improbable hypothesis – that extra teaching could not only not have a positive effect, but even have a negative effect on the level of knowledge, the model predicts an increase in people's average level of knowledge.

In more concrete terms, this very simple model tells us, for example, that achievement in English, German, or any other kind of knowledge may very well increase among average children of school age, whereas teachers of English, German or any other subject tend, for *good reasons*, to have the impression that 'the level is falling'.

The *beliefs*, therefore, of teachers are in no way illusions. On the contrary, they perceive reality *as it is*. The false belief stems in this case from the application of a principle which is so banal that it is rather difficult to imagine situations where it could mislead us. Can there be a more innocuous principle than that which tells us to see whether x is y to decide whether x is y? Nevertheless, there are indeed cases, as my rudimentary example shows, where this principle can become a machine generating false ideas.[26]

One could cite numerous examples in the same vein where subjective rationality seems to give rise to false ideas or beliefs – where, in other words, the knowing subject endorses false ideas for good reasons. I will merely offer two further examples in order to suggest that this mechanism has quite a general application.

According to one of the more widely accepted aspects of Keynesian theory, tax increases normally have deflationary effects: they reduce purchasing power, which leads to a fall in demand for goods and services and, in the end, lower prices. However, when directors of firms are asked whether they think that tax increases are inflationary or deflationary, most of them choose the first alternative.[27] Why is this? Simply because, exactly like the teachers in the previous example, their answer is based on their own immediate situation: tax increases affect firms' overheads, so they try to pass on these increased costs by raising prices.

Similar examples are rife: for instance, many people think that mechanization causes unemployment. This conviction is also based on *good reasons*. A simple calculation in fact shows that, at the local level, replacing human labour by machines can lead to a loss of jobs; but this local effect is not inconsistent with an *overall* opposite effect. Since the new machines have to be designed, manufactured, serviced, maintained, improved, replaced, and so on, they may overall create more jobs than they destroy.

However, this (possible) positive effect is visible only on an overall abstract level, whereas the negative effect may be immediately perceptible at the local level and easily accessible by a simple calculation.[28] As in the previous example, people who believe that mechanization causes unemployment are in no way the victim of an *illusion*. On the contrary, they believe what they see. The false belief of which, in this case, knowing subjects are the victims simply stems from confidence meta-consciously placed in the ordinary *empiricist* principle which legend attributed to St Thomas: to find out if x causes y, see whether x is in fact the cause of y.

Of course, people ask themselves questions of the kind 'is x the cause of y?' at every moment of the day. A principle often used to answer them, and it is a principle justifiably regarded as valid, is to see whether y tends to appear when x is present. If, on only a small number of occasions, I observe that I have difficulty in sleeping after drinking three glasses of wine, I conclude that . . . wine stops one sleeping.

Like the previous one, this principle can, however, lead to false beliefs. This has been shown by instructive experiments in cognitive psychology, of which the following is an example.[29]

A group of nurses was each given a set of a hundred casenotes with imaginary information on patients, relating to the presence (or absence) of a given symptom, and the diagnosis (or not) of a particular illness. The distribution was as shown in table 9.1.

Table 9.1

Symptom	Illness		
	Yes	*No*	*Total*
Yes	37	33	70
No	17	13	30
Total	54	46	100

The correlation between these two variables is not only very low, it also goes in the 'wrong' direction.[30] In fact, the illness was diagnosed *slightly more frequently* when the symptom was absent than when it was present. However, a high proportion (85 per cent) of nurses were convinced that the symptom was the effect of the illness.

Why was this? Because they were starting from the principle that when two characteristics are present in *thirty-seven* cases, one can conjecture that they are causally linked. After all, are not *two or three* sleepless nights from drinking too much alcohol enough to conclude that there is a causal link?

It is clear that the nurses are no more irrational than the subjects in the Feldman–Simon example: like them, they base their conjecture on principles of very general validity. In this sense, they have *good reasons* for endorsing a false causal link.

The conclusion is that, although sound methodological principles – seeing if *x* is *y* in order to decide whether *x* is *y*; asking oneself if *y* frequently follows *x* in order to decide whether *x* causes *y* – generally give rise to correct ideas, they may also very often lead to the establishment of false beliefs.

b) When respectable ideas or theories give rise to false beliefs

Similarly, respectable ideas can give rise to false conclusions.

Several studies of belief in supernatural phenomena have led to remarkable findings. Although belief in the existence of God tends, according to some of these studies, to be less the higher the level of education, the incidence of other types of belief tends to increase with the level of education. This is the case, for instance, with belief in psychological action at a distance or in extraterrestrial beings. In one of these experiments, 48 per cent, 62 per cent and 73 per cent of people educated respectively to primary, secondary and university level said they believed in the existence of extraterrestrial beings.[31]

There are two types of interpretation of these findings. The first one – probably the most common – is to interpret them as *irrational* (the subjects have no *reason* for believing that . . . , but . . .). However, closer analysis would perhaps show that these beliefs stem from conjectures based on good reasons. In effect, people whose secondary or higher education made them familiar with the history of science will have learnt that many concepts, entities or mechanisms which were long regarded as inconsistent with the very notion of science in the end became part of the corpus of scientific knowledge. The notion of physical action at a distance is a good example of this; though at certain times in the history of physics it was rejected as unacceptable, at others it was accepted.

I have no proof of the validity of this interpretation. Sociologists, who usually take a *naturalistic* view of *homo sociologicus*, rarely bother themselves with the reasons which subjects they observe might have for believing what they believe. It is, however, plausible that respondents with a high level of education arrive more readily at considerations such as 'Why should the advance of knowledge not accept the idea of *psychic* action at a distance, in the same way that it led to *physical* action at a distance becoming part of the scientific corpus?'

In other words, it is probable that, on some matters, subjects with a high level of education have *good reasons* for being less sceptical or less critical than those who are less familiar with the history of science.

To summarize this example ironically, I would say that faith in the virtue of methodical doubt can occasionally lead to an excess of credulity.

c) When respectable mental processes give rise to false beliefs

Very often, false ideas are produced by the confidence which the knowing subject normally invests in crucial processes such as induction.

Since Hume, we have known that this process, though lacking a clear basis, is indispensable not only to scientific knowledge, but to ordinary knowledge as well.

It can, however, give rise to false beliefs, as we see from the example of children who are asked to look at two triangles which are similar but of different size (ABC being bigger than A'B'C'),[32] and to answer some questions:

Q. Is side AB bigger than A'B'?
A. 'Yes', say all the children.
Q. Is BC bigger than B'C'?
A. 'Yes.'
Q. Is AC bigger than A'C'?
A. 'Yes.'
Q. Is the perimeter of ABC bigger than that of A'B'C'?
A. 'Yes.'

Q. Is the area of ABC bigger than that of A'B'C'?
A. 'Yes.'
Q. Is the sum of the angles in ABC bigger than that in A'B'C'?
A. 'Yes' . . .

Formally impeccable processes such as the syllogism, which in most cases lead to correct beliefs, can also give rise to false beliefs. I am not thinking here of Sophistic uses of correct deductive procedures, which have long been recognized and to which Pareto, for example, devotes much attention, making them a central part of his grammar of *derivations*. For instance, he showed that natural law theorists use reasoning processes which are formally impeccable, but which labour under the disadvantage that the word 'nature' tends to change meaning from one argument to another:[33] they read like syllogisms, they look like syllogisms, but they are not syllogisms.

What I have in mind is quite different and has not really been analysed by theorists of knowledge and belief.

Let us consider, for example, the following deductive theory: on average, the social origin of individuals influences their level of education, which in turn influences their social class. From these statements, the conclusion is that, if the strength of the relationship between social class at birth and level of education reduces over time, the relationship between status at birth and as an adult must also diminish. This deduction is perfectly correct. The words have the same meaning in different statements. We are not dealing therefore with the classic case which Pareto and his followers examine at some length. This line of reasoning is thus very likely to give rise to a sound belief, since this will be based on reasoning which is . . . correct.

But this theory also contains – like any theory – *implicit* statements. Generally speaking, these mental harmonics are no real problem. Sometimes, however, they may make the conclusions which subjects draw from their arguments weaker than they think. In the present example, the reasoning implicitly regards it as self-evident that the first relationship (between social origin and level of education) can change without the second relationship (between level of education and social status) being affected. This *a priori* is dealt with in an implicit way, because it is common in this kind of reasoning. However, since the first relationship cannot reduce in strength unless the general level of education increases, the second one cannot remain constant.[34] Here a false belief is produced by the application of a process which is usually valid to a case where it is not. In the same way one can, by imitating a model, reproduce it correctly, but also, in certain cases, distort it, as shown in the Simon example at the beginning of this chapter.

However the Feldman–Simon experiment, contrary to the impression which it may give, has also the advantage of showing that *subjective* rationality can give rise to false beliefs not only in the context of ordinary knowledge, but also in that of scientific knowledge. Although there is a closer check on scientific theories than those produced by ordinary knowledge, they nevertheless also contain all kinds of implicit statements which are in most cases innocuous and without consequence, but which in other cases can establish false ideas.

The example just given illustrates the distortion effects which can be produced by an *a priori* commonly used with justification by the knowing subject in all sorts of circumstances – that changes in variables do not affect constants. Similarly, the belief that a rent freeze will favour tenants implicitly assumes that the freeze does not affect supply of housing. As in the previous case, 'syllogistic' reasoning is inappropriate, because it assumes the unchanging nature of factors that are variable.

It would be easy to give examples where distortion of inference stems from confidence placed quite naturally in forms of reasoning that are useful and often trustworthy.

For instance, excessive confidence is placed in the principle of transitivity. As we saw earlier,[35] the relationship of 'resemblance' is intuitively interpreted as transitive, whereas in very ordinary cases, such as those envisaged by Wittgenstein, it may very well not be so: G_1 may well look like G_2, and G_2 like G_3, without G_1 and G_3 having anything in common. On the other hand, however, it is true that, in most cases, it is relevant to assume that the relationship of resemblance is transitive.[36]

Of course, this kind of distortion – due to the confidence normally given to forms of reasoning that are widely accepted – could itself be the object of a whole chapter. My aim here is merely to emphasize its importance.

Overall, the idea of *subjective* rationality is not only interesting for the study of decision-making.[37] It also allows us to outline a paradigm useful for the development of cognitive sociology and, more generally, for the analysis of beliefs.

This notion is an essential concept for all human sciences. To replace spontaneous irrational explanations by rational (in the *subjective* sense) explanations of behaviour and beliefs is one of the major ways forward in these disciplines.

The misuse of explanations of an irrational kind stems not only from the spread of popular Marxism and Freudianism. It derives also from a hallowed philosophical tradition – seen particularly in the moralists – that false ideas are never brought about by *reasons*. How could it be otherwise given that we want only *good* reasons to be the real cause of beliefs, and that we assimilate *good reasons* to objectively valid reasons?

The idea of *subjective rationality* is not just one concept among several. It invites us to look in a different way at behaviour and beliefs.

It may even be a time-bomb at the heart of the human sciences. If they take it seriously, economists can no longer be happy with the *a priori* psychology with which they honour *homo oeconomicus*. For their part, sociologists can no longer readily content themselves with explanations of behaviour or beliefs which are of an irrational type.

We can even go further and ask ourselves if the traditions behind the various 'human sciences' do not owe their differences to the fact that they have too long been in agreement on minimizing the cognitive aspects of behaviour.[38]

NOTE ON THE DEFINITION OF THE NOTION OF RATIONALITY

Understanding the behaviour of an actor is usually a matter of understanding the *reasons* or the *good reasons*. In this sense and in this sense only, the Weberian conception of *understanding* implies the postulate of the *rationality* of the social actor. This is not to say that it regards human beings as rational, since it is not dealing with human beings, but with *social* actors. The postulate of rationality is in other words a methodological principle and not an ontological assertion. Moreover, this notion of rationality is broader than that of classical philosophy or economics. If one agrees to define this notion *ostensively*, behaviour is rational if one can provide an explanation of the type: 'The fact that actor X behaved in manner Y is *understandable*: in fact, in the situation in question, the actor had good reasons for doing Y'.

This *ostensive* (or *deictic*) definition means that we can sketch in the boundary between rationality, in the sense in which this notion is understood here, and irrationality. For example, one cannot say: 'the mother had *good reasons* to smack the child, because she was angry.' Such a sentence immediately gives an impression of absurdity. However, one can say: 'the mother had *no reason* to smack the child, *but* she was angry'; her behaviour was *understandable*, but not *rational*. On the other hand, there would be no problem in saying: 'Calvinists had good reasons for reinvesting profits, because they were convinced that . . .'.

To underline the considerable difficulties with the definition of the notion of rationality, one needs only to remember in passing that Popper[39] suggests a broader definition of it, and agrees that one can regard an act as rational when the actor can give reasons for it, whatever these may be.

This short discussion allows us to come up with three types of definition of the notion of rationality. The first definition, which we can call *narrow*, says that behaviour is rational when it is based on objectively sound reasons: for example, I look left and right before I cross the road because I might *in fact* be knocked down if I do not. At the other extreme, Popper suggests a definition which could be called *broad*: behaviour is rational when it is based on reasons, whatever the nature of these reasons. Thirdly, in the spirit of a writer such as Weber, or nowadays Herbert Simon, an *intermediate* definition could be suggested: behaviour is rational when it can be explained by a sentence beginning '*X* had good reasons for doing *Y*, because . . .', without risking objection, and without oneself having the feeling of having said something incongruous.

The first definition means that we have to call irrational behaviour which most people would find reasonable. Popper's broad definition has the opposite defect of regarding as rational behaviour which is inspired by fanaticism or madness. As for the intermediate definition, though it is more acceptable, it has the disadvantage of giving a conclusion which can be misleading – that the notion of rationality can be defined semantically, but not formally. It is based on the fact that a phrase such as '*X* had *good reasons* for doing *Y*, because *X* believed that *Z* . . .' can either make sense or make no sense at all, and would regard *Y* in the former case as rational, and in the latter case as irrational. It follows that a belief can – or cannot – be accepted as a reason depending on the nature of the belief in question. In fact, the phrase '*X* had good reasons for doing *Y*, because *X* thought that *Z* . . .' makes sense if it can be completed by a set of statements which also make sense, such as 'because *Z* was true', 'because *Z* was probable', 'because *Z* was plausible', or more generally 'because *X* had good reasons to believe *Z*, because . . .', and so on.

We may find it uncomfortable to accept that a concept cannot be properly defined and that we have, as here, to rely on semantic criteria. In fact, several philosophers, and major ones at that, from Kant through Ryle to Wittgenstein, have shown that it was often naive to try to associate a particular definition with certain concepts.[40]

Perhaps this goes for 'rationality' as for 'truth', and perhaps it is impossible to attach a proper definition to these vital concepts. To use the vocabulary of the previous chapter, we are dealing here with *polythetic* terms.

If we accept this *ostensive* definition of the concept of rationality, used – more often implicitly than explicitly – in the sociology of action, it is easier to understand why Weber used quite naturally – that is, without feeling the need to justify himself – the phrase 'value rationality' (*Wertrationalität*). Many writers, such as Lukes,[41] were put out by this expression, since they concentrated on the *narrow* definition of the notion of rationality. Here it does seem difficult to agree that we can speak of value rationality – if the actor's reasons have to be objective, they cannot take the form of value judgements. On the other hand, the notion of *Wertrationalität* is no longer contradictory if it is applied to acceptable statements of the kind '*X* had good reasons for doing *Y*, because *X* believed in the normative statement *Z* and had good reasons for believing *Z*, because . . .'

This ostensive conception of the notion of rationality avoids the excesses of the broad and the narrow definition. It also means that we can distinguish varying *types* of rationality. Weber[42] felt the need for this typology, and, as we know, identified four main forms of action: rational actions in the teleological sense, rational actions in the axiological sense, traditional actions and affectively determined actions. It is not certain, however, that this distinction between *purposive* rationality (*Zweckrationalität*) and *value* rationality (*Wertrationalität*) is sufficient to exhaust the subject of types of rationality.

The ostensive definition of rationality (behaviour *Y* is rational if one can say of it '*X* had good reasons for doing *Y*, because . . .') means in any case that we can create a more productive set of types of rationality based on the nature of the considerations introduced by the 'because'. For example, we can have:

1) . . . because *Y* corresponds to *X*'s interests (or preferences);
2) . . . because *Y* is the best way for *X* to achieve the aim which *X* set himself or herself;
3) . . . because *Y* derives from normative principle *Z*; *X* believes in *Z*, and *X* has good reasons for believing in it;
4) . . . because *X* has always done *Y*, and there is no reason to question this practice;
5) . . . because *Y* derives from theory *Z*; *X* believes *Z* and has good reasons for believing it; and so on.

These various cases, like others which could be added to this list, are frequently encountered, not only in social sciences, but also in the explanations we come up with spontaneously in everyday life for behaviour which we observe. Moreover, they correspond to simple distinctions. Despite this, the words which try to describe them are not permanently fixed. In the first example, we can speak of *utilitarian* rationality. The second can be regarded as providing an implicit definition of the notion of *teleological* rationality (*Zweckrationalität* in Weber). The third implicitly defines *axiological* rationality (*Wertrationalität* in Weber). In the fourth example, we can speak of *traditional* rationality, and this case shows that, of actions inspired by tradition, some can be regarded as rational. These are the ones to which we can apply an acceptable explanation of the kind '*X* had good reasons for doing *Y*, because *X* had always done it and had no reason to question the practice.' Others, however, are irrational: those where it is said that '*X* had no reasons for doing *Y*, but tradition required that . . .'. The fifth example implicitly defines what might be called *cognitive* rationality.

Finally, the ostensive definition of rationality allows us to resolve the difficulties arising from the fact that one can speak not only of the rationality of *actions* or *behaviour*, but also of the rationality of *beliefs*. The answer to this problem often consists, as Jarvie and Agassi pointed out,[43] in accepting that the word 'rationality' has different meanings in the two contexts. The definition suggested above steers clear of these difficulties, since the good reasons of actors are conceived as capable – or incapable – of bringing beliefs into play.

10

Simmel and the theory of knowledge

The previous chapters were all variations on a model by Simmel. This one serves as an appendix to locate this model in Simmel's theory of knowledge as developed in two of his books, particularly in *The Philosophy of Money*.

Simmel's *The Philosophy of Money* is a remarkable, though difficult, book. It deals with a host of interlinked themes, each of which is of considerable scope and difficulty: what is the origin of values? what are the consequences of the spread of money on social relationship? on human thinking? It therefore includes arguments from what we would call economic sociology and economic psychology, and analyses from the sociology and philosophy of knowledge; other studies are from the social psychology of everyday life, such as his brilliant analysis of the implicit but rigorous rules about the choice of gifts in modern societies. All these matters intermingle as in a musical composition where philosophy, sociology, economics and psychology are inextricably linked. The length of the book, the insistent repetition of the themes and their interlinking, give to the whole work something of the character of a Mahler symphony.

Is money for Simmel merely a pretext – a topic on which to graft his variations? One thing at least is certain: above and beyond the overlong episodes, the breaks, the abrupt changes, there is a great consistency and also a great stability of thought, which are even clearer if one compares *The Philosophy of Money* with other books and particularly with *The Problems of the Philosophy of History*.

In this chapter I will try to show this consistency in respect of one of the main themes of the book – knowledge. This themes constantly preoccupied Simmel. The question of the nature of knowledge in the field of history and the social sciences, and the question of the objectivity of these disciplines, are the main themes in *The Problems of the Philosophy of History*.[1] They also figure largely in *The Philosophy of Money*. In view of the importance and the subtlety of Simmel's answers to these questions, I wanted to bring out their force and consistency.

MONEY AND KNOWLEDGE

Why does the theme of knowledge figure so largely in a book about the philosophy of money? Quite simply because, according to Simmel, the spread of money throughout modern societies profoundly affected human thought. Like Durkheim, and later Parsons, Simmel points out that social relationships tend to become impersonal in modern societies. However, Simmel goes much further than the two sociologists. He argues that, with the development of a money economy, goods became measurable and thereby acquired an objective value. For instance, money has an influence not only on the way we evaluate things, but also on the way we apprehend the relationship between things and their value. Before economies took on a distinct monetary character, values had a strong subjective dimension. The development of money led to an objectification of values: we see value as a property of things, which it clearly is not, since an object has no value in the sense, for example, that it has a colour.[2]

This analysis leads to the crucial point that knowledge and the human representation of the world can depend on sociological variables, particularly – and the aim of *The Philosophy of Money* is to show this – the spread of a monetary economy.

Other analyses in The *Philosophy of Money* show why the theme of knowledge figures so largely in the book: the development of a monetary economy, says Simmel, helped to affect and blur the way we distinguish between means and ends. What accompanied this, and was made possible by it, was the increased complexity of societies, which meant that the ultimate finalities of acts performed by individuals tend to escape them. Chinese weavers make cloth which, unknown to them, will be sold in Hamburg. Unlike artisans in the past, they are unaware of the final destination and the ultimate aim of their acts. They therefore tend to see only the next link in the 'teleological sequence' to which they belong: their aim can no longer be to try to adapt their product to the wishes of the final recipient, but to produce as much as possible at the best price. In the nature of things, they cannot pull back the chain; they cannot take means for ends. One could say that, in a complex society, actors cannot see the *destination*, or, to put it differently, the *meaning* of their work.[3]

At a deeper, or at any rate subtler, level, a monetary economy favoured, according to Simmel, the spread of quantitative thinking. With it, the realm of the measurable expanded, so that in the end everything was regarded as able to be measured, including the most subjective and elusive psychological states, such as sensations. On this, Simmel was obviously impressed by the psycho-physiological writing of Weber and Fechner, which he interpreted as presaging not only quantitative methods in the whole of the human sciences, but especially a quantitative view of the world.

However, and it has to be said straightaway, Simmel in no way falls into, the trap of sociologism. This is immediately apparent from the fact that the very basis of the phenomenon of value is, according to him, linked to the essence of humanity and in this sense is trans-historical. The origin of values lies in what is most subjective in humankind: wants. Simmel argues that objects have a value only in proportion to the sacrifices which we accept in order to obtain them.[4] In economic exchange, we sacrifice one thing (or, if money exists, a sum of money) to obtain another. Even Robinson Crusoe, despite the solitude in which he found himself, indulged in exchange: when he decided on a particular activity, he thereby renounced other activities regarded as desirable, but less desirable than the one chosen. The very existence of values is therefore the effect of universal psychic mechanisms.

The appearance of money profoundly influenced the way in which values are perceived by social actors. In fact, as soon as the value of goods is measured in money, the very basis of this value becomes hard to perceive for subjects, who can no longer see that value is grounded in wants, that it arises from their mediation between mutually incompatible wants, and that it is crystallized by exchanges which make this mediation more satisfying for the participants. The consequence is that subjects see things as having a value which is not only supra-individual, but objective.

Let us note in passing that it is hard not to see the influence of Carl Menger in these arguments. As Hayek rightly points out,[5] Menger's *Grundsätze*, as well as his *Untersuchugen über die Methoden der Sozialwissenschaften*, are based on methodological principles very close to those which Max Weber proposed for sociologists: one of them is what today we would call 'methodological individualism', and what Menger infelicitously called the 'atomistic method'. Two things must be added to Hayek's remarks: firstly, that these principles are not only shared by Simmel, but borrowed by Weber from Simmel's *The Problems of the Philosophy of History*, as the beginning of *Economy and Society* indicates; secondly, Simmel himself adopts not only Menger's methodology, but part of his theory.

Of course, the development of money not only modified subjects' perception of the relationship between things and their value. Generally speaking, the evolution of which the development of money is both the factor and the main symptom led, according to *The Philosophy of Money*, to a real sea change in human thinking, which moved from the singular to the universal mode, from the subjective to the objective mode, from the qualitative to the quantitative mode, and from the substantialist to the relativist mode.[6]

I will return later to the mediations which allow us to understand these relationships, and which is my main theme in this chapter. For the moment, I merely state that, according to Simmel, the development of a monetary economy went hand in hand, overall, with an upheaval in the frameworks of human thought. This is why it is rightly considered that *The Philosophy of Money* contains both a treatise on sociology and a treatise on the philosophy of knowledge.[7]

SIMMEL'S PHILOSOPHY OF KNOWLEDGE

I will now try to identify the main elements of the theory of knowledge which Simmel outlines in *The Problems of the Philosophy of History* and *The Philosophy of Money*. I will deal first with his philosophy of knowledge.

a) A relativist philosophy

To begin at the simplest level, let us recall first that Simmel never concealed his debt to Kant. He clearly recognizes it in *The Problems of the Philosophy of History*, where references to Kant are numerous. *The Philosophy of Money*, although it has no references to Kant, is profoundly Kantian in the sense that the role of the *a priori* in knowledge is one of the major aspects of the theory developed in it.[8] Moreover, the extensive nature of Simmel's thinking on the question of the *a priori* of knowledge shows how important it was for him.[9]

However, once this theme has been posited, Simmel distances himself from Kant: Simmel's *a priori* are not universal and atemporal, but variable in time and space, and even variable from one subject to another. Moreover, they are not reducible to a finite set of categories: their diversity and complexity mean they cannot be enumerated or described. Furthermore, it is as if they are stratified and slotted into each other. Overall, however faithful Simmel is to Kant, his conception of the *a priori* is very different from that of Kant, and perhaps more acceptable in so far as the origin of Simmel's *a priori* is infinitely less mysterious than that of Kant's, as I will try to show later.

Despite distancing himself from Kant, Simmel says that his theory of knowledge is 'relativist', that is, Kantian. We should immediately say that the word 'relativism', as used by Simmel, does not have the same meaning which it has nowadays in British or American writing on the philosophy of knowledge, where it has become synonymous with 'scepticism'. Let us avoid any misunderstanding by saying that today's 'relativists' usually conclude, from the fact that there is no knowledge without *a priori*, that there can be no certain and objective knowledge. Simmel merely follows the German usage of the time by saying that any theory which postulates the existence of an *a priori* is 'relativist'. However, for neo-Kantian relativists, the existence of *a priori* in no way implies this sceptical conclusion.

We can describe Simmel's starting point by what today we refer to as *complexity*: our immediate experience consists of a host of varied and jumbled sensations which, in this state, make no sense to us. We have to put some order into them, select them, arrange them. This, however, has to be done according to certain principles.

It is difficult to determine the origin of these principles. Here, Simmel merely says that perhaps they are, at least initially, suggested to the knowing subject by their basic needs. In other words, human knowledge, like animal 'knowledge', has a practical origin. A true representation is therefore first and foremost a useful representation of particular conditions of life. However, Simmel warns us straightaway not to confuse the true with the useful, even though the latter may lead to the former. Of course, no truth can claim to be absolute: an absolute truth must be conceived as a literal copy of the real world: but such a copy is virtually inconceivable, since for us the simplest object represents an inexhaustible multitude of sensations. However, though our representations cannot claim to be absolute truth, they are nevertheless not arbitrary, since a representation without contact with the real world would be of no use.

By giving *a priori* a crucial role in knowledge, Simmel rejects any *realist* conception of knowledge. However, because these *a priori* become significant only when they are, as it were, confirmed by reality, he also rejects any *conventionalist* conception, that is, any theory where the exclusive basis of truth is agreement between knowing subjects.

There is another reason, according to Simmel, why a realist theory of knowledge – one which argues that knowledge is the 'mirror of nature' – is unacceptable. It is because human thinking, by a necessity which is its own, proceeds by inference from principles: the human mind is made in such a way that it requires evidence before it recognizes truth.[10] However, these principles can have no absolute basis.

In his remarks to which I am referring here, Simmel is giving the first hints of what Hans Albert later called Münchhausen's trilemma.[11] Taking his cue from a remark by Schopenhauer on Spinoza's notion of *causa sui*, Albert says that the principles on which all deductive reasoning is based must, in the nature of things, either be posited without further justification, or else derive from other principles themselves based on existing principles, thus setting up an infinite regress, or else derive in a circular manner from their own consequences. Simmel does not state this 'trilemma' in as formal a way as Albert, but several times in both *The Philosophy of Money* and *The Problems of the Philosophy of History*, he refers to the three cases envisaged by Albert, and shows that he is perfectly aware that deductive thought cannot escape the trilemma of arbitrariness, circularity or infinite regression.

b) A non-sceptical relativism

Two things therefore invalidate realist theories of knowledge: firstly, the fact that knowledge must be based on principles and that it cannot be based on absolute principles, and secondly, the finitude of the knowing subject faced with the complexity of the world.

Simmel's attack on realism in the name of neo-Kantian relativism is, I repeat, one of the major themes of *The Problems of the Philosophy of History*, a book devoted to the epistemology of history and the human sciences: it is impossible, says Simmel, to take literally Ranke's famous adage,[12] and describe historical and social phenomena 'as they really are'. In *The Philosophy of Money* Simmel refines this theory by generalizing it. In effect, he suggests without ambiguity that the same analysis should be applied to the whole of knowledge: chemists and biologists, he argues, are in the same boat as historians or sociologists. Neither group can have access to reality as it is.

We can note in passing that *The Philosophy of Money* shows very clearly how far removed is Simmel from writers such as Dilthey – particularly his later work – or Habermas.[13] Where these writers see a difference in nature between sciences of interpretation and sciences of explanation, Simmel sees them as identical.

However, we must again stress the fact that, though Simmel's theory rejects realism, it nevertheless does not lead to scepticism.[14] It is no doubt because he was aware of this possible misunderstanding that the final section of *The Problems of the Philosophy of History* is called 'Against scepticism'. In *The Philosophy of Money*, he similarly emphasizes on several occasions that his relativism in no way leads to scepticism. Once again, Simmel's relativism has therefore nothing to do with the 'relativism' of contemporary philosophers and sociologists of science such as Feyerabend, Barnes or Bloor.[15] In *The Philosophy of Money* he bases his rejection of scepticism on a theory of the 'natural selection' of knowledge.[16] In other words, when there are two competing theories, the one which survives is the one which best allows us to get to grips with the real world and which, in this sense, is the nearest to it.

Moreover, although the useful is sometimes hiding behind the true,

Simmel's approach does not give rise to a pragmatism which would make the true dissolve into the useful. It is possible that some frameworks of thought, forms or *a priori* within which human thinking develops were progressively *formed* for reasons of utility. Historians of science have reminded us often enough that chemistry developed from alchemy, and that the latter was far from disinterested. At the same time, however, for the form to be productive, there has to be a correspondence with reality. The example of medicine is perhaps more relevant in this respect than that of chemistry. The pragmatic origin of this corpus of knowledge is hardly in doubt, but this does not imply that there are not medical theories which are true and medical theories which are false – that is, theories which correspond to reality and those which it rejects.

Simmel tries to clarify his position on this point by considering the example of geometry. Geometrical theorems, he points out, are deduced in a way which is non-circular and rigorous from what are posited as first principles. Therefore, in the framework of the principles defining a particular geometry, a given statement can without ambiguity be said to be true or false. The geometry in question, however, cannot *in itself* be said to be true or false, since by the nature of things it is based on principles which cannot themselves have a logical basis. However, the reasons why it was able to develop was perhaps that the point of view on which it is based met certain needs. In any event, though one cannot assess the truth of the geometry in question, one can appreciate its utility.

Simmel therefore puts pragmatism in its proper place: he sees the categories of true and useful at the same time as subtly interlinked, but also as mutually irreducible.

c) Realism and the philosophy of spontaneous knowledge

According to Simmel, the theory of spontaneous knowledge is more often realist than conventionalist or relativist. In fact, it is rare for knowing subjects to see that the useful can give rise to the 'true'. This is why they often, *without further thought*, 'grace the useful with the noble name of true'. On the other hand, they rarely see, and accept with reluctance, the idea that all objects can be looked at from a large number of different viewpoints.

The first reason for the popularity of this realist conception of knowledge is that knowing subjects tend to objectify, even substantify, what is only a relationship. This theme also appears in *The Problems of the Philosophy of History*, where it is illustrated by the example of the 'unconscious': very often, says Simmel, when we do not know what leads us to do a particular thing, we say that we acted according to unconscious motives. Then, without thinking about it, we often transform this acceptable statement, which merely shows our ignorance of the causes of our act, into a statement implying the existence of an entity – the 'unconscious'.

Similarly, we often conceive of a true statement not for what it is, that is, a point of view – non-arbitrary – about things, but as an objective property of things.

This tendency to objectification and substantification is further reinforced by the fact that the viewpoints on the basis of which 'true' statements can be established are often supra-individual in nature. In other words, they are institutionalized and have the 'objective' characteristic common to all institutions.

For example, chemistry, physics and biology consider the same objects from different principles or viewpoints. Once again, the absence of neutrality implied by the very notion of 'viewpoint' in no way means that chemists or physicists have to renounce the notion of truth. On the contrary, it is on the basis of their principles that specialists in these various disciplines can establish true statements and distinguish them without ambiguity from false ones.

However, since the principles that implicitly define the 'viewpoint' from which they are located have a supra-individual validity, these specialists are easily convinced of the objective truth of their statements, more specifically because they describe the world as it is. The principles that define chemistry and make possible a chemist's 'viewpoint' about things constitute what Simmel, once again showing Kant's influence, calls a 'form'.[17] Such a 'form' shows the institutionalization of a certain way of apprehending reality. However, we tend to forget its relational status and to believe that the chemist is describing things as they are. This is not, and cannot be, the case.

This realist illusion is further reinforced by the fact that knowledge accumulates and is transmitted from generation to generation, and this increases the possibility that the pragmatic origin of some of our knowledge and some of its 'forms' escapes us.

Here we need to refer to an important point which we have not been able to mention until now: although he is anxious, in *The Philosophy of Money*, to outline a general theory of the phenomenon of value, Simmel raises the possibility that not only what we regard as 'true', but also what we regard as 'beautiful', was – at least initially – what would have first been seen as useful.[18] Subsequently, the argument goes, the mechanisms for the transmission of ideas, values and 'forms' from one generation to the next tend to wipe out in the subject's mind the pragmatic origin of the aesthetic values attached to a particular object.

There is, finally, another reason – perhaps the most important, or at any rate the most subtle – why realism is the most popular theory of knowledge. This is that the complex nature of human thinking is often hidden from thinking subjects themselves. Because of their finitude, they can have in their minds at any one time only a limited set of statements. They therefore may not see, for example, that they are reasoning in a circular manner probably more often than they think. The case in point which Simmel refers to several times is the following. Assume that we are reasoning thus:

1) $A \rightarrow B \rightarrow C$
2) A

---

3) C

If we were aware of Münchhausen's trilemma, we would have only limited confidence in conclusion C, to which the combination of the first two statements leads. For we would see that the soundness of C cannot be greater than that of A. In reality, when we indulge in reasoning of this kind, we see it as potentially legitimating our belief in C. This of course is possible only if we are convinced of the validity of A. Why are we convinced of this? Often, argues Simmel, because we are thinking of other statements which are present in our mind only metaconsciously, and which are the basis of our confidence in A. For example:

4) $C \rightarrow A$

No doubt statement 4) reinforces the soundness of 2), since A is no longer a simple assertion. However, this extra soundness is illusory, since statements 1) to 4) constitute circular reasoning. For 4) to contribute to the firmness of our belief in C, not only does 4) need to be present in our mind, but at the same time it should not be the object of our attention.

Why do these adventitious statements remain metaconscious? Precisely because we cannot keep together more than a handful of statements.[19] This is why any reasoning includes a conscious part and a metaconscious part, or, to put it another way, an explicit part and an implicit part.

The theme of finitude plays a significant role in Simmel's theory of knowledge, and there are many variations on this theme in both *The Problems of the Philosophy of History* and *The Philosophy of Money*.[20] Further, the fact that the networks of causes cannot be seen in all their complexity, but must be read on the basis of *a priori*, explains why there are sectoral histories (for example, a history of manners, a history of art, and so on) but no universal history. There is also of course in this analysis, and linked to the theme of the finitude of thought, the idea that there can be no knowledge without a point of view.

We need to pause here to look at the word 'metaconscious',[21] which I have been using in my analysis. It is not used by Simmel, who speaks rather of 'unconscious'. However, not surprisingly, he never uses this word in the substantialist sense as used by Freud – at least in the latter's earlier writing.[22] Simmel calls 'unconscious' those statements or representations, for example, on which our reasoning is based at a particular moment, but which are not present in our consciousness. This is why the word 'metaconscious' perhaps has the advantage of avoiding the confusion and ambiguity of the word 'unconscious'.

The statement that ideas, beliefs and representations of the knowing subject always consist of a conscious part and a metaconscious part is a constant theme of Simmel's writing. Not only does our reasoning always have a submerged part, but the value we attribute to objects stems from procedures of comparison that are partly metaconscious.[23] For example, a statement such as 'this work is beautiful' stems from a series of twofold comparisons between comparable works which are not of course present in the mind of the subject when the statement is being made. Similarly, the ends as well as the means[24] of the act are always partly conscious and partly metaconscious.

The significance of this category which I am proposing to call 'metaconscious' derives, as we have seen, from the combination of the finitude of the acting and knowing subject and the complexity of reality. Its presence is seen in the fact that, in everyday life as well as in our more controlled activities such as scientific research, we use all kinds of representations and statements that are not directly present in our contemplation. We regard these statements as 'self-evident',[25] which is why they remain implicit. However, at the same time, they can play an essential role in consolidating our beliefs.

d) *Philosophy and social science*

It must also be said that Simmel's relativism leads him to a definition and a legitimation of philosophy, which is to be expected of a book that has the word 'philosophy' in its title.

The existence of philosophy, he says, is justified by the fact that any discipline is based on principles or *a priori* which cannot be justified within the discipline itself. Moreover, any discipline deals with its object of study only on the basis of a particular viewpoint, and only asks those questions about this object which can be answered within this framework. For example, economics takes the phenomenon of value as a given, but it has nothing to tell us about the origin of this phenomenon as such.

The vacuum which specific disciplines cannot by their very nature hope to fill constitutes, according to Simmel, the field of philosophy. In particular, the philosophy of money looks at questions which economics does not touch, to the extent that they cannot be answered within the framework of economics itself.

Simmel's relativism therefore leads him to reject the positivists' conclusions. Whereas they called for the elimination of philosophy in favour of positive disciplines, Simmel's view is that philosophy is eternal, since its existence is the consequence of the very nature of human knowledge.

It must be added that Simmel also destroys an illusion frequently held by philosophers when they claim that they are establishing the foundations of science: philosophy can no doubt reflect on the principles of science, but it cannot provide their foundation; the principles it would claim to be using to build this foundation would themselves have to have a foundation. To escape these illusions, Simmel says ironically, we need to regard each fundamental principle not as the final one, but as the penultimate one.[26] This is where we can clearly see Simmel's anti-positivism, and the big gap between him and Auguste Comte's faithful disciple Durkheim. We can also see what later distinguished him from writers such as Carnap.

e) To sum up . . .

In trying to summarize Simmel's philosophy of knowledge by reference to the most fundamental principles on which it is based, the first point is his argument that the phenomenon of knowledge derives from a triple need on the part of the social subject: a need to put order into sensations which are very varied, a need to hierarchize and satisfy wants and a need for economy of thought. The second point is that these needs are, according to Simmel, satisfied by mobilizing *a priori*, which always imply the active participation of the subject, even if the latter is not aware of this. Thirdly, these *a priori* are confronted with reality, and accepted or rejected according to the results of this confrontation.

One of Simmel's aphorisms perhaps best encapsulates his relativist philosophy of knowledge: the notion of truth has meaning, and access to the truth is possible, he says in effect, not '*although* it [truth] is relative, but *because* it is relative'.[27]

To conclude on Simmel's philosophy of knowledge, I will simply note not only Simmel's originality, but also what I think can be seen as his philosophical relevance *for us*: nowadays, the philosophy of science seems divided between *realism*, which continues to represent the spontaneous philosophy of specialist and layperson alike, and *relativism* (in the sense used by British and American writers, rather than by Kant or Simmel), which is very popular in international circles of the philosophy and sociology of science, and whose success is perhaps due to its 'break' with the realism of common sense.

Simmel rejects both these philosophies, not only by identifying their weaknesses, but also by proposing in their place a theory which is finely shaded and – at least in my view – credible and compelling.

SIMMEL'S SOCIOLOGY OF KNOWLEDGE

It is now clear why Simmel's philosophy of knowledge leads him naturally to outline a *sociology* of knowledge. As we have seen, since he regards knowledge as a point of view based on a perspective, it is only possible through the mobilization of *a priori*. However, as I have said, Simmel's *a priori* have neither the fixed nor the universal nature which Kant's *a priori* have. Moreover they are, as it were, stratified.

According to Simmel, the phenomenon of value is in itself universal, and derives from the fact that human beings are the site of incompatible wants between which they have to mediate. This characteristic is responsible for the formation of the world of values. However, though it is the condition which makes values possible, it does not determine their content. Similarly, the complexity of the real world and the finitude of the knowing subject introduce an imperative of ordering and classification. Categories such as 'cause', 'means' or 'end' play a universal role in this ordering, but they are used in practice in different ways.

For example, it seems that, for Simmel, there is a first level of *a priori* above which one sees more contingent levels, depending on social circumstances and therefore pertaining to the social sciences. This is why the *philosophy* of knowledge has to be extended into a *sociology* of knowledge, which in its turn assumes a philosophy of knowledge.

a) Its methodology

However, and this is a very important point, Simmel does not fall into the hypothesis of the social conditioning of ideas but, on the contrary, always stresses the mutual influence of social conditions and ideas. In this respect, he avoids both the excesses of Durkheim's sociologism and the extravagances of Marxist, and especially neo–Marxist, materialism.[28]

More specifically, concerning this question of the social determination of ideas, Simmel makes inferences from one of his favourite themes. In *The Philosophy of Money*, as in several other works, he emphasizes the fact that reality is made up of a jumble of causes and effects that are indiscernible as such to the knowing subject. He repeatedly affirms the circular nature of real causality, which he represents by the notion – a frequent theme in his writing – of 'reciprocal action' (*Wechselwirkung*). It is only because we are incapable of apprehending this complexity that we tend to simplify causal relationships and to see them unilaterally.

This means that, when applied to the methodological point we are looking at, Simmel sees social conditions and ideas as linked by reciprocal causal relationships. He says this directly in his own way: 'the soul depends on the world as much as the world depends on the soul.' By this he means that our ideas cannot be entirely independent of social conditions, but they cannot be directly dependent on them either.

Despite this, he says that we should not be surprised that there are two contradictory or, more precisely, contrary theories – the materialist theory and the idealist theory – and that they have an influence on this question. Both are examples of our tendency to transform circular causal relationships into unilateral causal relationships. Both contain a part of truth. At the same time, both are false, even though each has the upper hand when it comes to the other.

I do not need to stress the importance of this idea: it shows that we tend to regard predicates as *contradictory* (idealist/materialist, subjective/objective, realist/conventionalist, and so on), whereas in reality they *are* not. This is because by default we apply fundamental logical principles (the principle of *contradiction*, of the *excluded middle*) to situations to which in fact they do not apply.[29]

These methodological principles are systematically applied by Simmel when he analyses particular systems of ideas, as is shown in his brilliant analysis of Christianity in *The Philosophy of Money*. This is introduced by a look at former times where people's lives had a price depending on their social rank, as in the institution of blood money (*Wergeld*). In Anglo-Saxon England, it cost 2,700 shillings to kill the king, about fifteen times more than the price of killing a peasant. *Cum grano salis*, Simmel even propounds a philological hypothesis: the word *shilling*, he argues, comes from an old Saxon word *skillen* (to kill).

With Christianity, however, the principle of the equal worth of everybody was propounded. This is seen in the notion of the soul, which Simmel regards as the symbolic transposition of the principle. Because God wanted people to be equal in dignity, he gave them all a soul, which is supposed to be all that is best in them. Simmel treats the creation of the notion of the soul in an admiring way, as a superb intellectual innovation. At the same time, he suggests that the reason why there is a symbolic affirmation of everybody's equal value is that these former times were dominated by a form of thinking which he calls *substantialist*. The real meaning of the notion of soul is 'relational': it affirms everybody's equality of dignity. This real meaning has little to do with the representations, or even the substantialist images which the notion conveys and which describe the soul as a hidden and secret *part* of the individual. We can also note in this respect that Simmel's analyses of the notion of the soul are very close to Durkheim's in *The Elementary Forms of the Religious Life*.[30]

However, we also have to say that Christianity is analysed by Simmel as proposing representations consistent with *evolution*, but not caused by it. The myths of Christianity were acclaimed on the one hand because they gave dignity to the most dispossessed, and on the other hand because the universalism which they introduced in symbolic language corresponded to the changes arising from the increased complexity of societies. We see that Simmel is looking at the relationships between ideas and social conditions as an example of reciprocal relationships, of *Wechselwirkung*: as with Christianity, ideas can be autonomous and represent an authentic creation; but they are also more or less consistent – from the point of view of form as well as substance – with the expectations of the audience they address.

Later, with the spread of what we sometimes call modernity, and with the development of a monetary economy, the substantialist mode of thinking tends to lose ground, says Simmel. The affirmation of the equality of dignity takes on new forms: what socialism on the one hand and liberalism on the other have in common with Christianity is that they affirm the equal dignity of all. No doubt the form varies between different examples, but the substance is partly identical, says Simmel. Here he harks back to a theme of Nietzsche, which he refines and clarifies: while it is true that Christianity is more particularly consistent with the interests of the dispossessed, it is also in harmony with the tendency to universalization characteristic of modernity.[31]

Finally on this point, one can speak of Simmel's originality in relation to many sociologists of knowledge: ideas are not reflections of reality, they are not even conditioned by it; they are rather creations whose influence varies with the extent to which they are consistent, in form and substance, with the expectations, modes of thought and interests of a particular audience.

Here, Simmel is foreshadowing one of the main aspects of Max Scheler's sociology of knowledge;[32] for Scheler the role of social factors is particularly in the selection of ideas (a 'sluice-gate' role, he calls it); the actual origin of ideas is explained in a very minor and partial way, he argues, by social variables. For example, certain social and historical contexts favour a mechanistic view of the world; but the very existence of this view is not explained socially – it must be seen as one element of a relatively unchanging stock of possible views.

Simmel's rejection of unilateral determinism in the sociology of knowledge and culture can be illustrated by several examples, but I will give just one further one: his analysis of fashion. The notion of fashion, says Simmel, is a recent one; it appeared with modern forms of stratification as soon as social mobility was extensive enough for some members of each class to identify themselves symbolically, by imitating their manners and tastes, with the class just above them, in the hope that they could accede to that class. Fashion, says Simmel (and here he is close to Thorsten Veblen),[33] is therefore a class phenomenon.

However, at the same time, he does not draw the conclusion that artistic preferences can be seen sociologically as deriving from supposed collective class preferences.[34] For him, beauty is not what the ruling class defines it to be. There is an important quotation on this point: we follow fashion, says Simmel, *so long as we lack assurance in our aesthetic judgements.*

There is, after all, an objectivity of aesthetic values.[35] On this point, Simmel again follows Kant – the Kant of the *Critique of Judgement* – but he modernizes him by saying that a beautiful work is one which gives the impression of necessity, of coherence, of the dependence of the parts on the whole. He ties in this Kantian theme with an idea borrowed from Goethe: the artist is free in the first moments, but the initial conditions, once they have been established by the first strokes of the brush, the first bars of a score or the first lines of a novel, make the rest *necessary*. No doubt these initial conditions can in certain cases be inspired in the artist by the latter's social experiences, but they are in no way enough to qualify the work aesthetically.

It is clear that one reason why Simmel rejects aesthetic relativism, as he rejects cognitive relativism (I am using the word 'relativism' in the modern sense), is that beauty and truth are answers to vital questions.[36] These categories cannot therefore be reduced to illusions, not even social illusions.

The sociology of knowledge and culture does not therefore imply that the autonomy of the subject is eliminated, but rather that one recognizes it and appreciates, to use Simmel's frequent phrase, the 'freedom of the spirit' in human beings. It does not imply that values become dissolved in social conditions but, on the contrary, that one recognizes their objectivity. The beauty of a musical score, any more than the truth of a mathematical proposition, cannot derive from a convention, even one which is the work of an invisible hand.

Let us note in passing at this point that what is perhaps even clearer is another of the reasons why Simmel never accepted the idea of a break between philosophy and sociology: the sociology of knowledge and culture can no more answer every question about tastes, ideas or artistic preferences than economics can answer every question about money. Sociology can explain the enthusiasm of the non–connoisseur for Beethoven or of the layperson for Newton as the effect of snobbery or conformism, but not that of the connoisseur or expert. The sociology of knowledge can no more replace the philosophy of knowledge and epistemology than the sociology of art can replace aesthetics.

There is an essential conclusion to be drawn from these remarks, which remains implicit in Simmel: education as a liberator.

Another interesting theme in Simmel, which presages some of Pareto's arguments in his pendulum theory of ideologies, is the following: as we have seen, an essential characteristic of human thought is, according to Simmel, that it has to cope with the elusive complexity of what is real and what simplifies. This operation involves the mobilization of *a priori*. For example, a materialist is somebody who places emphasis, in the complex and always circular networks of causes and effects, on the signs or symptoms of the influence of social conditions on ideas. This is not wrong, says Simmel, it is simply not the whole picture. It is unacceptable as soon as the *a priori* cannot be apprehended, as soon as they ensnare the materialist subjects into being unaware of the existence of this part of their thinking. Conversely, the idealist is somebody who insists on the autonomy of the thinking subject, and on the independence of intellectual creations from social conditions. We can see that, when Simmel says both are right, he is not indulging in eclecticism, but is actually applying a very precise theory.

This theory can be generalized: the complexity of the real world, the need to simplify thinking, and the fact that all thinking includes a metaconscious part explain why many systems of representation seem to be elements of an alternative. One can be monist like Spinoza, or dualist like Descartes. One can be evolutionist or not. In the first case, one can have a pessimistic or an optimistic view of historical evolution. Regarding knowledge, one can be a realist or not. Still anxious to master the complexity of the real world, one can also adhere to the 'social conception of the world' – is Simmel thinking here of the sociological imperialism of Comte and Durkheim, or that of Marx? – or swear only by 'historism',[37] which was very popular in Simmel's time and which was destined to reappear in the 1960s adorned with the finery of novelty.[38]

All these viewpoints are based on *a priori*. All of them have an element of truth. This is why they are objectively important and socially influential.

It is clear that here we are far removed from the theory of ideology as illusion. Like Pareto, that other great sociologist of knowledge, Simmel sees that two propositions have to be linked – that it is impossible at the same time to see any system ending in *-ism* as true and to regard it as devoid of meaning. Pareto puts forward a similar argument: the task of the sociologist is to bring out the meaning of ideas which at first sight are strange, dubious or false. However, Simmel has the advantage over Pareto of being specific, of explaining why false ideas gain the upper hand and why dogmatic systems tend to appear in twos.

Simmel's evaluation of Marx is illuminating in this respect. He admires him, and recognizes his creative power: Marx developed his *viewpoint* with incomparable inspiration, says Simmel in *The Problems of the Philosophy of History*; and, in *The Philosophy of Money*, he says that the influence of Marxian thought derives from its having propounded a message consistent in form and substance with the expectations of certain groups of people. At the same time, Simmel argues, one can be Marxist only by failing to notice the restrictive nature of the principles on which this viewpoint is based. In other words, one cannot be Marxist unless one is blind.[39]

b) Some theses

Simmel applies these ideas to views about the modern world. Some people see in modernity the extension of the alienation of the individual, others see the development of individual autonomy. This theme is also a significant one in *The Philosophy of Money*, and it sufficiently distinguishes Simmel from most other writers for us to look further at this point.

The rationalization of the world which goes with a monetary economy, he says, in itself legitimates neither a pessimistic nor an optimistic view of history. On this theme as on others, we see that Simmel is far removed from the banalities contained in discourse on 'modernity', and that he is more 'secular' than Max Weber. For Simmel, the two views justify each other, which is why he stresses both the liberating and the alienating effects of money. It is true that money liberates. For example, payment in money was a major factor in freeing the medieval peasant from the lord's tutelage. It even contributed significantly to the downfall of feudalism. However, it is also true that money 'alienates'; for example, the extension of 'teleological sequences' means that social subjects are very often ignorant of the finalities of their own actions.

Simmel nowhere suggests that we can draw up an objective balance sheet of these divergent effects – this could only be subjective. We see why somebody such as Walter Benjamin did not really appreciate statements such as these.[40]

This point allows me to move from questions of method to questions of substance, and to say that, on matters of substance, there is in *The Philosophy of Money* an interesting sociology of *modern* knowledge and culture. I will not go very far into this point, since it covers a multitude of specific studies which are easily accessible and which I do not intend to summarize. I will simply indicate those characteristics that, according to Simmel, separate traditional societies from modern societies from the viewpoint of knowledge and culture.

I will not go back either to the theme of the influence of a monetary economy on values, or the fact that the latter are seen in the modern world as *objective* and *quantifiable*. Nor will I examine further, despite its importance, the hypothesis that money prepared the way for scientific thinking by facilitating – not necessarily determining – a formalist view of things, and by suggesting that the most diverse objects could, in a certain way and from a certain viewpoint, be compared, measured and, as it were, deprived of their substance and their singularity.

The possibility of quantifying, measuring and formally apprehending all objects, the very idea of being able to make statements of universal validity about the world, are all characteristics of scientific thinking which, according to Simmel, are analogous to the properties of money: its *formal* character, its 'indifference' to the qualitative content and the singularity of things.[41]

However, once again, we must not regard the relationship between a monetary economy and science in a causal and unilateral way. Simmel's suggestion is rather that money and its properties inspired in social actors a paragon which, as it were, gave them the idea of transposing it to other levels.

Not only does the development of money, at least to a certain degree, explain the big divide created by the appearance of scientific thinking, but, by bringing about a universalist view of phenomena and by favouring the creation of the category of the universal, the development of a monetary economy also facilitated the appearance of a *social* category unknown up to then – intellectuals. The appearance of this social type was difficult, argues Simmel, so long as substantialist thinking reigned supreme, with its world peopled by singular entities; but it became possible when the autonomous existence of a world of ideas was recognized. 'Intellectuals' were then able to replace theologians. From then on, Socrates was no longer banished from the city; on the contrary, he became an honoured citizen. Sometimes, intellectuals were granted unfamiliar power, as in the case of Robespierre, who has a visible effect on Simmel.

However, money did not only facilitate the appearance of intellectuals, it also brought about an intellectualization of life and the development of individualism – that is, a view which allowed people to consider themselves as bearers of universality.[42]

Another theme linked to the previous one, which we have already encountered and which figures largely in *The Philosophy of Money*, is that of the disappearance of substantialist thinking in modern societies.

In traditional societies things have an essence, and they tend to be incommensurable; they are endowed with singularity. Discontinuity prevails. Moreover, visible things and invisible things – Plato's ideas, for instance – have in common that they are regarded as endowed with a substantial reality. With modernity, on the other hand, these substances disappear. Intellectuals and scientists – the characteristic personages of modernity – create and manipulate all kinds of abstract entities that do not exist, even though they themselves tend to substantify them. The abstract retranslation of the Christian notion of the soul into the language of modern individualistic morality is an example of this transformation: the same idea is conceived in a *substantial* way in the first case, and in a *relational* way in the second.[43]

Simmel sees in Greek thought the proof that substantialism is typical of traditional thinking: substantialism is dominant here. He cautiously propounds moreover another hypothesis: perhaps the inalienability of real property in Greece made it difficult for the category of abstract universality to appear. Simmel does not say that his hypothesis could explain why there was no experimental science in Greece, but this emerges from his analyses.

Simmel says that the dominance of substantialism in Greece explains why those who moved away from it towards nominalism, Sophists and Socrates were all the victims of public condemnation.

It was money which finally established nominalism. By providing a concrete and visible model of reality of which the esssence is purely 'relational', money in fact facilitated the move, characteristic of modernity, from substantialism to relativism and nominalism.[44] It amounted to nominalism in action, as it were. It certainly presents itself in a material way, but the symbols which represent it became more and more impalpable over time. After gold, silver and leather money came paper money, cheques and bills of exchange. Money became more and more manifestly and ostensibly symbolic as its use increased. As soon as this process of dematerialization is sufficiently advanced, one cannot ignore that its function is to symbolize the relationships between individuals wanting goods to which they give different values.

Economic theory, or more particularly the representations of money in economic doctrines and policies as described by historians, also follows, says Simmel, this path from substantialism to nominalism. Fiscalism and mercantilism also indicate a substantialist conception of money: mercantilists believe that the economic vitality and political power of a country are measured directly by the quantity of money in state vaults. They even say that this amount of money is a causal factor in the other variables. The physiocrats' critique can be seen as a divergence from this substantialism. In Adam Smith and liberalism, and in Marx himself, the relational nature of money is better perceived, until it emerges into the spotlight. However, Simmel suggests that substantialist thinking still has some hold in the age in which he was writing: he sees an indication of this in resistance to the introduction of cheques.[45]

Simmel goes even further down this road and prophesies that nominalism and relativism are likely to prevail in all forms of thinking:

just as in the end we saw that money had a symbolic and relational character, so substantialist views of society are likely to disappear.[46]

Similarly, argues Simmel, we would probably understand that every theory is based on *a priori* and that, though one can cling tightly to the notions of truth and objectivity, one has also to give up trying to achieve absolute knowledge.

The long analysis of *The Philosophy of Money* therefore concludes on an optimistic note: the gentle move from substantialism to relativism should forewarn us against fanaticism and dogmatism . . .[47]

Once in a while does no harm; it is rare to catch this German Socrates red-handed in wishful thinking.

Notes

NOTES TO PREFACE

1 T. Parsons, *The Structure of Social Action* (McGraw Hill, New York, 1937).
2 *The Theory of Communicative Action* (vol. 1, Beacon Press, Boston, 1984; vol. 2, Polity Press, Cambridge, 1987); orig. pubd as *Theorie des kommunikativen Handelns* (Suhrkamp, Frankfurt am Main, 1981).
3 C. Perelman and L. Olbrechts-Tyteca, *The New Rhetoric: a treatise on argumentation* (University of Notre Dame Press, Notre Dame, IN, 1969); orig. pubd as *La Nouvelle Rhétorique: traité de l'argumentation* (Presses Universitaires de France, Paris, 1958), 2 vols.
4 *Ibid.*, conclusion.
5 Cambridge University Press, New York and London, 1958.
6 J. Habermas, in *Knowledge and Human Interests* (Heinemann, London, 1978 (1972)); orig. pubd as *Erkenntnis und Interesse* (Suhrkamp, Frankfurt an Main, 1968), stresses the 'dialogical' nature of knowledge. By introducing the idea that subjects are capable of not seeing their own reasoning better than their interlocutor, Simmel provides a concrete basis for this principle.
7 I gave a more general outline analysis of this phenomenon in *An Analysis of Ideology* (Polity Press, Cambridge, 1989); orig. pubd as *L'Idéologie ou l'origine des idées reçues* (Fayard, Paris, 1986). The present book is in fact a development of chapter 8 of this work.
8 To the classical definition to believe = *für wahr halten* (to regard as true), I therefore add the condition that what one regards as such is not, or is not very likely to be.
9 J. Elster (ed.), *The Multiple Self* (Cambridge University Press, London, 1986).
10 See in particular: 'Subjective rationality and the explanation of social behavior', public lecture, Max Planck Institut für Sozialforschung, rev. version pubd in *Rationality and Society*, 1, 2 (October 1989), pp. 173–96; 'Common sense and the social sciences', *International Sociology*, 3, 1 (1988), pp. 1–22; 'On relativism', in *Studies on Mario Bunge's 'Treatise on Basic Philosophy'*, ed. P. Weingartner and G. Dorn (Rodopi, Amsterdam, 1990); 'Should we believe in relativism?', in *Wege der Vernunft*, ed. A. Bohnen and A. Musgrave (Mohr, Tübingen, 1990); 'Die Erkenntnistheorie in Simmels *Philosophie des Geldes*',

Zeitschrift für Soziologie, 6 (December 1989), pp. 413–25; 'Subjective rational-ity and the theory of ideology', public lecture, University of Chicago, rev. version pubd in *Social Structure and Culture*, ed. H. Haferkamp (De Gruyter, Berlin and New York, 1989), pp. 269–87; 'Why social scientists tend to see the world as overordered', *Philosophica*, 44, 2 (1989), pp. 15–31; 'Razionalitá soggettiva e disposizioni', in *Il soggetto dell'azione: paradigmi sociologici ed imagini dell'attore sociale*, ed. L. Sciolla and L. Ricolfi (Angeli, Milan, 1989), pp. 27–50.

NOTES TO CHAPTER 1

1 *De l'esprit géométrique*, section II, 'De l'art de persuader', in B. Pascal, *Oeuvres complètes* (Gallimard, Paris, 1954), p. 592.
2 K. Mannheim, *Ideology and Utopia* (Routledge & Kegan Paul, London, 1954 (1929)).
3 For example, Barnes, Bloor and so on (see references in Chapter 7). Cf. F. Isambert, 'Un "programme fort" en sociologie de la science?', *Revue Française de sociologie*, 26, 3 (1985), pp. 485–508.
4 Pascal, *op. cit.*, p. 592.
5 Logic dictates that there should also be a type IIc corresponding to 'observable non-affective causes', which would cover, for example, cases where a chemical substance influences the subject's beliefs.
6 For example, R. Needham, *Belief, Language and Experience* (Basil Blackwell, Oxford, 1972) hails Lévy-Bruhl as the founder of cultural relativism, claiming that he was the first to see the difficulties of communication between cultures, which Peter Winch, for instance, emphasized (since each element of culture C is linked to the totality of that culture, observers from culture C′ cannot easily transpose into their language statements by subjects belonging to culture C). Credit should be given to Lévy-Bruhl for formulating an explanatory model which many analysts of the phenomena of knowledge use unconsciously. As will be seen in Chapter 2, many present-day cognitive psychologists think that ordinary knowledge obeys a logic that is different from scientific knowledge. In doing this, they rediscover the notion of 'prelogical mentality', even if they do not use the term. See, on Lévy-Bruhl, the classic book by J. Cazeneuve, *Lévy-Bruhl* (Presses Universitaires de France, Paris, 1963).
7 L. Lévy-Bruhl, *La mentalité primitive* (Presses Universitaires de France, Paris, 1960 (1922)); *The Notebooks on Primitive Mentality* (Basil Blackwell, Oxford, 1975), orig. pubd as *Les Carnets de Lévy-Bruhl* (Presses Universitaires de France, Paris, 1949); *L'Expérience mystique et les symboles chez les primitifs* (Alcan, Paris, 1938); *L'Âme primitive* (Presses Universitaires de France, Paris, 1963).
8 *La Mentalité primitive*, pp. 19–20.
9 The adjective 'mystical' indicates, according to Lévy-Bruhl, 'belief in forces, influences, actions imperceptible to the senses, but nevertheless real', *ibid.*, p. 30.

10 *Ibid.*, p. 77.

11 *Ibid.*, p. 31.

12 E. Durkheim, *The Elementary Forms of the Religious Life* (Allen & Unwin, London, 1915); orig. pubd as *Les formes élémentaires de la vie religieuse: le système totémique en Australie* (Presses Universitaires de France, Paris, 1990 (1912)).

13 R. Boudon, *The Analysis of Ideology* (University of Chicago Press, Chicago; Polity Press, Cambridge, 1989), orig. pubd as *L'Idéologie ou l'origine des idées reçues* (Fayard, Paris, 1986), chapter 2.

14 R. Boudon, *op. cit.*, and 'L'acteur social est-il si irrationel (et si conformiste) qu'on le dit?', in *Individu et justice sociale*, ed. F. Terré (Seuil, Paris, 1988), pp. 219–44.

15 R. Boudon, *La logique du social* (Hachette, Paris, 1983 (1979)), pp. 252–5.

16 E. Durkheim, *The Elementary Forms of the Religious Life*, p. 415 et seq. See the remarkable essay by R. Horton, 'Lévy-Bruhl, Durkheim and the scientific revolution', in R. Horton and R. Finnegan, *Modes of Thought* (Faber, London, 1983); and also C. Lévi-Strauss, *The Savage Mind* (Weidenfeld & Nicolson, London, 1972), orig. pubd as *La pensée sauvage* (Plon, Paris, 1983 (1962)).

17 The power of attraction which this hypothesis tends to exercise is all the stronger, and the existence of an established theory is all the more effectively prolonged, in that, as the so-called Duhem–Quine theory indicates, when a theory seems to be incompatible with observed data, one cannot determine what in the theory indicates, when a theory seems to be incompatible with observed data, one cannot determine what in the theory ought to be changed. Attempts at correcting it therefore start with a series – which can be a lengthy one – of trial and error approaches.

18 One cannot be happy with comparing the procedures of magicians with those of scientists by suggesting the former has recourse to immunizing auxiliary hypotheses, and the latter to independently testable auxiliary hypotheses, to correct a theory which is incompatible with certain facts. For example, there is nothing to say that a hypothesis such as 'the ritual was not carried out according to the prescribed rules' cannot be regarded as independently testable.

19 M. Weber, *Economy and Society: an outline of interpretative sociology* (Bedminster Press, New York, 1968); orig. pubd as *Wirtschaft und Gesellschaft* (Mohr, Tübingen, 1922).

20 Durkheim to a certain extent follows Tylor, though he also criticizes him. On this point, see T. Settle, 'The rationality of science vs, the rationality of magic', *Philosophy of the Social Sciences*, 1 (1971), pp. 173–94.

21 This 'psychology' is of course *ideal-typical* rather than descriptive.

22 T. Settle, *op. cit.*

23 M. Mauss, 'Esquisse d'une théorie générale de la magie', in *Sociology and Psychology* (Routledge & Kegan Paul, London, 1979), orig. pubd as *Sociologie et anthropologie* (Presses Universitaires de France, Paris, 1983 (1922)), pp. 1–141.

24 A. Oberschall, 'Cultural change and social movements', paper given to the Conference of the American Association of Sociology, 1989. See also K. Thomas, *Religion and the Decline of Magic* (Penguin, Harmondsworth, 1973).

25 Other factors must be taken into account to explain variations in this phenomenon. Witchcraft developed particularly in the most 'modern' parts of sixteenth-century Europe. This variation has to be compared with the penetration of modern ideologies (neo-Platonism), which was greater in Southern Germany or Northern Italy than in Spain or Southern Italy. However, Oberschall also points out that trials for witchcraft are costly and that only rich communities with a sufficient surplus can institutionalize them. From this stems the surprising correlation between the development of 'modernity' and that of witchcraft in sixteenth-century Europe.

26 Lévy-Bruhl, in *The Notebooks on Primitive Mentality*, almost totally disowned his theory of 'primitive mentality'. The text which shows most clearly Lévy-Bruhl's turnaround is probably his letter to Evans-Pritchard after the latter's publication of an article on primitive mentality: *Revue philosophique*, 4, (1957), pp. 407–13.

27 See Chapter 9 for an example taken from *On Suicide*; also R. Boudon, *Theories of Social Change . . .* and *The Unintended Consequences of Social Action* (St Martin's Press, London, 1982); orig. pubd as *Effets pervers et ordre social* (Presses Universitaires de France, Paris, 1979 (1977)), pp. 131–56.

28 R. Boudon, *The Analysis of Ideology*, p. 98.

29 In particular analyses, Pareto often abandons model IIc in favour of model Ib. Cf. R. Boudon, 'Le phénomène idéologique: en marge d'une lecture de Pareto', Lettura Fulvio Gerrini, *L'Année sociologique*, 34 (1986), pp. 87–126.

30 See J. Elster, *Making Sense of Marx* (Cambridge University Press, Cambridge, 1985).

31 The frequently quoted expression of Weber: *deutend verstehen* ('Soziologie [ist] eine Wissenschaft, welche soziales Handeln deutend verstehen und damit in seinem Ablauf und seinen wirkungen ursächlich erklären will' . . . 'Handeln [ist] mit einem subjektivem Sinn verbunden') either had no meaning or else means: finding a theory capable of being introduced by a formula of the type 'X had good reasons for doing or believing Y, because . . .'.

32 A complete taxonomy would include a class IId corresponding to '*non-affective and observable causes* (not having the status of *reasons*). Hallucinations caused by the ingestion of chemical substances would, for example, fall within this category.

33 S. Toulmin, *The Uses of Argument* (Cambridge University Press, New York and London, 1958), and C. Perelman and L. Olbrechts-Tyteca, *The New Rhetoric*.

34 C. Perelman, *L'Empire rhétorique* (Vrin, Paris, 1977).

35 Toulmin, for example, rejects neo-Marxist sociology of law which – carrying on classical tradition in a different way – argues that judicial reasons *are in fact* covering reasons.

36 T. Kuhn, *The Structure of Scientific Revolutions* (University of Chicago Press, Chicago, 1962); G. Holton, *The Scientific Imagination* (Cambridge University Press, Cambridge, 1978) and *Thematic Origins of Scientific Thought: Kepler to Einstein* (Harvard University Press, Cambridge, MA, and London, 1973); J. Ziman, *Reliable Knowledge: an explanation of the grounds for belief in science* (Cambridge University Press, Cambridge, 1978).

37 K. Popper, 'La rationalité et le statut du principe de rationalité', in *Les*

fondements philosophiques des systèmes économiques, ed. E.-M. Claassen (Payot, Paris, 1967), pp. 142–50.

38 For example, C. Lévi-Strauss, *La pensée sauvage*; R. Horton and R. Finnegan, *Modes of Thought*; E. Gellner, *Legitimation of Belief* (Cambridge University Press, Cambridge, 1974); M. Hollis and S. Lukes, *Rationality and Relativism* (Basil Blackwell, Oxford, 1982).

39 R. Nisbett and L. Ross, *Human Inference* (Prentice-Hall, Englewood Cliffs, NJ, 1980).

40 J. S. Mill, *On Fallacies: book v of a system of logic, ratiocinative and inductive* (Routledge & Kegan Paul, London, 1974).

41 A. Downs, *An Economic Theory of Democracy* (Harper, New York, 1957).

42 A special number of *Revue économique*, 40, 2 (March 1989), *L'Economie des conventions*, is a measure of this renewal.

43 J. B. Grize, *De la logique à l'argumentation* (Droz, Geneva, 1982); J. B. Grize (ed.), 'Discours, savoir, histoire', in *Revue européenne des sciences sociales*, 17 (1979), and especially *Pensée naturelle, logique et langage: hommage à Jean-Blaise Grize* (Université, Neuchâtel, 1983). See also R. Martin, *Pour une logique du sens* (Presses Universitaires de France, Paris 1983); R. Schrank and R. P. Abelson, *Scripts, Plans, Goals and Understanding* (Wiley, New York, 1977); N. Rescher, *Hypothetical Reasoning* (North Holland, Amsterdam, 1964) and *Plausible Reasoning* (Van Gorcum, Amsterdam, 1976).

44 R. Rorty, *Philosophy and the Mirror of Nature* (Basil Blackwell, Oxford, 1980).

45 G. Simmel, *The Problems of the Philosophy of History* (Free Press, New York, 1977); orig. pubd as *Die Probleme der Geschichtsphilosophie* (Duncker & Humblot, Munich, 1905 (1892)).

46 These different models have been applied or developed in recent writing. G. Vignaux, in *L'Argumentation* (Droz, Paris and Geneva, 1976), particularly chapters 6 to 8, adopts the perspective characteristic of Toulmin. (Today, this writer is more interested in analysing the relationship between language activities and knowledge activities, and in highlighting the importance of enunciative relationships in our representation of reality: *Le Discours acteur du monde: énonciation, argumentation et cognition* (Ophrys, Paris, 1988). On the other hand, D. McCloskey, *The Rhetoric of Economics* (University of Wisconsin Press, Madison, 1985), or R. Edmondson, *Rhetoric in Sociology* (Macmillan, London, 1984) follow the Perelman tradition. J. -F. Revel suggests, in *La Connaissance utile* (Grasset, Paris, 1989), that La Rochefoucauld's model should be applied to contemporary examples, since he thinks it will explain the intellectual distortions . . . of journalists.

47 I tried to show in *The Analysis of Ideology* that this type of dissemination characterized modern ideologies, such as developmentalism or the 'dependancy theory', which are based on scientific-type reasoning from which hyperbolic conclusions are drawn.

48 Adherence to sophistical theories is also a classic sociological problem dealt with at length by Pareto. In *The Analysis . . .*, I stressed the importance of communicative distortions in the explanation of this phenomenon.

49 See on this point, for example, J. Bouveresse, *Le Philosophe chez les autophages* (Minuit, Paris, 1984), or A. Mingat, P. Salmon and A. Wolfelsperger,

Méthodologie économique (Presses Universitaires de France, Paris, 1985), chapter 5.

50 Cf., for example, Hume, *An Enquiry Concerning Human Understanding*, V, 2; J. S. Mill, *op. cit.*, 1, 5, 2; F. Brentano, *Von der Klassifikation der psychischen Phänomene*, II, 1 (F. Meiner, Hamburg, 1959); C. Peirce, *Collected Papers* (Harvard University Press, Cambridge, MA, 1931), 5, p. 397; R. Needham, *Belief, Language and Experience*; J. Hintikka, *Knowledge and Belief* (Cornell University Press, Ithaca and London, 1961); H. H. Price, *Belief* (Allen & Unwin, London, 1969), etc.

NOTES TO CHAPTER 2

1 'Good reason' is often, in philosophical usage, an equivalent of 'reasons with an objective foundation', as, for example, in G. J. Warnock, 'Every event has a cause', in *Logic and Language*, ed. A. Flew (Basil Blackwell, Oxford, 1963), pp. 95–111. I think 'ordinary' usage is richer and sometimes corresponds to subjective reasons in the sense in which H. Simon uses the term, and it is this meaning which I take here. Cf. Chapter 9.

2 R. Nisbett and L. Ross, *Human Inference* (Prentice-Hall, Englewood Cliffs, NJ, 1980).

3 By interpreting the adjective 'rational' as shorthand for 'X had *good reasons* for . . ., because', all ambiguity is avoided and we are going back to the origin of the word 'rational', a polysemic word with different uses which have in common only the ability to be formulated as above. For a fuller discussion on this point, see Chapters 8 and 9, and particularly the final section of this chapter on the definition of rationality.

4 This example appears in the stimulating work of economic epistemology by A. Bonnafous, *Le Siècle des ténèbres de l'économie* (Economica, Paris, 1990).

5 J. M. Bochenski, *The Methods of Contemporary Thought* (Reidel, Dordrecht, 1965).

6 This theoretical 'consensus' is a necessary but not a sufficient condition to make a reason a 'good reason' in the sense in which I am using the term. In fact the most irrational beliefs can also be the object of a consensus. I do not think it is possible to define criteria which allow us to distinguish in any mechanical way between 'good' and 'bad' reasons. After all, there are no criteria to distinguish mechanically between truth and falsehood. Cf. Chapter 8 on this point.

7 I cannot here embark on a philosophical discussion on induction. Few people agree that it is possible to produce hypotheses exclusively from empirical data, and in no way am I assuming that here. By 'inductive process' I mean quite simply the process by which one tends – in ordinary as well as in scientific knowledge – to regard conjectures such as 'x(y)', 'x causes y', and so on as acceptable when, for instance, one has verified $x(y_i)$ from all the examples of y_i which one has been able to observe. Of course, one then has to ask whether this 'generalization' is in fact acceptable. What interests me here is that many distortions arise from the fact that other conjectures are also introduced implicitly, for instance, that the y_i observed are 'representative' of the totality of y_i.

8 A. Tversky and D. Kahneman, 'Availability: a heuristic for judging frequency and probability', *Cognitive Psychology*, 5 (1973), pp. 207–32.

9 The number of paths in A is 8^3, since they can go from any cross in the top line through any cross in the middle line to any cross on the bottom line. Similarly, the number of paths in B is 2^9. But $8^3 = (2^3)^3 = 2^9 = 512$.

10 There are ten possibilities for the first stop and nine for the second. But these 90 possibilities become 45 $[(10 \times 9)/2]$ since the combination of stop x and stop y is the same as stop y with stop x. Similarly, there are respectively 10, 9 and 8 possibilities to *eliminate* a first, second and third stop, in other words, to *choose* seven stops. However, these possibilities amount only to $(10 \times 9 \times 8)/(2 \times 3) = 120$ separate choices (since combinations $xyz, xzy, \ldots, zyx$ are identical). In the case of four (or six) stops, the number of *choices* is: $(10 \times 9 \times 8 \times 7)/(2 \times 3 \times 4) = 210$.

11 In fact, the question was systematically put for all values of the variable 'number of compulsory stops' between two and eight.

12 See references to this phrase in Chapter 3.

13 R. A. Shweder, 'Likeliness and likelihood in everyday thought: magical thinking in judgements about personality', *Current Anthropology*, 18, 4 (December 1977), pp. 637–59.

14 C. Lévy-Strauss, *La Pensée sauvage* (Plon, Paris, 1982 (1962)).

15 'Some scholars have viewed magic as a relatively effective set of procedures for acquiring knowledge and exercising control over one's environment, comparable to scientific canons of enquiry', R. A. Shweder, *op. cit.*, p. 637.

16 B. Malinowski, *Magic, Science and Religion* (Doubleday, Garden City, NY, 1954).

17 S. J. Tambiah, 'Form and meaning in magical acts: a point of view',. in *Modes of Thought*, ed. R. Horton and R. Finnegan (Faber, London, 1973), pp. 230–48. L. Wittgenstein, 'Bemerkungen über Frazer's "The Golden Bough"', *Synthese*, 17 (1967), 233–53.

18 R. A. Shweder, *op. cit.*, p. 637.

19 Others are referred to in Chapter 10.

20 R. A. Shweder, *op. cit.*, p. 643.

21 The line of reasoning followed by Shweder's subjects can be summarized (assuming that 'many' is associated with a threshold p_0) as

$2x(y)?$

[If 'often' $x(y)$, i.e., $p[x(y)] > p_0$, then $x(y)]$*

$p[x(y)] > p_0$

$x(y)$

22 For example, Shweder's theory is itself illustrative of 'Simmel effects'.

23 See Chapters 3 and 9 for a fuller discussion of this point.

NOTES TO CHAPTER 3

1 G. Simmel, *The Philosophy of Money* (Routledge & Kegan Paul, London, 1978); orig. pubd as *Philosophie des Geldes* (Duncker & Humblot, Leipzig, 1900).

2 G. Simmel, *The Problems of the Philosophy of History* (Free Press, New York,

1977); orig. pubd as *Die Probleme der Geschichtsphilosophie* (Duncker & Humblot, Leipzig, 1905 (1892)).

3 in *Economy and Society: an outline of interpretative sociology* (Bedminster Press, New York, 1968); orig. pubd as *Wirtschaft und Gesellschaft* (Mohr, Tübingen, 1922).

4 G. Simmel, *The Problems . . .*, p. 62.

5 *Ibid.*, p. 46.

6 *Ibid.*, pp. 46–7.

7 *Ibid.*, p. 46.

8 *Ibid.*, p. 58.

9 On 'paradigms', see T. Kuhn, *The Structure of Scientific Revolutions* (University of Chicago Press, Chicago, 1962). On 'thema', see G. Holton, *Thematic Origins of Scientific Thought* (Cambridge University Press, Cambridge, 1974). On 'conjectures', see K. Popper, *Conjectures and Refutations* (Routledge & Kegan Paul, London, 1969). On 'frames', see for example, E. Goffman, *Frame Analysis* (Harper, New York, 1974), A. Tversky and D. Kahneman, 'The framing of decisions and the psychology of choice', *Science*, 211, 4481 (January 1981), pp. 453–58, or S. Lindeberg, 'Choice and culture: the behavioral basis of cultural impact of transactions', in *Society and Culture*, ed. H. Haferkamp (De Gruyter, Berlin, 1989), pp. 175–98.

10 G. Simmel, *The Problems . . .*, p. 43.

11 F. Hayek, *New Studies in Philosophy, Economics and the History of Ideas* (Routledge & Kegan Paul, London, 1978), chapter 17.

12 G. Simmel, *The Problems . . .*, p. 43.

13 G. Simmel, *The Philosophy of Money*, p. 140. This passage immediately precedes the quotation at the beginning of this chapter.

14 Obviously, according to Hume, it is *habit* which explains why we believe that the sun will rise tomorrow.

15 I am taking this from the concrete example usually used by Peirce to illustrate his typology of the forms of reasoning. Cf. note 16. I put 'reasoning' in inverted commas to show that inductive 'reasoning' does not meet the requirements which logic usually places on reasoning.

16 Popper denies that induction can represent anything other than the expression of a conjecture, but agrees that the search for conjectures is essential in scientific life.

17 The three forms of reasoning distinguished by Peirce can be defined from the following example from C. Hartshorne and P. Weiss (eds), *Collected Papers of Charles Sanders Peirce* (Harvard University Press, Cambridge, MA, 1931), vol. 1, *Elements of Logic*, p. 2623:

Deduction
  Rule: All the beans from this bag are white (A).
  Case: These beans are from this bag (B).

  Result: These beans are white (C).
Induction (corresponding to the permutation BCA):
  These beans were in the bag.
  These beans are white.

All the beans in the bag were white.
Abduction (corresponding to the permutation ACB)
All the beans from this bag are white.
These beans are white.

These beans are from the bag.

Of course, only the first syllogism is valid. Peirce is well aware that the second one is a sophism, and he is obviously seeking not to suggest some extension of logic, but to identify the procedures deployed in knowledge. As for 'abduction', the approach has been to regard it as simply describing the process of looking for and formulating conjectures. See N. Rescher, *Peirce's Philosophy of Science* (Notre-Dame University Press, London, 1978).

18 In *Objective Knowledge* (Clarendon Press, Oxford, 1973), Popper presents extreme cases – not very convincing ones, it must be said – destined to show that the inductive propositions which are apparently most sound can be taken in default: bread which nourishes can also kill through ergotism; the sun sets every day, except within the polar circles. On Popper and the problem of induction, see the remarkable book by P. Jacob, *L'Empirisme logique* (Minuit, Paris, 1980), p. 124 et seq.

19 This explanation can be considered as refining Hume's. Hume in fact sees clearly that the reason why we believe our inductions is that we complete, more or less consciously, by *a priori* principles the information at our disposal.

20 A. Tversky, D. Kahneman and P. Slovic (eds), *Judgement under Uncertainty: heuristics and biases* (Cambridge University Press, New York, 1980). R. Nisbett and L. Ross, *Human Inference* (Prentice-Hall, Englewood Cliffs, NJ, 1980).

21 D. Bell, 'American exceptionalism', roneotyped.

22 The analysis by S. M. Lipset, in *The First New Nation* (Doubleday, New York, 1967), of the reasons why, in urban environments otherwise perfectly comparable, crime is much higher in the United States than in Canada, gives us another classic example of convincing causal imputation diverging from the usual statistical rules. The classic study by P. Lazarsfeld and A. Barton, 'Some functions of qualitative analysis in social research', in *Sociology*, ed. S. M. Lipset and N. Smelser (Prentice-Hall, Englewood Cliffs, NJ, 1961), pp. 95–122, identifies some of the cases where causal imputation diverges from canonical methods.

23 On the ambiguity of the notion of cause, see also Chapter 6.

24 Cf. Chapter 2.

25 R. Nisbett and L. Ross, *op. cit.*, p. 92.

26 *Ibid*, pp. 115–16.

27 See Chapter 1.

NOTES TO CHAPTER 4

1 Though many of the points in Popper's theory today seem questionable, others are still crucial. One of the major problems of the human sciences is

that they often readily accept *ad hoc* theories. Referring back to the example in Chapter 2, theories such as Lévy-Bruhl's on primitive mentality are frequent. *Ad hoc* theories often enjoy a brief notoriety because they are very close to theories usually stemming from common sense, and common sense likes to play its part. Though the falsifiable/verifiable distinction is not as relevant as Popper claims, the distinction between an *ad hoc* theory and a non-*ad hoc* theory is still crucial – in effect, an *ad hoc* theory tells us nothing.

2 The *methodological* nature of Popper's thought has been highlighted by G. Radnitzky, 'Méthodologie popperienne et recherche scientifique', *Archives de Philosophie*, 42, 1 (1979), pp. 3–40; 42, 2 (1979), pp. 295–325.

3 K. Popper, *The Logic of Scientific Discovery* (Hutchinson, London, 1972).

4 Popper defines it as follows: 'the falsifying mode of inference here referred to . . . is the *modus tollens* of classical logic. It may be described as follows: let p be a conclusion of a system t of statements . . . We may then symbolize the relation of derivability (analytical implication) of p from t by '$t{\rightarrow}p$' which may be read 'p follows from t'. Assume p to be false [then] we regard t as falsified', *ibid.*, p. 76.

5 *Ibid.*, p. 41.

6 *Ibid.*, p. 76.

7 A. N. Whitehead, *Introduction to Mathematics* (Williams & Norgate, London, 1921).

8 On Popper's theory of probability, see, for example, R. Bouveresse, *Karl Popper* (Vrin, Paris, 1981).

9 I. Lakatos, 'Falsification and the methodology of scientific research programs', in *Criticism and the Growth of Knowledge*, ed. I. Lakatos and A. Musgrave (Cambridge University Press, Cambridge, 1974), pp. 91–196.

10 Another way of saying it is *fallibilist*.

11 Popper, *op. cit.*, p. 278.

12 *Ibid.*, p. 279.

13 *Ibid.*, p. 280.

14 This point had already been made by Duhem and then taken up by Quine, so it is called the *Duhem–Quine thesis*.

15 Following on from Durkheim (and Duhem), Lakatos, *op. cit.*, stressed that it was often very difficult to determinate whether an observation *in fact* contradicts a theory, and also that it was difficult to know whether this contradiction is sufficient reason for abandoning the theory. Kuhn, in *The Structure of Scientific Revolutions* (University of Chicago Press, Chicago, 1962), is also not saying anything different from Durkheim when he argues that the decision to keep or abandon a theory is largely subjective. Cf Chapter 1.

16 The strongest criticism of some of those who accuse Popper of positivism is that he did not go far enough in his relativism.

17 Cf Chapter 3, note 17. The *modus ponens* is the paradigm of *deductive* reasoning. Let us call its three propositions A, B, and C. The 'abductive' equivalent of the *modus ponens* is the permutation ACB in this form of reasoning, and therefore corresponds to the 'reasoning' (not valid in logic, but corresponding to a procedure common in cognitive processes):

$$p \rightarrow q$$
$$q$$
$$\overline{}$$
$$p$$

The 'abductive' permutation in the sense in which Peirce uses it does correspond to induction in Popper's sense (cf. *The Logic of Scientific Discovery*, p. 40, where induction is defined as 'the inference of theories on the basis of singular statements "verified by experience"'). For Peirce, it is the permutation BCA which corresponds to 'induction', that is:

$$p$$
$$q$$
$$\overline{}$$
$$p \rightarrow q$$

18 Peirce in fact uses the phrase 'abductive reasoning' in different ways. Firstly, as we have seen, to indicate the case where recourse is had to a *rule*, for example, a casual hypothesis, to account for an observation: if the road is wet, it is because it has been raining, since when it rains the road is wet:

$$p \rightarrow q$$
$$q$$
$$\overline{}$$
$$p$$

As Habermas says in *Knowledge and Human Interests* (Heinemann, London, 1978 (1972)), p. 137, Peirce also uses *abduction* (as well as *hypothesis*) to indicate the case where one notes or assumes p, and then introduces the hypothesis $p \rightarrow q$ to explain q. This is not induction, but abduction, since there is a hypothesis and not just a generalization.

19 G. Radnitzky, 'La perspective économique sur le progrès scientifique: application en philosophie de la science de l'analyse coût-bénéfice', *Archives de philosophie*, 50 (April–June 1987), pp. 177–98.

20 For the sake of convenience, I use w, as is sometimes the convention, for the 'exclusive *or*' (*aut* in Latin: *either* one of the terms *or* the other, but *not both*), as in:
$$x(y) \; w \; x'(y) = [x(y) \; v \; x'\,(y)] \; \& \sim [x(y) \; \& \; x'(y)].$$

21 G. Holton, *Thematic Origins of Scientific Thought: Kepler to Einstein* (Harvard University Press, Cambridge, MA, and London, 1973).

22 *Ibid.*, p. 139.

23 In some cases, answer regarded as exclusive to begin with cease to be so (for example, the theory of light is no longer regarded as necessarily emission *or* wave). Other answers, however, are by the nature of things mutually exclusive, as the Millikan–Ehrenhaft debate shows.

24 Experiments consisting essentially of showing that charges in drops of liquid passing through an electric field vary discontinuously (Holton, *op. cit.*, p. 180 et seq.).

25 Popper, *op. cit.*, p. 270, rejects the idea of truth, but in a later note (p. 274 n. 1), accepts it in relation to Tarski's theory. In *Conjectures and Refutations*, the idea of truth is presented as indispensable. Nevertheless, if the theory of

refutation is valid, it is impossible to be convinced of the truth of a theory, even if it is true (I am ignoring the case of verifiable theories which Popper treats as atypical).

26 D. Buican, *Histoire de la génétique et de l'évolutionnisme en France* (Presses Universitaires de France, Paris, 1984).

27 *Ibid.*, p. 345.

28 D. Buican, *La Révolution de l'évolution* (Presses Universitaires de France, Paris, 1989), p. 228.

29 When it is an *empirical* question, it will be only under certain conditions that a question '$x \ w \sim x$?' will lead to the conclusion that x, for example, is *true* (because $\sim x$ has been recognized as false). An empirical question is never reduced completely to a formal question. However, this assertion has no bearing on the following points: many empirical questions take the form of an alternative or a sequence of alternatives; in this case, verification and falsification are symmetrical; and vice versa, the theory of falsification applies only to *some* questions.

30 There are also theories which are verifiable and non–refutable, and they are what gives Popper the biggest problems. Nevertheless they may sometimes have a perfectly valid basis. Cf., for example, the psychological theory 'when one does somebody a service, the reaction may be that person's gratitude, or ingratitude, or hostility'.

31 Although Popper placed great *explicit* emphasis on the open nature of scientific research, he *implicitly* regards as *self-evident* the fact that some episodes in the history of science which in fact constitute a context of the type $[p \ v \ p' \ v \ . \ . \ .]^*$ – such as the debate on the nature of light – have to be seen as representative of the very *essence* of scientific research.

32 See on this point P. Jacob, *L'Empirisme logique* (Minuit, Paris, 1980), p. 134.

33 K. Popper, *Objective Knowledge: an evolutionary approach* (Clarendon Press, Oxford, 1972), pp. 29–30.

34 Examples of *verifiable* theories are given in Chapter 8. Durkheim's theory of magic or Weber's theory of American religiosity can be regarded as verified in the sense that every statement in them is acceptable and accounts for the relevant findings.

35 A. Boyer, *K. R. Popper: une épistémologie laïque?* (Presses de l'Ecole normale supérieure, Paris, 1978), p. 19, quotes an interesting text from Pascal (reply to Father Chritmas, 29 October 1647): 'to make a hypothesis obvious, it is not enough that all phenomena follow on; instead, if one of these phenomena is followed by something contrary, this is enough to ensure its falsity' – a passage which reaffirms the *modus tollens* rather than anticipates the theory of falsification.

36 A. Lancelot, 'Partis politiques', *Encyclopaedia universalis* (EU, Paris, 1972), 12, pp. 579–83.

37 H. Hotelling, 'Stability in competition', *Economic Journal*, 39 (March 1929), pp. 41–57.

38 It spawned several developments, for example, G. Tullock's attempt to extend it to a multidimensional 'issue space', in *Toward a Mathematics of Politics* (University of Michigan Press, Ann Arbor, 1967).

39 A. P. Lerner and H.-W. Singer, 'Some notes on duopoly and spatial competition', *Journal of Political Economy*, 45 (April 1937), p. 145.

40 A. Smithies, 'Optimum location in spatial competition', *Journal of Political Economy*, 49 (February 1941), pp. 423–39.

41 H. Hotelling, *op. cit.*, p. 54.

42 This point illustrates what in *The Analysis of Ideology* (University of Chicago Press, Chicago; Polity Press, Cambridge, 1989) I called 'communication effects'. The hyperbolic nature of the theories tends to be reinforced – by mechanisms which I attempted to describe – during the course of their dissemination.

43 *Loc. cit.*

44 R. Merton, *Social Theory and Social Structure* (Free Press, Glencoe, IL, 1961), pp. 466 and 475. The form of argument used by Granet is to be found in most cultural relativists, for example, B. Whorf and D. Bloor.

NOTES TO CHAPTER 5

1 A simpler, if not more accurate, description than 'erotetic' (pertaining to questioning; cf, erotetic logic).

2 Cf, Chapter 3, note 9.

3 Several examples were given in Chapter 4.

4 E. Durkheim, *The Elementary Forms of the Religious Life* (Allen & Unwin, London, 1915); orig. pubd as *Les formes élémentaires de la vie religieuse* (Presses Universitaires de France, Paris, 1912), p. 49, n. 1.

5 *Ibid.*, p. 56.

6 *Ibid.*, p. 59.

7 *Ibid.*, p. 60.

8 *Ibid.*, p. 62.

9 *Ibid.*, p. 68.

10 *Ibid.*, p. 55.

11 *Ibid.*, p. 73.

12 *Ibid.*, p. 78.

13 *Ibid.*, p. 80.

14 *Ibid.*, p. 80.

15 *Ibid.*, p. 85.

16 *Ibid.*, p. 192.

17 *Ibid.*, p. 195.

18 *Ibid.*, p. 198.

19 *Ibid.*, p. 199.

20 *Ibid.*, p. 206.

21 For details on Durkheim's theory of religion, see the useful book by W. S. F. Pickering, *Durkheim's Sociology of Religion* (Routledge & Kegan Paul, London, 1984).

22 As Maurice Clavelin has pointed out to me, this distinction evokes Duhem's criticism of crucial experience: if we believe in crucial experience, we postulate (without saying so) that two theories – for example, the wave

theory (*p*) and the emission theory (*q*) of light – are contradictory, that is, $p = \sim q$, or, what amounts to the same thing, *p w q*. In fact, the procedure of the crucial experience can be formulated as: 1) *p w q*, 2) $p \rightarrow r$ (*r* = light moves faster in air than in water), 3) $q \rightarrow \sim r$, 4) *r* (from experience), 5) $\sim q$ (by 3 and 4), 6) *p* (by 5 and 1).

23 Durkheim, *op. cit.*, p. 198.

24 As well as *ontological a priori* of this kind, a theory can include *ethical a priori*. See J. Largeault, *Enigmes et controverses* (Aubier, Paris, 1980), chapter 10, which shows how ethical considerations enter into relativism. See also, on the ethical dimension of Wittgenstein's theory of magic, my article 'La théorie de la rationalisation et l'explication des croyances', *Philographies* (Crocus, Nantes), pp. 283–93. I do not touch on these kinds of *a priori* in this book, but limit myself to *formal, simple a priori*.

25 *Cognitive* relativism, as distinct from *ethical* relativism and *aesthetic* relativism.

26 Cf. Chapters 3 and 10.

27 See in particular: E. Gellner, *Legitimation of Belief* (Cambridge University Press, Cambridge, 1974); J. Passmore, *Science and its Critics* (Rutgers University Press, New Brunswick, NJ, 1978); J. Largeault, *op. cit.*; J. Bouveresse, *Le Philosophe chez les autophages* (Minuit, Paris, 1984); M. Hollis and S. Lukes, *Rationality and Relativism* (Blackwell, Oxford, 1982); I. Scheffler, *Science and Subjectivity* (Hackett, Indianapolis, 1982); P. Thuillier, *Les Savoirs ventriloques* (Seuil, Paris, 1983); N. Stockman, *Antipositivist Theories of the Sciences* (Reidel, Dordrecht, 1984); H. Atlan, *A tort et à raison* (Seuil, Paris, 1986).

28 F. Isambert, 'Un "programme fort" en sociologie de la science?', *Revue francaise de sociologie*, 26, 3 (1985), pp. 485–508.

29 D. Bloor, *Knowledge and Social Imagery* (Routledge & Kegan Paul, London, 1976); K. Hübner, *Die Wahrheit des Mythos* (Beck, Munich, 1985); T. Kuhn, *The Structure of Scientific Revolutions* (University of Chicago Press, Chicago, 1962).

30 This is based on my article 'On relativism', in *Treatise on Basic Philosophy*, ed. P. Weingartner and G. Dorn (Rodopi, Amsterdam, 1990).

31 T. Kuhn, *op. cit.*

32 P. Feyerabend, *Against Method: outline of an anarchistic theory of knowledge* (NLB, London, 1975).

33 D. Bloor, *op. cit.*

34 K. Hübner, *op. cit.*

35 'Selbst die grössten Erfolge von Theorien sagen nicht das geringste über ihre Wahrheit'. *Die Wahrheit . . .*, p. 252.

36 Hübner uses the classical notations of logic. F(*a*), or more simply F*a* = 'the predicate F applies to the subject *a*'. Here, the predicate F = 'falls in *t* from height *h*'.

37 C. Hempel, 'The function of general laws in history' in *Aspects of Scientific Explanation and Other Essays in the Philosophy of Science* (Free Press, New York, 1965).

38 W. H. Dray, *Laws and Explanation in History* (Oxford University Press, Oxford, 1957), *Philosophy of History* (Prentice-Hall, London, 1964). Also Dray (ed.), *Philosophical Analysis and History* (Harper, New York, 1966).

39 I developed this in *Theories of Social Change: a critical appraisal* (Polity Press,

Cambridge, 1966); orig. pubd as *La Place du désordre* (Presses Universitaires de France, Paris, 1984), basing my analysis particularly on Weber.

40 More precisely, they tend to require that 'laws' included in a sociological explanation are exclusively psychological propositions which might be regarded as obvious.

41 'Wissenschaftliche in Basissätze ausgedrückte Tatsachen, sind also niemals rein empirisch gegeben', Hübner, *op, cit.*, p. 247.

42 'Diese Axiome definieren die allgemeine Art und Weise, mit der die Wirklichkeit wissenschaftlich betrachtet wird', *ibid.*, p. 250.

43 'Rein empirisch ist ausschliesslich, dass sich unter der Bedingung von ST_1, die vorhin gekennzeichnete Ergebnismenge E_2 ereignet', *ibid.*, p. 251.

44 *Ibid.*, p. 250.

45 Based on an analysis of certain Greek myths, Hübner shows that the structure of the explanation of myths is not *formally* different from that of the scientific explanation just analysed. C.f. *Die Wahrheit . . .*, chapter 17.

46 Preference for one theory or another, depending on the facts themselves loaded with *a priori*, also cannot be based on objective reasons.

47 'Damit glaube ich also nur "zu Ende gedacht" zu haben, was sich bereits seit Jahrzehnten innerhalb der Wissenschaftstheorie, dieser von der Selbstreflexion der Wissenschaft bis zu ihren bohrenden Selbstzweifel hendelnden philosophischen Disziplin, abgezeichnet hat', *Die Wahrheit . . .*, pp. 413–14. According to this passage, thinking of the development of science as having to be considered exactly like any other historical phenomenon – the history of manners, for example – would be the conclusion drawn from the wide debate stretching from the Vienna Circle to Feyerabend.

48 'Die von der Wissenschaft erfasste Wirklichkeit ist demnach nicht die Wirklichkeit an sich, sondern sie ist stets auf bestimmte Weise gedeutete. Die Antworten, die sie uns gibt, hängen von unseren Fragen ab', *Die Wahrheit . . .*, p. 254. The last sentence of this passage is the crux: 'The answers is [reality] gives us depend on our questions.'

49 'Das bedeutet keineswegs, dass damit die Wissenschaft einem schranklosen Relativismus preisgegeben ist', *Die Wahrheit . . .*, p. 255.

50 *Questions Concerning Certain Faculties Claimed for Man*, V, p. 259 et seq.

51 J. Habermas, *Knowledge and Human Interests* (Heinemann, London, 1978 (1972)).

52 H. Albert, *Traktat über kritische Vernunft* (Mohr, Tübingen, 1975 (1968)).

53 Cf. Chapter 4.

54 In several of his works, particularly 'The myth of the framework', in *The Abdication of Philosophy*, ed. E. Freeman (Open Court, La Salle, II, 1976), pp. 23–48.

55 G. Radnitsky and W. W. Bartley III (eds), *Evolutionary Epistemology: rationality and the sociology of knowledge* (Open Court, La Salle, II, 1987), give many examples of the way in which the survival of scientific theories depends on selection processes identical with those presiding over the choice of hypotheses in a judicial investigation. The fact that the selection can be *subjective* in the short term does not imply that it is in the long term. On the contrary, a theory is perceived as condemned when it becomes *objectively* impossible to sustain it.

56 The fact that an answer is *dependent* on the question (or an observation in a theory) in no way implies that the question *affects* the answer (or that the theory *affects* the observation). This implication is also an effect of the strict *a priori* which Hübner introduces (either all the statements in an argument are *objective* or not]★, ['objective' = gross basic statement or proposition deduced mechanically from basic statements]★). In fact, answers are always dependent on questions but may or may not be affected by them. For example, if a majority prefers A to B, B to C and C to A ('Condorcet' effect), the order in which the questions are put *affects* the final choice. If the choice between A and B is put first, B is eliminated and C becomes the collective choice. On the other hand, if the group is first asked its preference between B and C, then between A and B, A is the collective choice. There are therefore cases where questions do *affect* answers; but there are obviously others where this contamination does not happen.

57 This point is emphasized by I. Scheffler, *Science and Subjectivity* (Hackett, Indianapolis, 1982). Generally speaking, the *framework* in which Hübner is located – like Kuhn, moreover – forbids him to take account of certain classic distinctions: Scheffler's distinction between 'theoretical proposition' and 'observation proposition'; Wittgenstein's between 'seeing *x*' and 'seeing *x* as'; Quine's between 'ontology' and 'ideology'. Put simply: Sherlock Holmes and Dr Watson may see the same things even though they have different ideas about these things.

58 For example, according to Feyerabend as well as Kuhn, the theory of relativity is different from the Newtonian system because it is based on another ST, system. Cf. Feyerabend, 'Explanation, reduction and empiricism', in *Minnesota Studies in the Philosophy of Science* (University of Minneapolis Press, Minneapolis, 1962), vol. III; Kuhn, *op. cit.*

59 T. Kuhn, 'Reflections on my critics', in *Criticism and the Growth of Knowledge*, ed. I. Lakatos and A. Musgrave (Cambridge University Press, Cambridge, 1970), 5, 'Irrationality and theory choice', pp. 259–78.

60 *The Structure . . .*, p. 107, quoted in *Reflections . . .*, p. 260.

61 *Ibid*, p. 194.

62 The case of Priestley is often referred to in this book, as it is in Bloor. Evans-Pritchard's example of the Azande also appears frequently in the two writers . . . as well as in most relativist philosophers and sociologists of science.

63 Kuhn, *op. cit.*, pp. 156–7.

64 *Ibid.*, pp. 99–100.

65 *Ibid.*, p. 71.

66 Cf. also Chapter 9.

67 An allusion to Popper's falsification theory.

68 Kuhn, *op. cit.*, pp. 170–1.

69 This is in any event convincingly argued by D. Buican, in *Histoire de la génétique et de l'évolutionnisme en France* (Presses Universitaires de France, Paris, 1984).

70 *The Structure . . .*, pp. 170–1: '[N]othing that has been or will be said makes it a process of evolution *toward* anything'.

71 This restrictive framework confirms another conclusion from Kuhn's (and Feyerabend's) theories: that the (sociological or historical) study of the

conditions in which a theory is implemented is relevant in judging claims of scientific knowledge to objectivity and truth.

72 I gave examples of these paradoxes in *The Analysis of Ideology* (University of Chicago Press, Chicago; Polity Press, Cambridge, 1989), chapter 6.

73 'Man darf nämlich zweifeln, erstens, ob es Gegensätze überhaupt gibt', *Jenseits von Gut und Böse*, § 2.

74 P. Jacob, *L'Empirisme logique* (Minuit, Paris, 1980), p. 88.

NOTES TO CHAPTER 6

1 On the symbolist interpretation of magic, cf. Chapter 9. See also Chapter 1.

2 See, for example, R. Nisbett and L. Ross, *Human Inference* (Prentice-Hall, Englewood Cliffs, NJ, 1980).

3 The devastating effect of this *a priori* on the human sciences has been the object of a great deal of attention. See, for example, the withering attacks by J. Van Rillaer, *Les Illusions de la psychanalyse* (Mardaga, Brussels, 1980), or J. Elster, 'L'Obsession du sens', in *Le Laboureur et ses enfants* (Minuit, Paris, 1986), p. 90 et seq.

4 As is seen clearly in *Unended Quest* (Collins, Glasgow, 1976), where Popper describes his intellectual struggles with Alfred Adler or the Vienna Circle.

5 *Critique of Pure Reason*, Book II, chapter 2, 3rd section (analogies from experience).

6 G. J. Warnock, 'Every event has a cause', in *Logic and Language*, ed. A. Flew (Basil Blackwell, Oxford, 1966), pp. 95–111.

7 *Ibid.*

8 J. S. Mill, *System of Logic* (Longmans Green, London, 1898 (1843).

9 *Ibid.*

10 M. White, *Foundations of Historical Knowledge* (Harper & Row, New York and London, 1965).

11 O. Ducrot, *La Preuve et le dire* (Mame, Paris, 1978), chapter 5: 'La notion de cause'.

12 Note also that in *Dire et ne pas dire* (Hermann, Paris, 1972), Ducrot stressed, following Collingwood among others, the role of implication in ordinary thinking.

13 J. Passmore, 'Explanation in everyday life, in science and history', in *History and Theory*, II, 2, (1962), pp. 105–23.

14 M. White, *op. cit.*

15 K. Popper, 'The myth of the framework', in *The Abdication of Philosophy*, ed. E. Freeman (Open Court, La Salle, IL, 1976), pp. 23–48.

16 L. White, *Medieval Technology and Social Change* (Clarendon Press, Oxford, 1962).

17 R. Boudon, *La Place du désordre* (Presses Universitaires de France, Paris, 1984).

18 A. D. Hirschman, *Essays in Trespassing* (Cambridge University Press, Cambridge, 1981).

19 L. Pellicani, *Saggio sulla genesi del capitalismo* (Sugar, Milan, 1988), chapter 2,

'Il mito weberiano del calvinismo'; 'Weber and the myth of Calvinism', *Telos*, 75 (1988), pp. 57–85.

20 S. N. Eisenstadt, 'The Protestant ethic thesis in analytical and comparative context', *Diogenes*, 59 (1967), pp. 25–46; L. Schneider, *Sociological Approach to Religion* (Wiley, New York, 1970); R. Boudon, 'Interprétation, explication, idéologie', *Encyclopédie philosophique* (Presses Universitaires de France, Paris, 1989), vol. I, pp. 241–54.

21 This point has been made by, among others, M. Polanyi, *Personal Knowledge* (University of Chicago Press, Chicago, 1958); G. Holton, *Thematic Origins of Scientific Thought: from Kepler to Einstein* (Cambridge University Press, Cambridge, 1974) and *The Scientific Imagination* (Cambridge University Press, Cambridge, 1974).

22 As Ducrot points out (*La Preuve . . .*, p. 104), this condition is equivalent to the logical implication which is defined as:

$p \rightarrow q$ if and only if $\sim (p \ \& \sim q)$.

23 For example, R. Aron, *Main Currents in Sociological Thought* (Weidenfeld & Nicolson, London, 1965), vol. 2, pp. 11–69; orig. pubd as *Les Etapes de la pensée sociologique* (Gallimard, Paris, 1983 (1964).

24 Basic Books, New York, 1975.

25 W. F. White, *Street Corner Society* (University of Chicago Press, Chicago, 1955); P. Robert, *Les Bandes d'adolescents* (Ouvrières, Paris, 1966); A. K. Cohen, *The Culture of the Gang* (Free Press, Glencoe, IL, 1955).

26 P. Veyne, *Comment on écrit l'histoire* (Seuil, Paris, 1971), pp. 127–30, rightly stresses the ambiguity of the notion of 'profound causes'.

27 The works of Maurice Cusson, who avoids the pitfall of unicausal explanations, highlight the fertility of this theory. See *Le Contrôle social du crime* (Presses Universitaires de France, Paris, 1983) and *Croissance et décroissance du crime* (Presses Universitaires de France, Paris, 1990).

28 E. E. Evans-Pritchard, *Witchcraft, Oracles and Magic among the Azande* (Clarendon Press, Oxford, 1968 (1937).

29 S. Steinberg, *The American Melting Pot* (McGraw-Hill, New York, 1974).

30 The data given in table 6.1 indicate the proportion of university teachers of a particular religion (for example, Protestant) in a particular discipline (for example, agriculture) in relation to the proportion of Protestant teachers in all universities, that is, $(N_{pa}/N_a)/(N_p/N)$. The statistics are sensitive to the relative dimension of the three religious groups, as seen in the following arithmetic example:

Discipline	Numbers of Protestants	Numbers of Catholics	Protestant representation	Catholic representation
1	480	20	1.06	0.44
2	180	20	0.99	1.1
3	160	40	0.88	2.2
4	180	20	0.99	1.1

Another statistic (*odd ratios*) is more neutral: it is obtained by relating the number of Catholic farmers divided by the number of Protestant farmers to the number of non-farming Catholics divided by the number of non-farming Protestants, that is $(N_{ca}/N_{pa})/(N_{ca}/N_{pa})$.

31 See the reservations of L. Pellicani, *Saggio sulla genesi del capitalismo* (Sugar, Milan, 1988).

32 Max Weber, *The Protestant Ethic and the Spirit of Capitalism* (Allen & Urwin, London, 1976 (1904–5)), orig. pubd as *Die protestantische Ethik und der Geist des Kapitalismus* (Mohr, Tübingen, 1920); R. Merton, *Science, Technology and Society in Seventeenth Century England* (Howard Fertig, New York, 1970).

33 The importance of the similarity between cause and effect in causal imputation had already been pointed out by Hume. This is another important *a priori*: by default, the tendency is to prefer as a cause something which resembles the effect to be explained. In this sense, relationships of similarity, far from being, as Lévy-Bruhl thought, characteristic of 'prelogical mentality', are an important ingredient in causal inference, and this applies to ordinary thinking as well as to methodical thinking.

34 This had already been clearly seen by D. Friedman, 'Normative and rational explanations of a classic case: religious specialization in academia', in *The Microfoundations of Macrosociology*, ed. M. Hechter (Temple University Press, Philadelphia, 1983), pp. 90–114.

35 Defined in each discipline by the extent to which the rate of increase of first degrees was greater than the rate of increase of doctorates.

36 Cf., for example, M. Cusson, *Croissance . . .*

37 D. Buican, in *Histoire de la génétique et de l'évolutionnisme en France* (Presses Universitaires de France, Paris, 1984), showed that the resistance in France to Darwin or Mendel, up to and sometimes after the Second World War, is partially explained by a spirited resistance to the idea that order can be brought about by chance. In my book *The Analysis of Ideology*, I quoted the fascinating case of E. Hagen, who refused to recognize the *contingent* nature of phenomena in economic development which he himself had identified.

38 Cognitive psychology has shown that a causal relationship between X and Y tends to be readily accepted when there is a substantial similarity between X and Y.

NOTES TO CHAPTER 7

1 C. Perelman and L. Olbrechts-Tyteca, *The New Rhetoric: a treatise on argumentation* (University of Notre Dame Press, Notre Dame, IN, 1969); orig. pub as *La nouvelle rhétorique, traité de l'argumentation* (Presses Universitaires de France, Paris, 1958), I, § 31, pp. 163–4.

2 R. Rorty, *Philosophy and the Mirror of Nature* (Princeton University Press, Princeton, 1979).

3 *Ibid.*, p. 146.

4 In the model assimilating knowledge with contemplation, 'there is no way to relate the reception of forms into the mind to the construction of proposi-

tions' (*ibid.*, p. 146). Kant substitutes '*knowing that*' for '*knowing of*', but, fixed in the Cartesian framework, raises a new rhetorical question – 'how to get from the inner space to the outer space' (*ibid.*, p. 147).

5 This is the argument of Richard H. Popkin in his remarkable book on the history of scepticism, *The History of Scepticism from Erasmus to Descartes* (Van Gorcum, Assen, 1964), chapter 3: that Montaigne, putting his genius at the disposal of the Catholic tradition, was indulging (in *In Defence of Raymond Sebond*) in a pure exercise of rhetoric and not, as the traditional interpretation of this book claims, in an exposition of his own philosophical convictions.

6 G. Balandier, *Le Désordre* (Fayard, Paris, 1988), p. 241: 'the assertion that people produce neither the true nor the false, but 'the existing' (Paul Veyne) no longer appears provocative; P. Veyne, *Les Grecs ont-ils cru à leurs mythes?* (Seuil, Paris, 1983).

7 In 'Les intellectuels et le second marché', *Revue européene des sciences sociales*, 28, 87 (1990), pp. 89–104, I tried to explain the reasons why the human sciences swing violently between an aesthetic interpretation and a cognitive interpretation of their objectives.

8 *Op. cit.*, p. 178.

9 This is an interesting example of the restrictive logical framework which I examined on Chapter 5: the view that an idea should be legitimated *either* by its objective validity, *or* by its social value, is often taken as read, but is in fact only a conjecture.

10 Simmel, *The Problems of the Philosophy of History* (Free Press, New York, 1977); orig. pub as *Die Probleme der Geschichtsphilosophie* (Duncker & Humblot, Munich, 1892).

11 This example refers to a completely abstract system with no bearing on the physical world. Therefore the multiplicity of 'truths' observed in it refers to neither of the two cases considered here.

12 The attraction of Mandelbrot's theory of fractal objects (*Les Objets fractals, forme, hasard et dimension* (Flammarion, Paris, 1975)) and of its famous application to the problem of the length of the coast of Brittany no doubt stems from the same analysis: the length of the coast of Brittany *is* indeterminate since it depends on the accuracy of the measuring instrument in coping with indentations. If measured by an infinitely accurate instrument, it would be of infinite length; if a crude instrument is used, this length would reflect the crudeness of the measure. M. Serres jokingly says, in *Le Passage du Nord-Ouest* (Minuit, Paris, 1980), that in any event this length would be included in a *finite* quantity of concrete . . .

13 M. Weber, 'Protestant sects and the spirit of capitalism', in *The Protestant Ethic and the Spirit of Capitalism* (Allen & Unwin, London, 1976 (1904–5).

14 R. K. Merton, *Social Theory and Social Structure.* (Free Press, Glencoe, IL, 1957).

15 The word 'functional' is of course ambiguous. I am employing it here in its normal meaning when it is used *non-metaphorically* Cf. R. Boudon, 'La notion de fonction', *Revue française de sociologie*, 8, 2 (1967), pp. 198–206 (repr. in R. Boudon, *La crise de la sociologie* (Droz, Geneva, 1971), pp. 205–13); and J. Elster, *Ulysses and the Sirens* (Cambridge University Press, Cambridge, 1979), p. 28. Of course the word 'function' can be and often is, used *metaphorically*.

16 Up to now, I have frequently used the adjective *true* and its derivatives (*to verify*, and so on). It is perhaps now time to make it clear that I usually use the word in the sense of Aristotle (say, of the being that it is, of the not-being that it is not), or, what amounts to the same thing, of Tarski's correspondence theory. I have to say, however, that there are contexts where I do not think this theory is applicable. It *is* applicable when, for example, one asks oneself whether a descriptive proposition is true. Leaving aside the case of formal 'truths', it is not applicable, for example, in the case of a theory such as Durkheim's theory of magic (cf. Chapter 1): all that can be said is that all the propositions of this theory are acceptable, in the sense that they describe quite ordinary psychological mechanisms, that they are correctly linked to each other, that they account for the *explanandum* and its variations in time and space, and so on; but there is no means of making any *reality* correspond to this theory, not even by thought, so that here one is in a quite different situation from the one which relates, as correspondence theory claims, the statement 'the snow is white' to the reality of the whiteness of snow. Here again, we can take Kant literally: it is impossible to define the notion of *truth*. To which must be added, however, that it is possible to define it in ways which are *locally* valid. Cf. Chapter 8.

17 L. Moulin, 'Les origines religieuses des techniques électorales et délibératives modernes', *Revue internationale d'histoire politique et constitutionelle* (April–June 1953), pp. 106–48.

18 J. Buchanan and G. Tullock, *The Calculus of Consent* (University of California Press, Berkeley, 1967).

19 S. Popkin, *The Rational Peasant* (university of California Press, Berkeley, 1979).

20 C. Lévi-Strauss, *The Elementary Structures of Kinship* (Eyre & Spottiswoode, London, 1969), orig. pubd as *Les Structures élémentaires de la parenté* (Presses Universitaires de France, Paris, 1967 (1945); 'The future of kinship studies', *Proceedings of the Royal Anthropological Institute* (1965), pp. 13–22.

21 Malinowski wrote a thesis on Mach. E. Gellner, '*Zeno of Cracow* or *Revolution at Nemi* or *The Polish Revenge*: a drama in three acts', in *Culture, Identity and Politics* (Cambridge University Press, Cambridge, 1987), pp. 47–74.

22 I am referring to a loose movement inspired by sociologists influenced by Comte (such as Durkheim), but of whom G. A. Lundberg, *Foundations of Sociology* (McKay, New York, 1964 (1939)), is probably the best example. The neo-positivism – linked to the so-called logical empiricism movement – of O. Neurath and especially C. Hempel also had some influence on social science.

23 A point clearly seen by Mannheim (Cf R. Boudon, *The Analysis of Ideology* (University of Chicago Press, Chicago; Polity Press, Cambridge, 1989), chapter 3), but also by Windelband and Rickert.

24 Gellner clearly shows that Malinowski's machismo is also explained by the fact that his Polishness meant he was suspicious of evolutionist anthropology, as he was of history. The latter discipline seemed to him very ideological: the Battle of Hastings is remembered because the landed aristocracy is a significant group in England. This approach set Malinowski on the road of the ahistorical and synchronic language used by economists but still to be

extended to other human sciences. With Malinowski, it is no longer change, but stability, that needs to be explained. A criticism of history which echoes Malinowski is to be found in M. Ferro, *L'Histoire sous surveillance* (Calmann-Lévy, Paris, 1985).

25 P. Ricoeur, *Temps et récit* (Seuil, Paris, 1983), I.

26 Monism of this kind can be seen in the debate between R. W. Fogel and G. R. Elton (in *Which Road to the Past? Two views of history* (Yale University Press, New Haven, 1983); both these eminent historians agree that history has an *essence*.

27 In anthropology there is also a conflict between 'geneticists' (such as G. Balandier) and 'structuralists' (such as Lévi-Strauss).

28 'Ob das Verständnis des Singulären zur *Allgemeingültigkeit* erhoben werden kann', quoted by J. Habermas in *Knowledge and Human Interests* (Heinemenn, London, 1978 (1972)), p. 214; the latter argues that Dilthey is artificially saving the notion of objectivity by the philosophy of life.

29 I am again taking this word in the very broad sense, as in Weber's example of Protestant sects or Buchanan and Tullock's studies on majority rule.

30 J. Passmore, 'Explanation in everyday life, in science and in history', *History and Theory*, 2 (1962), pp. 105–23.

31 A. Oberschall proposed a *functional* explanation of this phenomenon in 'Culture Change and Social Movements', 84th Annual Meeting of the American Association of Sociology, San Francisco, 9–13 August, 1989 (roneo-typed). See Chapter 1.

32 An argument sometimes used to save the principle of the uniqueness of truth in the case where a phenomenon is explained by two valid and incommensurable theories is to say that these truths are *complementary*. The tautological aspect of the argument gives away its *rhetorical* nature.

33 S. N. Eisenstadt, 'The Protestant ethic thesis in analytical and comparative context', *Diogenes*, 59 (1967), pp. 25–46; L. Schneider *Sociological Approach in Religion* (Wiley, New York, 1970); R. Boudon, 'Explication, interprétation, idéologie', *Encyclopédie philosophique* (Presses Universitaires de France, Paris, 1989), vol. 1., pp. 241–54.

34 K. Marx and F. Engels, *Werke* (Dietz, Berlin, 1968), vol. 39, p. 97.

35 E. Durkheim, *The Rules of Sociological Method* (Macmillan, London, 1982), p. 26.

36 I note in passing that, unlike Bloor, I am here suggesting getting rid of the traditional asymmetry which argues that adherence to *true* ideas is explained *teleologically* and adherence to *false* ideas *causally* (see, on this traditional view, Chapter 1 above), by arguing in principle that we must try to explain every belief in a way which is not *causal*, but *teleological*. K. Dixon, in *The Sociology of Belief* (Routledge & Kegan Paul, London, 1980), rightly points out that the weaknesses of the sociology of knowledge stem from its adherence to the *causal* world.

37 D. Bloor, 'Wittgenstein and Mannheim on the sociology of mathematics', *Studies in the History and Philosophy of Science*, 4, 2 (1973), pp. 173–91; in *Knowledge and Social Imagery* (Routledge & Kegan Paul, London, 1976).

38 P. Winch, *The Idea of a Social Science* (Routledge & Kegan Paul, London, 1958).

39 L. Wittgenstein, *Remarks on the Foundations of Mathematics* (Basil Blackwell, Oxford, 1967), orig. pubd as *Bemerkungen über die Grundlagen der Mathematik* (Suhrkamp, Frankfurt am main, 1974); and especially *Philosophical Investigations* (Basil Blackwell, Oxford, 1968).

40 On the *teleological/causal* distinction is here superposed the *endogenous/exogenous* one, about which much has also been written, again under the influence of the principle of the uniqueness of truth: the constant question was whether the history of science should be interpreted on the basis of exogenous or endogenous factors. This question is destined to remain unanswered. However, the interest it arouses shows the ease with which one takes adjectives denoting opposites as contradictory, and also shows the strength of the principle of the uniqueness of truth. In the same way, studies on whether the history of science is *rational* or *irrational* receive no attention. In this case, the two adjectives do not have the meaning which I am giving them here: in fact they magnify the previous distinctions.

41 *Knowledge and Social Imagery*, p. 93.

42 *Ibid*, p. 86.

43 *Ibid*, p. 143.

44 Cf. Chapter 5.

45 Cf. the distinction pointed out by Mannheim – which Bloor argues should be removed – between *relational* propositions (variable in time and space and able to be explained *causally*) and *universal* propositions. I discussed this distinction in *The Analysis of Ideology* (University of Chicago Press, Chicago; Polity Press, Cambridge, 1989).

46 *Knowledge and Social Imagery*, chapter 6. One could analyse in the same way Bloor's reference to Diophantus, who accepted only a *positive* solution or solutions – when these exist – as solutions to second degree equations. This obviously does not show that Diophantus lived in a cultural world incommensurable with ours, but simply that he had *reasons* – having regard to the state of mathematics at the time – for considering only positive solutions, just as Aristotle had reasons for not regarding $\sqrt{2}$ as a number.

47 Cf. Chapter 6.

48 B. Latour and S. Woolgar, *Laboratory Life: the social construction of scientific facts* (Sage, London, 1979).

49 *Ibid.*, pp. 180–2.

50 *Ibid.*, pp. 179–80.

51 *Ibid.*, p. 177 n. 15.

52 *Ibid.*, p, 177. The idea of inversion means that, once a fact is stamped as such, the statement which corresponds to it is regarded as the product of this fact, whereas, according to the authors, the fact exists only because there is a factual statement corresponding to it.

53 *Ibid.*, p. 183.

54 See also B. Latour, *Science in Action* (Open University Press, Milton Keynes, 1987), and the special number of *L'Année sociologique*, 36 (1986), ed. B.-P. Lécuyer and B. Latour.

55 Latour and Woolgar, *op. cit.*, p. 179.

56 H. Reichenbach, *Experience and Prediction* (Chicago University Press, Chicago, 1938).

57 Or the distinction which G. Holton makes between science made and science in the making.

NOTES TO CHAPTER 8

1 V. Pareto, *Traité de sociologie générale* (Droz, Paris and Geneva, 1968 (1916)).
2 M. Black, *Models and Metaphors* (Cornell University Press, Ithaca and London, 1962), p. 32.
3 E. Goffman, in *Frame Analysis* (Harper & Row, New York, 1974), speaks of *keying* to indicate this allocation of an expressive activity to a *type* ('it's theatre', 'it's serious music', and so on). This concept can be applied also to the verbal atoms which words or phrases are ('it's a metaphor', and so on). These *keying* operations can happen perfectly straightforwardly even when we are unable to define the type to which we are attaching a particular phenomenon ('it's classical music', and so on).
4 R. Boudon, *Theories of Social Change: a critical appraisal* (Polity Press, Cambridge 1986; orig. pub. as *La place du désordre* (Presses Universitaires de France, Paris, 1984)), pp. 138–46.
5 R. Boudon, *A quoi sert la notion de structure?* (Gallimard, Paris, 1968).
6 G. Ryle, *The Concept of Mind* (Hutchinson, London, 1949).
7 *Critique of Pure Reason*, Part II, 'Introduction', III.
8 E. Goffman, *op, cit.*, chapter 7.
9 J. W. N. Watkins, in 'Ideal types and historical explanation', in *Readings in the Philosophy of Science*, ed. H. Feigl and M. Brodbeck (Appleton Century, New York, 1953), pp. 723–43, pointed out that the concept of ideal type had two meanings in Weber, and he called them 'holistic' and 'individualistic'. It is perhaps more precise to say that Weber uses the notion of ideal type in a sense close to our modern notion of *model* (thus the theory of American religiosity in his article on Protestant sects in the United States is simplified and, in that sense, 'ideal' like any 'model'), but also to characterize the particular nature of conceptualization in historical science.
10 Durkheim, *The Elementary Forms of the Religious Life* (Allen & Unwin, London, 1915 (1912)).
11 *Philosophical Investigations* (Basil Blackwell, Oxford, 1968), § 66. On Wittgenstein, see particularly J. Bouveresse, *La Parole malheureuse* (Minuit, Paris, 1971); J. Hartnack, *Wittgenstein und die moderne Philosophie* (Kohlhammer, Stuttgart, 1960).
12 'Betrachte z. B. einmal die Vorgänge, die wir "Spiele" nennen. Ich meine Brettspiele, Kartenspiele, Ballspiel, Kamfspiele, usw. Was ist allen diesen gemeinsam? – Sag nicht es *muss* ihnen etwas gemeinsam sein, sonst hiessen sie nicht "Spiele" – sondern *schau*, ob ihnen etwas gemeinsam ist. Denn wenn du sie anschaust, wirst du zwar nicht etwas sehen, was *allen* gemeinsam wäre, aber du wirst Ähnlichkeiten, Verwandschaften sehen, und zwar eine ganze Reihe'.
13 *Philosophical Investigations*, 967: '*Ich Kann diese Ähnlichkeiten nicht besser charakterisieren als durch das Wort 'Familienähnlichkeiten'*'.

14 R. Needham, 'Polythetic classification: convergence and consequences', *Man*,
10, 3 (September 1975), pp. 349–69. J. Ziman, in *Reliable Knowledge*
(Cambridge University Press, Cambridge, 1978), stresses that most concepts
in the human sciences *are* vague concepts. In *A quoi sert la notion de structure?*
(Gallimard, Paris, 1968), I pointed out the *polysemic* nature of the concept of
structure.

15 See Chapter 9.

16 The previous remarks are not the end of the debate. The example of game
theory and, more generally, the theory of decision-making in a situation of
uncertainty arguably shows that the definition of the notion of rationality
inevitably varies with the structure of the situation where the individual is.
For example, rationality is of a Waldian type in certain interactions with
nature, and Savagian or Laplacian in others. In situations of interaction
between actors, the maximin strategy, for example, is 'rational' or 'irrational'
depending on the structure of the interaction system. *Within these two contexts*,
the notion of 'rationality' is therefore polythetic. *A fortiori*, it is even more
complex when one examines simultaneously all the contexts in which it
appears.

17 Debates about terms such as 'intelligence', 'disposition', and so on also show
the difficulty of escaping from the idea that there can be a 'thing' corresponding to an undefinable word.

18 C. Perelman and L. Olbrechts-Tyteca, *The New Rhetoric: M a treatise on
argumentation* (University of Notre Dame Press, Notre Dame, IN, 1969),
§ 58.

19 $d_A/^m = 10/25 = 0.4$
$d_B/^m = 12/40 = 0.3$.
One can, moreover, use for this operation the *median* as well as the *average*.

20 The standard deviation (square root of the average of the squares of deviation
from the average) of distribution A is: $\sigma_A = 12.75$. That of B is: $\sigma_B = 14.14$.
Taking the average as the unit of measure, the indices of inequality are:
$\sigma_A/M_A = 0.51$; $\sigma_B/M_B = 0.35$.

21 This is the so-called Gini coefficient: $G_A = 0.275$; $G_B = 0.35$. This coefficient
is by no means free from criticism, although it has a kind of cult status: in fact,
it would inevitably identify inequalities in a strictly egalitarian society where
all individuals had exactly the same aggregate income during their lives.

22 As is shown by the value of the coefficients of regression: $f_A = 60/100–20/300$
$= 16/30$; $f_B = 70/100–30/300 = 18/30$.

23 I suggested this coefficient in *Mathematical Structures of Social Mobility*
(Elsevier, Amsterdam, 1973). In A, the *maximum* number of shifts of class is
180 (assuming marginal quantities to be fixed), and the *minimum* number is 20
(*structural* mobility). There could therefore be a *theoretical non-structural mobility*
of 180–20 = 160. The *real non-structural mobility* of 60–40 = 20 gives $B_A = 40/
160 = 0.25$. In the same way, in the case of B, *maximum* mobility is 200,
minimal or *structural* mobility is 0 (since margins do not change from one
'generation' to the next). Hence $B_B = 60/200 = 0.3$.

24 This is the Yasuda coefficient: in A, if their class at birth had no influence on
present class, 20 persons born into class I would now be in class I, with 140

shifts between classes; and since the *minimal* or *structural* mobility in this case is 20, the *theoretical non-structural mobility (corresponding to the condition of class at birth having no influence on present class)* would be 140–20 = 120. Relating this to *observed non-structural* mobility gives: $Y_A = (60–20)/(140–20) = 0.33$. Similarly $Y_B = 60/150 = 0.4$.

25 F. Waismann, 'Verifiability', in *Logic and Language* (first series), ed. A. Flew (Basil Blackwell, Oxford, 1952), p. 120.

26 M. Hesse, *The Structure of Scientific Inference* (University of California Press, Berkeley, 1974), chapter 1, showed that words such as 'sky', 'land', 'fish', 'man' and so on are much less descriptive than they seem. They are indissolubly linked with causal laws, like the concepts of 'atom' or 'proton'.

27 P. Besnard, *L'Anomie* (Presses Universitaires de France, Paris, 1987); M. Masterman, 'The nature of a paradigm', in *Criticism and the Growth of Knowledge*, ed. I. Lakatos and A. Musgrave (Cambridge University Press, Cambridge, 1974).

28 *Philosophical Investigations*, § 1: the 'Augustinian' view is, according to Wittgenstein, where 'the words of the language designate objects' ('die Wörter der Sprache benennen Gegenstände'). Although all words do not designate objects, it would be going too far to say, inversely, that no word designates an object.

29 The distinction between 'notions' and 'concepts' correlates with that between 'polythetic terms' and 'non-polythetic terms'.

30 T. Kuhn, *Scientific Development and Lexical Change*, Thalheimer Lectures, Johns Hopkins University, Baltimore, 12–19 November 1984.

31 Popper points out, in *Conjectures and Refutations* (Routledge & Kegan Paul, London, 1969), that it is *neo-Marxism* in particular which, by refusing to take account of the fact that Marxist theory had been refuted and by developing strategies of immunization, comes close to the intrinsically irrefutable theory which psychoanalysis is. Cf. J. Bouveresse, 'Une illusion de grand avenir', *Critique*, 346 (March 1976), pp. 292–306.

32 It would be more accurate to speak of neo-Darwinian theory rather than Darwinian theory, since historical Darwinism was less restrictive regarding the explanatory mechanisms it encompassed.

33 In Chapter 4

34 In its variants, Darwinism nevertheless contains statements on reality (such as the hypothesis that the environment does not influence the frequency of mutations).

35 I. Lakatos, 'Falsification and the methodology of scientific research programs', in *Criticism and the Growth of Knowledge*, ed. I. Lakatos and A. Musgrave (Cambridge University Press, Cambridge, 1970), pp. 91–196.

36 Cf. Chapter 1

37 P. Feyerabend, *Against Method: outline of an anarchistic theory of knowledge* (NLB, London, 1975).

38 *Ibid.*, p. 186.

39 *Ibid.*, p. 187.

40 *Ibid.*, p. 195.

41 *Ibid.*, p. 188.

42 *Ibid.*, p. 198.

43 *Ibid.*, p. 202.

44 *Ibid.*, p. 204.

45 *Ibid.*, Chapter 17. B. Whorf, *Linguistique et anthropologie* (Denoël, Paris, 1969).

46 Like Kuhn, Feyrabend confirms this idea by considerations taken from the psychology of form, *op. cit.*, p. 221 et seq.

47 *Ibid.*, p. 230.

48 *Ibid.*, p. 250. This text reveals of course Wittgenstein's influence, even though Feyerabend's conception of language is not very Wittgensteinian. Cf. note 37.

49 This 'contradiction' between the motivations of scientists and the finalities of their role is easily resolved when it is seen that the progress of knowledge belongs to the category of *unwanted* effects, which is a classic one in sociological analysis.

50 *Lexikon der Musik* (Fischer, Frankfurt an Main, 1986), article on 'Debussy'.

51 It is because he conceives of the notion of 'science' as non-polythetic, and because his search for a 'demarcation' criterion led him to be exclusively interested (as Laudan pointed out) in the confrontation between theory and phenomena, that Popper, against his will, was often regarded as 'positivist'. The reasons why Feyerabend and Habermas call him this are different, and stem particularly from the fact that Popper tries to make the normative rules of science into universal rules, valid also in the fields of ethics and politics. Cf. Feyerabend, *Against Method*, p. 163.

52 Using Popper as a starting point, I have summarized the debate about the demarcation criteria between science and metaphysics. It would be interesting to do a similar analysis of the very full debate by philosophers, sociologists and anthropologists concerning the distinction between science and magic.

53 It is also to be noted that the impossibility of describing the 'demarcation' between science and non-science is sometimes interpreted as stemming from the fact that there is arguably not *one*, but *several* sciences with their 'own criteria of scientificity'. This profoundly false idea is behind many artifices: every science tries to establish the truth and to separate the objective from the subjective, while making sure it does not go too far in any way in terms of its audience. However, what should be particularly noticed from my present standpoint is that there is in this outline the 'Augustinian' conception which Wittgenstein speaks of: every science has *its* essence. This polytheist conception of science, like Feyerabend's 'anarchist' conception of science, are both based on the same argumentative axis – that [every word indicating an authentic reality is non-polythetic]*, hence: [a word which cannot be defined designates nothing]*.

54 *The Structure of Scientific Revolutions* (Chicago University Press, Chicago, 1970 (1962), p. 160.

55 *Ibid.*, p. 160.

56 *Ibid.*, p. 162.

57 *Ibid.*, p. 163.

58 My aim is not to introduce a discussion about Kuhn's thought, the importance of which has given rise to a huge body of writing to which the

reader is referred; I merely wish to show here that the most unexceptionable theories may contain innocuous *formal a priori* which can completely change the conclusions we might draw from them.

59 *The structure* . . . , p. 170.

60 Without saying so explicitly, the Kuhnian revolution proposes to replace the notion of *truth* by that of *normality*.

61 In Chapter 7.

62 Cf. Chapter 4.

63 L. Laudan, *Progress and its Problems* (Routledge & Kegan Paul, London, 1977).

64 *Ibid.*, p. 50.

65 Questions of this type were raised not only in physics, but also in physiology, in the second half of the eighteenth century. Cf. Laudan, *op. cit.*, p. 59.

66 As Zahar and Koertge point out (cf. Laudan, *op. cit.*, p. 232). One of the important points made by Laudan is also that of the distinction between research traditions and theories. This notion ties in with that of 'paradigm', but it has the edge in that it stresses the evolutive and polythetic aspect of general frameworks in which scientific research is located. In my articles 'Notes sur la notion de théorie dans les sciences sociales; *Archives européennes de sociologie*, 11 (1970), pp. 201–51 (rep. in R. Boudon, *La Crise de la sociologie* (Droz, Geneva, 1971), pp. 159–204), and 'Théorie', in *Dictionaire critique de la sociologie*, ed. R. Boudon and F. Bourricaud (Presses Universitaires de France, Paris, 1986), I suggest distinctions between the different *types* of theories close to those of Laudan.

67 Laudan (*op. cit.*, p. 74) rightly points out that conceptual problems play no part in Kuhn's consideration of the progress of theories. The same is true of Lakatos: 'All Lakatos' measures of progress require a comparison of the empirical content of every member of the series of theories which constitute any research program' (*ibid*, p. 77). Laudan goes further and rightly considers that the whole Popperian tradition reveals this 'empiricist' aspect. However, this 'empiricism' is less one of principle than a result of a 'non-polythetic' view of the notion of progress like all the notions used by these philosophers of science.

68 Cf. Chapter 7

69 Which is not true of the 'psychological' statements in *The Protestant Ethic and the Spirit of Capitalism*.

70 Cf. Chapter 2

71 This is not the appropriate place to develop a 'theory of truth'. Let us merely say that the correspondence theory – like any theory – is applicable only to certain cases. In other words, we can go along with Kant: there are no universal criteria of truth. Which does not imply – unless one claims that the concept of truth is *either* empty *or* non-polythetic – that truth does not exist.

72 Most analysts of the books on which I have based my argument consider that the *sociology* or the *history* of science is the only possible *philosophy* of science. This is true, for example, of Kuhn, Feyerabend, Bloor or Hübner.

73 Common to Feyerabend, Kuhn or Bloor, but expressed particularly clearly by Hübner, for example.

74 P. Feyerabend, *Farewell to Reason* (Verso, London, 1987).

NOTES TO CHAPTER 9

1 On this I have been helped by conversations with Herbert Simon, as well as by the comments of K. Brown and R. A. Shweder in 'Subjective rationality and the explanation of social behaviour', *Rationality and Society*, I, 2 (October 1989), pp. 173–96.

2 H. Simon, *Models of Bounded Rationality* (MIT Press, Cambridge, MA, 1982), II, 8.1.

3 The notion of rationality is a polythetic notion (cf. Chapter 8). There is no proper definition, and one can only give a deictic definition of it: behaviour or belief Y are *rational* if one can say of them 'subject X has good *reasons* for doing (or believing) Y, because . . .'; they are *irrational* if one can say of them 'subject X has no reasons for doing (or believing) Y, *but* . . .'. Formal definitions of 'rationality' are obtained by applying a generally undesirable *reduction* in the content of the concept. It is just as reductive to define rationality by reference to the notion of *objectively* valid reasons as it would be, to take Wittgenstein's example, to define the concept of game by reference to the criterion of competition.

4 Simon, *op. cit.*, 134.

5 J. Feldman, 'Simulation of behaviour in the binary choice experiment', in *Computers and Thought*, ed. E. A. Feigenbaum and J. Feldman (McGraw-Hill, New York, 1963), pp. 329–46.

6 In fact, their conjectures are less abstract and less clear than I am suggesting: they know that the sequence is random, but they nevertheless try to identify structures which will allow them to guess the result of the next throw, by, for example, 'bringing back into line' the sequences which they think contradict the idea of chance. However, the result is the same: the 'imitation' strategies of chance lead them to act as if they had decided to produce a random sequence governed by the same parameter as the sequence produced by the person conducting the experiment.

7 Since $(0.8 \times 0.8) + (0.2 \times 0.2) = 0.68$.

8 Since $(0.5 \times 0.5) + (0.5 \times 0.5) = 0.5$.

9 M. Weber, *Gesammelte Aufsätze zur Wissenschaftslehre*, 2 vols (Mohr, Tübingen, 1951 (1922)); K. Popper 'La rationalité et le statut du principe de rationalité', in *Les fondements philosophiques des systèmes économiques*, ed. E.-M. Claassen (Payot, Paris, 1967), pp. 142–50.

10 Cf. Chapter 2.

11 D. Hume, *Essays, Moral, Political and Literary*, (Oxford University Press, Oxford, 1963 (1741–2)).

12 *Ibid.*, p. 58.

13 I am obliged to Kevin Brown for this comment.

14 Hume, *op. cit.*, p. 59.

15 A. Downs, *An Economic Theory of Democracy* (Harper & Row, New York, 1957).

16 The analysis that follows summarizes and completes the one that appears in Chapter 1.

17 For more detail on Lévy-Bruhl, see Chapter 2.

18 L. Wittgenstein, 'Bemerkungen über Frazer's *The Golden Bough*', in *Sprach-*

analyse und Soziologie, ed. R. Wiggershaus (Suhrkamp, Frankfurt am Main, 1975), pp. 37–58.

19 J. Beattie, *Other Cultures* (Cohen & West, London, 1964).

20 Cf. Wittgenstein, *op. cit.*: 'Die Magie aber bringt einen Wunsch zur Darstellung; sie aüssert einen Wunsch.'

21 R. Horton, 'Tradition and modernity revisited', in *Rationality and Relativism,* ed. M. Hollis and S. Lukes (Basil Blackwell, Oxford, 1982), pp. 201–60. See also K. Thomas, *Religion and the Decline of Magic* (Penguin Books, Harmondsworth, 1973).

22 E. Durkheim, *The Elementary Forms of the Religious Life* (Allen & Unwin, London, 1915); M. Weber, *Economy and Society,* (Bedminster Press, New York, 1968), orig. pub as *Wirtschaft und Gesellschaft* (Mohr, Tübingen, 1922).

23 Cf. Chapter 2 for a more detailed discussion.

24 I suggested in *La Logique du social* (Hachette, Paris, 1979) that, on the basis of these texts, Durkheim could be regarded as a writer close to Weber, in the sense that he seems anxious to see social phenomena that interest him as the product of *understandable* actions or attitudes, even though, in his doctrinal writing inspired by positivism, he tries to eliminate completely the subjectivity of social actors from scientific discourse.

25 Durkheim's analysis here foreshadows A. Hirschman's *tunnel effect*: 'The changing tolerance for income inequality in the course of economic development', in *Essays in Trespassing* (Cambridge University Press, Cambridge, 1980), pp. 39–58. I myself tried to show that effects of this type underlay other hypotheses, such as Tocqueville's hypothesis that actors' subjective dissatisfaction increases as their objective situation improves, in *The Unintended Consequences of Social Action* (St Martin's Press, London, 1982), orig. pubd as *Effets pervers et ordre social* (Presses Universitaires de France, Paris, 1989 (1977)).

26 I suggested in *The Analysis of Ideology* (University of Chicago Press, Chicago; Polity Press, Cambridge, 1989) that these types of effects should be called 'position effects'; I gave several examples of them analogous to the one shown here. This case in point was clearly identified by a pioneer of the sociology of knowledge: G. de Gré, *The Social Compulsions of Ideas: toward a sociological analysis of Knowledge* (Transaction Books, New Brunswick, NJ, 1979 (1941)), chapter 3, pp. 35–112; there was a timely reminder of the work of this writer by F. Chazel in 'Institutionnalisation de la sociologie de la connaissance aux Etats-Unis: l'apport de Gérard de Gré, *Revue française de sociologie,* 28, 4 (1987), pp. 663–77.

27 G. Katona, *Psychological Analysis of Economic Behavior* (McGraw-Hill, New York, 1951).

28 This case in point can be seen as an application of Tversky and Kahneman's 'availability heuristics'.

29 R. A. Shweder, 'Likeness and likelihood in everyday thought: magical thinking in judgements about personality', *Current Anthropology,* 18, 4 (1977), pp. 637–58.

30 $f = 37/70 - 17/30 = -0.04$.

31 J. B. Renard, *Les Extraterrestres* (Cerf, Paris, 1988). Findings of a similar type are given in D. Boy and G. Michelat, 'Croyances aux parasciences: dimen-

sions sociales et culturelles', *Revue française de sociologie*, 27, 2 (1986), pp. 175–204.

32 N. Balacheff, 'Processus de preuve et situations de validation', *Educational Studies in Mathematics*, 18 (1987), pp. 147–76.

33 *The Mind and Society: a treatise on general sociology* (Dover, New York, 1963), chapters 9, 10 and 11.

34 R. Boudon, *L'Inégalité des chances* (Hachette, Paris, 1979 (1973)).

35 In Chapter 8.

36 The same goes for the implication relationship. One is justified in usually conferring on it – metaconsciously – the property of transitivity, since it is true that:

$$[(a \rightarrow b) \ \& \ (b \rightarrow c)] \rightarrow \geqslant a{-} > c).$$

But the property of transitivity is no longer assured with certainty if the presence of *a* makes that of *b* no longer *certain*, but *more probable*. By default, there will be a tendency, in a case like this, to assume transitivity.

37 For example, great use of it is made in the sociology of organizations. Cf. M. Crozier and E. Friedberg, *L'Acteur et le système* (Seuil, Paris, 1977).

38 In a stimulating book, *La Marginalité créatrice: fragmentation et croisement des sciences sociales* (Presses Universitaires de France, Paris, 1990), M. Dogan and R. Pahre examine the current breakdown of boundaries between the 'established' social sciences, and the resulting fragmentation. They rightly emphasize that this abolition of boundaries is positive: innovation in fact is a result particularly of hybridization between philosophy, psychology, sociology, economics, and so on. It is perhaps time, however, to go back to the simple idea that *action* is the theme common to all human sciences, and to remember that there is virtually no action without beliefs.

39 In 'La rationalité et le statut . . .' (see note 9).

40 Cf. Chapter 8.

41 S. Lukes, 'Some problems about rationality', *Archives européennes de sociologie*, 8, 2 (1967), pp. 247–64.

42 M. Weber, *Economy and Society* (Bedminster Press, New York, 1968) I, 1.

43 'The problem of the rationality of magic', *British Journal of Sociology*, 17, 1 (March 1967), pp. 55–74.

NOTES TO CHAPTER 10

1 *The Problems of the Philosophy of History* (Free Press, New York, 1977).

2 Despite this, values are objective: they constitute a world which duplicates the real world: *The Philosophy of Money* (Routledge & Kegan Paul, London, 1978), p. 65; orig. pubd as *Philosophie des Geldes* (Duncker & Humblot, Leipzig, 1900).

3 See also, in *The Philosophy of Money*, p. 505 the theme of how technological development led to an intellectualization of machines and a deintellectualization of workers.

4 *Ibid.*, pp. 92, 100, 107.

5 *New Studies in Philosophy, Economics and the History of Ideas* (Routledge & Kegan Paul, London, 1978), chapter 17.

6 *The Philosophy of Money*, p. 18.

7 To which must be added that this relationship derives from the very notion of form. For Simmel, social evolution produces frameworks of thought which tend to be regarded by social subjects as self-evident; see *The Philosophy of Money*, p. 298. For example, for the Greeks the notion of substance and the distinction between substance and accident is a self-evident distinction, *ibid.*, p. 302. They therefore dislike intensely those who, like the Sophists, quibble at such notions.

8 In *The Philosophy of Money*, Plato is the most frequently quoted philosopher. It is not that Simmel is in any way a Platonist, but for him Platonic *ideas* seem to show quasi-allegorically the objectivity of the world of values; moreover, they illustrate the tension between substantialism and relativism, to which he continually refers here.

9 For Simmel, abstraction, implicitly defined by him as the manipulation of *a priori*, is a constituent of human thought: *The Philosophy of Money*, p. 91.

10 *Ibid.*

11 H. Albert, *Traktat über die kritische Vernunft* (Mohr, Tübingen, 1975). Cf. chapter 5, p. 000.

12 The meaning of Ranke's adage is often distorted: 'History has been given the task of judging the past, forming its contemporaries, and thereby serving the future. This essay does not assign itself such elevated tasks. It simply tries to show what really happened' (*'wie es eigentlich gewesen ist'*), *Zur Geschichte der germanischen und romanischen Völker* (1824).

13 W. Dilthey, *Der Aufbau der geschichtlichen Welt in den Geisteswissenschaften* (Suhrkamp, Frankfurt am main 1981 (1914)).

14 *The Philosophy of Money*, p. 115.

15 P. Feyerabend, *Against Method: outline of an anarchistic theory of knowledge* (NLB, London, 1975); B, Barnes, *Interest and the Growth of Knowledge* (Routledge & Kegan Paul, London, 1977); D. Bloor, *Knowledge and Social Imagery* (Routledge & Kegan Paul, London, 1978).

16 Close to the one developed by, for example, W. W. Bartley in *Evolutionary Epistemology, Rationality and the Sociology of Knowledge* (Open Court, Peru, ILH, 1986). The counter-argument to the principle of the natural selection of ideas is that many scientific ideas have no practical application (such as cosmogonic theories).

17 As soon as we can see the Kantian inspiration of Simmel's use of the notion of 'form', it seems to me as uninstructive to speak, as is sometimes done, of the 'formal' or 'formist' sociology of Simmel as it would be to speak of the 'formal' or 'formist' philosophy of Kant.

18 *The Philosophy of Money*, p. 81.

19 *Ibid.*, p. 132.

20 *Ibid.*, p. 140, and also many passages in *The Problems of the Philosophy of History*.

21 Cf. Chapter 3 and Chapter 8.

22 I am referring here to the argument of A, MacIntyre in *The Unconscious: a*

conceptual analysis (Routledge & Kegan Paul, London, 1973 (1958)). He sees the 'early' Freud as *substantialist*, that is, as trying to explain psychic manifestations by reference to a substantified unconscious, and the 'later' Freud as *descriptive*.

23 For the argument that values derive from unconscious comparisons, *The Philosophy of Money*, p. 168 and p. 175. On the unconscious, *ibid.*, p. 423.

24 For the argument that the long-term consequences of action are less present in the consciousness than proximate consequences, see *The Philosophy of Money*, p. 303.

25 *Ibid.*, p. 304.

26 *Ibid.*, p. 128.

27 *Ibid.*, p. 143.

28 As Merton pointed out in *Social Theory and Social Structure* (Free Press, Glencoe, ILH, 1957), chapter 12, Marx's sociology of knowledge in no way repudiates the autonomy of law, science and other forms of thought. This is why we must be careful to distinguish Marx from neo-Marxist philosophers and sociologists, for whom all ideas are often the product of social conditions. Similarly, we must distinguish Durkheim from the neo-Durkheimians. For example, in M. Granet's *La Pensée chinoise*, there is a much more radical sociologism than in Durkheim's *The Elementary Forms of the Religious Life* or even in the article by Durkheim and Mauss, 'De quelques formes primitives de classification', *L'Année sociologique*, 6 (1901–2), pp. 1–72.

29 Cf. Chapter 5.

30 For references to the intellectual antipathy between Durkheim and Simmel, see S. Mesure, 'Simmel et l'irruption du social', *Commentaire*, 43 (Autumn 1988), pp. 830–3.

31 *The Philosophy of Money*, pp. 390, 465. This does not imply that there are no differences on other points between 'socialism' and 'individualism': *ibid.*, 225–30. On socialists' hatred of money: *ibid.*, p. 321.

32 *Problems of a Sociology of Knowledge* (Routledge & Kegan Paul, London, 1979), orig. pubd as *Die Wissensformen und die Gesellschaft* (Der neue Geist, Leipzig, 1926).

33 *The Theory of the Leisure Class* (New American Library, New York, 1953 (1899)).

34 Like Veblen, Simmel categorically refuses to explain tastes systematically by reference to social factors. Sociology can interpret only the most external and superficial aspects of the processes of aesthetic valorization. The 'connaisseur' is attracted by a particular work because it represents a totality that is original, coherent and *objectively* powerful. The notion of 'point of view' is here at the furthest limits of its application. It is totally unacceptable to say that aesthetic phenomena can be analysed from the aesthetic point of view *or* the sociological point of view. What is true is that there are phenomena which are the concern of sociology, such as those analysed by Veblen or Quentin Bell (*On Human Finery* (Hogarth Press, London, 1976)), and others which are not. 'Pleasure' grounds, cumbersome crinolines, African *fattening houses*, or the 1920s taste for 'flappers' are explained by social causes, but not the fact that *Macbeth* or *Madame Bovary* are honoured as classics. Simmel is here emphasiz-

ing a distinction in relation to *aesthetic* values which was later also stressed in relation to *cognitive* values by the founder of the sociology of knowledge, Karl Mannheim (*Ideology and Utopia* (Routledge & Kegan Paul, London, 1954)): belief in the truth of the statement 'usury is immoral' is determined by social causes, but not belief in '2 + 2 = 4'.

35 *The Philosophy of Money*, p. 109.

36 *Ibid.*, p. 81.

37 A view that there can be no objective interpretation of the historical past, since every observer and every age reads the past with the spectacles of the time. Historism is a diachronic variant of cultural relativism (illustrated, for example, by Peter Winch) whereby there can be no non-distorted communication between different cultures (cf. Chapter 7). 'Historism' should not be confused with 'historicism' in Popper's sense – a concept indicating theories which claim to see in the historical and social world laws just as rigorous as those in the natural world.

38 On monism and dualism, see *The Philosophy of Money*, p. 136 and 146; on materialism, *ibid.*, p. 139; on the fact that there can be legitimately divergent views on evolution, *ibid.*, p. 64, and also numerous passages in *The Problems of the Philosophy of History*.

39 This is why it is hardly surprising that Simmel seems to be the pet hate of György Lukács in *The Destruction of Reason* (Merlin, London, 1980), orig. pubd as *Die Zerstörung der Vernunft* (Aufbau, Berlin, 1955), and by Ernst Bloch in *Geist der Utopie* (Suhrkamp, Frankfurt an Main 1964). It must be said that, although Simmel is extremely indulgent towards Marx, he does not refrain from attacking the Marxist intellectuals or German social democracy of his time.

40 B. Valade, 'Georg Simmel: la sociologie et l'expérience du monde moderne', *Encyclopaedia Universalis-Universalia* (1988).

41 *The Philosophy of Money*, pp. 158, 161.

42 *Ibid.*, p. 395.

43 *Ibid.*, pp. 190, 126.

44 *Ibid.*, p. 198.

45 The medieval notion of the 'just price' and the taboo about usury similarly presuppose a substantialist view: *ibid.*, p. 149, 220ff. On the substantialist nature of 'mercantilism' and 'fiscalism', *ibid*, p. 235. On the relational nature of money, *ibid*, pp. 183, 292.

46 I will not go into detail here on this important point (which I analysed in my introduction to the French translation of *The Problems of the Philosophy of History*), namely that if there is one area in Simmel where one needs to be aware of the need to move from substantialism to relativism, it is that of the social sciences. They can make progress only by a critique of the substantialist illusion. This implies substituting individualism for methodological holism, as Simmel shows very clearly in passages which I quoted in 'Individualisme et holisme dans les sciences sociales', in *Sur l'individualisme*, ed. P. Birnbaum and J. Leca (Presses de la Fondation nationale des sciences politiques, Paris, 1986), pp. 45–59. The fact that 'every phenomenon which seems to constitute some new unit above individuals . . . [is in fact resolved] in the reciprocal actions

exchanged by the individuals' does not imply that there is no need to recognize the existence of the supra-individual, in the sense that subjects encounter a state of the world, ideas, or a social organization which impose themselves on them. Cf. *The Philosophy of Money*, p. 220.

47 *Ibid.*, p. 511.

Index